Mao's Third Front

In 1964, the Chinese Communist Party (CCP) made a momentous policy decision. In response to rising tensions with the United States and the Soviet Union, a top-secret massive military industrial complex in the mountains of inland China was built, which the CCP hoped to keep hidden from enemy bombers. Mao named this the Third Front. The Third Front received more government investment than any other developmental initiative of the Mao era, and yet this huge industrial war machine, which saw the mobilization of fifteen million people, was not officially acknowledged for over a decade and a half. Drawing on a rich collection of archival documents, memoirs, and oral interviews, Covell Meyskens provides the first history of the Third Front campaign. He shows how the militarization of Chinese industrialization linked millions of everyday lives to the global Cold War, merging global geopolitics with local change.

Covell F. Meyskens is Assistant Professor in the National Security Affairs Department at the Naval Postgraduate School.

Mao's Third Front

The Militarization of Cold War China

Covell F. Meyskens
Naval Postgraduate School, Monterey, California

CAMBRIDGE
UNIVERSITY PRESS

CAMBRIDGE
UNIVERSITY PRESS

University Printing House, Cambridge CB2 8BS, United Kingdom

One Liberty Plaza, 20th Floor, New York, NY 10006, USA

477 Williamstown Road, Port Melbourne, VIC 3207, Australia

314–321, 3rd Floor, Plot 3, Splendor Forum, Jasola District Centre, New Delhi – 110025, India

79 Anson Road, #06–04/06, Singapore 079906

Cambridge University Press is part of the University of Cambridge.

It furthers the University's mission by disseminating knowledge in the pursuit of education, learning, and research at the highest international levels of excellence.

www.cambridge.org
Information on this title: www.cambridge.org/9781108489553
DOI: 10.1017/9781108784788

First published 2020

A catalogue record for this publication is available from the British Library.

Library of Congress Cataloging-in-Publication Data
Names: Meyskens, Covell F., 1978– author.
Title: Mao's third front : the militarization of Cold War China / Covell F. Meyskens, Naval Postgraduate School, Monterey, California.
Description: Cambridge, United Kingdom ; New York, NY : Cambridge University Press, 2020. | Includes bibliographical references and index.
Identifiers: LCCN 2019053353 (print) | LCCN 2019053354 (ebook) | ISBN 9781108489553 (hardback) | ISBN 9781108784788 (ebook)
Subjects: LCSH: China – Economic policy – 1949–1976. | Defense industries – China. | China – History, Military.
Classification: LCC HC427.9 .M47 2020 (print) | LCC HC427.9 (ebook) | DDC 338.4/73550095109045–dc23
LC record available at https://lccn.loc.gov/2019053353
LC ebook record available at https://lccn.loc.gov/2019053354

ISBN 978-1-108-48955-3 Hardback

Contents

Tables

Figures

Maps

Abbreviations

CCP	Chinese Communist Party
GMD	Guomindang
ICBM	intercontinental ballistic missile
PLA	People's Liberation Army
PRC	People's Republic of China
RMB	*renminbi* – Chinese currency
SOE	state-owned enterprise

Acknowledgements

This book began as the consequence of a coincidence. I had just finished my PhD comprehensive exams, and I still had yet to settle on a dissertation topic. So, what I did was look through John K. Fairbank's textbook on Chinese history and see what I could find that matched my interests in the Mao era and the Cold War, and that had occurred in Sichuan province, since my PhD adviser Jacob Eyferth had contacts there that I knew would be valuable for carrying out a research project. Flipping through the pages of Fairbank's book, I came upon a brief mention of the Third Front. Having little idea what it was, I searched around for more information and uncovered a couple of articles by Barry Naughton which laid out the Third Front's centrality to the political economy of late Maoist China. Intrigued by the idea of studying a topic that not only touched on geopolitics, economic development, and social history but was also understudied, I decided to make the Third Front into the focus of my dissertation.

Looking back at that decision, I have often thought my younger self to be foolhardy for choosing to research the Third Front due to the problems that its size and complexity posed for making it into a manageable topic of study, to say nothing of the problems with acquiring sources on an issue directly related to Chinese national security. The fact that I was able to make the Third Front into the subject of this book was only possible thanks to the collegiality, guidance, and friendship of many people. My interest in the Cold War came from reading Bruce Cumings. It was his work on Cold War East Asia that initially sparked by intellectual interest in East Asian political economy and that brought me to the University of Chicago to pursue a PhD. The citations to his writings in the pages to follow are a testament to Bruce's influence.

If it were not for Jacob Eyferth, this project would not exist. It was only because he had conducted research in Sichuan that I came to learn about the Third Front. Jacob has over the years always been willing to go over drafts and talk through ideas, consistently challenging me to sharpen my analysis, flesh out my conceptual framework, and make links with the existing historiography. After arriving in Chicago, I met Michael Geyer. An early conversation with him played a formative role in helping me to think through how to take the many issues related to the Third Front and divide them up into discrete chapters. I came to know Ken Pomeranz about halfway through my dissertation. My research has been enriched from his extensive advice. To Ken and Jacob, I owe my still limited ability to think like a social historian. Both at Chicago and after, I also learned much from banter about academic affairs with Max Bohnenkamp, Anne Rebull, Guoquan Seng, Nianshen Song, Limin Teh, Saul Thomas, Jake Werner, and Hai Zhao.

The research for this book was made possible by multiple Foreign Language and Area Studies Fellowships, a Republic of China Language Fellowship, a Fulbright-Hays Doctoral Dissertation Research Abroad Fellowship, a Fulbright Institute of International Education Fellowship, a write-up fellowship from the University of Chicago's Center for East Asian Studies, and the Naval Postgraduate School's Research Initiation Program. I would also like to express my gratitude to Liu Shilong and Chen Bo of Sichuan University for all that they did to facilitate my field-work in Southwest and Central China as well as Chen Yongfa and Yu Miing-lin for hosting me at Academica Sinica's Institute of Modern History. An abundance of thanks is especially due to Chen Donglin and Xu Youwei who put me in touch with their contacts and generously discussed with me what they knew about elite politics and everyday life at the Third Front.

Over the past four years, I have been fortunate to have a supportive group of colleagues at the Naval Postgraduate School. Mo Hafez and Clay Moltz have provided consummate mentorship on how to chart out a scholarly career while at the same time navigating the specificities of working for the U.S. Department of Navy. Having draft chapters productively critiqued by Naaz Barma, Anne Marie Baylouny, Anne Clunan, Erik Dahl, Ryan Gingeras, Mike Glosny, Wade Huntley, Dan Moran, Afshon Ostovar, Jessica Piombo, James Russell, Zach Shore, Rachel Sigman, and Chris Twomey all profoundly contributed to the clarification of the book's aims. Chris Darnton's comments on a draft book introduction were particularly helpful, as have been his thoughtful responses to my ample questions about scholarly life writ large. Teaching at the Naval Postgraduate School has endowed me with an invaluable sounding board, as conversations with students have given me insights into how military folk think about national security, the policies that states implement to shore up national defense, and the multiple motivations that inform people's experiences of military service.

Presenting research-in-progress at academic venues also significantly contributed to writing this book. Participating in scholarly events organized by Jennifer Altehenger, Denise Ho, Aaron Moore, Gai Hershatter, Emily Honig, Malcolm Thompson, Fabio Lanza, Melissa Dale, Karl Gerth, Joshua Howard, and Jessica Dahl all provided stimulating forums to discuss different aspects of the book with members of the Chinese studies community. I learned much as well from Association of Asian Studies' conference panels organized with Judd Kinzley, Jeremy Tai, Scott Relyea, Harrison Kim, Aaron Moore, Jaewoong Jeon, Maggie Clinton, and Hou Li. It was at AAS where I met Fabio Lanza, who not only helped me to traverse the travails of the publishing process, but also read multiple drafts, gave pointed criticism, and talked over my many queries. Anonymous reviewers' astute comments also pushed me to dig deep, develop the book's conceptual framing, and locate and mobilize more sources. The process of revising the book gained an additional boost from judicious comments by Karl Gerth, Mindy Smith, Alex Day, and Barry Naughton. Lucy Rhymer has, likewise, been a model editor, and Natasha Whelan, James Baker, and Podhumai Anban have skillfully shepherded the book through the production process. I would also like to thank John Hopkins University Press and Routledge for allowing me to use previously published materials in chapter 3 and 5.[1]

This book would have never come to fruition without the solicitude of my wife Hsin-Hui Tseng and support of my family members. I knew that it was clearly time to finish the dissertation when our two-year old daughter Ya-Yen began talking about how she was collecting materials for a chapter for her dissertation, and I knew that I was talking too much about my book when she started offering advice on how to revise it at the dinner table. Finally, I dedicate this book to the millions of people who gave their lives to building the Third Front and have shared their varied experiences in interviews, memoirs, and archival documents.

[1] Parts of chapter 5 are from the following article. Covell Meyskens, "Third Front Railroads and Industrial Modernity in Late Maoist China, *Twentieth-Century China*, Volume 40, Issue 3, October 2015, pages 238–260. Published by Johns Hopkins University Press. Parts of chapter 3 are from this article. Covell Meyskens, "Building a Dam for China in the Three Gorges Region, 1919–1971." In *Water, Technology, and the Nation-State*, edited by Erik Swyngedouw and Filippo Menga, 207–222. London: Routledge, 2018.

Introduction

On January 13, 1978, an article appeared on page four of the *People's Daily* that at first glance was of no particular significance. It was about a man named Zhang Xianzhong who worked at a rural cotton-processing factory in Hubei province. A fire had recently broken out at his workplace, and he had run around with an extinguisher to protect machinery and cotton. Zhang's determination to safeguard China's collective property was impressive, and his "revolutionary heroic spirit of putting his life on the line" was worthy of praise.[1] In the 1970s the Chinese press was awash with similar stories, but buried near this article's end was a detail that was not at all run-of-the-mill. Zhang had "participated in Third Front construction." The phrase "Third Front construction" had never before appeared in the *People's Daily*. If someone had wondered what the Third Front was, the article offered no hints. It merely stated that Zhang had "participated in Third Front construction" and left it at that. If someone had asked around about the Third Front, most people would have been able to provide no information. Even if someone knew about it, they would have probably feigned ignorance since the Chinese Communist Party (CCP) had told them that the Third Front had to be hidden from China's Cold War enemies – the United States and the Soviet Union. The concealment of the Third Front from public view might be unremarkable if it were small. Yet the Third Front was anything but tiny.

The Third Front was, in the words of Barry Naughton, "a purposive, large-scale, centrally directed program" to construct "a huge self-sufficient industrial base area" in the mountains of inland China "to serve as a strategic reserve in the event of China being drawn into war" with the United States or the Soviet Union.[2] To build the Third Front, the Party mobilized roughly 15 million workers and one million family

1 "Lei Feng shi de minbing Zhang Xianzhong," *Renmin ribao*, January 13, 1978.
2 Barry Naughton, "The Third Front: Defence Industrialization in the Chinese Interior," *China Quarterly* 115 (1988): 351.

members.[3] With a price tag of 20.5 billion RMB (*renminbi* – Chinese currency), the Third Front was the most expensive industrialization campaign of the Mao era, costing more than the combined total of both the First Five Year Plan and the Great Leap Forward.[4] Nearly thirty years ago, Barry Naughton pointed out the Third Front's centrality to the political economy of late Maoist China, noting that "with the exception of petroleum development, the central government's industrialization policy between 1965 and 1971 *was* the Third Front."[5] In the intervening decades, the Third Front has largely fallen out of view in Western scholarship.[6]

Drawing on recently available sources, I aim to retrieve the Third Front from the Cold War shadows where the CCP stashed it for safekeeping.[7] A history of Mao's China without the Third Front is like a history of the Soviet Union that does not consider preparations for war with the capitalist West and Nazi Germany.[8] In both cases, a historian would be omitting the profound national consequences of international military tensions. This book shows that the geopolitical antagonisms of the Cold War deeply shaped Communist Party efforts to re-engineer China into a socialist industrial nation and contributes to the growing number of studies which have demonstrated that international security concerns militarized government attempts to make China modern from the late Qing into the Mao era.[9]

The Third Front dramatically altered the economic trajectory of the People's Republic of China (PRC). Prior to its start, Party leaders were

[3] The Appendix will explain how I calculated this number.

[4] These calculations only include investments in capital construction. They do not include the long-term economic costs. For statistics on capital construction investment, see Guowuyuan sanxian jianshe tiaozheng gaizao guihua bangong shi sanxian jianshe bianxie zu, *Sanxian jianshe* (Beijing, 1991), 32.

[5] Barry Naughton, "Industrial Policy during the Cultural Revolution: Military Preparation, Decentralization, and Leaps Forward," in *New Perspectives on the Cultural Revolution*, eds. William A. Joseph, Christine P.W. Wong, and David Zweig (Cambridge, MA: Harvard University Press, 1991), 158. Italics in the original.

[6] It is not mentioned, for example, in Maurice Meisner, *Mao's China and After: A History of the People's Republic* (New York: The Free Press, 1999). Jonathan Spence, *The Search for Modern China* (New York: W.W. Norton, 2012). Andrew G. Walder, *China under Mao: A Revolution Derailed* (Cambridge, MA: Harvard University Press, 2015).

[7] I discuss the historiography of the Third Front in the section titled "Bringing the Third Front In."

[8] Stephen Kotkin, *Magnetic Mountain: Stalinism as Civilization* (Berkeley: University of California Press, 1995). Lennart Samuelson, *Plans for Stalin's War-Machine: Tukhachevskii and Military–Economic Planning, 1925–1941* (New York: Palgrave MacMillan, 2000).

[9] Some examples are Hans van de Ven, "The Military in the Republic," *China Quarterly* 150 (1997): 352–374. Rana Mitter, "Modernity, Internationalization, and War in the History of Modern China," *Historical Journal* 48:2 (2005): 523–543.

preoccupied with recovering from the Great Leap Forward, which had been intended to create a communist society and rapidly boost heavy industry but instead produced economic depression and famine. After the Great Leap, the CCP leadership had slowed down the pace of industrialization and invested more in coastal regions and the production of consumer goods. The Third Front put China on a very different path. It shifted China's economic center of gravity towards inland regions, and it remade quickly expanding heavy industry into a top national priority. Afraid that the United States or the Soviet Union could demolish Chinese industry with a few air raids or nuclear strikes, nearly 400 state-owned enterprises were moved from coastal cities to clandestine mountain locations.[10] This policy shift had significant consequences. It reduced coastal development, intensified consumer austerity, and militarized Chinese developmental strategy. If the CCP had stuck with its original plans, this choice would have probably led to less funding for inland industry, wider regional economic differences, and the pillars of modern industrial society becoming less entrenched in the Chinese interior.

The Third Front campaign also gave a second life to some of the Maoist economic techniques that had underpinned the Great Leap. With the inauguration of the Third Front, the Party again proclaimed that China should learn from how the CCP dealt with the underdevelopment of domestic science and technology during the revolutionary war era.[11] Like the Red Army, managers of Third Front projects should not view the scarcity of technical personnel, industrial equipment, and foreign aid as an insurmountable obstacle to the advancement of Chinese socialism. They should be self-reliant and mobilize any available resources into quasi-military campaigns that leaned heavily on large labor brigades to rapidly enlarge China's economic base. If anyone even so much as urged alternative policies, they ran the risk of being denounced as traitors who supported American or Soviet developmental methods over Chinese.

Last and not least, the Third Front provides a window onto how people within China responded to the CCP's attempts to socially engineer a population that conformed to Maoist principles. According to Maoist norms, when someone received a transfer order to the Third Front, they were supposed to willingly pack up their lives to participate in constructing a secret heavy-industrial base in China's mountainous hinterlands. Once someone became a Third Fronter, they were never supposed to want to be

[10] Zhao Dexin, *Zhonghua renmin gongheguo jingji shi 1967–1984* (Zhengzhou: Henan renmin chubanshe, 1991), 183.

[11] Sigrid Schmalzer, "Self-Reliant Science: The Impact of the Cold War on Science in Socialist China," in *Science and Technology in the Global Cold War*, eds. Naomi Oreskes and John Krige (Cambridge, MA: MIT Press, 2014), 79.

anything else. They had to make the Third Front their life for as long as the Party needed. If they encountered hardships, it was politically incorrect for them to complain. They were supposed to remain wholeheartedly committed to struggling to build a Maoist version of industrial modernity in the Third Front even if that meant engaging every day in taxing manual labor at a remote construction site, only to return at night to a group canvas tent to eat a barebones meal and sleep on a thatched mat far away from family. In practice, people's responses to participation in the Third Front were shaped by a variety of socioeconomic, political, and geographic factors and only sometimes personified the CCP's prescriptions.

The Origins of the Third Front

The first known mention by Mao Zedong of the Third Front dates from 1964. Mao recommended building it after reading a General Staff report in April that year. The report noted that most Chinese industry was in fourteen big coastal cities prone to air raids or a nuclear strike, and so the General Staff suggested researching measures to guard against a sudden attack.[12] Mao proposed the Third Front as a solution to this security predicament at State Planning Commission meetings in May. Mao asserted that in the nuclear age China must have "a rear defense area [and] . . . prepare to go the mountains," like the Party had done in its battles against Japan and the Guomindang (GMD).[13] The Third Front was that military safe haven. China had to be divided up into three war zones: a First Front along the coast and in the northwest, a Second Front behind the coast, and a Third Front in the southwest. In the last area, Mao ordered a heavy-industrial base to retreat to in the event of a foreign occupation. This area was subsequently named the Big Third Front.[14] Mao wanted coastal enterprises relocated to the Big Third Front and to assist in developing heavy industry in inland areas. To further bolster national security, Mao demanded at a Politburo meeting on June 8 that every province set up a military industrial complex, or, as it was later called, a Small Third Front.[15] Then, on June 16, Mao told the Politburo to

[12] Chen Donglin, "Sanxian jianshe," in *Zhongguo gongchandang yu sanxian*, ed. Chen Donglin (Beijing: Zhonggong dangshi chubanshe, 2015), 4. The official editor of this volume is Chen Xi. Multiple Chinese scholars have told me that Chen Donglin edited this volume, and so I have listed him in this role.

[13] Mao Zedong, "Yao ba Panzhihua he lianxi dao Panzhihua de jiaotong, mei, dian jianshe de gao qi lai," May 27, 1964, in *Zhongguo gongchandang yu sanxian*, ed. Chen Donglin (Beijing: Zhonggong dangshi chubanshe, 2015), 43.

[14] Zhonggong zhongyang wenxian yanjiushi, *Zhou Enlai zhuan, Volume 4* (Beijing: Zhongyang wenxian chubanshe, 1998), 1768.

[15] Mao, "Yao ba Panzhihua he lianxi dao Panzhihua de jiaotong," 43. Mao Zedong, "Mei ge sheng dou yao you yi, er, Sanxian," June 8, 1964, in *Zhongguo gongchandang yu sanxian*, 52.

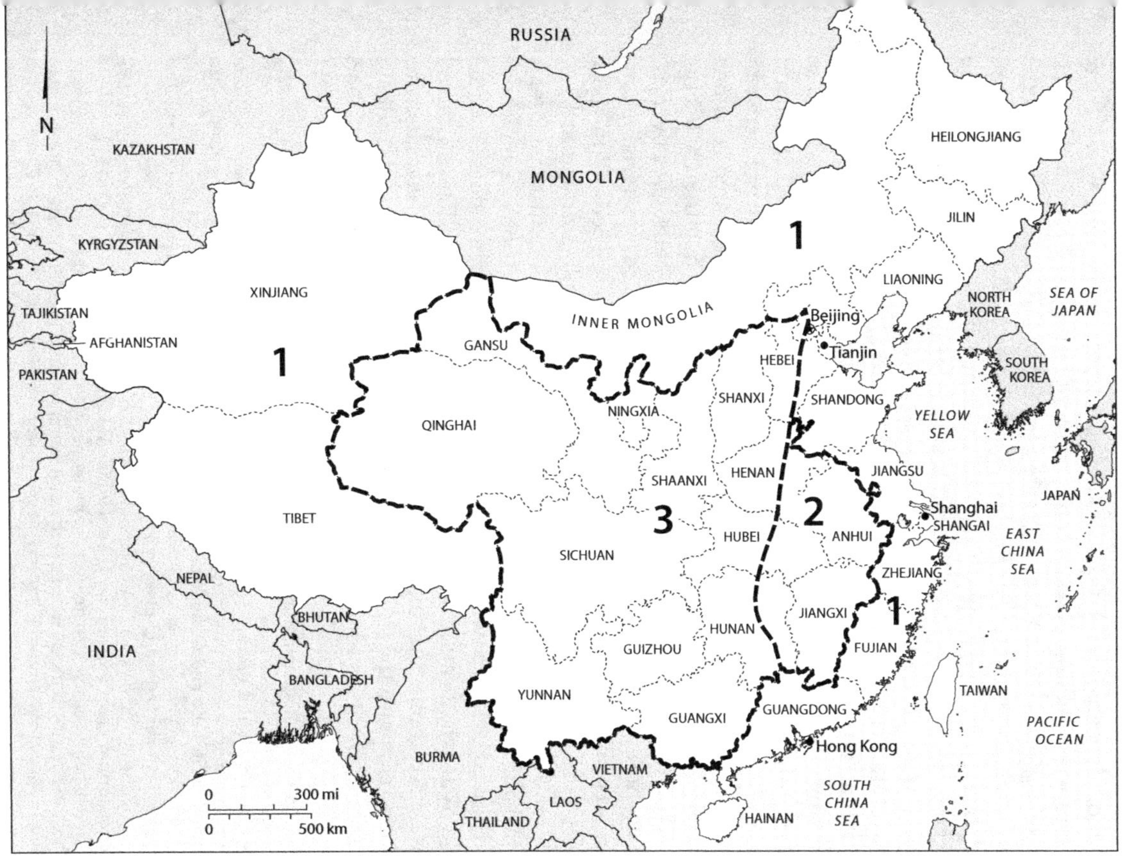

Map 0.1 The First, Second, and Third Fronts

form militias in every county, so that localities did not have to rely on the Party center or the People's Liberation Army (PLA). Only then could China be undefeatable.[16]

Mao advocated constructing the Third Front at the time when Party leaders were making preparations for the Third Five Year Plan. In the preceding year, Deng Xiaoping, vice premier Liu Shaoqi, director of the Planning Commission Li Fuchun, and a few other top leaders had sketched out a rough plan that was informed by the aftermath of the Great Leap.[17] Spurred on by the Taiwan Straits crisis of 1958, CCP leaders tried in the Leap to follow the example of Stalin's rapid industrialization drive between 1929 and 1941 and make China into a major industrial and military power by severely curbing consumption and directing all resources into a large militarized campaign to increase heavy industry.[18] During the Leap, the Party also invested in inland heavy industry to act as a rear base and reduce the economic gap between the coast and the interior.[19] In the end, the Leap precipitated a famine that killed around 30 million people and brought to a halt the CCP's big push to augment industry.[20] Deng Xiaoping and his colleagues oversaw the economy's recovery. Investment was drastically cut, material incentives were reintroduced, and rural markets were reopened. With these policy measures, the Party was able to revive economic production.[21]

This developmental approach, however, did not address China's increasing international vulnerability. In the early 1960s, China was a technologically scrawny military power with no weighty allies, and the Cold War was heating up in Asia. Chiang Kai-shek in Taiwan talked ceaselessly about retaking mainland China and launched several commando raids into the southeast. China fought a border war with India in 1962, and Beijing's friend-turned-bitter-enemy – the Soviet Union – had

[16] Mao Zedong, "Difang dangwei yao gao junshi, yao junbei da dan bu yao huangzhang," June 16, 1964, in *Zhongguo gongchandang yu sanxian*, 53.

[17] Naughton, "Third Front," 352. Chen Donglin, *Sanxian jianshe: Zhanbei siqi de xibu kaifa* (Beijing: Zhonggong zhongyang dangxiao chubanshe, 2013), 43–45. The group also included Bo Yibo and Chen Yun.

[18] John Garver, *China's Quest: The History of the Foreign Relations of the People's Republic of China* (Oxford: Oxford University Press, 2016), 113, 131, 143.

[19] Judd Kinzley, "Crisis and the Development of China's Southwestern Periphery: The Transformation of Panzhihua, 1936–1969," *Modern China* 38 (2012): 574–576.

[20] There is an extensive debate on how many people died during the Great Leap famine. I follow Andrew Walder, who puts the number at around 30 million. See Walder, *China under Mao*, 169. Frank Dikötter, *Mao's Great Famine: The History of China's Most Devastating Catastrophe, 1958–62* (London: Bloomsbury, 2010), 324–334, has given a much higher estimate of 50 million. As Walder has noted, this higher estimate "cannot be reconciled with age-specific population data." Walder, *China under Mao*, 364–365.

[21] Barry Naughton, *The Chinese Economy: Transitions and Growth* (Cambridge, MA: MIT Press, 2007), 71–72.

sided with New Delhi. Making matters even worse, in the wake of the Sino-Soviet split, Moscow had stationed hundreds of thousands of troops on China's northern border.[22] In 1964, Sino-Soviet tensions reached a new level when the CCP publicly claimed that the Soviet Union faced the "danger of capitalist restoration" since Soviet leader Nikita Khrushchev's "revisionist clique" had installed itself atop the party-state as a "new Soviet bourgeoisie" and endorsed rising income inequality. China also accused the Soviet Union of giving up on the defense of international socialism against imperialism by showing interest in a policy of peaceful existence with American empire.[23] Beijing, in stark contrast, saw Washington as a major imperial threat. The United States had waged war against China in Korea, and American military bases and security alliances were geared towards stymieing socialism's global influence and undermining postcolonial and decolonizing states.

When Deng Xiaoping and his colleagues started work on the Third Five Year Plan in 1963, they did not give first consideration to China's worsening security environment. They advocated continuing with post-Great Leap policies and concentrating on agriculture and coastal areas for industrial development.[24] Mao, on the other hand, was concerned that post-Great Leap policies exhibited signs of Soviet revisionism and that his colleagues in the Party center were steering China towards a Soviet-style capitalist resurgence. In the months following Mao's first proposal of the Third Front in May 1964, he often switched in meetings between pressuring his colleagues to construct the Third Front and warning them that there was a significant risk that Soviet revisionism could take hold in China. Meanwhile, Deng Xiaoping, Liu Shaoqi, and Li Fuchun only partially supported the Third Front and continued to stress the Third Five Year Plan's original coastal and consumer focus. It was only after the Gulf of Tonkin incident in early August caused Party leaders to worry that a Sino-American war was about to explode that they firmly backed the Third Front campaign.[25] After the Third Front campaign started, Mao made a series of assertive actions. In December 1964, he accused Liu Shaoqi, Li Fuchun, and Deng Xiaoping of sidelining him in the policy-making process. In January 1965, he said that Liu Shaoqi was a revisionist like Khrushchev, and he formed a "small planning committee" to take over work on the Third Five Year Plan which did not include Liu, Deng, or Li.[26]

[22] Chen, "Sanxian jianshe," 4–5. Garver, *China's Quest*, 182.

[23] Roderick MacFarquhar, *The Origins of the Cultural Revolution, Volume 3, The Coming of the Cataclysm, 1961–1966* (New York: Oxford University Press, 1997), 363.

[24] Naughton, "Third Front," 351. [25] Chen, *Sanxian*, 44–54.

[26] Chen, *Sanxian*, 72–73. MacFarquhar, *Origins of the Cultural Revolution*, 426–427, 430.

Instead, the committee was headed up by oil minister Yu Qiuli, whom Mao admired for successfully establishing the Daqing oilfield through forced-draft industrialization during the Great Leap, an accomplishment which supplied large quantities of much-needed oil to China's petrol-poor economy.[27] Following Mao's criticism of Li Fuchun, Yu Qiuli effectively took over as Planning Commission director. As for Deng and Liu, they remained involved in Third Front planning. However, Mao told a small number of high-ranking leaders that he thought Liu and Deng were trying to set up "separate kingdoms."[28] Mao's undercutting of his colleagues' authority around the same time that he urged building the Third Front raises the question of whether the Third Front was part of an effort by Mao to advocate for the revival of a fast-paced large-scale industrialization drive similar to the Great Leap while simultaneously pre-emptively pushing back against potential critics of this policy change.

According to Barry Naughton, when Mao suggested prioritizing national security and building the Third Front, he received wide support from the CCP leadership.[29] In his book on the Third Front, Chinese historian Chen Donglin presents a more complicated picture. He claims that Mao's and the central Party's decision was based on "how to handle the small possibility of war" since "ignoring that possibility . . . would be gambling with the nation's fate."[30] Chen provides no archival documents as support. What he does provide is evidence of meetings in which Mao and other Party leaders presented conflicting views about China's economic future and disagreed about the necessity and size of the Third Front. The historian Chen Jian has asserted that the start of the Third Front campaign fits with Mao's tendency to treat "international tension . . . as a useful tool for domestic mobilization," but had few sources with which to substnantiate his claim.[31] Based on the materials Chen Donglin presented and on recently published documentation, I argue that Mao employed international tensions to overcome resistance from his colleagues to undertaking the Third Front campaign, and that

[27] "Zhongyang guanyu chuanda 'shiyou gongye bu guanyu daqing youtian huizhan qingkuang de baogao' de tongzhi," in *Gongye xue daqing xianji lu ji shiliao xuanbian*, ed. Zhonggong Daqing shiwei dangshi yanjiushi (Beijing: Zhongyang wenxian chubanshe, 2004), 29–30.

[28] Chen, *Sanxian*, 71.

[29] Naughton, "Third Front," 351. Lorenz Lüthi concurs with this view. "The Vietnam War and China's Third-Line Defense Planning before the Cultural Revolution, 1964–1966," *Journal of Cold War Studies* 10 (2008): 26, 32–33. Li Danhui and Yafeng Xia agree with Naughton too. *Mao and the Sino-Soviet Split, 1959–1973* (Lanham: Rowman and Littlefield, 2018), 95.

[30] Chen, *Sanxian*, 100.

[31] Chen Jian, *Mao's China and the Cold War* (Chapel Hill: University of North Carolina Press, 2001), 13, 214–215.

they ultimately only backed down when Washington ramped up its military involvement in Vietnam after the Gulf of Tonkin incident.

America's strong response to the Gulf of Tonkin incident is well known. On August 7, 1964, Congress granted President Johnson the power "to take all necessary measures to repel any armed attack against the forces of the United States and to prevent further aggression."[32] Johnson then authorized bombing North Vietnam and sending troops into the South. By the end of 1965, the United States had 184,300 troops in the South, and by the end of 1967, American planes had dropped 864,000 tons of explosives on the North. Most Pentagon analysts expected American military power to cause the North Vietnamese to realize that they could not defeat Washington and retreat to engaging in small skirmishes and propaganda campaigns. And yet, Communist forces never backed down, in part because Johnson dreaded that dispatching ground forces into North Vietnam would provoke a huge Chinese intervention like it had in the Korean War.[33]

China's response to the Gulf of Tonkin incident has received less attention. In preparation for a possible war with the United States, Beijing commenced the Third Front campaign. On August 12, Zhou Enlai approved the construction of a massive industrial system in southwest China consisting of Panzhihua Steel in Sichuan, the Liupanshui coal mines in Guizhou, and three railroads connecting the provinces of Sichuan, Yunnan, and Guizhou.[34] Then, on August 19, Li Fuchun, vice premier Bo Yibo, and chief of the general staff Luo Ruiqing issued a report. According to its terms, no new industrial projects could be built in fifteen large cities mainly along the coast; all new projects had to be concealed in the mountains, and industrial enterprises, universities, and research institutes had to relocate to the Third Front.[35] By supporting these policies, the Party radically altered the direction of the Third Five Year Plan.

The greenlighting of the Third Front campaign switched the Third Five Year Plan's focus from consumption and material incentives to heavy industry and austere living. By backing the Third Front's establishment, the Party center also reoriented investment inland and ended the post-Great Leap moratorium on mass-mobilizing resources for big industrial projects. Lastly, by deciding to build an industrial base in the

[32] Robert J. McMahon, *The Limits of Empire: The United States and Southeast Asia since World War II* (New York: Columbia University Press, 1999), 113, 116.
[33] Mark Philip Bradley, *Vietnam at War* (Oxford: Oxford University Press, 2009), 110–112.
[34] "Zhou Enlai deng pizhun Lu Zhengcao guanyu jiasu xiajian Chengkun deng xinan tielu de bao gao," August 12, 1964, in *Zhongguo gongchandang yu sanxian*, 57–60.
[35] Chen, "Sanxian jianshe," 8–9.

mountains, Party leaders made Cold War military pressures dominant in economic affairs and imprinted the guerilla tactics of the CCP's revolutionary base areas into the physical layout of China's economic geography. When Party leaders launched the Third Front in August 1964, they not only propelled militarized rapid industrialization policies back into the motor of the national economy, they also joined the long list of statesmen fighting the last war.[36]

Third Front Construction: An Overview

When Mao and his lieutenants initiated the Third Front campaign, they did not fully reinstate Great Leap policies. To begin with, the Third Front was not a nationwide aboveboard movement which granted localities power to instigate projects. It was a covert campaign whose developmental spotlight shone on western and central China. Authority was also more concentrated. Central ministries planned and administered the Big Third Front in co-ordination with Third Front offices in regional, provincial, and municipal committees, while county towns operated Third Front support offices to oversee the mobilization of local labor and supplies for construction projects. The Office of the National Defense Industry performed the same function for the Small Third Front in conjunction with provincial and municipal committees, while again relying on county Third Front support offices to direct local resources to building sites.[37]

The Third Front campaign also did not revive the utopian ambition of leapfrogging into communism. After the Great Leap, austerity without the promise of an abrupt rise in material welfare became the national norm. But the goal of austerity was not asceticism. The aim was building socialism. What made austerity seem to become an end in itself was that the time horizon for achieving socialism was not an immediate prospect. It was a process whose accomplishment was put off into the indefinite future.[38] Repressed consumption was not evenly distributed across China's social landscape. Especially important was the Party's decision to enforce a residence permit system which provided significantly more socioeconomic benefits to urban than to rural residents and only very rarely sanctioned urban–rural migration or relocation to cities higher up

[36] Jack Snyder, *The Ideology of the Offensive: Military Decision Making and the Disasters of 1914* (Ithaca: Cornell University Press, 1984).

[37] Guowuyuan, *Sanxian*, 24–26.

[38] On austerity in Mao's China, see Maurice Meisner, *Marxism, Maoism, and Utopianism: Eight Essays* (Madison: University of Wisconsin Press, 1982), 118–131. Ci Jiwei, *Dialectic of the Chinese Revolution: From Utopianism to Hedonism* (Stanford: Stanford University Press, 1994), 134–167.

in the urban hierarachy.[39] The Party, however, did not entirely abandon the aspiration to provide labor with broad welfare benefits, though policy makers restricted the material embrace of the social welfare state to state-owned enterprises, which every single Third Front work unit was.[40]

On the other hand, there were notable similarities between the Third Front and the Great Leap. The Party again sought to socially engineer a labor force that treated the attainment of socialist modernity as dependent upon the expression of certain ideas and attitudes. To qualify as a good socialist person, someone had to embody the objectives of Maoism. Workers had to go wherever the Party needed them most, and when they arrived there they had to take the masses as a more powerful force for building socialism than modern technical knowledge and skills. Laborers and their families were also supposed to be self-reliant, to defer consumption, and to painstakingly struggle to raise economic output out of a desire for ideological recognition rather than material rewards. As for central leaders, they integrated into the Third Front many large industrial projects originally pursued during the Great Leap, and they resurrected some aspects of the Great Leap's approach to development. Once again, the Party leadership approved the mobilization of huge regiments of labor to hasten the accumulation of industrial resources. This time around, though, all projects had to be camouflaged as much as possible in undisclosed mountain locations for security reasons.

To back up potential front lines along the coast, the central Party endorsed in late 1964 the establishment of Small Third Front military industrial complexes in the mountains of Guangdong, Guangxi, Fujian, Shandong, Zhejiang, Jiangsu, Anhui, Jiangxi, and Hebei, and in Beijing's western highlands.[41] Party leaders, meanwhile, focused Big Third Front construction on the southwest. Hundreds of projects had no precedent. For instance, Party leaders sanctioned a conventional-weapons complex

39 Tiejun Cheng and Mark Selden, "The Origins and Social Consequences of China's *Hukou* System," *China Quarterly* 139 (1994): 667.

40 On social welfare in China after the Great Leap, see Nara Dillon, *Radical Inequalities: China's Revolutionary Welfare State in Comparative Perspective* (Cambridge, MA: Harvard University Press, 2015), 278–282.

41 Cui Yinan and Chen Junfeng, "Sanxian jianshe yu Guangxi chengzhen fazhan yanjiu," *Guangxi shehui kexue*, February 25, 2018. Zhong Jianying, "Liushi niandai fujian de 'xiao sanxian'," *Fujian dangshi yuekan* 5 (1998): 23–25. Xie Zhongqing, "1960 niandai Shanghai zhiyuan Jaingxi xiao sanxian jianshe yanjiu," *Jingangshan daxue xuebao* 31:6 (2016): 69–76. Liu Jianmin, "Lun Hebei 'xiao sanxian' jianshe" (PhD diss., Hebei shifan daxue, 2004). Zhang Qing, "Shandong 'xiao sanxian' gongye yicun diaocha baohu yanjiu" (master's thesis, Shandong jianzhu daxue, 2013). Su Taolin and Zhang Huijian, "20 shji 60 niandai Beijing xian sanxian jianshe," *Dangdai Beijing yanjiu* 1 (2014): 47–49. Yang Hanqing and Liang Xiangyang, "20 shiji qishi niandai Guangdong de xiao sanxian jianshe," *Hong guangjiao*, July15, 2015.

scattered in the mountains around Chongqing, so that if enemy troops attempted to enter Sichuan, they would run into a wall of firepower.[42] To further bolster regional industrial capabilities, the central Party signed off on an electronics base and aerospace complex in northern Guizhou. In Sichuan, central ministries set up a large cement plant in Emei, a steel factory in Jiangyou, a nuclear complex along the western edge of the Chengdu plain, an aerospace base and electronics complex scattered between Chengdu and Mianyang, and manufacturing complexes around Chongqing that produced trucks, precision instruments, river boats, and seafaring vessels.[43]

The central Party also pumped resources into projects attempted during the Great Leap. The Metallurgy Ministry resurrected construction of Panzhihua Steel in Sichuan, Jiuquan Steel in Gansu, and Shuicheng Steel in Liupanshui in western Guizhou, where the Coal Ministry re-mined local deposits to fulfill Panzhihua's energy needs along with carbon deposits around Chongqing and in western Sichuan. The Railroad Ministry restarted work on the Chengdu–Kunming Railroad to link Panzhihua to the outside world, and it again began laying the Guiyang–Chongqing and Guiyang–Kunming lines.[44] The Oil Ministry poured more funds into developing natural-gas fields in Luzhou in eastern Sichuan, and the First Machine-Building Ministry rehabilitated the Second Heavy Industry Works in Deyang in Sichuan's west to manufacture factory machinery. Central leaders also resuscitated large projects in central and northwest China – such as the Danjiangkou Dam in Hubei and the Liujiaxia Dam in Gansu – but they mainly conducted preparatory regional surveys and planning for new industrial ventures.[45]

The first phase of Third Front construction was thrown into disarray in 1966 when Mao extended his criticism of Soviet revisionism to the entire country in the opening salvos of the Cultural Revolution, and Red Guards followed Chairman Mao's order in his big-character poster "Bombard the Headquarters" to struggle against "cadres from the central down to the local levels" who were suspected of betraying China's socialist project and enforcing "a bourgeois dictatorship."[46] Third Front construction picked back up in 1969 in response to Sino-Soviet border clashes at Zhenbao Island. Taking place shortly after the Soviet invasion of Czechoslovakia in

[42] Yu Ronggen and Zhang Lanqi, eds., *Dangdai Chongqing jianshi* (Chongqing: Chongqing renmin chubanshe, 2003), 227–228.

[43] Guowuyuan, *Sanxian*, 108–109, 117, 143–145, 147, 150–151.

[44] Guizhou sheng liupanshui difang bianzuan weiyuanhui, *Liupanshui sanxian jianshe zhi* (Beijing: Dangdai zhongguo chubanshe, 2003), 3–4.

[45] Chen, *Sanxian*, 268–269, 287–289, 313–314.

[46] Roderick MacFarquhar and Michael Schoenhals, *Mao's Last Revolution* (Cambridge, MA: Belknap Press, 2006), 90.

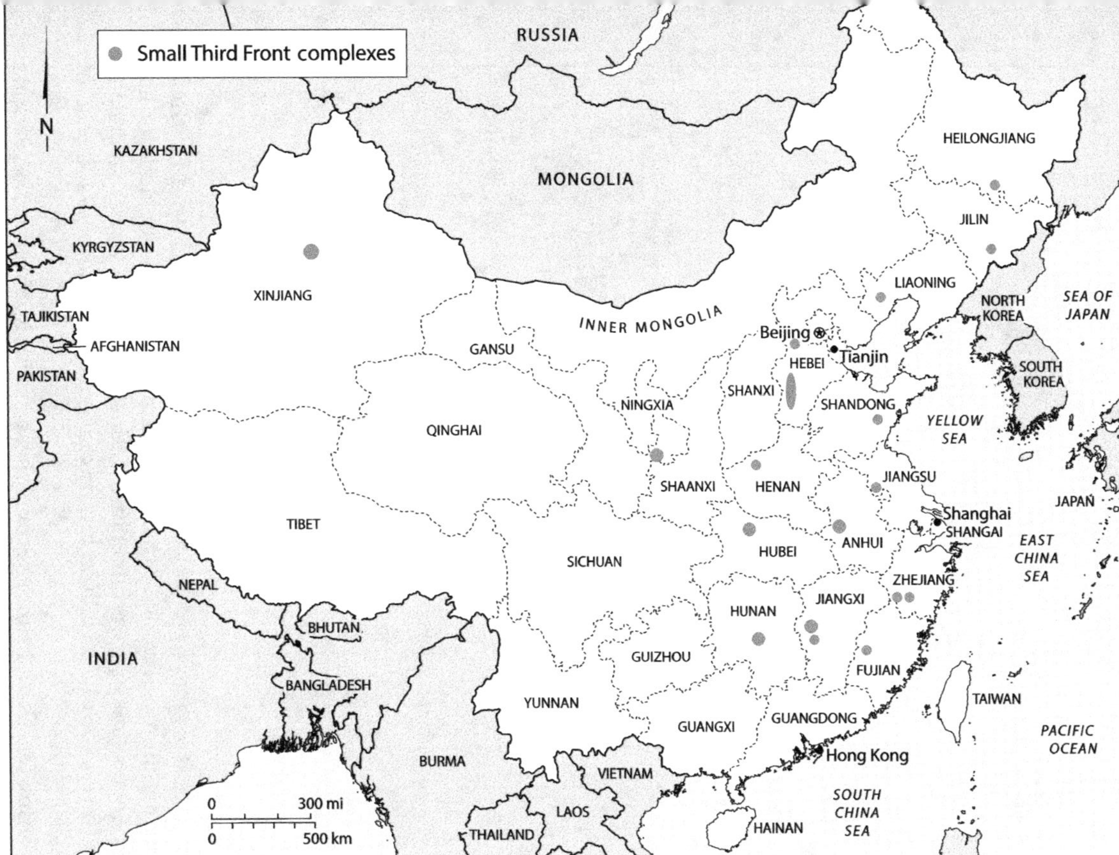

Map 0.2 The Small Third Front

Map 0.3 The Third Front in southwest China

1968, CCP leaders were concerned that Soviet leader Leonid Brezhnev might act more aggressively than he had in Czechoslovakia and not just send Soviet tanks steamrolling into China to reaffirm Soviet leadership over international socialism but make good on Moscow's threat of a nuclear strike.[47]

During the Third Front's second phase, building continued on existing Small Third Front facilities, and a few more complexes were added in the

[47] Garver, *China's Quest*, 278–280.

northeast, Ningxia, and Xinjiang closer to probable battle lines.[48] The central Party also jump-started Big Third Front projects put on hiatus in the southwest due to the fracas of the Cultural Revolution, while shifting Big Third Front construction's geographic focus to central China and the northwest. Like in the Third Front's first phase, central planners incorporated several large Great Leap projects into construction plans, such as the Hunan–Guizhou, Beijing–Liuzhou, and Xiangfan–Chongqing Railroads. The central Party also reinvigorated work on the Second Automobile Works and a Three Gorges hydropower station by setting in motion the founding of the Gezhouba Dam and making the small Hubei town of Shiyan into a new motor city.[49] The Coal Ministry additionally rekindled mining ventures in northern Shaanxi, southern Henan, northern Ningxia, and southern Inner Mongolia. The Chemical Ministry expanded plastics production around Lanzhou, and the Oil Ministry renewed drilling of oilfields in Hubei, Henan, and the Shaanxi–Gansu borderlands.[50]

Party leaders authorized several new ventures as well. Fearing that Soviet artillery units might soon rush across the flatlands of northern China and seize Beijing, the Central Military Commission ordered a cluster of tank manufacturers in southern Shanxi.[51] Military planners also demanded a helicopter complex in Jiangxi; a military truck complex and an aerospace base in southern Shaanxi; another aerospace base and shipbuilding complex in western Hubei; and light-arms manufacturers in the western half of Henan, Hubei, and Hunan.[52] The strategic calculus behind this sprawling mesh of firepower was to force an enemy to encounter at every step the persistent barrage of a storm of steel.[53] Central ministries also funneled resources into regional electricity infrastructure and founded several mainstays of inland China's power sector, such as the Qinglin Thermal Plant in Shaanxi, the Wu River Dam in Guizhou, an electrical grid linking the southwest and northwest, and another power grid connecting central and north China.[54]

In 1972, the Third Front's second phase tapered off when China balanced against Soviet aggression by establishing friendlier relations with the United States. The improvement of Sino-American relations

[48] Li Rui and Wang Chunlei, "Heilongjiang xiao sanxian jianshe diaocha yu pingjia," *Suihua xueyuan xuebao* (2015): 22–24. Wang Enbao, "Liaoning zai zhiyuan 'xiao sanxian' zhong de gongxian," *Dangshi zongheng* (August 2011). Zhou Mingzhang, "Sanxian jianshe yu Ningxia chengshihua," *Ningxia shehui kexue* (June 2018). Chen, *Sanxian*, 217.

[49] Chen, *Sanxian*, 265–267, 286–287. [50] Chen, *Sanxian*, 307–308, 313–315, 318–319.

[51] Wang Ziyun, "Shanxi sanxian jianshe de yanjiu," *Shanxi qingnian guanli ganbu xueyuan xuebao*, December 20, 2004.

[52] Chen, *Sanxian*, 294–295. Guowuyuan, *Sanxian*, 148–154, 173.

[53] Guowuyuan, *Sanxian*, 151–154. [54] Chen, *Sanxian*, 281.

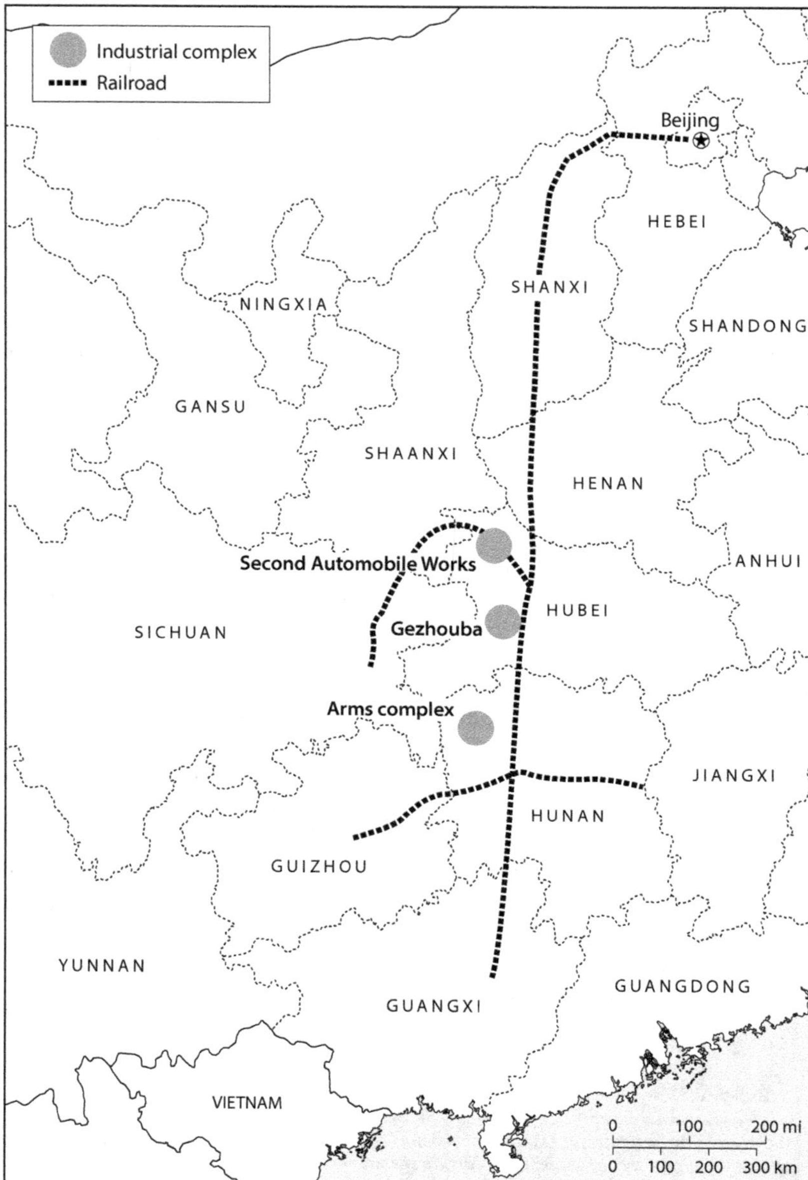

Map 0.4 The Third Front in south-central China

removed the sense of impending crisis that had powered the quick-paced developmental policies that burst onto the national scene with the Great Leap and surged a final two times in the Third Front campaign.[55] With the easing of Cold War tensions, the Party leadership directed the national economy away from militarized industrialization. With this epochal shift, the Third Front lost its centrality to Chinese development strategy. What did not fade away, but rather remained as cornerstones of national development, were inland China's larger industrial base, which firmed up the region's connections with the rest of the nation, and the CCP's commitment to carrying out big region-making industrial initiatives.

Bringing the Third Front In

Barry Naughton revealed the Third Front's importance in a pair of pioneering articles in 1988 and 1991. His attention to the Third Front is the exception in the West. Over the past few decades, only a few authors have studied the Third Front. Mel Gurtov and David Bachman have discussed enterprise restructuring in the 1980s.[56] Judith Shapiro has dedicated part of a chapter to the environmental damage caused by a few projects.[57] Jeremy Brown has written a section of a chapter on the experiences of urban and rural people at one factory.[58] Lorenz Lüthi has penned an article on central planning up to 1966.[59] When other scholars bring up the Third Front, they usually cite Naughton and agree with his verdict that the Third Front was an "immensely costly" program that had "a negative impact on China's economic development."[60] There are two exceptions. Chris Bramall has argued that the Third Front was a factor behind economic growth in Sichuan, and Chen Chao has analyzed group governance in a Third Front factory.[61] The above studies add to our

[55] For the Great Leap, see Garver, *China's Quest*, 130–133, 142–145.

[56] David Bachman, "Defence Industrialization in Guangdong," *China Quarterly* 166 (2001): 273–304. Mel Gurtov, "Swords into Market Shares: China's Conversion of Military Industry to Civilian Production," *China Quarterly* 134 (1993): 213–241.

[57] Judith Shapiro, *Mao's War against Nature: Politics and the Environment in Revolutionary China* (Cambridge and New York: Cambridge University Press, 2001), 142–159.

[58] Jeremy Brown, *City versus Countryside in Mao's China: Negotiating the Divide* (New York: Cambridge University Press, 2012), 173–183, 190–199.

[59] Lüthi, "Vietnam War," 26–51.

[60] Naughton, "Third Front," 351. See, for instance, John King Fairbank, *China: A New History* (Cambridge, MA: Belknap Press of Harvard University Press, 1992), 398–399.

[61] Chris Bramall, In *Praise of Maoist Economic Planning: Living Standards and Economic Development in Sichuan since 1931* (Oxford: Clarendon Press, 1993), 101–103. Chen Chao, *Toleration: Group Governance in a Chinese Third Line Enterprise* (Basingstoke: Palgrave MacMillan, 2018).

knowledge about the Third Front's composition, consequences, and social dynamics. Nonetheless they only offer a piecemeal picture.

Chinese research is more extensive. Starting in the 1980s, a trickle of articles began to appear. In the last two decades, this trickle has become a steady stream. Particularly important are monographs by Chen Donglin and He Haoju on the entire Third Front and edited volumes by Xu Youwei and Chen Donglin on the Small Third Front.[62] Chinese studies acknowledge the Third Front's economic difficulties and harsh living conditions, but their overall outlook is Whiggish, and they highlight how the Third Front contributed to the Party's ongoing project of developing western China.[63] Although Chinese historians present a generally positive portrayal of the Third Front, it would be a mistake not to draw on their research for this reason. Not only do Chinese scholars have unique access to archival documents, participants, gray literature, and classified materials, but their studies also contain many valuable insights into the complexities of everyday life, the Third Front's economic impact, and elite decision making.

Beyond these Third Front studies, most Chinese histories of the 1960s exhibit the same tendency as Western scholarship. They attend to the two big events which bookend the decade – the Great Leap and the Cultural Revolution – and they chart out Mao's conflicts with his colleagues after the Leap and his assertion of dominance through struggles in the cultural sphere, culminating with the Cultural Revolution.[64] This focus on cultural disputes has led scholars to often characterize the late 1960s and early 1970s as the Cultural Revolution decade. This narrative underappreciates that the commencement of the Third Front campaign brought about a monumental change in Mao's disagreements with his colleagues over economic policy. Cold War concerns thrust rapid development strategies back into the center of the national economic agenda, where they remained until more amiable Sino-American ties imparted to China a more favorable security climate in the early 1970s. Through examining the Third Front, this book brings a central pillar of Chinese industrial policy back into historical comprehension of Mao's China.

[62] Chen, *Sanxian*. He Haoju, *Sanxian jianshe yu xibu da kaifa* (Beijing: Dangdai Zhongguo chubanshe, 2003). Xu Yuwei and Chen Donglin, eds., *Xiao sanxian jianshe yanjiu luncong* (Shanghai: Shanghai daxue chubanshe, 2015). Xu Yuwei and Chen Donglin, eds., *Xiao sanxian jianshe yanjiu luncong: Xiao sanxian jianshe yu guofang xiandaihua* (Shanghai: Shanghai daxue chubanshe, 2016).

[63] See, for instance, Chen, *Sanxian*, 252. He, *Sanxian*, iv.

[64] For example, see Pang Songzhu, ed., *Mao Zedong shidai de Zhongguo* (Beijing: Zhonggong dangshi chubanshe, 2007). Pang Xianzhi and Chongji Jin, eds., *Mao Zedong zhuan 1949–1976 xia* (Beijing: Zhongyang wenxian chubanshe, 2004), 1388–1425.

More broadly speaking, Chinese and English histories of the Mao era regularly refer to the Cold War when discussing big international events like the Korean War or the Sino-Soviet split. Yet only diplomatic historians frequently take the Cold War as a major category of analysis.[65] Their research has demonstrated that foreign policy under Mao was shaped by Party leaders' determination to overcome China's century of humiliation by foreign imperialist countries.[66] Social historians, on the other hand, have a tendency to center their analyses on examining society from the bottom up, resulting in historiographic endeavors which tell us much about processes internal to China but push the Cold War almost completely into the background.[67] It is too early for students of Chinese history to heed Matthew Connelly's advice and "take off the Cold War lens," since many have yet to put it on.[68] By studying the Third Front, this book aims to push forward the emerging body of scholarship that descends from the heights of elite politics and elucidates the ways in which the Cold War's ramifications extended far beyond the chambers of diplomats into the inner workings of Chinese political economy, patterns of everyday life, and frameworks of meaning.[69]

The Global Cold War and China's Militarized Modernity

According to Odd Arne Westad, the central driving force behind the global Cold War was the conflict between the Soviet Union and the United States

[65] Chen, Mao's China. Lorenz M. Lüthi. *The Sino-Soviet Split: Cold War in the Communist World* (Princeton: Princeton University Press, 2008). Jeremy Friedman, *Shadow Cold War: The Sino-Soviet Competition for the Third World* (Chapel Hill: University of North Carolina Press, 2015). Gregg Brazinsky. *Winning the Third World: Sino-American Rivalry during the Cold War* (Chapel Hill: University of North Carolina Press, 2017).

[66] Michael H. Hunt, *The Genesis of Chinese Communist Foreign Policy* (New York: Columbia University Press, 1996). Michael M. Sheng, *Battling Western Imperialism: Mao, Stalin, and the United States* (Princeton: Princeton University Press, 1997). Chen, *Mao's China*.

[67] Some examples are Jeremy Brown and Matthew D. Johnson, eds., *Maoism at the Grassroots: Everyday Life in China's Era of High Socialism* (Cambridge, MA: Harvard University Press, 2015). Huaiyin Li, *Village China under Socialism and Reform: A Micro-History, 1948–2008* (Palo Alto: Stanford University Press, 2009).

[68] Matthew Connelly. "Taking Off the Cold War Lens: Visions of North–South Conflict during the Algerian War for Independence," *American Historical Review* 105 (2000): 739–769.

[69] Some examples are Jeremy Brown, "From Resisting Communists to Resisting America: Civil War and Korean War in Southwest China, 1950–1951," in *Dilemmas of Victory: The Early Years of the People's Republic of China*, eds. Jeremy Brown and Paul G. Pickowicz (Cambridge, MA: Harvard University Press, 2007), 105–129. Austin Jersild, *The Sino-Soviet Alliance: An International History* (Chapel Hill: University of North Carolina Press, 2014). Garver, *China's Quest*. Sigrid Schmalzer, *Red Revolution, Green Revolution: Scientific Farming in Socialist China* (Chicago: The University of Chicago Press, 2016). Nicholai Volland, *Socialist Cosmopolitanism: The Chinese Literary Universe, 1945–1965* (New York: Columbia University Press, 2017).

over the meaning and direction of European modernity and their international efforts to transform the global order in order to demonstrate the universality of their respective ideologies.[70] American modernity stressed individual freedom, antistatism, market capitalism, containing communism, and a strong faith in the power of technology.[71] On the other hand, Soviet modernity prioritized turning poor peasant societies into developed nation-states that not only were made up of industrial workers, but also elevated their social status and looked after their welfare. In pursuit of this end, Soviet modernizers strived to eliminate market transactions which were taken to be an obstacle to the foundation of a new socialist order based on equality, justice, and raising the social standing of the underprivileged.[72]

In Cold War China, there existed a third Maoist version of modernity. Like the Bolsheviks, the first generation of CCP leaders were anticapitalists who wanted to make a weak agrarian country into a strong industrial state and create a new society with socialist ways of behaving.[73] Similar to Moscow, Beijing also did not think of the Cold War in John Lewis Gaddis's famous phrase as a period of "great power peace."[74] They considered the postwar world to be in a period of ongoing conflict in which China had directly fought against America in the Korean War, the capitalist camp constantly besieged socialist states, and the United States and European countries regularly interfered militarily in decolonization and the affairs of postcolonial states.[75]

Chinese apprehension towards the Cold War is visible in the way that it was talked about, or rather was *not* talked about. Throughout the Mao era, the term "the Cold War" (*leng zhan*) never figured prominently in national discourse. Between 1950 and 1963, it averaged annually only 198 appearances in the *People's Daily*, compared to 2,499 times in the *New York Times*.[76] At the time of the Third Front's height (1964–1971), the expression "the Cold War" fell almost completely out of use, showing

[70] Odd Arne Westad, *The Global Cold War: Third World Interventions and the Making of Our Times* (New York: Cambridge University Press, 2005), 4.

[71] Westad, *Global Cold War*, 9. [72] Westad, *Global Cold War*, 40.

[73] Kotkin, Magnetic Mountain, 14. Yinghong Cheng, *Creating the "New Man": From Enlightenment Ideals to Socialist Realities* (Honolulu: University of Hawai'i Press, 2009), 48–126. Jochen Hellbeck, *Revolution on My Mind: Writing a Diary under Stalin* (Cambridge, MA: Harvard University Press, 2006).

[74] John Lewis Gaddis, "The Long Peace: Elements of Stability in the Postwar International System," *International Security* 10 (Spring 1986): 100. On the Soviet Union, Vladislav M. Zubok, *A Failed Empire: The Soviet Union in the Cold War from Stalin to Gorbachev* (Chapel Hill: University of North Carolina Press, 2009).

[75] On the Korean War, see Chen Jian, *China's Road to the Korean War: The Making of the Sino-American Confrontation* (New York: Columbia University Press, 1994). On Chinese anti-imperialism abroad, see Friedman, *Shadow Cold War*. On the Cold War more broadly, see Chen, *Mao's China*.

[76] Proquest Historical Newspapers, *The New York Times*, "Cold War."

up in the pages of the *People's Daily* only twelve times per year, while it remained a mainstay of American public discourse. Thus we can say that on a semiotic level, the Cold War never happened in Mao's China because the CCP never viewed the conflict between capitalism and socialism as cold from the late 1940s into the 1970s.

Chinese conceptions of the Cold War were similar to those of other Third World countries whose national strivings were subjects of geopolitical intrigue and military posturing that sometimes morphed into armed conflict.[77] They were shot through with examples of American and Soviet activities imperiling Chinese interests at home and abroad.[78] Chinese foreign policy was also rooted in the CCP's understanding of the purpose of the international socialist movement. Party leaders thought, as Jeremy Friedman has argued, that anti-imperialism should be the principal concern of revolutionary activities worldwide, and that state socialism would bring about a shift in the global balance of power by economically developing countries that even in the age of decolonization were still subject to the geopolitical dominance of imperialist nation-states.[79] Beijing endeavored to persuade Third World nations to adhere to China's geopolitical stance and cautioned them against siding with the Soviets or Americans in the Cold War since they coveted hegemony over the Third World, and their capitalist and revisionist inclinations would generate social and economic inequality. The CCP counseled the Third World instead to take up the Maoist approach to modernity, whose policies of rural revolution, guerilla warfare, self-reliance, and equality promotion purportedly offered the surest way to both preserve national independence and become a socialist country.[80]

The PRC's attempt to contain the influence of Soviet revisionism, American imperialism, and global capitalism was not limited to the international realm. It also had a domestic correlate.[81] In this regard,

[77] Heonik Kwon, *The Other Cold War* (New York: Columbia University Press, 2010).

[78] James L. Hevia, *English Lessons: The Pedagogy of Imperialism in Nineteenth-Century China* (Durham, NC: Duke University Press, 2003), 334–338. Shen Zhihua and Li Danhui, *After Leaning to One Side: China and Its Allies in the Cold War* (Stanford: Stanford University Press, 2011), 167–195.

[79] Friedman, *Shadow Cold War*, 2.

[80] On Chinese critiques of Soviet foreign policy, see Sergey Radchenko, *Two Suns in the Heavens: The Sino-Soviet Struggle for Supremacy, 1962–1967* (Stanford: Stanford University Press, 2009). Nicholas Khoo, *Collateral Damage: Sino-Soviet Rivalry and the Termination of the Sino-Vietnamese Alliance* (New York: Columbia University Press, 2011);and Friedman, *Shadow Cold War*. On Chinese critiques of American foreign policy, see Brazinsky, *Winning the Third World*.

[81] Andrew G. Walder notes this trend in "Cultural Revolution Radicalism: Variations on a Stalinist Theme." In Joseph, Wong, and Zweig, *New Perspectives on the Cultural Revolution*, 41–61.

China was of a piece with other Cold War states which treated the geopolitical project of containment as a struggle for hearts and minds on the home front.[82] Nefarious social elements were perceived to be operating within China which supported Soviet and American practices, and so both the CCP and the Chinese people had to remain vigilant, steadfastly fight against their influence, and strive to realize Maoist objectives. Only then could China prevent foreign enemies from gaining sway over the body politic, subverting the Chinese revolution from within, and derailing China's march towards socialist modernity. The irony is that the CCP's drive to curb American and Soviet pull within China made containing them into one of the most pressing domestic concerns. Such was the dialectical logic of national insecurity in the global Cold War.[83]

The international strains of the Cold War led to a pronounced militarization of Mao's China. The militarization of modern China, however, did not begin with the Cold War. As Hans van de Ven has argued, in both the nineteenth and twentieth centuries military ways of thinking deeply influenced leading ideas about how to modernize China.[84] The centrality of military practices to Chinese conceptions of modernity was closely related to the country's loss of eight wars between the First Opium War in 1840 and World War II. Faced with defeat after defeat, top officials came to think that the primary purpose of statecraft was the pursuit of wealth and power in order to strengthen China's ability to defend its sovereignty.[85] Leading late Qing reformer Liang Qichao put forth a position that was widely held by subsequent Chinese thought-leaders. He asserted that since modernity was an "age of struggle among nations for the survival of the fittest,"[86] the government had to back industrialization and fashion a new Chinese people that had a solid work ethic, "a strong sense of nationalism [and] a militaristic mentality."[87]

[82] Charles S. Maier, "The Politics of Productivity: Foundations of American International Economic Policy after World War II," *International Organization* 31 (1977): 607–633. Elaine Taylor May, *Homeward Bound: American Families in the Cold War Era* (New York: Basic Books, 1988).

[83] Laura McEnaney, "Cold War Mobilization and Domestic Politics: The United States," in *The Cambridge History of the Cold War, Volume 1*, ed. Melvyn P. Leffler and Odd Arne Westad (Cambridge: Cambridge University Press, 2010), 420–441. David Priestland, "Cold War Mobilisation and Domestic Politics: The Soviet Union," in Leffler and Westad, *The Cambridge History of the Cold War, Volume 1*, 442–463.

[84] Van de Ven, "The Military in the Republic," 373.

[85] Stephen R. Halsey, *Quest for Power: European Imperialism and the Making of Chinese Statecraft* (Cambridge, MA: Harvard University Press, 2015), 6.

[86] Liang Qichao, "Renewing the People," in *Sources of Chinese Tradition: From 1600 through the Twentieth Century*, compiled by Wm. Theodore de Bary and Richard Lufrano (New York: Columbia University Press, 2000), 289.

[87] Cited in Cheng, *Creating the "New Man,"* 51.

Drinking from the same anxious well of national precarity, GMD founder Sun Yat-sen devised a comprehensive development plan for China in 1920, and he endorsed a period of military tutelage during which the GMD would remold the populace from a "heap of loose sand" into disciplined citizens devoted to building the nation and protecting it from foreign harm.[88] CCP leaders shared Sun's belief that an enlightened Party knew best how to modernize China, or as Mao said, paint upon China's "poor and blank" slate "the freshest and most beautiful" socialist society.[89] Both the GMD and CCP's militarized paternalistic views of China's modernization are instances of what James Scott has labeled high modernism; that is, "the aspiration to the administrative ordering of nature and society ... [by] high-level administrators ... [of] all aspects of social life in order to improve the human condition."[90]

In the Third Front campaign, the Party pursued five goals that were intimately linked to its overhauling of China into a socialist industrial society. First, the Third Front manifested the Party's determination to industrialize China and transform its natural resources into engines of economic growth. Second, the Third Front aimed to rebalance the regional weight of China's industrial geography from the coast to the interior. Party leaders viewed China's coastal-heavy economy as a legacy of imperialism, and Mao echoed widespread Party sentiments when he called for rectifying regional disparities in his 1956 speech on the "Ten Great Relationships."[91] Third, the Party sought, as part of the Third Front campaign, to make citizens that gave first priority in all their affairs to the construction of a socialist China. Fourth, CCP leaders undertook the Third Front to ensure the security of the socialist regime that they had spent most of their lives devising and defending.[92]

Intertwined with the above four goals was a fifth and final one. The Third Front responded to the Party's resolve to redress China's

88 William C. Kirby, "Engineering China: The Origins of the Chinese Developmental State," in *Becoming Chinese*, ed. Wen-hsin Yeh (Berkeley: University of California Press, 2000), 138–143.

89 The quote is from Mao Zedong, "Introducing a Co-operative," April 15, 1958, *Marxists Internet Archive*, accessed June 23, 2017, www.marxists.org/reference/archive/mao/selected-works/volume-8/mswv8_09.htm For succinct discussions of these issues, see Paul A. Cohen, "The Post-Mao Reforms in Historical Perspective," *Journal of Asian Studies* 47 (1988): 518–540. Joseph Esherick, "Ten Theses on the Chinese Revolution," *Modern China* 21 (1995): 45–76.

90 James C. Scott, *Seeing Like a State: How Certain Schemes to Improve the Human Condition Have Failed* (New Haven: Yale University Press, 1998), 88.

91 Nicholas R. Lardy, *Economic Growth and Distribution in China* (New York: Cambridge University Press, 1978), 10–13, 152–157.

92 For a history of the first generation of CCP leaders, see William W. Whitson, *The Chinese High Command: A History of Communist Military Politics, 1927–71* (Santa Barbara: Praeger, 1973).

humiliation by imperialists. According to Party doctrine, China endured a hundred-year saga of foreigners trampling on its sovereignty from the First Opium War in the late 1830s to the Allied victory over Japan in World War II.[93] Party leaders carried out the Third Front to reduce the risk that a Sino-American or Sino-Soviet war would result in China once again losing sovereignty over its territory. Mao cited as inspiration for the Third Front Chiang Kai-shek's failure to set up sufficient inland industry prior to World War II. As a result, when Japan invaded in 1937, the GMD was forced to retreat inland to a small industrial base when the heat of battle was already scorching hot. Mao argued that China should also learn from the negative example of Stalinist Russia, which did not build an adequate rear base in the 1930s, and so Moscow had to relocate industry in the 1940s when the Nazis were already on the Red Army's heels.[94] In the following two sections, I lay out how the CCP attempted to achieve these five goals and give a preliminary assessment of their performance.

Maoist Developmental Strategy and Cold War Insecurity

Structuring Communist Party efforts to defend Cold War China through the Third Front campaign was a Maoist approach to science and technology. Sigrid Schmalzer has traced Maoist views of technoscience to the revolutionary fountainhead of Yan'an. Faced with the superior technological might of the GMD and the Japanese, CCP leaders decided that if they favored foreign machinery and foreign-trained experts, they could not confront pressing economic needs. Party elites thought that the only way they could build up economic capabilities was to pursue a strategy of self-reliance which emphasized native techniques, mass mobilization, and applied science.[95] This style of development was applied to the economic sector as well as to the military realm, where self-reliance meant making up for scarce industrial weaponry by employing rural militias to supply front lines and bleed the morale out of enemy forces through a war of attrition.[96]

93 David Apter and Tony Saich, *Revolutionary Discourse in Mao's Republic* (Cambridge, MA: Harvard University Press, 1994), 92. The losses included the Second Opium War, the Sino-French War, the First Sino-Japanese War, the eight-power invasion during the Boxer Rebellion, the Russo-Japanese War in Manchuria, Japan's Twenty-One Demands, Japan's invasion of Manchuria, and the Japanese invasion of 1937. For a book-length statement of this view, see Hu Sheng, *Imperialism and Chinese Politics* (Beijing: Foreign Languages Press, 1955).

94 Mao Zedong, "Yao yanjiu Sitalin je Jiang Jieshi de cetui," November 26, 1964, in *Zhongguo gongchandang yu sanxian*, 119–120.

95 Schmalzer, "Self-Reliant Science," 79.

96 Xiaobing Li, *A History of the Modern Chinese Army* (Lawrence: University of Kansas Press, 2007), 55–56, 68–72. For the classic statement of this strategy, see Mao Zedong, *On*

When CCP leaders founded the People's Republic, they leaned to the Soviet side in the bipolar Cold War world and implemented in the First Five Year Plan the Soviet policy of establishing a socialist industrial society through central planning agencies supervising the staged growth of large capital-intensive projects in both the economic and military spheres.[97] During the Great Leap, Mao and his colleagues sought to accelerate China's transition into a communist economy.[98] Judging Soviet-style development insufficient to achieve this utopian goal, CCP leaders replaced it with a strategy that Mao dubbed "walking on two legs."[99] The central idea was that national development did not have to depend solely on machinery and technically skilled labor. The Party could adapt the Yan'an way of self-reliance and mass mobilization into a strategy of rapid industrialization and make use of limited domestic machinery and skilled workers while simultaneously compensating for their lack by channeling China's large rural population into building infrastructure with available local materials. Contrary to Soviet methods, the key motivator for labor was ideological praise, not material inducements. The main leaders in the industrialization process were also not central planners. They were local officials who could start projects on their own and who, as Judith Shapiro has shown, organized labor along military lines, enforced military-like discipline, and used militarized terminology to describe the industrialization of natural environments.[100]

In the wake of the Great Leap's failure, the future of Maoist developmental strategy was far from certain. Chinese national security was also on very shaky ground since Beijing lost Moscow as a security guarantor and a provider of industrial goods when the Sino-Soviet alliance fell apart in the early 1960s. Worried about the prospect of having to fight a war with the United States or the Soviet Union completely on its own, the CCP advanced China's nuclear weapons program while acting on the belief that the best defense strategy was not based on nuclear arms.[101] China was not in the same technological league as the United States or the

Guerilla Warfare, 1937, *Marxists Internet Archive*, www.marxists.org/reference/archive/mao/works/1937/guerrilla-warfare, accessed June 25, 2017.

97 On the economic side, see Deborah A. Kaple, *Dream of a Red Factory: The Legacy of High Stalinism in China* (New York: Oxford University Press, 1994). Hua-yu Li, *Mao and the Economic Stalinization of China, 1948–1953* (Lanham: Rowman and Littlefield, 2006). On the military side, see Li, *Modern Chinese Army*, 113–146.

98 Dali Yang, *Calamity and Reform in China: State, Rural Society, and Institutional Change since the Great Leap Famine* (Stanford: Stanford University Press, 1996), 33–34.

99 Carl Riskin, *China's Political Economy: The Quest for Development since 1949* (New York: Oxford University Press, 1987), 117.

100 Shapiro, *Mao's War*, 70–75.

101 Ralph Powell, "Great Powers and Atomic Bombs Are 'Paper Tigers'," *China Quarterly* 23 (1965): 55–63.

Soviet Union. Chinese air and ground troops could not ward off American or Soviet planes. Nor did the Chinese military have a - guaranteed second strike to dissuade the United States or the Soviet Union from launching a nuclear attack. On October 16, 1964, Beijing carried out its first successful nuclear test, but it could only hit Soviet cities when the DF-4 intercontinental ballistic missile came online in 1971, and it could only target the whole United States when the DF-5 was deployed in 1981.[102]

To deter American or Soviet aggression, the CCP loudly proclaimed that China had a people's army of ideologically committed citizens ready to fight a protracted ground war. Lin Biao described this military threat in the preface to the *Little Red Book* as China's "spiritual atom bomb."[103] Since a large Sino-foreign hot war never happened in the late 1960s and early 1970s, it is hard to say how this strategy would have held up in battle. It is also unclear whether the threat of a protracted war with China figured into Soviet calculations to pull back from the brink of war in the late 1960s. What is certain is that the fear of Chinese forces rushing into North Vietnam and waging a protracted people's war like in Korea in the early 1950s kept the United States from trying to roll back communism anywhere closer to China's borders than the seventeenth parallel.[104]

At the time of the Vietnam War, the Third Front was the defensive industrial backbone of Chinese national security strategy. With the Third Front, CCP leaders reconceptualized the entire country as one giant battlefield in which society and economy were militarized in advance in preparation for the perceived threat of a surprise attack. If foreigners invaded, they would have to fight through the First, Second, and Third Fronts to achieve victory, and all along the way they would confront militias supplied with light arms by Small Third Front arsenals stationed in the mountains of many provinces. Chinese citizens not mobilized for the Third Front did not know that the national economy had been spatially reconfigured in anticipation of an imminent war. Nor did they understand that one big reason why scarcity was endemic to daily life was that huge quantities of resources were being funneled inland since Party leaders had determined that the eastern seaboard would likely be occupied or reduced to rubble in the event of a Sino-Soviet or Sino-American war.

[102] John W. Lewis and Xue Litai, *China Builds the Bomb* (Stanford: Stanford University Press, 1988), 212–214.

[103] Alexander C. Cook, ed., *Mao's Little Red Book: A Global History* (New York: Cambridge University Press, 2014), 1.

[104] George McTurnan Kahin, *Intervention: How America Became Involved in Vietnam* (New York: Knopf, 1986), 336, 338–342.

The layout of Third Front projects was also imbued with Cold War anxieties. Concerned that the military could not defend the nation's skies, central planners applied a programmatic high-modernist formula. Enterprises had to be ensconced within mountains, split up into pieces, and distributed over large areas, so that it would be more arduous for enemy planes to locate and destroy them.[105] The central Party additionally responded to Chinese insecurity in the Cold War by reinstating in the Third Front campaign the Great Leap's emphasis on austerity, mass mobilization, and militarized rapid development. The Party, however, exchanged the Great Leap's focus on local initiative for the Soviet policy of centralized authority over the building of large industrial projects.

The construction of Third Front ventures was closely tied to what Michael Szonyi has termed Cold War time. That is a period in which local activities were profoundly affected by international political affairs and decision making in Beijing, Washington, and Moscow.[106] When a great-power war appeared imminent in 1964 with the United States and in 1969 with the Soviet Union, the Chinese leadership endeavored to accelerate national preparations for battle by inscribing Maoist military stratagems into the Third Front's construction process. In accordance with the guerilla tactic of concentrating forces for key conflicts, millions of industrial workers and tons of industrial equipment were transferred to industrial outposts in the interior.[107] Nearby rural residents were mobilized in even bigger numbers to serve as the crack troops of militia construction brigades, and they were commanded to carry in local handicrafts to make up for shortages of industrial machinery.

At Third Front construction sites, work habits became unglued from clock time and became subject to what Gail Hershatter has characterized as "campaign time."[108] During building campaigns, the normal eight-hour workday was trumped by the demands of a state of emergency which induced a particular form of what E.P. Thompson has designated as task-oriented time. But where Thompson's notion of task-oriented time often implies a more leisurely, less top-down approach to finishing a work task, campaign time was inexorably enmeshed with commands from above to

[105] Guowuyuan, *Sanxian*, 21–22.

[106] Michael Szonyi, *Cold War Island: Quemoy on the Front Line* (Cambridge, Cambridge University Press, 2008), 4.

[107] Guowuyuan, *Sanxian*, 22, 26–29.

[108] On campaign time, Gail Hershatter, *The Gender of Memory: Rural Women and China's Collective Past* (Berkeley: University of California Press, 2011), 237–246. For the dynamics of mass campaigns, see Gordon Bennett, *Yundong: Mass Campaigns in Chinese Communist Leadership* (Berkeley: Center for Chinese Studies China Research Monographs, 1976).

quicken construction schedules and raise economic output.[109] People were instructed to work as much as possible since a war of invasion might at any moment come crashing through the horizon into the present.

According to Barry Naughton, Third Front labor produced three major economic achievements. It created a railroad grid in isolated parts of China, increased the development of mineral resources, and established some fairly efficient factories.[110] For Naughton, the Third Front's limited successes were not worth their high costs. It is Naughton's view that if Party leaders had pursued "alternative, more measured, industrialization strategies," they could have attained "the same level of development of Third Front areas combined with a significantly higher level of output for Chinese industry as a whole."[111] The core of this alternative development strategy would have involved focusing China's scarce capital on more developed coastal regions whose existing industrial base would have helped to stimulate more industrial growth than the remote underdeveloped areas that made up the Third Front.

I partially agree with Naughton's assessment of the Third Front. Many projects were not economically viable in the long run because their location and product line were closely linked to military concerns. Some projects were also impetuously built, and their construction dragged on for years. This is partly attributable to security pressures speeding up construction. The Cultural Revolution played a significant role too, since administrators and skilled workers came under attack for supposedly stabbing Maoist China in the back and supporting Soviet revisionism and a capitalist road for the country. Nationwide fights against perceived internal threats collided with the Third Front in 1966 and almost completely supplanted its construction with internecine clashes in 1967 and 1968. I additionally share Naughton's position that the Third Front helped to build out railroad networks and increase mining operations in inland China, a point which Chris Bramall has elaborated on in his research on infrastructure development in Sichuan during the Mao era.[112]

However, I argue that the Third Front fostered the CCP's resolve to build industrial systems that reshape the economic makeup of whole regions. The central product of the Party's efforts at region making was the expansion in inland China of what Astrid Kander and her colleagues have singled out as the three large development blocks that serve as the core of industrial economies. The first development block is the collection

[109] E.P. Thompson, "Time, Work-Discipline, and Industrial Capitalism," *Past & Present* 38 (1967): 59–61.
[110] Naughton, "Third Front," 375. [111] Naughton, "Third Front," 380–381.
[112] Bramall, *Maoist Economic Planning*, 113.

of industries whose chief source of energy is coal. The second is the technological system that revolves around oil, and the third is the assemblage of technologies whose driving energy source is electricity. The formation of these development blocks not only entailed producing more electricity, coal, and oil. It also involved the establishment of factories that produced iron-made and petrochemical goods, the construction of railroads that connected inland provinces to nationwide distribution systems, building roads which served a growing automobile industry, and forging electrical grids that tied together several provinces and powered an expanding manufacturing sector.[113]

I also maintain that the Third Front was the only policy that economic planners considered in the mid-1960s that favored industrializing inland China. The only other policy choice discussed by Party leaders was the original draft of the Third Five Year Plan composed by Deng Xiaoping and other high-ranking officials. Their plan made no mention of pursuing large-scale inland industrialization. The Third Front was the sole policy the central Party articulated to address the economic divide between the coast and the interior. If the Party had not backed the Third Front, regional economic discrepancies would have likely become bigger since the only other policy option existing at the time did not make reducing them into a political priority.

Maoist Social Engineering and Cold War Norms

The Communist Party under Mao not only sought to industrialize socialist China. It also endeavored to forge a new socialist man that adhered to Maoist standards of behavior. The Daqing oilfield was the public face of Chinese efforts to build a new socialist industrial person in the 1960s and 1970s. Daqing was the model that everyone knew about from the national press which incessantly urged industrial workers to imitate Daqing labor's ascetic industriousness, so that China might make more headway on the road to socialist modernity.[114] The Third Front campaign was the huge hidden side of Chinese industrial policy. Third Front workers never became objects of national veneration since, like other Cold War statesmen exposed to the heat of intense geopolitical friction, Chinese leaders presumed that whatever was publicly perceptible was militarily vulnerable.[115] Sequestered in the

[113] Astrid Kander, Paolo Malanima, and Paul Warde, *Power to the People: Energy in Europe over the Last Five Centuries* (Trenton: Princeton University Press, 2014).

[114] For the associated history, see Hou Li, *Building for Oil: Daqing and the Formation of the Chinese Socialist State* (Cambridge, MA: Harvard University Press, 2018), 95–134.

[115] Joseph Masco, *The Theater of Operations: National Security Affect from the Cold War to the War on Terror* (Durham, NC: Duke University Press, 2014), 124–138. For a history of

shadows, the Third Front offered a massive canvas for the CCP's political experiment of fashioning a new socialist person through what Michel Foucault has characterized as technologies of power that regulate people's conduct and channel individuals towards particular ends.[116]

On the one hand, the Party sought to suppress practices discursively associated with China's Cold War competitors – the United States and the Soviet Union. These practices included prioritizing personal interests, preferring office work, advocating more gradual development, seeking comfort, favoring the use of machinery, and giving technical personnel authority over decision making. Diametrically opposed to these politically flawed practices were ways of thinking and behaving that were appropriate conduct for a loyal Maoist. Counted within this ideological domain were being self-reliant, championing collective interests, making the most out of local resources, believing that the masses could overcome any difficulty, and strenuously working to build socialism wherever and with whomever the CCP designated as best.[117]

The experiences of Third Front participants provide evidence of how the precepts of Maoist social engineering operated in practice. As Neil Diamant has shown in his book on family reform in Mao's China, the Party's quest to manufacture a new socialist people produced numerous unintended consequences.[118] In the case of the Third Front, laborers were injured and died in workplace accidents, and they self-segregated along regional lines and the urban–rural divide.[119] With stories of shared sacrifice, CCP propaganda ideologically papered over socioeconomic divisions between urban and rural areas *and* inland regions and the coast. But Third Front participants could see spatial divides in China's economic geography, and they knew in what places they would rather be.

Many urban recruits begrudgingly moved away from the relative affluence of coastal and northeastern towns for a new life in mountainous hinterlands. Upon arriving in the Third Front, many urbanites quickly longed to leave impoverished inland areas and work at state-owned enterprises with extensive welfare provisions in centrally located cities.

civil defense, see Edward M. Geist, *Armageddon Insurance: Civil Defense in the United States and Soviet Union, 1945–1991* (Chapel Hill: University of North Carolina Press, 2019).

116 Michel Foucault, *Technologies of the Self: A Seminar with Michel Foucault*, eds. Luther H. Martin, Huck Gutman, and Patrick H. Hutton (Amherst: University of Massachusetts Press, 1988), 18.

117 For quotes about these practices, see Mao Tse-tung, *Quotations from Chairman Mao Tse-tung* (New York: Bantam Books, 1967), 102–114.

118 Neil J. Diamant, *Revolutionizing the Family: Politics, Love, and Divorce in Urban and Rural China, 1949–1968* (Berkeley: University of California Press, 2000), 9–11.

119 Brown, *City versus Countryside*, 173–183, 190–199. Chen, *Toleration*, 76–87.

Some individuals later found meaning in their work while other people's perceptions tracked in the other direction. They set out with a desire to assist in building socialist industry, only to become disillusioned. Some people expressed discontent by deploying the weapons of the weak and shirking work.[120] Some called for improvements in living and working conditions. Others demanded to be sent home and fought with management personnel. Some individuals became so disgruntled with Third Front life that they ended their own. Policies which devalued advanced schooling and foreign techniques made some participants cherish technical skills even more. In the above respects, Third Fronters were like groups – such as sent-down youth and the Xinjiang Construction Corps – which often did not live up to the CCP's expectation that they be indifferent to where and with whom they served socialism, no matter how poor, remote, and isolating their work assignments were.[121]

The Party, likewise, sapped popular support by conflating socialist modernity with austerity and heavy-industrial production. As Ci Jiwei has observed, the resultant endemic consumer shortages prompted inadvertent desires for better material conditions that went against the Maoist principle of collective asceticism.[122] Rural folk, on the other hand, generally held a more positive view of the Third Front and desired access to the version of socialist modernity that Third Front work units made available to employees in the form of special schools, hospitals, residential areas, and cultural centers. No matter what side of the urban–rural divide someone came from, participant desires to take part in the Third Front often ran contrary to Maoist norms and stemmed just as much from a yearning to secure a richer material life as from an ardor to safeguard socialism from China's Cold War rivals.

While the Third Front campaign unquestionably generated many unplanned effects, the consequent variety of different experiences does not place in doubt, as Jerry Brown and Matthew Johnson have suggested, "the credibility of a unified national narrative" or "whether 'Mao's China' ever existed at all."[123] The Third Front campaign, on the contrary, points to the power of the centralizing Maoist state to reduce the complexity of social, economic, and political affairs to administrative formulas which

[120] James C. Scott, *Weapons of the Weak: Everyday Forms of Peasant Resistance* (New Haven: Yale University Press, 1985), 34–35.

[121] On sent-down youth, see Thomas P. Bernstein, *Up to the Mountains and Down to the Villages: The Transfer of Youth from Urban to Rural China* (New Haven: Yale University Press, 1978). Michel Bonnin, *The Lost Generation: The Rustification of Chinese Youth, 1968–1980* (Hong Kong: Chinese University Press, 2013). On the Xinjiang Construction Corps, see Tom Cliff, *Oil and Water: Being Han in Xinjiang* (Chicago: The University of Chicago Press, 2016).

[122] Ci, *Dialectic*, 134–167. [123] Brown and Johnson, *Maoism at the Grassroots*, 15.

circumscribed the ways that people lived, thought, and used resources.[124] Vital to this process of governmental simplification were the many Third Front participants who acted according to the mottos of Maoism.[125] Whether people did so voluntarily or by force of circumstance, there is much evidence that recruits listened to the Party's directives and struggled to realize them in their daily lives.

Central planners ordered industry in isolated mountains and delineated what categories of people could be politically trusted for classified projects. Local officials, in turn, supervised recruitment campaigns in which workers had to publicly declare their determination to construct the Third Front. Project managers also applied Maoist ideas to the building process and organized campaigns which stressed local self-reliance, working relentlessly, and valuing the progress of socialism more than family life, consumption, or regional location. Laborers hurried to achieve project targets, hollowed out mountains, and concealed factories inside. Managers kept consumption to a minimum, and they commended laborers whose conduct echoed Maoist ideals.

Although not all Third Front participants perceived Maoist ideals to be ideal, some people regarded their own life goals to be reflected in the objectives of China's party-state and wanted to be paragons of Maoism.[126] This trend was especially pronounced among people who had performed revolutionary work for the CCP for so long that it was hard to determine where their life ambitions ended and the Party's began.[127] Some young people, who were born around the time of the PRC's founding and had grown up under the Red Flag, also wanted to accomplish the political and economic missions that Chairman Mao and the Party set out for them.[128] Some people of this sort put serving the revolution before family and sought to mirror in their own daily activities

[124] Scott, *Seeing Like a State*, 23. For an analysis of this trend in Cultural Revolution cultural production, see Laikwan Pang, *The Art of Cloning: Creative Production during China's Cultural Revolution* (London: Verso Books, 2017).

[125] On the social effects of governmental simplification in the legal realm during the Mao era, see Jennifer Altehenger, *Legal Lessons: Popularizing Laws in the People's Republic of China, 1949–1989* (Cambridge, MA: Harvard University Asia Center, 2018).

[126] Other books which make this point are Hershatter, Gender of Memory, 99–128, 213–232. Schmalzer, *Red Revolution*, 24, 156. Wang Zheng, *Finding Women in the State: A Socialist Feminist Revolution in the People's Republic of China, 1949–1964* (Berkeley: University of California Press, 2017).

[127] On the bonds holding together senior Party members, see Apter and Saich, *Revolutionary Discourse in Mao's Republic*, 141–183.

[128] Similar trends have been observed in Anita Chan, *Children of Mao: Personality Development and Political Activism in the Red Guard Generation* (Basingstoke: The Macmillan Press, 1985). Guobin Yang, *The Red Guard Generation and Political Activism in China* (New York: Columbia University Press, 2016). Margaret Tillman, *Raising China's Revolutionaries: Modernizing Childhood for Cosmopolitan Nationalists and*

the ethic of hard work and spartan living espoused by Party propaganda. There was one goal of the Maoist state which many Third Fronters looked favorably upon despite dissatisfactions with adverse working and living conditions. They were eager to contribute to China's industrial strengthening, and to this day many people still talk proudly about how, thanks to their strenuous labor, inland China transformed into a more developed region.

Sources and Chapter Outlines

When I started this project in 2011, the first place I went was Chengdu to examine the city archive. The archivist politely told me that I could look over the catalog and nothing else. Discouraged but resolved to find documentary sources I moved on to Chongqing, where I had a contact at the archive. Initially, this connection proved fortuitous, and I copied files on relocated factories and railroad building. Then, suddenly someone realized that the Third Front was related to national defense, and I was only allowed to read files after an archivist had confirmed that no pages were labeled "classified" (*jimi*) or "secret" (*mimi*). This constraint made it almost impossible to continue research since even documents about providing food to a Third Front work unit were sometimes marked as classified.

I was subsequently advised to inform archives that I was interested in a more innocuous-sounding subject, like "industrial development" (*gongye fazhan*). This is what I did when I gathered documents at the Sichuan Provincial Archive during the 2012–2013 academic year. The materials I collected contained information on factories moved inland, building new work units, and central government and provincial policies between 1964 and 1966. There was more limited documentation on Cultural Revolution conflicts in 1967 and 1968. Not wanting to restrict my study to the first few years of the Third Front, I searched for archives with online catalogs that indicated accessible materials for both the 1960s and 1970s. The places I found were the Shanghai Municipal Archive and the Hubei Provincial Archive.

At the Hubei Provincial Archive, I photocopied files on railroads, hydropower stations, and the Second Automobile Works, as well as central government and provincial reports. In Shanghai, I hired a Chinese graduate student to copy a list of archival files that I had located in the online catalog on the moving process, the Small Third Front, and factional conflicts during the Cultural Revolution. I was denied entry to the Panzhihua Municipal Archive and provincial archives in Guizhou, Shaanxi, Liaoning, and Jilin. Committed

Liberated Comrades, 1920s–1950s (New York: Columbia University Press, 2018), 160–209.

to finding more archival sources, I looked to published collections. Most important for my research on elite politics is a selection of central government documents about the Third Front assembled by Chen Donglin.[129] I also located a few collections by cities on the Chengdu plain, the Shaanxi Provincial Archive, and the Panzhihua Party history office. This last resource has been particularly valuable, as it contains roughly 600 pages of central, provincial, and municipal documents about the building of Panzhihua.[130]

Doyens of China studies Timothy Cheek and Stuart Schram have alerted students of the Mao era to the fact that published CCP documents have likely been altered by editors.[131] Following Cheek's lead, I have worked to address this issue by checking for alternative versions of documents in publications, such as the biographies of Party leaders and the *Jianguo yilai zhongyao wenxian* series. While some documents are duplicated in other sources, I have not found significant differences. Many documents are also not available elsewhere, and they contain a wealth of information about the thinking of top Party leaders, the policy-making process, and the steel town of Panzhihua. We cannot discount the fact that some published documents may have been changed. One factor that suggests that they are reliable is that they make frequent references to sensitive issues, which Cheek has pointed out are often omitted, such as tensions between Party leaders, discontent with government policies, and discussions of policies that did not work.[132]

When I began researching the Third Front eight years ago, I was aware that archivists would consider my topic to be "sensitive" (*mingan*) and uninclined to grant me access. I thus early on took inspiration from pioneering historical garbologists – Michael Schoenhals and Jeremy Brown – and sought to obtain relevant materials from other sources.[133] From book markets and private collections, I have acquired over fifty memoirs and around a dozen document collections that were distributed to work units in

[129] Chen Donglin, ed., *Zhongguo gongchandang yu sanxian jianshe* (Beijing: Zhonggong dangshi chubanshe, 2015). Chen Xi is officially credited as the editor. I have been told by multiple sources that Chen Donglin was the editor, and so I have attributed the editorship to him here.

[130] Zhonggong Panzhihua shi dangshi yanjiushi, ed., *Panzhihua kaifa jianshe shi wenxian ziliao xuanbian* (Panzhihua: Zhonggong Panzhihua shiwei dangshi yanjiushi bian, 2000).

[131] Timothy Cheek, "Textually Speaking: An Assessment of Newly Available Mao Texts," in *The Secret Speeches of Chairman Mao: From the Hundred Flowers to the Great Leap Forward*, ed. Roderick MacFarquhar, Timothy Cheek, and Eugene Wu (Cambridge, MA: Harvard University Press, 1989), 86, 91.

[132] Timothy Cheek, ed., *Mao Zedong and China's Revolutions: A Brief History with Documents* (New York: Palgrave, 2002), 39.

[133] Jeremy Brown, "Finding and Using Grassroots Historical Sources from the Mao Era," December 15, 2010. *Dissertations Reviews*, http://dissertationreviews.org/archives/310, accessed October 31, 2018.

the 1960s and 1970s. I also scoured provincial, municipal, and factory gazetteers for information about the Third Front and collected volumes containing Chinese government statistics about the Mao-era economy. Scholars are widely aware that official Chinese statistics are not always completely reliable due to a mixture of underreporting, overreporting, and breakdowns in the statistical system. I have, nonetheless, made use of Chinese government statistics, especially in Chapter 5, because no one has yet generated an alternative data set which is convincingly more reliable.[134]

To further fill out the empirical base of this study, I additionally performed 120 interviews with Third Front participants. The first set of interviews occurred in 2011 in Chengdu, Chongqing, and Deyang, followed by interviews in 2012 and 2013 in Shiyan, Wuhan, Xi'an, Panzhihua, Chongqing, Zizhong, and Chengdu; in 2016 in Chengdu, Deyang, and Pengzhou; and finally in 2018 in Beijing and Shanghai. The way that I located most interviewees was through a digital version of the snowball method.[135] I searched for online memoirs about the Third Front and emailed their authors. Respondents would occasionally offer to set up a group interview. Afterwards, I would arrange follow-up meetings with individuals and their contacts. The second way I came into contact with interviewees was through Chen Donglin, who put me in touch with a Party historian in Panzhihua. Interviews in Panzhihua were abruptly cut short when a local official became concerned that I was learning too much about the negative side of local history and told his contacts to no longer talk with me. A few people continued to meet and connect me with their friends. But most people subsequently refused to sit for an interview. The final way that I found interviewees was through Chinese friends in the United States who introduced me to the children of Third Front workers who were in their late thirties and forties. With them, I talked about what it was like to grow up at the Third Front.

"Third Front children" (*sanxian zidi*), as they called themselves, did not make up the bulk of my interviewees. I interviewed seven of them. The rest were people in their mid-sixties to early eighties who had come to the Third Front in their late teens to thirties. Nearly all were men. Only nine interviewees were women, and their husbands tended to talk over them when I directed questions towards them. Not wishing to offend my interlocutors, yet also wanting to hear women's voices, I made repeated attempts to give them a forum to air their perspectives, usually to little

[134] Naughton, *The Chinese Economy*, 13. Chris Bramall, *Chinese Economic Development* (London: Routledge, 2009), 97, 101, 290–291.

[135] I took my methodological cue from William Hurst, *The Chinese Worker after Socialism* (Cambridge: Cambridge University Press, 2009), 10.

avail, since they and their spouse were used to homosocial conversations. In this regard, my study is different from Gail Hershatter's work on the 1950s which relies mainly on female voices.

On the other hand, I, like Hershatter, turned to oral history because I was concerned that the memories of individuals who had participated in the Third Front were rapidly becoming inaccessible as people passed away. I also encountered a similar issue to other historians who have drawn on written memoirs or engaged in oral-history work on Mao's China.[136] People are remembering events that occurred four or more decades ago, and the experiences of the intervening years have affected the meaning of past events.[137] To account for the distorting effects that time has on how people recall the past, I have endeavored to confirm information in individual memories with archival documents, as well as work in the opposite direction and check what I learned from archival sources with interviewees and written memoirs. In some cases, it has not been possible to cross-check oral interviews and written memoirs with archival materials. At times, this is because interviewees and written memoirs discussed topics that archival documents either do not mention or only bring up in passing. Most important for the purposes of this study are the nuances of everyday life.

When I performed interviews, I did not stick to a script, and I only gave questions in advance if people demanded them. I found that making conversations less structured and letting people wander in their thoughts made them less inclined to rush through the questions they thought I wanted them to address. This meant that sometimes sessions would weave for hours between a whole slew of topics related to me, them, China, and everything in between, and only occasionally be about the Third Front. On the flip side, the open-ended interview format meant that people would sometimes in the middle of a discussion veer off in another direction and recollect memories of personal loss and hardship which I lacked the temerity to ask directly about. When I raised questions, I focused on mundane affairs. I posed questions about topics such as housing arrangements, cultural activities, work routines, available transport, the natural environment, family life, medical facilities, and schooling. Even when I brought up more momentous events, like being recruited for the Third Front, I inquired about rudimentary issues, such as how companies sent off recruits.

[136] Some studies are Jacob Eyferth, *Eating Rice from Bamboo Roots: The Social History of a Community of Handicraft Papermakers in Rural Sichuan, 1920–2000* (Cambridge, MA: Harvard University Press, 2009). Hou, *Building for Oil*. Schmalzer, *Red Revolution*. Wang, *Finding Women*. Cliff, *Oil and Water*.

[137] Hershatter, *Gender of Memory*, 5.

I rarely directly quote interviews in this book. This is because I only sometimes recorded sessions. People who took part in the Third Front were told for decades by officials that their work was classified, and they were even paid a subsidy on top of their regular monthly wage to protect national secrets. The interlocking of people's lived experiences with national security made many interviewees very concerned about divulging confidential information to a foreigner, especially one like me who came from the place that they had long thought of as their enemy – "American imperialism" (*Meidi*). I did not want to make interviewees even more wary of talking by taping our discussions, and so at times I did not.

Taken together, the written and oral sources undergirding this book provide information about all aspects of the Third Front campaign. They not only illuminate more technical issues, such as resource allocation and organizational structures. They also give a ground-level view of the multitude of ways that people experienced China's campaign to bolster its industrial defenses before the Cold War turned hot. I will leave it to the reader to judge whether the memories interviewees told me, and the stories contained in written memoirs, left out negative details because their authors or editors were worried about presenting China in an unfavorable light.

I begin my study of the Third Front by describing in Chapter 1 the post-Great Leap policy climate out of which the Third Front originated. When the Great Leap failed, a group of leaders centered on Liu Shaoqi reaffirmed top-down control and promoted higher consumption, lower growth targets, and coastal development. Mao Zedong viewed these policies as being dangerously close to Soviet revisionism and wanted to push China onto a different economic path. I argue that Mao utilized growing American and Soviet animosity to tar post-Great Leap policies as a threat to national security and launch a new Maoist approach to building socialism in China in the Third Front campaign. Mao and his colleagues set up the Third Front to be different from the Great Leap, which had relied on bottom-up mass mobilization and simple technologies. In contrast, the Third Front fused low- and high-tech methods in a centrally planned project to covertly industrialize inland areas in anticipation of a future conflict with Cold War rivals.

Chapter 2 examines how the Communist Party recruited millions of workers to construct the Third Front. Party officials sought to socially engineer a labor force that embraced Maoist norms and disregarded any difficulties that moving to remote inland areas brought to their family, workplace, or own person. People responded to recruitment in various ways. Some people thought of expanding inland industry as a way of manifesting their devotion to Chinese socialism. Many others were more concerned about the material benefits and burdens that Third Front participation would bring to their region, factory, family, or self. Shanghai leaders urged central planners not to neglect the coast, whereas the administrators of inland provinces requested more skilled workers and industrial equipment. Urban residents fretted over what sort of housing, schooling, and cultural activities would be available in China's impoverished hinterlands. Rural youth, on the other hand, were generally eager to earn higher wages. But many of their parents were worried about the loss of household labor and the possibility that their children might be injured or die in a workplace accident. Overall, my research illustrates that the consequences of enlisting in the Third Front were not always clear and that the value of being involved varied according to one's geographical, social, and economic position.

Chapter 3 discusses how the Third Front was constructed. It shows that the Party militarized the Third Front by hiding projects in secure locations, speeding up construction in the face of military pressures, and requiring participants to emulate the Red Army's strategy of local self-reliance. At the start of the Cultural Revolution, Mao intensified the militarization of the Third Front when he urged ousting capitalist roaders who ostensibly supported changing China into a Soviet-style revisionist state. I maintain that this last form of militarization transformed enmity towards Cold War foes into a struggle against domestic forces, a strategy Mao successfully deployed in previous instances. Assaults on capitalist roaders were undertaken to attain numerous political objectives. Some workers aired grievances about poor living conditions. Others demanded the right to go home. As for Party leaders, they claimed that critics of the Third Front were allied with foreign agents. The CCP made use of this latter assertion to restore political discipline and revitalize the Third Front when the Soviets appeared poised to attack in 1969. The same Maoist discourse created obstacles to the Third Front's success by attacking experts and slow development.

Chapter 4 chronicles everyday life in the first Third Front project that Mao Zedong ever proposed – the steel town of Panzhihua located deep in the mountains of southern Sichuan. I demonstrate that Maoist ideas about how to build Chinese socialism had a profound impact on the daily affairs of Panzhihua. In accordance with Maoism's productivist ethos, central and local officials focused on increasing production and poured tons of resources into building high-tech industry. Workers, meanwhile, were housed for years in barracks-style tents and provided with a bare minimum of consumer goods. Many residents of Panzhihua did not experience the austerity of everyday life in ways that the Party considered appropriate to a good Maoist subject. Some recruits did not accept the CCP's expectation that they be satisfied with building socialism wherever the Party decided. Others tired of their hectic work schedule and grew bored of Panzhihua's limited cultural life. Urban recruits desired to be with family in distant locations and move to a city higher up in China's socioeconomic order. Rural folk also wished to be with family, but in contrast to urbanites they considered gaining access to the welfare provisions of a state-owned enterprise to be a route out of rural poverty. On both sides of the urban–rural divide, practices of daily life became the contested ground of Maoist developmentalism.

Chapter 5 assesses the CCP's efforts to industrialize China during the Third Front campaign. I demonstrate that the Third Front constrained development by dedicating economic resources to costly projects in the interior instead of focusing on less expensive coastal endeavors. The Cultural Revolution also lifted construction costs by hindering project completion. The Third Front, however, was the sole economic policy that Party leaders formulated at the time to develop inland areas, and despite its many problems, it helped to lessen regional economic differences. The industrialization of inland China in turn provided a foundation for post-Mao economic growth by accelerating the movement of regional resources, linking the interior more tightly into national networks, and cultivating the CCP's aspiration to industrialize entire regions.

The epilogue analyzes the CCP's shift away from the Maoist developmental model behind the Third Front in the wake of Sino-American rapprochement. With the warming of Sino-American relations, Party leaders no longer thought that China had to undertake a big industrialization drive in preparation for war. Beijing, however, vacillated about how close it should become to Washington until Mao died in 1976, and Deng Xiaoping placed China firmly on the American side in the Cold War. In this new international climate, CCP leaders felt secure enough to publicly mention the Third Front for the first time. The Chinese people were also no longer required to be developmental soldiers who disregarded personal comforts and participated in militaristic campaigns to shore up Chinese industry. At peace with the United States, the Chinese Communist Party drew down its Cold War ramparts and made China into a nation of civilians.

1 The Coming of the Third Front Campaign

This chapter examines the policy environment out of which the Third Front campaign emerged. I look at both foreign and domestic affairs because the Communist Party's decision to launch the Third Front was the product of international and national currents in the late 1950s and early 1960s. On the domestic front, the CCP leadership entered the tail end of its first decade in power with high hopes. The First Five Year Plan, undertaken with Soviet guidance, had produced significant economic growth, and the Party foresaw even greater achievements with the Second Five Year Plan. However, rather than continuing to follow Soviet advice, Party leaders under Mao Zedong's direction decided to devise China's own model of socialist development in the Great Leap Forward.

Unlike the Soviet model, the Great Leap did not stress central command and extensive planning. Its developmental emphasis was on local areas mobilizing all available resources for big infrastructure projects. Party leaders anticipated that after a few years of intense work, China would acquire an industrial base large enough to sustain a communist society which could provide equably for the material needs of its all members. This is not what happened. The Great Leap turned into an economic catastrophe. After the Great Leap collapsed, it was not at all clear what would become of China's attempt to invent its own way to construct a socialist industrial society, as the Party's most urgent concern became resolving a nationwide famine that killed around 30 million people.[1] With China's economy in turmoil, the central Party instituted a period of economic adjustment and put off commencement of the Third Five Year Plan until 1966. Mao, in the meantime, allowed Liu Shaoqi and a few other high-ranking leaders to revive the economy by implementing a lower rate of investment, a more measured speed of development, more funds for consumer industries, and a larger role for markets and material incentives.[2]

[1] Walder, *China under Mao*, 333. [2] Naughton, *Chinese Economy*, 72–73.

In the early 1960s, not only did the CCP have to overcome extreme economic difficulties, but also Beijing faced a very fragile international situation. The Sino-Soviet alliance fell apart, and Moscow turned from a potential ally in any armed conflict into a military competitor. At the same time, the United States, which already had tens of thousands of troops stationed in East Asia, increased its military participation in the Vietnam War.[3] Mao and his colleagues agreed that the best way to deal with China's increasingly challenging security climate was to acquire nuclear weapons while preparing to fight a protracted people's war in the event that the Americans or Soviets invaded. The first known reference to a national security policy that foreshadowed the Third Front was made in 1960 by minister of national defense Lin Biao, who advocated readying the country for war by relocating industry and military units to inland mountains.

The central Party did not at first act on Lin Biao's recommendation. Mao resurrected Lin's suggestion to move industry inland during early conversations about the Third Five Year Plan in 1964. Mao argued that initial drafts of the Third Five Year Plan, produced by Liu Shaoqi and his colleagues, had paid insufficient attention to China's perilous security situation and wrongly emphasized developing the coast and raising living standards. To make China more secure, the Party had to alter the Third Five Year Plan and recenter it on transferring resources to inland regions to build a big secret heavy-industrial base, a project Mao named the Third Front. Through a close examination of recently accessible Chinese materials, I show that Mao employed international tensions to push through this rapid industrialization project.

When Mao first recommended constructing the Third Front in May 1964, his policy suggestion did not receive broad backing from Party leaders. Liu Shaoqi and a few other leaders engaged in foot dragging. They proposed undertaking surveys and carrying out planning. I argue that Liu and his colleagues acted in this way because they were reluctant to engage in a large industrialization drive so soon after the Great Leap, and they wanted to continue the more gradual developmental path of the previous few years which favored building up coastal areas and lifting consumption. Mao held a very different view of post-Great Leap economic policies. Mao thought that they were leading the Chinese economy in the wrong direction, and that if they were not reversed, China might

[3] On American involvement in Vietnam in the early 1960s, see Marilyn B. Young, *The Vietnam Wars 1945–1990* (New York: HarperCollins, 1991), 89–123. On Sino-Soviet relations in the early 1960s, see Lorenz Lüthi, *The Sino-Soviet Split: Cold War in the Communist World* (Princeton: Princeton University Press, 2008), 157–272. Li and Xia, *Mao and the Sino-Soviet Split*, 45–92.

become a revisionist country like the Soviet Union, where Mao maintained that a privileged bureaucratic elite had gained power under Khrushchev's leadership and revived capitalism.[4]

During meetings about the Third Five Year Plan, Mao let his colleagues know that pursuing the Third Front was a military necessity and that he considered backing another approach to Chinese development to be revisionist and an inadequate response to foreign threats. At first, Party leaders largely held their ground and insisted on making increasing consumption the core plank of the Third Five Year Plan. Encountering lukewarm support from his colleagues, Mao did not give up on the idea of constructing the Third Front. He pressed his longtime comrades in arms harder and asserted that China needed a strategic industrial rear to defend itself against its Cold War enemies. Mao even threatened to set up the Third Front on his own if the CCP leadership did not side with him on this crucial policy initiative upon which the fate of China's socialist revolution rested.

The Party center only endorsed building the Third Front when the United States bombarded North Vietnam after the Gulf of Tonkin incident, and a Sino-American war seemed impending.[5] When the central Party came out in favor of constructing the Third Front, plans to concentrate on coastal development and improve living standards were set aside. In their place, Chinese leaders instated a modified version of the Maoist policies that had structured the Great Leap. Chinese developmental strategy again became centered on a *levée en masse* of labor to accelerate heavy-industrial growth. Mao and other leaders, however, did not set up the Third Front to be a repeat of the Leap. They restricted the regional target of industrialization to inland China, unlike the Great Leap, which sought to develop the entire country. Central agencies also retained control over Third Front projects in contrast to the Leap, which granted local areas the power to independently commence economic initiatives.

In the Third Front, the Party also dropped the Leap's aspiration to make the PRC into a communist society with welfare guarantees for all Chinese. The CCP instead pursued a policy of generalized austerity while still striving to furnish a basic social safety net for state-owned enterprises – a policy which benefited every single Third Front company. The precedent for this top-down spartan approach to industrialization was the Daqing oilfield which the Party ordered national industry to pattern itself after in January 1964. Despite this command, central planners only approved a slew of new industrial projects when the Gulf of

[4] Meisner, *Mao's China*, 300. [5] Naughton, "Third Front," 353.

Tonkin incident triggered Party support for the Third Front in August 1964. As the CCP set out on this new militarized road to building socialist industrial modernity in China, Mao continued to push his colleagues to go faster and warned them about the danger of a capitalist resurgence. Mao's lieutenants fell in line behind his new industrial policy for China, though some remained concerned that the Third Front might cause the problems of the Great Leap to return.

International Insecurity and Maoist Military Strategy

In the early 1960s, China was in a vulnerable geopolitical position. Since the 1950s, the United States had surrounded China with a ring of military bases in Japan, South Korea, Taiwan, and the Philippines, and Washington had forged security arrangements with several countries in Southeast Asia.[6] China's exposure to attack by the United States became especially apparent when Beijing learned in 1959 that American spy planes were carrying out reconnaissance missions all over China, including above the capital.[7] Although anti-air raid brigades downed some American planes in the early 1960s, repeated transgressions of Chinese airspace made it clear that the PLA could not keep enemy aircraft at bay.[8] Beijing also did not have even one atomic bomb while the United States and the Soviet Union cumulatively possessed roughly 21,600 nuclear warheads in 1960, with over 90 percent in American hands.[9]

With the rupture of the Sino-Soviet alliance in the early 1960s, China's security situation became even more precarious. Ties between Beijing and Moscow had been strained for years. At the broadest level, the Chinese disapproved of the "great-power chauvinism" of the Soviet Union.[10] A more concrete issue that gnawed at Sino-Soviet relations was Moscow's hesitation to provide plans for a nuclear weapon.[11] Mao

[6] For a brief history of American involvement in East Asia during the Cold War, see Bruce Cumings, *Parallax Visions: Making Sense of American–East Asian Relations at the End of the Century* (Durham, NC: Duke University Press, 1999), 9–34, 205–226. For a more detailed history, see Michael J. Green, *By More Than Providence: Grand Strategy and American Power in the Asia Pacific since 1783* (New York: Columbia University Press, 2017), 245–362.

[7] Lüthi, *Sino-Soviet Split*, 166, 185.

[8] Nie Rongzhen, *Nie Rongzhen Huiyi lu* (Beijing: Jiefangjun chubanshe, 1986), 817. Han Zengtao, "Jiluo U2 feiji de ren: Ji kongjun zhandou yingxiong Yue Zhenhua." *Dangshi bocai* 9 (1996), 30–32. Yue Zhenhua. "Jiluo Mei zhi U-2 feiji zuozhan zhuiji," *Bai nian chao* 6 (2002): 17–22.

[9] Joseph Cirincione, *Bomb Scare: The History and Future of Nuclear Weapons* (New York: Columbia University Press, 2008), 26.

[10] Jersild, *Sino-Soviet Alliance*, 56.

[11] Shu Guang Zhang, "Between 'Paper' and 'Real Tigers': Mao's View of Nuclear Weapons," in *Cold War Statesmen Confront the Bomb*, eds. John Lewis Gaddis, Phillip

also despised Soviet premier Nikita Khrushchev's interest in a policy of peaceful coexistence of the socialist and capitalist blocs. Mao, as John Garver has noted, "saw Khrushchev's push for détente with the United States as unprincipled abandonment of the militant anti-imperialist principles followed by Lenin and Stalin," which Beijing still supported around the world.[12]

Mao let Khrushchev know his low opinion of him by repeatedly berating him to his face in the late 1950s.[13] Upset with Mao's insulting behavior and disapproving of the Great Leap, Khrushchev pulled out aid to China in 1960. Instead of softening his stance, Mao leaned into the Sino-Soviet split and had Chinese diplomats ramp up criticism of the Soviet Union at international events.[14] Moscow, meanwhile, dealt with the security consequences of the Sino-Soviet split by keeping over 100,000 troops stationed on the PRC's northern flank.[15] Enmeshed in the hostile geopolitical environment of the global Cold War, the CCP nearly doubled military expenditures between 1961 and 1963 to 19.1 percent of the state budget.[16]

While some senior Party members, such as Liu Shaoqi and Deng Xiaoping, had reservations about Mao's capability to direct Chinese development after the Great Leap turned into a massive famine, his status as a military strategist was another matter.[17] Even as Party leaders laid to rest Mao's ideas about how to modernize China's economy in the early 1960s, they still supported his ideas about national defense in the nuclear age. According to Shu Guang Zhang, Mao thought of the "bomb as nothing more than a conventional weapon of high explosiveness." It was, in Mao's words, "a paper tiger" which great powers used "to scare people" but did not determine "the outcome of a war." Battles were "decided by people, not by one or two new types of weapons."[18] Mao was, nonetheless, in favor of China obtaining nuclear arms because, "In today's world, if we don't want to be bullied by others, we should have

H. Gordon, Ernest R. May, and Jonathan Rosenberg (Oxford: Oxford University Press, 1999), 205–209.

12 Garver, *China's Quest*, 133. Friedman, *Shadow Cold War*, 58–59, 83–84.

13 Alexander V. Pantsov with Steven I. Levine, *Mao: The Real Story* (New York: Simon & Schuster, 2012), 130, 137.

14 Lüthi, *Sino-Soviet Split*, 179, 181, 190.

15 Lowell Dittmer, *Sino-Soviet Normalization and Its International Implications, 1945–1990* (Seattle: University of Washington Press, 1992), 188.

16 Guojia tongji ju, *Zhongguo tongji nianjian* (Beijing: Zhongguo tongji chubanshe, 1983), 449.

17 For an overview of the Party leadership's criticisms of Mao's economic policies after the Great Leap, see Walder, *China under Mao*, 180–188.

18 Zhang, "Between 'Paper' and 'Real Tigers'," 195–196.

atomic weapons by all means."[19] Other CCP leaders agreed and funneled funds into China's nuclear weapons program.[20]

Mao and other Party leaders, however, did not consider nuclear weapons to be enough to protect China against the military might of the Soviet Union and the United States, and so they also prepared to fight a ground war. The basic strategy for any future conflict was laid out by the Central Military Commission in 1956 and reaffirmed in 1960. The plan stipulated that if the United States and Japan came attacking from the north, then the PLA would attempt to block it from invading China. On the other hand, if the United States, along with Chiang Kai-shek's forces in Taiwan, attacked from the south, the CCP would allow enemy troops to venture deep into Chinese territory before the PLA and civilian militias launched counterattacks.[21] Marshal He Long explained in a 1960 speech why militias were a vital part of China's force structure. In any future war, "the enemy would certainly be able to" overcome border defenses. But before enemy forces entered China, they "would use missiles and nuclear bombs to destroy ... important military, political, and economic targets and then ... use paratroopers to occupy important towns and transport junctions and split the country up into pieces." This is why "the entire nation had to be armed" (*quan min jie bing*) and be ready to fight in militias behind enemy lines.[22]

The Party's vision of war in the early 1960s fit with both its history of waging protracted people's wars and China's very weak military position compared to its Cold War adversaries. Beijing's military assets at the time were far less than either Washington's or Moscow's. China's navy was puny. Its air force was almost nonexistent, and it had no atomic bomb to deter a nuclear strike. Even when China successfully tested an atomic bomb in October 1964, its nuclear arsenal was small, and it had no delivery system that could bomb Moscow until 1971 or the United States until 1981.[23] China had a large army, but it did not possess

[19] Zhang, "Between 'Paper' and 'Real Tigers'," 205.

[20] On China's pursuit of a nuclear weapon after the Sino-Soviet split, see John Wilson Lewis and Litai Xue, *China Builds the Bomb* (Stanford: Stanford University Press, 1988), 137–189.

[21] M. Taylor Fravel, "Shifts in Warfare and Party Unity: Explaining China's Changes in Military Strategy," *International Security* 42:3 (Winter 2017–2018): 53–59 and Table 1.

[22] Liao Guoliang, Li Shishun, and Xu Yan, *Mao Zedong junshi sixiang fazhan shi* (Beijing: Jiefangjun chubanshe, 1991), 525. Marshal Xu Xiangqian similarly highlights the importance of importance of militias in "Guanyu zhanzheng chuqi wenti," October 15, 1963, in *Xu Xiangqian junshi wenxuan*, ed. Guofang daxue di er bian yanjiushi "Xu Xiangqian zhuan" bianxie zu (Beijing: Jiefangjun chubanshe, 1993), 151. On militias in the early 1960s, see Elizabeth Perry, *Patrolling the Revolution: Worker Militias, Citizenship, and the Modern Chinese State* (Lanham: Rowman and Littlefield, 2006), 190–192.

[23] This is likely one reason for China's implementation of a no-first-use policy for nuclear weapons in 1964, because if Beijing first used nuclear weapons against either the United

much high-tech hardware. There was also no viable way of quickly improving the technological abilities of China's military since the Soviet Union was its enemy, and there was a Western embargo on trading arms with China from the early 1950s.[24]

Although central Party leaders supported Mao's ideas about guerilla warfare as a general national security strategy, there were limits to how far they put his military thought into practice. For instance, Lin Biao argued at a Central Military Commission meeting in February 1960 that the military must prepare for "enemies coming from the air," or else nuclear bombs could eliminate what the CCP had so painstakingly constructed in the preceding decade. Drawing on Mao's thought, Lin proposed a solution that recalled the CCP's wartime bases and prefigured the defense tactics embedded in the Third Front. He suggested "retreating inland, scattering, hiding, and taking up positions near and inside mountains," where "they could withstand a nuclear blast."[25] Lin's comments elicited no policy response.

In June 1960, Mao also invoked the military wisdom of the Party's revolutionary base areas with comments that foreshadowed the military strategy behind the Third Front. Mao declared, "The southwest and northwest are big rear defense areas. Most of the south-central region is a big rear defense area too ... Every military region needs to build a big rear defense area, and every province needs to build a big rear defense area." Later in 1960, Mao told a central Party conference, "We must prepare for war. We must not assume that all is peaceful under heaven. Every provincial-, municipal-, and central-level comrade must be mindful of military affairs."[26] At this point, no Party leaders acted on Mao's policy suggestions.

In January 1962, Lin Biao again anticipated the Third Front campaign when he argued at the "7,000 cadres conference" that Chiang Kai-shek in Taiwan might seize upon China's weakness after the Great Leap and attack Chinese cities. Since the PLA could not keep GMD forces contained in coastal areas, especially if the US Navy came to Chiang's aid,

States or Soviet Union, they could not carry out a devastating strike on either country, but they could likely count on one in return.

[24] For an overview of Chinese military capabilities at the time, see Li Ke and Hao Sheng, *Wenhua da geming de renmin jiefangjun* (Beijing: Zhonggong dangshi ziliao chubanshe, 1989), 279–311. On the embargo, see Richard A. Bitzinger and J. D. Kenneth Boutin, "China's defence industries: Change and continuity," in *Rising China*, ed. Ron Huisken (Sydney: Australian National University Press, 2009), 127.

[25] Lin Biao, "Zai jun kuda huiyi shang de jianghua," February 1960, in *Mao Zedong dui sanxian jianshe de youguan zhishi*.

[26] Mao Zedong, "Zai Shanghai huiyi shang de jianghua," June 14, 1960, in *Mao Zedong dui sanxian jianshe de youguan zhishi*.

Lin suggested having Chinese troops retreat to a "second front" around Suzhou and, if needed, to a "third front" near Huang Shan in Anhui to wage a protracted war. So that a military maneuver of this sort could be carried out with less difficulty if necessary, advance preparations should be undertaken in third-front and second-front areas. Lin also noted that this kind of defense policy could be applied nationwide. With the Chinese economy still impacted by the aftermath of the Great Leap Forward and the GMD taking no major military action against mainland China, the Communist Party did not follow up on Lin's recommendations.[27]

In January 1962, Lin also highlighted the importance of underground structures in the nuclear age. He gave as evidence subterranean complexes in America and people who survived the bombing of Hiroshima in air-raid shelters. According to Lin, China was especially fortunate because it "has so many tall mountains. If we build a cave, and a bomb is dropped on Mt. Tai, will it get rid of Mt. Tai? Will it push the Changbai mountains into the sea? That's impossible. If war erupts, we can go into caves" and then come out after the bombing is over and "attack with bayonets and grenades."[28] The Party center did not at this time begin building a large number of air-raid shelters. Lin's comments are, nevertheless, a very arresting statement of the applicability of Maoist tactics to rebutting a nuclear holocaust. Even if enemy forces bombarded China with nuclear weapons, the CCP could still prevail if troops literally retreated inside mountains only to later emerge for a counterassault with light arms.

The Cold War Heats Up

Alternate Politburo member Wang Jiaxiang tried to dial down international tensions in February 1962 by writing a letter to Mao in which he argued that the Party should not be overconcerned about the imminence of another world war. China could peacefully coexist with imperialism if it reduced funding for anti-imperialist movements, especially in Vietnam, where Beijing risked being pulled into a battle with the United States reminiscent of the Korean War. Mao rejected Wang's ideas, as he thought that wars of national liberation signaled the international success of Maoist-style socialism, whereas efforts to appease American imperialism and Soviet revisionism were signs of surrender to China's Cold War enemies.[29]

27 Naughton, "Third Front," 352.

28 Lin Biao, "Zai kuoda de zhongyang gongzui huiyi de jianghua," January 29, 1962, in *Mao Zedong dui sanxian de youguan zhishi*.

29 Garver, *China's Quest*, 166. Bertil Lintner, *China's India War: Collision Course on the Roof of the World* (Oxford: Oxford University Press, 2018), 83–84, 87–88.

Sino-Soviet relations deteriorated even more when roughly 60,000 Chinese Kazakhs and Uyghurs suddenly moved from Xinjiang across the border into the Soviet Union in April and May 1962. The Chinese government accused Moscow of being behind this incident, giving aid to "subversive activities" in Xinjiang and supplying "encouragement and assistance" to refugees. The Chinese Foreign Ministry even claimed that Moscow was "provoking a military rebellion" in Xinjiang.[30] A few months later, China's far western border became enflamed when military clashes broke out with India in October. Signaling the further decline of Sino-Soviet relations, Moscow not only backed New Delhi in this armed quarrel, but the Soviet Union also sent India military equipment in subsequent years.[31]

Another cause of strain between Moscow and Beijing was their conflicting views about where exactly their border was. From late 1962, the Chinese Foreign Ministry began to complain about territorial disputes and maintained that Soviet troops were repeatedly employing military force against China from territory that Beijing thought should rightfully be its own.[32] In March 1963, a *People's Daily* editorial significantly raised the stakes of Sino-Soviet territorial disagreements, asserting that the border between China and the Soviet Union was the result of unequal treaties that tsarist Russia had forced on China in the late nineteenth century. Moscow interpreted this historically charged viewpoint as a challenge to Soviet territorial sovereignty.

In order to shore up Soviet influence in the Far East, Moscow increased military aid to Mongolia.[33] In July 1963, the Kremlin formalized its military support for Mongolia, agreeing to upgrade its defenses and deploy more Soviet troops along the border. Over the next few years, Soviet forces in Mongolia jumped from around 200,000 soldiers to about a million.[34] In response to rising border tensions, China's Central Military Commission convened a conference on how to defend the border against the Soviet Union and Mongolia in September and October 1963, which concluded that China had to "be militarily prepared to deal with possible border conflicts provoked by" the Soviet Union.[35]

As Chinese tensions with the Soviet Union and Mongolia mounted, so did security pressures from the American-allied GMD in Taiwan. Between 1962 and 1965, the GMD carried out forty special forces raids on southeast China.[36] American animus towards China was also on the rise. Between September 1958 and April 1962, US Navy vessels entered

[30] Radchenko, *Two Suns*, 110.
[31] Garver, *China's Quest*, 182.
[32] Radchenko, *Two Suns*, 111.
[33] Li and Xia, *Mao and the Sino-Soviet Split*, 94.
[34] Chen, "Sanxian jianshe," 4.
[35] Li and Xia, *Mao and the Sino-Soviet Split*, 94.
[36] Chen, *Sanxian*, 77.

Chinese waters 144 times with a total of 261 ships, while 335 American planes flew through Chinese airspace 161 times.[37] Between January 1961 and June 1963, American aircraft flew twenty-four reconnaissance missions over China, including over the Lop Nor nuclear testing facility in Xinjiang and the Baotou plutonium processing plant in Inner Mongolia.[38] The United States was casting an ever-bigger military shadow over Southeast Asia too. Between 1961 and 1963, American forces in South Vietnam grew from around one battalion (900 men) to more than a full division (16,732).[39] The American media and government officials also incessantly discussed military activities that the Department of Defense could execute against communist China.[40]

In response to America's growing presence in Southeast Asia, the CCP provided North Vietnam with over 320 million RMB in military aid between 1956 and 1963 to wage guerilla warfare in South Vietnam. In 1962, a Vietnamese delegation warned Beijing that insurgent activities in the South might cause Washington to deploy air or land forces against the North. To harden up Vietnam's defenses, China agreed to equip 230 more battalions. In March 1963, chief of the General Staff Luo Ruiqing visited Hanoi and promised Chinese support in the event of an American attack. In May, Liu Shaoqi met with North Vietnamese leader Ho Chi Minh and pledged that Hanoi could "count on China as the strategic rear" if North Vietnamese efforts to liberate the South provoked an American reprisal.[41] Liu vowed that "the Chinese people, the CCP, and the Chinese government all firmly support ... the Vietnamese people's opposition to the American imperialist invasion and their patriotic and just struggle to fight for the peaceful unification of their motherland."[42]

In September 1963, Mao again mentioned the necessity of Chinese war-preparedness. This time he linked it directly to China's past century of imperial humiliation. "From the 1840s to 1940s ... nearly every single ... imperialist power invaded our country and defeated us." The sole exception was "the War of Resistance against Japan."[43] If China's

[37] Liu Zhiqing, "1962 nian de di san cai taihai weiji," *Dangshi bolan* 4 (2004): 9–13.

[38] Chen, "Sanxian jianshe," 5.

[39] Stanley B. Weeks and Charles A. Meconis, *The Armed Forces of the USA in the Asia-Pacific Region* (London: I.B. Tauris, 2004), 23.

[40] On American hostility towards China, see James M. Carter, *Inventing Vietnam: The United States and State Building, 1954–1968* (New York: Cambridge University Press, 2008), 113–148. Mark Atwood Lawrence, *The Vietnam War: A Concise International History* (New York: Oxford University Press, 2008), 68–82.

[41] Chen Jian, "China's Involvement in the Vietnam War, 1964–69," *China Quarterly* 142 (1995): 359–363.

[42] Song Yijun and Sun Yanbo, "Liu Shaoqi yu sanxian jianshe de lishi huigu he sikao," *Junshi lishi* 6 (2008): 12.

[43] Pang and Jin, *Mao Zedong zhuan 1949–1976 xia*, 1359.

economy did not improve, then it was inevitable that China would "receive a beating" from imperialist countries. Even though a world war might not take place, the Party still "had to take the possibility of coming under attack as the starting point of all work." This assertion is rather remarkable. No longer did the risk of the Cold War bursting into flames constitute a foreboding imagined future. The CCP had now to take securing the country against an enemy assault as their top priority and soon change China's "backward economic and technological status."[44]

One foreign enemy that Mao was particularly concerned about was the United States due its intensifying involvement in the Vietnam War.[45] As American military forces in Vietnam increased, the central Party sent orders to local officials to organize street protests which demonstrated to the world Chinese indignation towards US imperialism. Local officials also had to set up exhibitions which chronicled American oppression in Vietnam. Local government agencies took up central Party commands, mobilizing millions in anti-American marches and directing work units to visit exhibits denouncing the United States.[46]

In January 1964, the CCP's security concerns swelled even higher. Nuclear physicists were making significant advancements on China's atomic bomb project, and they were close to performing the first nuclear test. The Soviet Union and the United States were both known to be opposed to China's development of nuclear weapons, and they had signed a Limited Nuclear Test Ban Treaty in late 1963 that forbade aboveground testing, which Beijing interpreted as an affront to its nuclear ambitions.[47] Chinese intelligence reports also indicated that Washington might soon execute a pre-emptive strike on Chinese nuclear facilities, and so on January 31, Zhou Enlai ordered the nuclear program's relocation to sites that were "mountainous, dispersed, and hidden."[48] When Zhou Enlai uttered this phrase, he surely had no idea that just a few months later Mao would take this geographic concept and enshrine it at the heart of the Third Front's massive industrialization campaign.

[44] Mao Zedong, "Yao yi keneng aida wei chuda dian lai buzhu women de gongzuo," September 1963, in *Zhongguo gongchandang yu sanxian*, 39.

[45] Chen, *Sanxian*, 80.

[46] "Quanguo gedi jin sibai wan ren youxing," *Renmin ribao*, January 16, 1964. Denise H. Ho talks about these exhibitions in *Curating Revolution: Politics on Display in Mao's China* (Cambridge: Cambridge University Press, 2018), 123. Beijing Municipal Archive file 102–001-00351 is about how local work units mobilized Chinese against the war in Vietnam. I scanned it in 2012 but did not make copies. Now it is closed to the public, so I cannot cite exact files.

[47] Lüthi, *Sino-Soviet Split*, 252–272. [48] Chen, *Sanxian*, 299.

Initial Sketches of the Third Five Year Plan

When Zhou Enlai issued his directive to move China's nuclear program, Party leaders were in the process of drafting the Third Five Year Plan. In their initial reflections, there is no hint that they were considering beginning another big industrialization drive similar to the Great Leap. Quite to the contrary, they thought that the Party had to learn from the Leap's economic mistakes and move ahead cautiously. Liu Shaoqi, Deng Xiaoping, Li Fuchun, Bo Yibo, and a few others started work on the Third Five Year Plan in early 1963. At a meeting on February 20, director of the Planning Commission Li Fuchun indicated that the promotion of agriculture and consumables would be the core of the plan. Deng agreed that, "During the Third Five Year Plan, we must work hard to solve problems related to food, clothing, and daily essentials." In October, Bo Yibo remarked that it was necessary to reduce infrastructure construction. Liu Shaoqi agreed: "In the past," during the Great Leap,

> the infrastructure battlefront was too long. There were too many projects. Demands were too high and too rushed. Designs were done badly, and projects were hurriedly begun ... We only paid attention to increasing output and ignored quality. We set targets too high ... We must always remember these painful learning experiences.[49]

Similar sentiments informed the Party center's "preliminary thoughts" on the Third Five Year Plan put forward for the Central Committee's consideration in early 1964. The plan's priorities were agriculture, national defense, and basic industry, in that order. Agriculture was supposed to receive 20 percent of total investment, compared to 7.1 percent in the First Five Year Plan and 11.3 percent during the Great Leap.[50] Initial plans made no mention of rectifying the economic disparity between the coast and the interior.[51] The only reference to developing inland areas was a suggestion to build the Sichuan–Guizhou and Yunnan–Guizhou railroads, which Li Fuchun clarified meant only building part of each line.[52] Otherwise, the main focus of national development was to be the coastal areas.[53]

On April 29, the Central Secretariat held a meeting to discuss the Third Five Year Plan. Li Fuchun explained the plan's logic. "To advance agriculture, some defense, industry, and transportation projects have not been included. This is so that the country does not have more

[49] Song and Sun, "Liu Shaoqi yu sanxian jianshe," 13. [50] Chen, *Sanxian*, 44.

[51] "Zhonggong zhongyang guanyu yinfa di san wu nian jihua de san ge wenjian de tongzhi," May 2, 1964, in *Jianguo yilai zhongyao wenxian xuan bian* 18, ed. Zhonggong zhongyang wenxian yanjiu shi bian (Beijing: Zhongguo wenxian chubanshe, 1998), 442–514.

[52] Chen, *Sanxian*, 45. [53] Naughton, "Third Front," 351.

problems than it can cope with due to financial constraints." While Li did not directly reference the Great Leap here, his statement probably brought the Leap's problems into the minds of everyone in the room. Chief of the General Staff Luo Ruiqing agreed with Li: "This is the only safe way. If in the future there is not enough [for defense], we can think up another solution." Deng Xiaoping concurred that

> industry ought to still serve agriculture, basic daily needs, and national defense … After a few years, when there is no need to import grain, then we can free up some currency reserves to import some new technologies … Whatever the state of agriculture in the country is has to be made known and discussed by everyone. This is the real spear and gun.[54]

The Daqing Model Emerges

In late 1963, while Liu Shaoqi and his associates were hammering out the guiding ideas behind the Third Five Year Plan, another model of economic development began to come into the limelight whose central principles would become integral to the Third Front campaign. That model was the Daqing oilfield, whose construction was overseen by oil minister Yu Qiuli during the Great Leap. Faced with supply shortages and a bitterly cold winter in China's far northern province of Heilongjiang, Yu opted in 1960 to bring Mao's military ideas to bear on economic activities. Drawing on the Maoist tactic of gathering forces together to wage "a war of annihilation" (*jianmie zhan*), Yu mobilized over 50,000 workers in an "all-out battle" (*da huizhan*) to set up infrastructure. To motivate workers, Yu did not offer material inducements. He had laborers read Mao's works, so that they engaged in hard labor not for the sake of personal enrichment but out of fidelity to Mao and China's socialist enterprise.[55]

Directed by the Oil Ministry, the Daqing oilfield showed that when the Party consolidated economic authority within central ministries, the party-state could, in historian Hou Li's words, be "adept at … mobilizing resources, energy, and enthusiasm from the masses for a single project within a very short period of time."[56] Despite Daqing's success, the central Party had no intention in 1960 of making it into a model for other industrial ventures since China at the time was in the throes of the Great Leap famine. The Party's first major promotion of Daqing

[54] Chen, *Sanxian*, 44–46.

[55] For a firsthand account, see Yu Qiuli, *Yu Qiuli huiyi lu* (Beijing: Jiefanjun chubanshe, 1996), 636–666. For a social history of the battles to build Daqing, see Hou, *Building for Oil*, 29–62.

[56] Hou, *Building for Oil*, 62.

occurred at the National People's Congress in November 1963 when Yu Qiuli told congress delegates, of which Mao was one, that the oil industry was the one economic sector which far surpassed the production goals set by the Party during the Great Leap. The Oil Ministry had mobilized tens of thousands of people in a large militarized campaign, and they had struck a lake of black gold.[57] Without Daqing oil, much of China's motorized economy would have been powerless since China lost its main supplier of crude oil in the rancor of the Sino-Soviet split.[58]

On December 24, Beijing mayor Peng Zhen organized an event at which vice minister of oil Kang Shi'en relayed Daqing's accomplishments to over 56,000 cadres from the Beijing government, the State Council, and the Central Committee. During Kang's speech, Peng Zhen interjected and praised how workers at Daqing had made China self-sufficient in oil by "enduring hardships." Peng Zhen asserted that "if the entire country were to fight as hard as the people in Daqing had, there would be no limit to accelerating national development." When faced with a problem, Daqing workers had the "fighting style of the People's Liberation Army," were "well-disciplined," and "strived to accomplish glorious missions under harsh conditions."[59] Convinced that Daqing's militarized approach to economic development could serve as a model for industry nationwide, Mao had Yu Qiuli come to Zhongnanhai and give a brief on the Daqing oilfield to leading economic planners – Li Fuchun, Zhou Enlai, Deng Xiaoping, and Chen Yun.[60]

The following month, Mao proclaimed in a *People's Daily* editorial that the "whole nation must learn from the PLA," so that the entire population could become like its "heroic troops" and "fight hard battles." The article predicted that once all Chinese modeled their lives after soldiers, "The project of socialist construction will develop in leaps and bounds."[61] On February 5, the Party center presented the Daqing oilfield as a model of how to achieve fast-paced national development, telling industrial enterprises to emulate its "all-out battle" tactics.[62] On February 13 at an education work conference, Mao again lauded Daqing, remarking that its builders had with "a little investment" in "a short period of time" realized

57 Hou, *Building for Oil*, 96.
58 Arthur Jay Klinghoffer, "Sino-Soviet Relations and the Politics of Oil," *Asian Survey* 16 (1976): 541–542.
59 Hou, *Building for Oil*, 97.
60 Hou, *Building for Oil*, 98.
61 "Quanguo dou yao xuexi Jiefangjun," *Renmin ribao*, February 1, 1964.
62 "Zhongyang guanyu chuanda 'shiyou gongye by guanyu Daqing shiyou huizhan qingkuang de baogao' de tongzhi," February 5, 1964, in *Gongye xue Daqing wenxian bianji ji shiliao xuanbian*, ed. Zhonggong Daqing shiwei dangshi yanjiu shi (Beijing: Zhongyang wenxian chubanshe, 2004), 29–30.

"a great achievement."[63] Party praise for Daqing in the early months of 1964 did not lead to a big burst of industrial construction activity. That would only happen when China's leaders took up Mao's ideas about how to rework the Third Five Year Plan after the Gulf of Tonkin incident in August 1964 and started the Third Front campaign.

A New Vision for the Third Five Year Plan

Mao began to enunciate his own vision of what should be the primary objectives behind the Third Five Year Plan in mid-1964. Mao based his comments on a chief-of-operations report commissioned sometime in early 1964 by the General Staff's deputy chief Yang Chengwu.[64] The report evaluated how ready the national economy was for a sudden attack. Issued on April 25, the report noted that over half of China's industry and population were located in in fourteen cities with a population over one million mainly in the northeast and along the coast, which enemy bombers and nuclear missiles could easily reach. Railroad, water, and shipping infrastructure suffered from the same strategic defects. If the CCP did not improve the geographic arrangement of Chinese industry, foreign powers could unleash devastating floods and paralyze the economy at the beginning of any future war.[65] On May 9, Luo Ruiqing distributed the report to Mao and other members of the Central Standing Committee.[66]

After reviewing it, Mao met on May 10 and 11 with the leading small group of the Planning Commission to discuss the Third Five Year Plan. The commission's director, Li Fuchun, headed up the sessions. When Li suggested concentrating on the production of high-quality steel, Mao suddenly spoke out against the idea that "eating, clothing, and daily essentials" should be the core of the Third Five Year Plan and asked his colleagues what then would become of the steel industry, saying, "can [steel] eat? Can it wear clothes?" When Li Fuchun said that only part of some railroads could be built, Mao again expressed his disapproval and demanded that Panzhihua Steel in Sichuan and Jiuquan Steel in Gansu both be built.[67]

Although Mao did not explicitly say so, other leaders present knew that the construction of Panzhihua would require more than just building part

[63] Mao Zedong, "Guanyu jiaoyu geming de tanhua," February 13, 1964, in *Jianguo yilai Mao Zedong wengao, Volume 11*, ed. Zhonggong zhongyang wenxian yanjiu shi (Beijing: Zhongyang chubanshe, 1996), 22–24.

[64] Chen, "Sanxian jianshe," 4.

[65] "Zong can zuo zhan bu de baogao," April 25, 1964, in *Zhongguo gongchandang yu sanxian*, 55–56.

[66] Chen, "Sanxian jianshe," 4. [67] Chen, *Sanxian*, 46.

of some railroads. Establishing Panzhihua would necessitate huge investments in southwest China. The Railroad Ministry would have to lay the Chengdu–Kunming line through Panzhihua and the Guiyang–Kunming line through Liupanshui in Guizhou, where a new mining complex would have to be established to produce the coking coal that would be necessary for smelting steel in Panzhihua. Every one of these projects was gigantic.

The two railroads would have to pass through complex mountainous terrain, and together they covered an area over 1,600 kilometers long. Developing Liupanshui coal mines would demand large investments too. Geological surveys would have to be performed, mines would have to be dug, and coal-processing centers would have to be put up. On top of all these projects, Panzhihua Steel itself would have to be created in an area over 300 kilometers away from the nearest big city – Kunming – which itself did not have much of an industrial base. The Chinese government had tried to build these projects during the Great Leap as part of a larger effort to industrialize inland China, and the Party had dramatically failed, ceasing construction work on all related projects in 1962.[68]

Mao expressed to his colleagues that he was not fazed by the idea of starting up another big industrialization drive. Not mincing words about the importance of boosting steel output, Mao declared that if Panzhihua and Jiuquan Steel "aren't built, then I will never be at ease." Foreign pressures were mounting against China, and if the CCP had to "fight a war," Mao inquired, "what will we do? Until Panzhihua is built, I won't sleep well."[69] After hearing Li Fuchun remark that the Party needed to take a balanced approach to economic development, Mao said that Li was right that the CCP "can only do as many things as we have money for … In the past, we suffered losses, set revenue too high, and made the infrastructure construction battlefront too long."[70] Everyone at the meeting nodded their heads in agreement.[71]

In spite of cautioning against raising investment levels, when Li Fuchun mentioned that basic industry and transport infrastructure were still weak, Mao proclaimed that if this did not change, China "won't be

[68] Yang Chao, *Yang Chao zai Panxi* (Panzhihua: Panzhihua shi dangan bu, 2011), 14. Kinzley, "Crisis and the Development," 574–576. I do not discuss in detail here what would be required to build Jiuquan Steel because Mao talked much more often about Panzhihua Steel.

[69] Mao Zedong, "1964 nian 5 yue 10 ri zhi 11 ri zai jiwei lingdao xiaozu huibao di san ge wu nian jihua shexiang, dang yilun dao tielu, jiaotong, di san ge wu nian jihua zhi neng gao name duo shi de zhishi," in *Panzhihua kaifa*, ed. Zhonggong Panzhihua shi dangshi yanjiushi (Panzhihua: Zhonggong Panzhihhua shiwei dangshi yanjiushi bian, 2000), 6.

[70] Zhonggong zhongyang wenxian yanjiu shi, *Mao Zedong nianpu 1949–1976 di 5 juan* (Beijing: Zhongyang wenxian chubanshe, 2013), 348.

[71] Chen, *Sanxian*, 47.

able to sit comfortably and stand up straight. It will fall over." In Mao's opinion, the Chinese economy had "two fists – agriculture and the defense industry – and one ass – basic industry." While Mao said that it was "essential" that all three sectors be "set … up right," he singled out "basic industry" as being most important and stated that "there cannot be too much of everything else. They must be adjusted accordingly."[72]

When Deng Xiaoping suggested decreasing the amount of imported grain in exchange for more technological imports, Mao seconded his view, arguing that agriculture should be as self-sufficient as possible. "It should not borrow money from the state. Nor should it ask for things from the state." Mao reiterated, though, that the Third Five Year Plan could not repeat the Party's previous mistakes. "There needs to be some leeway" in the country's economic plan. "In the past, we talked about it, but we didn't do it. These past few years we did better. We should continue like this. We can't set state revenue too high. Setting it too high is dangerous. In the past we did and suffered losses. We set revenue too high and extended the infrastructure battlefront too long."[73] In Mao's opinion, it was "best to do less and well."[74]

Mao Insists on Building the Third Front

Mao's colleagues at first did not enact his recommendations on how the Party should revamp the Third Five Year Plan. On May 18, Li Fuchun repeated the original conception of the Third Five Year Plan. "Agriculture still has to have priority … and so some important railroads will either not be included or not be completely finished." As for the Jiuquan and Panzhihua steel plants, the time was not yet ripe to start them. Economic planners should only "actively prepare" for them.[75] On May 27, Mao summoned Liu Shaoqi, Zhou Enlai, Deng Xiaoping, Li Fuchun, Peng Zhen, and Luo Ruiqing to his bedroom. It was there that he first mentioned the idea of the "Third Front" and tried to impress upon leaders how essential it was to China's protection from international threats.

Mao criticized the original Third Five Year Plan for "not paying enough attention" to the Third Front.[76] Mao insisted, "now it must be

[72] Zhonggong zhongyang wenxian, *Mao Zedong nianpu*, 348. Chen, *Sanxian*, 47.
[73] "Fulu: Li Fuchun guanyu di san ge wunian jihua chubu shexiang de shuoming yaodian," May 1964, in *Jianguo yilai zhongyao wenxian xuan bian 18*, 523.
[74] Chen, *Sanxian*, 47.
[75] "Li Fuchun guanyu di san ge wunian jihua chubu shexiang de shuoming," May 18, 1964, in *Zhongguo gongchandang yu sanxian*, 41–42.
[76] Pang and Jin, *Mao Zedong zhuan*, 1361.

added on. In the next six years, the southwest needs to be given … industrial bases for metallurgy, the defense sector, oil, railroads, coal, and machine building."[77] Mao also gave some indication of where exactly the First, Second, and Third Fronts were. "The First Front is the coast. From the Baotou steel plant [in Inner Mongolia] to Lanzhou [in Gansu province] is the Second Front, and the southwest is the Third Front … In the age of atomic bombs, not having a rear defense area just won't do."[78] The Party had to avail itself of its revolutionary past and "prepare to go to the mountains, and there still needs to be a place to go." Mao made clear that that place was Panzhihua when Luo Ruiqing mentioned that the chief of staff was worried about the ability of reservoirs around Beijing to contain floods. Mao stated, "If there is a problem with Beijing, as long as there is Panzhihua, then the problem will be solved. If Beijing is flooded, we will still have Panzhihua … We should also build what Panzhihua needs in terms of transport, coal, and electricity."[79]

Mao reassured his colleagues that they need not worry about financing for the Third Front. "If there is not enough money … then you can use my publication royalties and wages." Resource shortages should also not prevent the Party from undertaking the Third Front campaign. "If we lack trains to build the Third Front, we can take a truck. If we lack trucks, we can still ride donkeys."[80] Mao was likely using hyperbole here to make light of a serious issue while at the same time signaling to Party elites that the Third Front had to be constructed no matter what. The most important project of all was Panzhihua Steel. If it was "not built," Mao reminded his colleagues, he wouldn't "be able to sleep."[81] Panzhihua Steel had "to be built quickly but not sloppily." The time had come for the Party "to solve the problem" of the lack of a rear base, and the Party had to act now. China was in the midst of "a race against time, to get ahead before the outbreak of war … to compress the First Front and move inland."[82] If everyone did not approve of this new policy line, Mao would not give up on it. He would himself "go to … Xichang [near Panzhihua] and hold a meeting" about founding the Third Front.[83]

Mao's vehemence about constructing the Third Front led Party leaders to pay more attention to it at a meeting on May 28. They exhibited varying degrees of interest. Zhou Enlai was the most effusive. He not

[77] Chen, *Sanxian*, 50. [78] Zhonggong zhongyang wenxian, *Mao Zedong nianpu*, 355.
[79] Mao, "Yao ba Panzhihua he lianxi dao Panzhihua de jiaotong," 43.
[80] Mao Zedong, "Zai wu ge fu zongli huibao sanxian jianshe wenti shi de zhishi," May 27, 1964, in *Panzhihua kaifa*, 6.
[81] Chen, *Sanxian*, 53.
[82] Mao Zedong, "Zai zhongyang gongzuo huiyi shang de jianghua," May 27, 1964, in *Panzhihua kaifa*, 6.
[83] Chen, *Sanxian*, 50.

only endorsed building Panzhihua. He also called for the development of basic industry in southwest China and the large-scale transfer of industrial enterprises to the region. Zhou praised Mao's "strategic thought," which highlighted how "China in the past was … semicolonial, and so … China's economic development was unbalanced."[84] He was unsure though how to handle "the layout of the First and Second Fronts," and he thought that the Party still had to figure out how to balance "eating, food, and daily essentials with the defense sector and basic industry." Zhou did not "blame the Planning Commission" for not sufficiently considering the Third Front. Rather, in line with the anti-Soviet sentiment of the day, he placed responsibility on the calculating methods learned during "the First Five Year Plan from the Soviet Union."[85]

Li Fuchun's support for the Third Front was a bit less expansive. He apologized for not previously "paying enough attention" to constructing the Third Front, and he thanked Mao for pointing out that the original ideas for the Third Five Year Plan "had not attended enough to rear areas." Sweetening his mea culpa with a compliment for Mao, Li added, "great minds think alike." And yet Li did not throw his weight behind the Third Front right away. He suggested putting off construction of Jiuquan Steel, and he only backed preparing to build Panzhihua and railroads between Chengdu and Kunming, Guiyang and Kunming, Hunan and Guizhou, and Chongqing and Guiyang.[86]

Liu Shaoqi thought that the Party should focus on preparing to build Panzhihua, Liupanshui, and the Chengdu–Kunming Railroad. Jiuquan Steel and other projects could be considered later. Right after Liu made this statement, Peng Zhen brought up Mao's remarks about using his royalties to pay for the Third Front, and Luo Ruiqing and Deng Xiaoping recalled Mao's comment that if they did not get behind the Third Front, then he would split with the Party center and go to Xichang to set up the Third Front on his own.[87] Liu Shaoqi appears to have been less concerned about how Mao might act than he was about the Third Front's potential economic consequences, warning his colleagues that there was "an incipient tendency, once things are relaxed a bit, then everyone completely relaxes." If this tendency continued, then the same problem of "infrastructure construction becoming too much" could happen again.[88] While Liu did not explicitly mention the Leap, everyone present was aware of what he was talking about.

[84] Zhou Enlai, "Guanyu di san ge wu nia jihua de ruogan wenti," *Dang de wenxian* 3 (1996): 15.
[85] Chen, *Sanxian*, 51.
[86] Li Fuchun, "Guanyu jihua anpai de ji dian yijian," *Dang de wenxian* 3 (1996): 21.
[87] Liu Shaoqi, "Gao xinan sanxian xianzai yao zhuoshu," *Dang de wenxian* 3 (1996): 20.
[88] Chen, *Sanxian*, 51–52.

CCP leaders also understood that given China's capital constraints the only way that they could accomplish Mao's order to "quickly build" the Third Front was implementing the same developmental strategy that they had deployed during the Great Leap. They would have to extend the hands of the state into the countryside and mobilize massive regiments of labor in militarized campaigns. The leadership's awareness of this fact is evident from Deng Xiaoping's remark that the only way to build Panzhihua was to fight "a war of annihilation." This expression was Party-speak for assembling large brigades of rural labor to construct economic infrastructure, like the CCP had done at the Daqing oilfield and during the Great Leap writ large. Deng was worried, like Liu Shaoqi, that the Third Front might be a prelude to another big wave of industrial construction, and so he added, "we can't rashly set up projects everywhere."[89]

Not satisfied with his colleagues' planning ideas, Mao pressed them to adopt new economic ways at a June 6 meeting.[90] Mao lashed out in particular at Li Fuchun, whom he accused of "learning the Soviet Union's method" of planning so well that it had "become a habitual force" in his thinking. Mao instructed him that "changing planning methods" was a revolutionary issue.[91] Mao went even further and alerted his colleagues that he was concerned about opponents of Chinese socialism within the Party. "What to do," Mao asked, "if the Party center gives rise to Khrushchev-style revisionism?"[92] After raising the possibility of an insider threat within the commanding heights, Mao turned to the topic of the Third Front, which for him did not just mean Panzhihua and a few other projects. It meant expanding basic industry and the defense sector in inland China. Mao also restated his assertion that the Third Front campaign was a military must because, "As long as imperialism exists, there is the danger of war. We are not imperialism's chief of staff. We don't know when it will fight a war." And so the Party "must work hard to build the Third Front."[93]

Preparing for a Protracted People's War

At the same June 6 meeting, Mao again threatened his colleagues, "if you don't build Panzhihua," then he would take matters into his own hands

[89] Li, "Guanyu jihua anpai de ji dian yijian," 21. [90] Chen, *Sanxian*, 52.

[91] Chen, *Sanxian*, 54.

[92] Xiao Donglian, *Qiusu Zhongguo: Wenge qian shi nian shi* (Beijing: Zhongguo dangshi chubanshe, 1999), 794.

[93] Sun Dongsheng, "Woguo jingji jianshe zhanlue buju de zhuanbian: Sanxian jianshe juece xingcheng shulue," *Dang de wenxian* 3 (1995): 44.

and "hold a meeting" in Panzhihua. Mao ramped up the intimidation factor, telling his colleagues that he would "ride a donkey" to get there.[94] Mao perhaps made this last comment for a comedic effect that strengthened its rhetorical force. It is possible that he also sought to remind Party leaders of when they rode donkeys for transportation in the revolutionary base areas.[95] The likelihood of this implicit reference to the CCP's history is supported by the fact that it was at this meeting that Mao told his colleagues that building a Big Third Front in the southwest would be insufficient to wage a protracted war. The Party also had to establish a Small Third Front in the First and Second Fronts, which "must also build defense industries and prepare base areas for guerilla warfare."[96]

At a follow-up meeting on June 8, Mao continued to harangue his colleagues about the emergence of revisionism in China, which he connected to challenges to his authority within the central Party. According to Mao, "in this country of ours, one-third of power is not in my hands. It is in the hands of enemies."[97] At the same meeting, Mao raised the issue of the Third Front, asking, "If enemies occupy our place, what are we going to do? Every coastal province must have some grenades, TNT manufacturers, and defense factories. I have talked about this for a few years, but nothing has been done." Likely because Mao was aware of his associates' hesitation to start another Great Leap-like campaign, he added, "Everyone agrees that Third Front construction must be done quickly but not carelessly."[98]

On June 16 at a Politburo meeting, Mao again warned about the dangers of China possibly losing its way and becoming a revisionist country like the Soviet Union.[99] At the same meeting, Mao also again expounded on the military importance of the Third Front, linking its construction to readying the country for a protracted people's war. In Mao's view, China could not just prepare for a war in which the United States "comes from Guangdong," since he was not sure that Washington would follow that strategy. Mao was also "not sure" if the United States would "come from the northeast" and "take the same road as the Japanese military."[100] There was also the possibility that America would "come from the Bohai Sea" and seek to blockade Beijing "like the English

94 Sun, "Woguo jingji jianshe," 44.
95 Joseph W. Esherick, "Tracking an Iconic Photograph," *PRC History Review* 1:3 (December 2015): 1–5.
96 Chen, "Sanxian jianshe," 7.
97 Zhonggong zhongyang wenxian yanjiu shi, *Liu Shaoqi nianpu* (Beijing: Zhongyang wenxian chubanshe, 1996), 585.
98 Mao, "Mei ge sheng dou yao you yi, er, sanxian," 52.
99 Zhonggong zhongyang wenxian, *Mao Zedong nianpu*, 363.
100 Mao, "Difang dangwei yao gao junshi," 53.

and French armies" during the Opium Wars "and the Eight-Power Coalition" during the Boxer Rebellion.[101]

Mao asserted that China had to be equipped to handle all these possibilities and that the best way for China to fight was to choose its battles. "If we can win a battle, then we fight. If we can't win a battle, then we retreat. If we can stop an invasion, then we stop it. If we can't stop an invasion, isn't it better to retreat?" In anticipation of the war of attrition that Mao envisioned, "every province, district, and county had to form militias." Local areas "must not rely on the center [or] ... on the PLA's millions of troops." Localities had to have militias to defend China, and the Party had to take advantage of the fact that China was "a big country" and had a very "long battlefront." The CCP "was duty-bound to defend our country's territory." But Party leaders had to be willing to give up territory. "If we can't defend it, we aren't going to go away." If the enemy enters into the cities, then we "will also enter into the cities and engage in street fighting and crawl into homes." No matter what China's enemies did, Mao was confident that the Party "will always fight."[102]

After hearing Mao's lecture about the need to stress war-preparedness, Li Fuchun took more interest in the Third Front. Yet he still did not approve building any projects; he only ordered the "Planning Commission to go and conduct surveys for three months" in the southwest as well as in Shanghai and the northeast since their enterprises would be the primary supplier of Third Front labor and equipment.[103] Zhou Enlai assisted Li Fuchun with preparations. On June 19, Zhou gathered representatives from the Planning Commission and fourteen ministries and discussed with them Mao's recent comments about the Third Front. He told them to establish an investigation team comprising cadres and experts and go immediately to the southwest to figure out what projects each ministry would undertake and where they would be located.

Zhou designated the Planning Commission as the group's leading work unit, and ministries appointed vice directors as representatives. On June 23, the group flew to Chengdu and met with the secretary of the Southwest Commission, and the provincial secretaries of Sichuan, Yunnan, and Guizhou. During their meeting, they established twelve special groups to study five big projects: a conventional-weapons complex around Chongqing, a steel complex around Panzhihua, the Chengdu–Kunming Railroad, a coal complex around Liupanshui, and the transfer

[101] Chen, *Sanxian*, 84. [102] Mao, "Difang dangwei yao gao junshi," 53.
[103] Chen, *Sanxian*, 61.

of machine-building factories to inland China. The group then set out to begin initial preparations for the Third Front.[104]

The Vietnam War and Approval of the Third Front

As the first surveys for the Third Front got underway, Beijing sought to firm up diplomatic ties in Southeast Asia. In July 1964, the CCP sent a delegation to Hanoi to meet with representatives of Laos and North Vietnam. Meeting participants concluded that the United States would probably soon station more land forces in South Vietnam and perhaps bombard the North. They also agreed that they should better co-ordinate military operations against the United States, and China reiterated its commitment to support Southeast Asian allies "by all possible and necessary means."[105]

As China strengthened its alliance against American imperialism in Southeast Asia, Mao took the Sino-Soviet split to another level, publicly professing in a pamphlet titled *On Khrushchev's Phony Communism and Its Historical Lessons for the World* that the Soviet Union was socialist in name but was becoming capitalist in practice. "The revisionist Khrushchev clique" ran the Soviet Union and "under the signboard of 'peaceful coexistence'," Khrushchev and his supporters had "been colluding with American imperialism, wrecking the socialist camp and … opposing the revolutionary struggles of the oppressed peoples and nations." Meanwhile, within the Soviet Union, Khrushchev had done away with "the proletarian character of the Communist Party of the Soviet Union" and paved "the way for the restoration of capitalism" by favoring the dominance of a "privileged stratum" that "appropriates the fruits of the Soviet people's labour and … secures high incomes in the form of high salaries … and a great variety of personal subsidies."[106]

In the same month that Mao authorized the publication of this anti-Soviet tract, border tensions between Moscow and Beijing escalated. Since the previous February, Beijing and Moscow had attempted to resolve border disputes, but by July, negotiations were on the ropes. To ensure border security, the Kremlin deployed more troops and ordered them to engage in regular training and military maneuvers. On July 2, Mao told Party leaders at a meeting of the Politburo that they should "not

[104] Dan Lanshan, "Sui Cheng Zihua diaocha: Da xinan sanxian jianshe," *Taiqian muhou* 6 (2010): 15–16. Zhonggong Panzhihua shiwei dangshi yanjiu shi bian, *Panzhihua kaifa jianshe da shiji* (Chengdu: Chengdu keji daxue chubanshe, 1994), 41.

[105] Chen, "China's Involvement," 360–361.

[106] Mao Zedong, *On Khrushchev's Phony Communism and Its Historical Lessons for the World*, *Marxists Internet Archive*, July 14, 1964, www.marxists.org/reference/archive/mao/works/1964/phnycom.htm.

only pay attention to the east" and be concerned about an attack by the imperialist United States. They also had to pay attention to "the north" and the threat of a Soviet attack. For socialist China to be secure, the CCP had to "prepare for war on both fronts."[107] In September, the General Staff responded to this change in Mao's threat perception by expanding Chinese defenses on the Soviet border and surveying border regions. So that China would be ready for a sudden Soviet assault, Chinese military personnel examined routes utilized by the Soviet troops during World War II to attack the Japanese and collected information about Soviet and Mongolian military activities.[108]

While Mao and other CCP leaders were worried about the possibility of a Sino-Soviet war, it was the American threat that caused the Third Front campaign to rapidly pick up speed and bureaucratic momentum a month prior to the Chinese military buildup on the Soviet border. The spark that set the prairie fire occurred not in China but in Vietnam. On August 4, the United States alleged that North Vietnamese boats attacked the USS *Maddox* without provocation in the Gulf of Tonkin.[109] In retaliation, the US Air Force showered bombs on North Vietnam on August 5. On the same day, Zhou Enlai and Luo Ruiqing suggested to Hanoi that China and Vietnam work more closely on handling the American threat. Just in case war suddenly exploded, the Central Military Commission put southern military units into a state of combat-readiness.[110]

Unable to sleep that night, Mao scribbled at 6 a.m. on the draft statement of Chinese opposition to the United States invading Vietnam, "If we are going to war, then I should change my travel plans," and canceled a previously scheduled inspection tour of the Yellow River.[111] Four days later, President Lyndon Johnson signed the Gulf of Tonkin Resolution, which led to the deployment of over 184,300 American troops to Vietnam by the end of 1965.[112] Meanwhile, within China, the PLA dispatched more units to south China, and Beijing declared its opposition to American activities in Vietnam and promised that "China would never fail to come to the aid of the Vietnamese."[113]

Preparing the home front for war, the Party rallied twenty million in anti-American protests between August 7 and 11. According to the

107 Li and Xia, *Sino-Soviet Split*, 95–96. The quote is on page 96.
108 Li and Xia, *Sino-Soviet Split*, 97–98.
109 Secretary of Defense Robert McNamara later admitted that the August 4 incident never happened, but an earlier one on August 2 had occurred. *The Fog of War: Eleven Lessons from the Life of Robert S. McNamara*, directed by Errol Morris (Los Angeles: Sony Pictures Classics, 2003).
110 Chen, "China's Involvement," 364.
111 Zhonggong zhongyang wenxian, *Mao Zedong nianpu*, 382.
112 Bradley, *Vietnam at War*, 111. 113 Chen, "China's Involvement," 365.

People's Daily, "protestors resolutely supported the Vietnamese people crushing American imperialism's armed aggression." The newspaper also connected the present conflict to the Korean War and cited a veteran who proclaimed that "the Chinese people already measured itself up to America's invading army in the battles of Korea and exposed the paper tiger of American imperialism." The article warned that if the United States did not back down, American troops would again be knocked "bloody and wounded."[114] While the Chinese press maintained an attitude of nationalist bravado towards the prospect of a Sino-American war, Mao indicated to Party leaders that they were not doing enough to fortify national security.

Mao made this point when he returned the General Staff's report on China's lack of military readiness to Luo Ruiqing on August 12. On the report, Mao noted, "The State Council's special small group [for the Third Front] had already been established," but as far he could tell, one thing was unclear: "has it started to work or not?"[115] Party leaders understood that the time for foot dragging was over. War with the United States was on the horizon, and arrangements for battle had to be made now. Later that day, Zhou Enlai approved a report by the first secretary of the Railroad Corps, Lu Zhengcao. Lu argued that China had to "adapt to the urgent needs of the situation in Southeast Asia" and establish a Southwest Railroad Engineering Force to mobilize 240,000 workers to construct the Chengdu–Kunming, Yunnan–Guizhou, and Sichuan–Guizhou railroads.

Lu Zhengcao did not directly mention the Daqing oilfield in his description of the Southwest Railroad Engineering Force. But there were clear similarities. Like at Daqing, power over Third Front rail projects would be concentrated in a single headquarters administered by the central government. Yet where Daqing's headquarters oversaw one project, the Southwest Railroad Engineering Force would supervise the building of a regional industrial system. The Railroad Ministry would take the lead and have authority over all planning and designs, and the acquisition and deployment of labor, funding, equipment, and raw materials. The Railroad Corps would operate as second in command and direct construction efforts. Zhou Enlai passed the report with his decision to Li Fuchun and Bo Yibo, who said that after "some discussion" with Luo Ruiqing they agreed that using "a military approach" was "a good method."[116]

114 "Fandui Meiguo qinlue Yuenan de langchao xi juan ge zhuyao chengshi: Quanguo yi qian duo wan ren shiwei youxing," *Renmin ribao*, August 10, 1964.

115 Chen, *Sanxian*, 55.

116 "Zhou Enlai deng pizhun Lu Zhengcao," August 12, 1964, in *Zhongguo gongchandang yu sanxian*, 57, 59.

On August 16, Li Fuchun headed up a Planning Commission meeting at which he declared that China's economic priorities had changed. The Vietnam War had escalated. The First Front was no longer secure, and the Third Front campaign was of the utmost necessity. To protect industry, Lin ordered "no new industrial projects" in the First Front. As for projects that "are in the process of construction, if they can be shrunk in size, then they should be shrunk." If an enterprise "can be split in two, then prepare to split it in two ... If an enterprise can be relocated, then relocate it." When enterprises are moved, they should not be relocated to big cities; they should follow the idea Lin Biao suggested in 1960 of "dispersing, backing into mountains, and hiding" defense industries. Not only "the Sichuan–Guizhou, Yunnan–Guizhou, and Chengdu–Kunming railroads must be built ... the Hunan–Guizhou Railroad must also be built." Li Fuchun was likely mindful that some of his colleagues atop China's party-state were not in favor of this new policy, as he asserted that people shouldn't think that "because we might prepare for ten years and not fight a war that we can delay and linger." Li firmly declared that the Party "must prepare for war."[117]

In spite of Li's more expansive view of the Third Front, Mao was still dissatisfied with his performance and urged him to pick up the pace, asking him, "why is Third Front construction so slow?" Li tried to defend himself by saying that the Party lacked the requisite funds and plans. Mao would not have it and rebuked the Planning Commission, saying that its planning methods were "inappropriate" and that its members "do not work hard."[118] Mao urged the central Party to speed up Third Front construction the next day at a meeting of the Secretariat. "When it comes to the Third Front," Mao declared, "the more enthusiasm the better. Even if it is a bit rough, that's fine." We must engage in "a race against time."[119]

On August 19, Li Fuchun, Bo Yibo, and Luo Ruiqing gave a report to Mao which ordered the immediate construction of the Third Front that was circulated to all central ministries, provinces, and cities.[120] Li and his partners stated that they had "met with all responsible parties, and everyone agrees that the Chairman's instructions [on the Third Front] and the report of the chief of operations are extremely important. It is a vital matter of our country's strategic defense that must be handled seriously

[117] Li Fuchun, "Zai guojia jiwei 1964 nian niandu jihua zuotanhui shang de fayan," August 16, 1964, in *Zhongguo gongchandang yu sanxian*, 61.

[118] Chen, *Sanxian*, 61.

[119] Mao Zedong. "Zhuxi he shuji chu guanyu sanxian jianshe deng wenti de zhishi," in *Panzhihua kaifa*, 7.

[120] Lüthi, "Vietnam War," 33.

and worked hard on to achieve."[121] Central ministries were assigned responsibility for projects relevant to their operations, and a special small group under the direction of Li Fuchun was founded within the State Council to oversee Third Front affairs. The report also repeated Li's directives from a few days prior about what to build and where to move enterprises. Lastly, the report broadened the scope of work units that should move inland to include institutions of higher education, scientific research institutions, and design institutes.

The report did not refer to the Party's wartime base areas. But the strategic logic behind them was embedded in the report in another way. The key words came from Zhou Enlai's directive eight months earlier to protect China's nuclear program by putting projects in "mountainous, dispersed, hidden" locations. Yet now the Party center imprinted this Maoist defense strategy into a major industrialization drive. The report also did not explicitly address how Third Front projects were to be built.

All Party leaders comprehended, though, that China could only accomplish Mao's order to rapidly construct a large number of industrial ventures in the southwest by mobilizing labor in "wars of annihilation," like the Oil Ministry had done at Daqing. By greenlighting Third Front construction, the Party transformed the policy of China studying the Daqing model from a proclamation into the driving principle behind a large, centrally directed, militarized industrialization campaign to re-engineer the economic composition of inland China. Post-Great Leap economic retrenchment was over, washed away by the militaristic aftermath of the Gulf of Tonkin incident and Mao's dogged insistence that a defensive industrialization initiative was the best way to address rising international threats.

Beginning a Militarized Industrialization Campaign

After Mao's colleagues approved construction of the Third Front, he still reprimanded them for not acting quickly enough. While listening to Bo Yibo's update on planning for the Third Front on August 20, Mao interjected that the CCP had to "learn a lesson from Stalin's experience." Before World War II, Stalin "didn't prepare fortifications … didn't prepare for an enemy attack, and … didn't relocate" industry.[122] Mao had told the Party to start work on the Third Front a long time ago, and "the Central Party Work Conference just talked for a really long time, and the

[121] "Li Fuchun, Bo Yibo, Luo Ruiqing guanyu guojia jingji jianshe ruhe fangbei diren turan laixi wenti de baogao," August 19, 1964, in *Zhongguo gongchandang yu sanxian*, 71–72.

[122] Zhonggong zhongyang wenxian, *Mao Zedong nianpu*, 391.

Chengdu–Kunming Railroad was still not implemented, as if you weren't worried about it." In the past, "the Hunan–Guizhou, Yunnan–Guizhou, and Sichuan–Guizhou railroads … had been worked on for several years, but nothing had come of it." Work on all of these railroads had to restart now. "If there weren't enough steel rails, then the rails of other lines can be torn up." So that the country would be ready for a protracted people's war, "Every province had to have a military division and arsenal." That way, if war came, the Party could re-enact its wartime military strategy of "striking when victory is possible and retreating when it isn't."[123]

On the same day, Mao's personal secretary, Chen Boda, launched an implicit attack on Li Fuchun, complaining to Li's assistant, Yang Bo, that the Soviet Union's decade-long influence in China had "caused a blind faith" in its "unreasonable planning system," which "had hurt us in many ways, especially in helping a revisionist regime to grow." According to Chen Boda, the Party "had to act according to Mao's instructions" and embark on its own "socialist industrial road."[124] Li Fuchun endeavored to accomplish Mao's orders. On August 24, Li updated Mao on the Third Front's progress, and he suggested that the Party set up a Southwest Base Construction Headquarters to oversee the planning and construction of a regional industrial complex. Li not only included in his proposal Panzhihua Steel; Liupanshui Coal; and the Chengdu–Kunming, Yunnan–Guizhou, and Sichuan–Guizhou lines; he also called for the expansion of existing steel plants in Kunming, Chongqing, Chengdu, and Guizhou; the revival of efforts to build a large heavy-industrial machinery factory in Deyang in Sichuan; the carrying out of surveys for the Hubei–Sichuan line; and making "comprehensive plans for all kinds of industry."[125]

Although Li's view of what projects the Third Front should include was becoming larger, Mao was still not pleased with his work, so much so that on August 27 he took Chen Boda's recommendations from a week earlier, gave them to Deng Xiaoping, and told him to have them discussed at a Central Party Work Conference.[126] On Chen's report, Mao scribbled a warning. If planning methods did not change within a year or two, then "it would be best to eliminate the current Planning Commission and set up a different organization." In late August, Mao informed Li Fuchun directly that he thought the Planning Commission "was not reporting their work"

[123] Zhonggong zhongyang wenxian, *Mao Zedong nianpu*, 391–392.
[124] Chen, *Sanxian*, 63.
[125] Li Fuchun and Bo Yibo, "Guanyu jianshe Panzhihua gangtie jidi gei Mao Zedong he zhonggong zhongyang de baogao," August 24, 1964, in *Zhongguo gongchandang yu sanxian*, 74–77. The quote is on page 77.
[126] Zhonggong zhongyang wenxian, *Mao Zedong nianpu*, 397–398.

to him and Liu Shaoqi, and he complained that Third Front construction had still not begun.[127]

On August 30, Deng Xiaoping gave the Third Front campaign a bureaucratic push forward, distributing central Party directives about the Third Front to all ministries and provinces and ordering their implementation. Deng followed up this decision with a Secretariat directive to "send railroad construction troops to building sites by the end of September ... First guarantee funding for Third Front needs and do what was possible with remaining funds for other areas ... Set up a railroad construction headquarters, a Southwest Preparation Office ... and give [the Third Front] whatever it needed." Deng also demanded the construction of an industrial complex around Panzhihua and Chongqing.[128]

On September 4, Mao told Zhou Enlai, Deng Xiaoping, and Bo Yibo to "remove Li Fuchun" from the planning of the Third Front.[129] They do not appear to have listened. In early September, Mao continued to rail against the Party's economic planning practices in the past and present. At a gathering in Hangzhou, Mao denounced the Party leadership for "stopping the construction of the Sichuan, Yunnan, and Guizhou railroads" in the early 1960s during the period of economic adjustment after the Great Leap. This policy decision "made no sense ... Not building Panzhihua also made no sense. Haven't we known for a long time that Panzhihua has a mine? Why didn't we build it? If you don't arrange for it to be done, then I will ride a donkey to Xichang."[130]

In spite of Mao's threats, Li Fuchun did not stop working on Third Front affairs, and Mao still discussed economic planning with him. During a meeting with Li on September 12, Mao again pointed to the Great Leap's major success story – the Daqing oilfield – as an excellent model for industrial development. "The Daqing oilfield has its own ethos and logic ... Yu Qiuli gathered all the resources of the petroleum sector to engage in a fierce battle. The people in Daqing had no roads, no food, and no houses, but they succeeded."[131] The next day, Li Fuchun wrote a letter to Mao explaining how he was currently reforming the way China conducted "economic work, planning work, and design work," so that they accorded with "Mao's thought and China's present international

127 Chen, *Sanxian*, 64. 128 Chen, *Sanxian*, 57–58.

129 "Mao Zedong, Zhou Enlai, and Deng Xiaoping deng dui Lu Zhengcao guanyu xinan tielu jianshe chubu buzhu de baogao de zhishi," September 1, 3, and 4, 1964, in *Zhongguo gongchandang yu sanxian jianshe*, 78.

130 Mao Zedong, "Zai Hangzhou dang jiangdao xiu xinan tielu, si tiao xian ding xi alai hai shi de zhishi," in *Panzhihua kaifa*, 7.

131 Hou, *Building for Oil*, 98–99.

situation." Li stated that in the past few years we "paid too much attention to the First Front, neglected the Third Front, and made the layout of industry unreasonable. We must strive in seven to ten years to change ... the country's industrial layout."[132] The apologetic character of Li's letter shows that he understood that Mao was upset with him and that his future status in the Planning Commission was uncertain.

Li's promised changes to the planning process shed light on what he thought would appease Mao. According to Li, the Party center had to "implement the Chairman's idea of waging wars of annihilation and the idea of scattering troops to defend all positions" when the Party was rearranging "the layout of the entire national economy." Here, Li Fuchun, like Lu Zhengcao before him, was drawing on the Daqing model of mobilizing huge amounts of militarized labor to rapidly complete industrial projects. Like both Lu Zhengcao and Mao, Li Fuchun did not envision the battlefield on which laborers would fight to be the same as the Great Leap. The war to develop Chinese industry would not play out throughout the entire country under the command of many different local leaders. Nor would the Third Front campaign pursue the Great Leap's utopian goal of furnishing extensive welfare guarantees to every single Chinese.

Rather, as Lu Zhengcao proposed for Third Front railroads, central agencies would administer the entire Third Front campaign and concentrate on developing heavy industry in a specific region. To achieve this goal, Li Fuchun advocated pursuing several tasks in the next decade. The Party should form a High Command, led by Mao and Liu Shaoqi, to supervise the entire Third Front.[133] Around 100 factories would move inland in just the next year. A conventional-weapons complex would be constructed around Chongqing in three years and another one around Jiuquan in five years. Panzhihua and its associated railroads would be completed in seven years. Surveys and building of the Hunan–Guizhou Railroad would be finished by 1968. Strategic storage depots would be established for oil, iron, salt, steel, cotton cloth, and other resources. In addition, "all newly constructed factories" would be "'small and complete' and not big and complete ... Nonproductive construction" would also have to "make do with what is available." In this last statement, Li was again taking inspiration from the Daqing oilfield, which, as historian Hou Li has said, promoted "industrialization without urbanization."[134] That is to say, industrial development occurred but it was not accompanied by the formation of urban social services or a consumer sector.

132 The quotes in the next paragraph are also from Li Fuchun, "Guanyu jingji gongzuo he jihua gongzuo gei Mao Zedong de huibao xin," September 11, 1964, in *Zhongguo gongchandang yu sanxian*, 81–84. The quotes are on pages 81, 83.

133 Chen, *Sanxian*, 65. 134 Hou, *Building for Oil*, 93, 133–134.

On September 21, Li stressed at a Planning Commission meeting that the Party had to treat the accomplishment of these objectives as part of a wider struggle against American imperialism and Khrushchev's revisionist clique, while "supporting the people of the world's revolutionary struggles." He also denounced the Soviet model of building "big and complete" industrial enterprises which had "large administrative buildings, a large social service sector, and nonproductive buildings whose standards were excessively high." The Third Front was not going to follow the Soviet example. China had to "without exception abolish" Soviet planning methods, and the Third Front campaign had to follow the indigenous Maoist methods of socialist development worked out at the Daqing oilfield. Third Front planners had to "make do with what is available" and build "small and complete" factories whose housing was "the local version of the rammed-earth residences" that had housed workers at Daqing, and only establish basic social services, so that more resources could go into productive uses.[135]

Not everyone in the Party center was at ease with the acceleration of the Third Front campaign. A source of particular anxiety was the displacement of Party concern about agriculture with a focus on heavy industry. Li Fuchun hinted at this when he noted in passing that vice premier Tan Zhenlin had suggested that "no matter if a village is in the First, Second, or Third Front, all are the Third Front." Li thought that Tan was "really correct."[136] Liu Shaoqi likely knew that Li Fuchun was worried that the Party would neglect agriculture, as it had during the Great Leap. Liu Shaoqi also probably suspected that Li was concerned that planning for the Third Front campaign was inadequate and overambitious, again like during the Great Leap, as Liu Shaoqi confided in Li Fuchun on October 18, "we must advocate being honest people, speaking honest words, and doing honest things. When we set up an economic plan, we must not let honest people suffer. We must not let people making false and exaggerated reports gain the advantage ... We must seek truth from facts."[137]

These remarks were dangerous ones that would have almost certainly incited Mao's resentment since, as Deng Xiaoping told a friend, the Great Leap was Mao's "sickness of the heart" (*xin bing*). Whenever anybody mentioned it, he became very upset.[138] The fact that Liu Shaoqi talked with Li Fuchun about his concerns suggests that he had reason to believe that Li shared his trepidation that the Third Front campaign might turn

[135] Li, "Zai quanguo jihua huiyi shang de jianghua," 88.
[136] Li, "Zai quanguo jihua huiyi shang de jianghua," 89.
[137] Song and Sun, "Liu Shaoqi yu sanxian jianshe," 14.
[138] Chen, *Sanxian*, 66.

into another Great Leap Forward in which baseless reports again became the economic norm.

Expanding and Accelerating Third Front Construction

Mao reacted differently to the Third Front's picking up bureaucratic steam. He urged his colleagues to expand their vision of what it should be.[139] On October 19, Bo Yibo and Li Fuchun were briefing Mao on the progress of the Third Front in the southwest and around Jiuquan in Gansu when Mao stressed that there was no need to compress the Third Front into the southwest and the Shaanxi–Gansu–Ningxia borderlands around Jiuquan since "there was also western Hunan, western Hubei, and western Henan."[140] When Li and Bo said that investment in agriculture might have to be reduced, Mao said, "that is the way it should be. Agriculture should mainly rely … on the [local] masses to do things," not on the central government.[141] After their meeting with Mao, Li and Bo traveled to the southwest to inspect the Third Front.[142]

During their trip, Li and Bo sent a report to Mao on November 9 to explain why they had discontinued work on many industrial projects in 1962. The report reads as a delayed response to Mao's critical remarks on this issue over the past few months. Li and Bo focused their comments on the previous attempt to construct Panzhihua between 1958 and 1962 during the Great Leap. They acknowledged that when building stopped,

> From the perspective of the present … there was construction that was necessary and that could have been done related to geological surveys, scientific testing and research, and building railroads. The problem was that there was no central objective; resources were spread too thin … too many people were mobilized, and preparatory work was insufficient.

Given these issues, Li and Bo concluded that ceasing construction in 1962 "was correct for most projects." The two exceptions were one tunnel for the Chengdu–Kunming Railroad and research on how to smelt Panzhihua's high-titanium-content iron ore. Otherwise, all projects had to be aborted because, in 1962, "There was much pressure to reduce labor." Central ministries lacked money to invest, and there "was not enough food to eat" for the 80,000 workers in the area. There was only enough food for 5,000 people. There had also been no co-ordination of projects. When a project was started there was "no unified, well thought-

[139] Chen, *Sanxian*, 66. [140] Zhonggong zhongyang wenxian, *Mao Zedong nianpu*, 420.
[141] Mao Zedong, "Yao wang yun gui chuan, shan gan ning, xiangxi xiang'e, xiangxi ji," October 19, 1964, in *Zhongguo gongchandang yu sanxian*, 92.
[142] Sun, "Woguo jingji jianshe," 45.

out arrangement of each project. The central government and local work units started projects independently." When projects were canceled, "There was no unified leadership" either. The Party center had to learn from this experience and make sure that this time it "paid attention to every aspect of organizational ... and co-ordination work."[143]

While Li Fuchun and Bo Yibo urged careful planning and co-ordination, Mao championed enlarging the Third Front campaign even more. On October 22, Mao commented on a report about war preparations in Guangdong. Officials there had responded to the possibility that the United States might expand its war of invasion to North Vietnam by developing plans to relocate enterprises to rear areas to set up a provincial military industrial complex that had electrical networks, communication systems, military roads, and educational and health facilities. Mao strongly approved of Guangdong's actions and ordered Liu Shaoqi and a few other top leaders to distribute Guangdong's report to all provinces for discussion.[144]

Mao did not think that the Party should wait and see how the American military behaved and only later build provincial military industrial complexes. The Party had to immediately "give first priority to defense industry construction ... gradually improve [China's] industrial layout," and "strengthen the Third Front" based on the principle of "fighting soon, fighting big, and fighting a nuclear war." And there was no time to waste. China had to "engage in a race against time and struggle to be fast."[145] On November 3, Zhou Enlai and Luo Ruiqing followed up on Mao's order with a directive for provinces in east China, north China, south-central China, and the northeast to "construct local defense industries, including firearms, bullets, land mines, grenades, and explosives." Provinces in these regions had also to "relocate some ... support factories from big cities to rear areas ... set up small coal mines, electrical plants, and necessary repair factories"; construct defense structures for transportation and communication networks; "stockpile grain, salt, oil, and other strategic resources"; and build backup schools and hospitals.[146]

[143] Li Fuchun and Bo Yibo, "Guanyu Panzhihua diqu gongye jidi jianshe shangma xiama jingyan jiaoxun de baogao," November 10, 1964, in *Zhongguo gongchandang yu sanxian*, 104–106. On government pressure to decrease the urban population after the Great Leap, see Brown, *City versus Countryside*, 77–107.

[144] Mao Zedong, "Dui Guangdong shengwei 'guanyu guofang gongye he sanxian beizhan gongzuo de qingshi baogao' de piyu," October 22, 1964, in *Zhongguo gongchandang yu sanxian*, 93.

[145] Mao, "Dui Guangdong shengwei 'guanyu guofang gongye he sanxian beizhan gongzuo de qingshi baogao' de pishi," 7.

[146] "Zhonggong zhongyang pizhuan Zhou Enlai, Luo Ruiqing guanyu yi er liang xian ge sheng shi qu jianshe ziji houfang he zhanbei gongzuo de baogao," November 3, 1964, in *Zhongguo gongchandang yu sanxian*, 96–98.

On November 26, Mao again met with Zhou Enlai, Liu Shaoqi, Li Fuchun, Deng Xiaoping, and Peng Zhen to discuss the Third Front. Mao was not pleased when Deng said that plans for railroads needed to be done soon. Mao thought that the Party "shouldn't drag its feet." If construction "can start, then it should start." Conscious of his colleagues' worries about the central Party losing control over the Third Front campaign, he stressed that the Third Front "should not have multiple leaders. Power must be monopolized by the Central Committee."[147]

Mao also elaborated on why he had designated the southwest as the Third Front's core. According to Mao, history had proven Sichuan's strategic advantages. During the Han dynasty, Sichuan's mountainous borders had given natural protection to Liu Bei's kingdom. Only one of his opponents had marched into Sichuan, but his troops had not found a way back out. More recently, the Japanese never overcame the geographic challenge of entering Sichuan during World War II, and so they never threatened Chiang Kai-shek in Chongqing. Japan's inland advance had an even harder time because of CCP guerilla attacks. In addition, Sichuan's plentiful farmland and people made it an ideal place for a rear base.[148]

Mao spoke up again when Li Fuchun indicated that it would take until 1975 to reach the steel production levels that Mao wanted for Third Front regions. Mao complained, "can't it be done quicker? Imperialism has not fought a war for twenty years. Will imperialism not fight a war?"[149] Mao also chastised Li for making the Planning Commission focus on insignificant matters. This "had to change." The Commission had to "concentrate on big issues. If it didn't change, then it really had to be dissolved."[150] As an act of contrition, Li organized a Planning Commission meeting to study Mao's ideas on December 1. Liu Shaoqi, Deng Xiaoping, and Zhou Enlai did not follow Mao in his criticisms of Li Fuchun. Instead, they emphasized that management of the economy had to be executed under a unified leadership. Each area could not run their own independent Third Front campaigns. The Party should take ten to fifteen years to build the Third Front, and power had to be concentrated in the hands of the Central Committee, Politburo, and Secretariat.[151]

[147] Zhonggong zhongyang wenxian, *Mao Zedong nianpu*, 438.
[148] Mao Zedong, "Yao yanjiu Sitalin he Jiang Jieshi de chetui," November 26, 1964, in *Zhongguo gongchandang yu sanxian*, 119–120.
[149] Zhonggong zhongyang wenxian, *Mao Zedong nianpu*, 438. [150] Chen, *Sanxian*, 68.
[151] Chen, *Sanxian*, 69.

The Small Planning Committee Takes the Lead

Mao's discontent with Li Fuchun and other central planners did not dissipate. After reading a December 7 Planning Commission report, Mao said it was "good, but it only has bones. There is no flesh, and it is totally boring." Mao hoped that in the next few months the Party center would make a plan that had "bones, flesh, and hair."[152] Mao's animosity towards his colleagues boiled over at his seventy-first birthday party on December 26. In attendance were central Party leaders, minister of oil Yu Qiuli, Daqing's most celebrated model worker "Iron Man" Wang Jinxi, and Qian Xuesen, who headed up China's nuclear weapons program.

During dinner, Mao expressed high praise for Daqing and the Oil Ministry, which "had a good work style." Mao denounced others who "ignore the Daqing model and are not willing to learn from it."[153] Making clear whom he had in mind, Mao later suddenly turned to Li Fuchun and barked, "You people never talk with me about anything – ah – you never tell me anything. Nowadays, I don't know about anything. You people are making independent kingdoms. You are really putting on airs."[154] Mao also reminded his colleagues about the dangers of revisionism taking hold within the Party, and he bemoaned the handling of the Four Clean-Ups movement.[155] Started in February 1963, Mao had hoped to have local cadres and mass groups use the Four Clean-Ups movement to criticize bourgeois capitalist and revisionist practices among local cadres. In Mao's opinion, Liu Shaoqi had foiled his intention.[156] Making known his rage, Mao growled, "Are the Four Clean-Ups going to be done or not? Contradictions between the inside and outside of the Party are merging. This is non-Marxist." He then blew smoke at Liu Shaoqi and Deng Xiaoping. Everyone was stunned into silence.[157]

In response to Mao's criticism, Party leaders met on December 26 and 27 to discuss how to alter economic planning. They decided that in addition to changing some members of the Planning Commission, they had to revolutionize planning work, modify their thinking, and be more activist. Li Fuchun also criticized his past conduct. Mao's wrath did not subside. On December 28, he again derided the central Party for having "at least two factions – a socialist faction and a capitalist faction."[158] On December 31, Li Fuchun convened a meeting of the Planning Commission in which he informed cadres at the bureau level and above about Mao's criticisms of planning work, and he issued a self-criticism.[159]

[152] Chen, *Sanxian*, 69. [153] Hou, *Building for Oil*, 99. [154] Chen, *Sanxian*, 71.
[155] Pang and Jin, *Mao Zedong zhuan*, 1372.
[156] MacFarquhar, *Origins of the Cultural Revolution*, 423. [157] Chen, *Sanxian*, 71.
[158] Xiao, *Qiusu Zhongguo*, 791. [159] Chen, *Sanxian*, 71.

Li's self-abnegation was all for naught. Mao had already started in late December to work on setting up a group to handle the management of the national economy. Mao chose as its head none other than the one-armed leader of the Daqing oilfield – Yu Qiuli. Upon appointing him, Mao told his colleagues that Yu's "one arm has a firmer hold than your two arms," and that he wanted Yu to "usher in a new work style" in economic planning.[160]

On January 3, 1965, Mao struck again, accusing Liu Shaoqi of having Four Clean-Ups work groups "study documents for forty days and never actually enter a village."[161] Later in January, Liu opposed making the rectification of capitalist roaders in the CCP part of the Four Clean-Ups Movement. Mao was so furious that he informed others that he considered Liu to be a traitor to the socialist cause just like Khrushchev.[162] In parallel to his attacks on Liu, Mao assigned Zhou Enlai to work with Yu Qiuli on forming a new economic planning staff. The leading members were Yu Qiuli, his ally in the Oil Ministry Lin Renjun, Mao's personal secretary Chen Boda, vice secretary of Zhejiang province Lin Hujia, and vice secretary of Beijing Jia Tingsan. This group became the so-called "small planning committee." Li Fuchun requested making its members vice directors of the Planning Commission. His proposal was approved, but his power was undermined.

Li remained the official director of the Planning Commission until 1975. Yu Qiuli, however, effectively took over as the commission's head in January, as Mao transferred authority over the Third Five Year Plan to the small planning committee. Mao ordered it to take building the Third Front as its primary objective and answer only to vice premier Zhou Enlai and himself. All other vice premiers were not supposed to interfere in their affairs. This included Deng Xiaoping, Luo Ruiqing, Li Fuchun, and Bo Yibo.[163] Other vice premiers were supposed to advise the small planning committee and implement its directives. Psychologically very troubled by recent events, Li Fuchun went in June 1965 to the ocean resort of Beidaihe to convalesce.[164]

On January 23, 1965, Mao met with Yu Qiuli to discuss the Third Five Year Plan. Yu told him, "The national economy after three years of adjustment ... already has a better base. Looking at every aspect of the current situation, future steps can be a bit bigger."[165] Mao agreed with Yu's assessment and then related the military logic of the Third Front to

160 Chen, *Sanxian*, 72. 161 Zhonggong zhongyang wenxian, *Mao Zedong nianpu*, 460.
162 Xiao, *Qiusu Zhongguo*, 792–793. 163 Chen, *Sanxian*, 73. 164 Chen, *Sanxian*, 71.
165 The quotes in the next two paragraphs are from "Mao Zedong tiqu Yu Qiuli 'sanwu' jihua he sanxian jianshe wenti shi de chahua," January 23–24, 1965, in *Zhongguo gongchandang yu san sanxian jianshe*, 135–136.

the CCP surviving the GMD's first three extermination campaigns against the Jiangxi base area in the 1930s. "Enemies were so many. Weapons were so little. We had so few people. We just had dozens of bullets for each gun, but we still won! Didn't we? Why can't we still win now?" Yu then turned to the issue of economic priorities, stating that "the Third Five Year Plan still must absolutely take agriculture as the base as the guiding principle. Agriculture cannot be relaxed." Mao took a very different stance.

Recalling the original principle behind the Third Five Year Plan, which emphasized food, clothing, and daily essentials, Mao stated that the fact that "people must eat and must wear clothes really can be a problem!" Mao, however, reassured Yu that the Party had learned from the Great Leap and "will not again exaggerate achievements or issue arbitrary and impracticable orders." Yu suggested that Third Front construction focus on "a few railroad lines, Panzhihua's steel complex, and … Liupanshui's coal complex." Mao disagreed. The Third Front could not just have railroads, steel, and coal; it also had to have "machine building, a chemical industry, defense factories," gas, and oil. Only then would the Third Front be well built. Yu remarked that "Third Front construction is going to be done by building up the country through thrift and hard work, and so at the start, we must build less non-productive buildings." Mao concurred and again made a reference to the Party's revolutionary history, observing that during the Chinese Civil War, "Our troops did not have nice houses to live in. And yet those who didn't have nice houses still routed those with nice houses."

While Mao expressed his support for the virtues of austere living, Liu Shaoqi became worried about the rapid increase in the capital construction budget, as the Third Front campaign went into high gear in 1965, and construction projects began to multiply in the southwest and northwest. At a Politburo meeting on May 11, Liu remarked, "Nationwide there are now 1,260-plus infrastructure projects." This was about the same as "the highest ever of 1,270 projects" during the Great Leap. "The battlefront is already extremely long. Every place and ministry must conscientiously control the inclination to lengthen the infrastructure battlefront … There are some projects that can be put off for later. We must pay attention. We must not again extend the infrastructure battlefront too far."[166]

On June 16, Mao convened another meeting with the small planning committee about the Third Five Year Plan at which he advocated plowing resources into infrastructure construction while still keeping investment

[166] Song and Sun, "Liu Shaoqi yu sanxian jianshe," 14.

levels within limits. Also in attendance were Zhou Enlai, Peng Zhen, Bo Yibo, Marshal Chen Yi, and minister of finance Li Xiannian. During his report, Yu Qiuli noted that in recent discussions "there has been one view," which maintains that the prioritizing of national defense over "eating, clothing, and daily essentials … violates the principle of taking agriculture as the base."[167] Mao retorted, "it should be violated. If it is not violated, then what can be accomplished? … Agriculture is doing better." Referring to the Great Leap, Mao said, "Now is not like then. During those three years, we issued arbitrary and impracticable orders. Now we are doing Dazhai … Agricultural investment … can still be reduced. In the past, too much money was wasted on agriculture."

Mao nonetheless cautioned against investing too much. Central planners had suggested allotting around 100 billion RMB between 1965 and 1970 for the Third Five Year Plan. Mao argued that if we "do so much in five years, we will be shaving off too much from the people …. Doing too much is not good … If we do fewer projects, then we can wage wars of annihilation," by which Mao meant big infrastructure projects. "We must not do a 100 billion RMB. We should do 80 or 90 billion RMB." In the Third Five Year Plan,

> There has to be a lot of wiggle room … You are being pressured by every area and every ministry. You also want to go faster, but don't you be pressured into speeding up too much! If we raise taxes too high and requisition too much grain from the people, they will get angry. That's not okay. Don't make things too tense.

Mao thus rejected a proposal to allocate 43 billion RMB for the Third Front. Mao wanted to allot no more than 33 billion RMB. Mao also opposed setting production targets too high. "Too much pressure cannot be placed on the people … This is a matter of principle." In all planning work, economic administrators had to consider three issues:

> First are the people. We cannot lose the people's heart. Second is waging war. Third is famine. Planning must consider these three factors. If we lose our connection with the people, then we have lost our way. If we do too much, then we will lose our links to the people.

A few days later, Mao fumed to his personal bodyguard Wang Dongxing about the Third Front's capital construction budget being too high. "How will the people get by? If we do so much building, then the food supply and transportation system will not be able to keep up." Supply bottlenecks would emerge and negatively affect the pace and quality of industrial construction. The Party "must not make the people

[167] The quotes in the next three paragraphs are from "Mao Zedong tiqu Yu Qiuli 'sanwu' jihua," 138–140.

angry. If they are angry, will it still be possible to fight a war?" Mao then made a revealing statement about how his own behavior over the last year had influenced his colleagues in the Party center. He remarked that he had "wanted them to set up the Third Front," but at first "they didn't listen and didn't do it." Then later "they did it and went all-out. Now it is too much … I've got to put them right, so they don't commit the same mistake in the future."[168]

Mao, however, had no intention of pulling back completely from the new militarized industrialization drive which the central Party had finally endorsed due to a mixture of Mao's persistence and China's worsening international security situation. As the Third Front campaign moved off the government's drawing board and became a policy that central economic planners were required to figure out how to realize, orders to mobilize labor to construct a secret military industrial complex went out across the country, thrusting the security challenges of the Cold War into the lives of millions.

[168] Mao Zedong, "Zai dazhang wenti shang yao you liangshou zhun bei," July 26, 1964, in *Zhongguo gongchandang yu sanxian*, 169.

2 Good People and Good Horses Go to the Third Front

How people experienced being mobilized for the Third Front is not always apparent. Some memoirs and archival documents give unadorned descriptions that have no specifics about individuals' thoughts or feelings. A typical instance comes from the recollections of Ma Deyou – an engineer who worked for four decades at the Second Automobile Works in Hubei province. "In late August 1966, I was transferred from the First Automobile Works to the Second Automobile Works. I was responsible for the preparatory work for the engine factory. On September 14, 1966, I left Changchun and . . . took part in surveying the location of the Second Automobile Works."[1] While we might wish that Ma offered more insights into how he reacted to being reassigned to the Third Front, there is a certain elemental truth in the stripped-down-to-basics way that Ma presents this life-changing event.

Ma, whether he wanted to or not, moved to the Third Front. The Party center had decided to carry out the Third Front campaign as part of their long-standing mission to build socialist industrial modernity in China, and so mobilization orders came cascading down from central government agencies in Beijing through provincial Party organizations into the offices of local work units and the lives of Chinese families and individuals. This chapter takes a deep dive into how the CCP mobilized Third Front labor and how different social groups responded to recruitment efforts. The chapter starts at the very top of the party-state with central Party discussions and policies regarding Third Front mobilization. Subsequent sections move progressively down the echelons of power and present the reactions of inland leaders; Shanghai officials; and finally specific factories, families, and individuals.

When Mao first brought up Third Front recruitment, his colleagues only supported assigning a small number of top officials to engage in

[1] Ma Deyou, "Xuexi Rao Bin 'keding xia da juexin, hua da liqi' de jingye jingshen," in *Shiyan wenshi di 8 ji erqi chuangye zhuanji*, ed. "Shiyan wenshi" di 8 ji bianshen weiyuanhui (Shiyan: Hubei Shiyan shi weiyuanhui wenshi he xuexi weiyuanhui, 2008), 197.

exploratory studies for a few select projects. Initial studies also did not endorse building the Third Front at once. They gave projections of labor and resource needs and expressed concern about how transferring a large number of people out of agriculture might impact rural areas. These worries stayed at the forefront of Party leaders' minds when they formally authorized establishing the Third Front and relocating enterprises to inland regions. Party elites knew that the only way that they could quickly industrialize the interior was to rely heavily on rural labor. Yet they also understood from the Great Leap that shifting rural residents away from agricultural to industrial work came with significant risks. So that too much labor was not pulled out of agricultural production, the Party center approved employing rural workers only part-time in construction brigades and militias for specific infrastructure projects. So that mobilization efforts were well co-ordinated and well built, Party leaders also mandated the use of centralized command structures to oversee Third Front operations, and they required that only "good people and good horses" (*haoren haoma*) be sent to the Third Front.[2]

This last regulation made Third Front recruitment distinctly different from the relocation of criminals to isolated labor camps and young people to remote areas during the sent-down-youth movement. Both of these endeavors were notoriously underfunded, and the latter targeted a certain age bracket, while the former was a form of punishment.[3] The Third Front, on the other hand, received special treatment from the Party center which ordered that it obtain "good horses" – that is to say, the best equipment and ample resources. Third Fronters were also subject to a background check which excluded groups, such as landlords and capitalists, whom the Party considered liable to support domestic or foreign forces hostile to Chinese socialism.

From an official perspective, being a Third Front recruit was thus a political privilege. It marked someone off as one of the "good people" which the CCP could count on to act like one of the dutiful servicemen in the song "Chairman Mao's Loyal Soldiers Listen Most Closely to the Party."[4] A recruit would go "wherever there is hardship … and make it their home. If the motherland needs them to" travel to the farthest corners of the country, they would "pack their bags and set out" for the

[2] Guowuyuan, *Sanxian*, 26–27. Chen Li, "Haoren haoma shang sanxian," *Zhongguo hangtian bao* 8 (2016): 5–6.

[3] On labor camps, see Ning Wang, *Banished to the Great Northern Wilderness: Political Exile and Re-education in Mao's China* (Ithaca: Cornell University Press, 2017). On sent-down youth, see Bernstein, *Up to the Mountains*. Bonnin, *Lost Generation*.

[4] "Mao zhuxi hao zhanshi zui ting dang de hua," *News of the Communist Party of China*, ht tp://cpc.people.com.cn/GB/64150/64154/4509287.html, accessed August 9, 2018.

battlefront. Once they arrived in the Chinese interior, they would seek to realize Premier Zhou Enlai order's to "engage in a race against time, change [China's] industrial layout, and speed up Third Front construction."[5]

Some people designated by the Party as politically reliable had reasons not to want to take part in the Third Front. Some central and provincial leaders thought that agriculture deserved more attention. Officials from big cities tried to limit the numbers of people and amounts of equipment they provided to inland areas. Some rural areas sought to retain local resources for themselves too. Urban workers were aware that their residency permit allowed them to inhabit cities with better socioeconomic conditions, and they were generally not interested in anyone in their family having their residency status changed to somewhere lower down the urban hierarchy. When the Party informed city residents that they or their children had to leave the upper urban stratum of Maoist society and settle in the mountains of the backwards interior, many people experienced depression, anger, and anxiety.[6] They did not aspire to be devoted Maoist soldiers who were indifferent to family concerns, residential location, and the material conditions of everyday life.

On the other hand, some workers in state-owned enterprises and graduates from technical schools and universities viewed the Third Front favorably because of its links to Maoist China's inequitable socioeconomic geography. The only option the Party gave urban recruits was going to the Third Front and receiving the welfare privileges granted to employees of state-owned enterprises. Otherwise, if they did not accept a transfer order, then they would lose their CCP membership and right to work in a state-owned enterprise. Rural recruits, on the other hand, were more inclined to consider inclusion in the Third Front to be advantageous since it was a socioeconomic step up out of the countryside into better-remunerated industrial work. Some rural parents, however, could not bear to part with their children and worried about their safety.

Other recruits experienced enrollment in the Third Front like some of their contemporaries involved in scientific farming, who, according to Sigrid Schmalzer, "embraced elements of state propaganda in ways that were meaningful and empowering to them."[7] Signing up to bring industry to impoverished areas was a way for some urban and country folk to express their commitment to China's socialist project. For other people,

[5] Zhou Enlai, "Wang zhongyang shuji chu huibao tigang," March 12, 1965, in *Zhongguo gongchandang yu sanxian jianshe*, 153.

[6] Jeremy Brown finds a similar trend among Tianjin sent-down youth assigned to the Third Front. See *City versus Countryside*, 179.

[7] Schmalzer, *Red Revolution*, 15.

engaging in the Third Front campaign was the next logical step in their life trajectory. Their personal narrative was already deeply interconnected with constructing socialism in China and fighting off its adversaries, and so it made sense to them that the next chapter of their life history would demand undergoing further hardships to protect China's socialist revolution from foreign enemies.

Moving towards Mobilization

Mao Zedong first suggested mobilizing China for the Third Front in May 1964. Panzhihua and Jiuquan Steel had to be built, and resources had to be moved out of the largest cities since tensions were rising with the United States and the Soviet Union, and over 60 percent of Chinese industry was concentrated in fourteen big cities mainly along the coast. On May 27, Mao complained to Liu Shaoqi, Zhou Enlai, Deng Xiaoping, and Li Fuchun, "we have ignored using the coast's existing economic base." They must now employ it to address the lack of "basic industry and a strategic rear."[8] Zhou Enlai took up Mao's proposal the following day at a meeting about the Third Five Year Plan. Zhou argued that "the Third Front is a big blank. We absolutely must construct it." At present, "the vast majority" of big cities "are in the First Front and the Second Front . . . so many of our best machine industries are in coastal cities." We should take them "and split one into two and two into four, then we can send [the pieces] to the Second Front or Third Front."[9] Other Party leaders were more hesitant and did not advocate relocating work units to inland China right away or assembling labor to construct Panzhihua.

Instead, they called for performing preparatory studies, and on June 26, the Party center founded an inter-ministry Panzhihua Investigation Team and dispatched it to the southwest to undertake surveys in conjunction with leading officials from Sichuan, Guizhou, and Yunnan.[10] On July 15, Mao criticized Party leaders for not yet relocating factories, asking rhetorically, "are we just going to give Shanghai's many factories to enemy forces? We can't do that."[11] Mao again declared that both Panzhihua and Jiuquan Steel "must be built." The Planning Commission promptly sent a team to Jiuquan to undertake two years of preparations.[12] This decision only required a small group to engage in prep work.

[8] Mao, "Yao ba Panzhihua he lianxi dao Panzhihua de jiaotong," 43.
[9] Zhou, "Yao jianli sanxian guandian," 45–46. [10] Dan, "Sui Cheng Zihua,"15–18.
[11] Chen, *Sanxian*, 142.
[12] Jiuquan gangtie gongsi jingli ban gong shi bian, *Jiuquan gangtie gongsi jianshe, fazhan shiliao* (Jiuquan: Jiugang yinshui chang, 1996), 251. Chen, *Zhongguo gongchandang yu sanxian jianshe*, 585.

Vice minister of railroads Lu Zhengcao made an early estimate of labor demands for the Third Front on August 11. He gave a ballpark figure of 200,000 to 240,000 people to erect three interprovincial railroads in the southwest. He proposed relying not on "a lot of civilian workers" since that would inevitably "increase the burden on villages ... Also training civilian workers to master the requisite technical skills would take a long time." Lu Zhengcao thought it was better to deploy 80,000 soldiers from the Railroad Corps, 60,000 workers from the Southwest Railroad Engineering Bureau, and workers from other railroad work units in China. He wanted by the end of 1964 "to have at least half arrive ... and in the first half of next year have all on site."[13] A month later, Lu walked back his recommendation to limit rural labor and suggested the Railroad Corps "recruit 100,000 new soldiers." These new recruits would principally come from the countryside.[14]

On August 16, Li Fuchun addressed the other major source of Third Front labor – big cities in the First, Second, and Third Fronts. Li asserted that the CCP should send people mainly from the First Front since it contained nine of China's most populous cities, whereas the Second Front had three, and the Third Front had two. If labor moved now, then in the event of war, China "would not be in danger because it will be prepared, and there will be no need to panic." Li admitted that moving resources to the Third Front was a "complicated issue," especially since it "not only included industrial enterprises but also scientific research institutes, design institutes, and colleges." Nonetheless, First Front work units that could split in two should prepare to do so.[15] While Li Fuchun talked about shifting resources inland, he did not issue any specific relocation orders.

Two days later the Panzhihua Investigation Team reported their findings to Zhou Enlai and Li Fuchun. In their report, they endorsed the idea of deploying the Railroad Corps to construct railroads, though they did not yet mobilize labor. Zhou and Li also suggested that the Party could use the "two labor systems" as a way to acquire workers.[16] According to this policy, set out by Liu Shaoqi during the Great Leap, rural residents were designated as "part-worker-part-peasant," and communes were permitted to allocate part of their labor time for agriculture and part for

[13] Lu Zhengcao, "Guanyu jiasu xiujian Chengkun deng xinan tielu de bao," August 11, 1964, in *Zhongguo gongchandang yu sanxian jianshe*, 79.

[14] "Fu: Lu Zhengcao guanyu xinnan tielu jianshe chubu buzhu de baogao," September 1, 1964, in *Zhongguo gongchandang yu sanxian jianshe*, 58–59.

[15] Li Fuchun, "Zai Guojia jiwei 1964 nian," 61–62.

[16] "Guojia jiwei Panzhihua diaocha gongzuo zu huibao tigang," August 18, 1964, in *Zhongguo gongchandang yu sanxian jianshe*, 63, 65–67. The quote is on page 63.

industry. In practice, this categorization of rural people was a way for administrators of industrial projects to draw workers out of the countryside and assign them temporarily to "construction brigades" (*shigong dui*) for infrastructure projects.[17]

On August 19, Li Fuchun, Bo Yibo, and Luo Ruiqing urged all ministries and provinces to co-operate on relocating from the First Front "existing old enterprises," especially those located in "industrially dense cities." All "factories that can split in two should reassign part of their enterprise to the Third Front and Second Front, and all factories that can move should have plans and established measures to relocate."[18] The following day, Mao was listening to Bo Yibo discuss plans to readjust the regional layout of Chinese industry when he reiterated the urgency of "every coastal province moving work units inland. Not only industry and transportation work units but also ... schools, academies of science, and design institutes ... Moving later is not as good as moving earlier." The CCP had to learn from Stalin's insufficient preparations for war, ready the country for an attack, and put work units in safer locations.[19]

The First Mobilization Orders

Li Fuchun and Bo Yibo issued the first mobilization orders of the Third Front campaign on August 24, 1964. Central and provincial officials had to funnel resources towards building Panzhihua along with three interprovincial railroads in the southwest, the coke town of Liupanshui in Guizhou, three military industrial complexes in Guizhou, and several power plants in the region. Li and Bo made the important decision of applying the concept of "two labor systems" to the Third Front. They backed this labor policy because "in Panzhihua ... there are very few people ... and so it was necessary to dispatch labor power from outside areas." Rural workers could be brought in for temporary positions building infrastructure; "Production and management cadres, technical cadres, and some skilled workers can be employed as permanent

[17] Liu Shaoqi, "Liang zhong laodong zhidu he liang zhong jiaoyu zhidu," May 30, 1958, in *Jianguo yilai zhongyao wenxian xuan bian 11*, ed. Zhonggong zhongyang wenxian yanjiu shi bian (Beijing: Zhongguo wenxian chubanshe, 1994), 338–342. Duan Feng, "Liu Shaoqi 'liang zhong laodong zhidu he liang zhong jiaoyu zhidu' de lilun yu shijian," in *Liu Shaoqi baizhou nian jinian: Quanguo Liu Shaoqi shengping he sixiang yantao hui lunwen ji (xia)*, ed. Zhonggong zhongyang wenxian yanjiu shi guanli bu (Beijing: Zhongyang wenxian chubanshe, 1999), 904–915.

[18] Li Fuchun, Bo Yibo, and Luo Ruiqing, "Guan yu guojia jingji jianshe ruhe fangbei diren turan laixi wenti de baogao," August 19, 1964, in *Zhongguo gongchandang yu sanxian jianshe*, 71–72.

[19] Mao Zedong, "Yixian yao banjia, erxian sanxian yao jiaqiang," August 20, 1964, in *Zhongguo gongchandang yu sanxian jianshe*, 73.

workers."[20] These two strategies of labor mobilization became the norm for the Third Front campaign. Urban workers were enlisted in technical and administrative positions as permanent workers, and rural labor was hired for short-term construction work.[21]

On August 30, Deng Xiaoping informed all ministries and provinces about Third Front construction, and he demanded that important factories, schools, and organizations in the First Front move to mountainous, dispersed, hidden places in inland regions.[22] Luo Ruiqing gave another push to mobilization efforts when he told attendees at a Defense Industry Work Conference on September 3 that relocations had to begin immediately. According to Luo, Mao had recently said at a central Party meeting that moving inland was a matter of life and death. It was like in 1927 when some intellectuals refused to go to the countryside, and then Chiang Kai-shek killed them. Mao thought, "if in 1965 there is still no movement," then their inaction "will be punished by history."[23] A few days later, Mao told Bo Yibo that saying no to a transfer order was unacceptable. When Bo informed Mao that the vice director of the Shanghai Coal Design Institute was unwilling to go to the Third Front, Mao said, "Fire him."[24] Mao also instructed Bo that anyone in the CCP who did not enroll should lose their Party membership.[25]

As the Third Front campaign got underway, the Party center founded centralized organizations to handle building the Third Front on September 11, 1964. At the very top was the Third Front Construction Support and Examination Small Group. It was placed under the direction of the Planning Commission and the Economic Commission and charged with "furnishing Third Front construction with physical ... and financial resources."[26] Vice director of the Economic Commission Gu Mu was assigned to lead the group. The Southwest Third Front Preparatory Small Group was established to oversee regional planning and construction efforts. Its leadership consisted of top officials from Sichuan, Guizhou, and Yunnan, as well as vice directors from fifteen central ministries. Sichuan's first Party secretary Li Jingquan was appointed as

[20] Li Fuchun and Bo Yibo, "Guanyu jianshe Panzhihua gangtie jidi," 76.

[21] Zhu Cishou, *Zhongguo xiandai gongye shi* (Chongqing: Chongqing chubanshe, 1990), 472.

[22] Chen, *Sanxian*, 57. [23] Chen, *Sanxian*, 142.

[24] "1964 nian quanguo jihua huiyi 'jihua huiyi qingkuang fanying' di 40 qi," September 24, 1964, in *Zhonghua renmin gongheguo jingji dangan ziliao xuanbian*, Zhongguo shehui kexueyuan, 453.

[25] Interview with Third Front scholar, Spring 2013.

[26] "Zhonggong zhongyang guanyu chengli xinan tielu jianshe zhihui bu deng jigou de jueding," September 11, 1964, in *Zhongguo gongchandang yu sanxian jianshe*, 73.

its head, and vice director of the Planning Commission Cheng Zihua was designated as its second in command.

The Southwest Third Front Preparatory Small Group then created one planning group to administer the Panzhihua industrial complex and another planning group to manage building a conventional-weapons complex around Chongqing. Vice director of the Planning Commission Cheng Zihua and vice minister of metallurgy Xu Chi were chosen to lead the Panzhihua group, and mayor of Chongqing Lu Dadong and vice minister of the Fifth Machine-Building Industry, which was in charge of conventional weapons production, were selected to direct the Chongqing complex.[27] In parallel, the Party center formed the Southwest Railroad Construction Headquarters to supervise railroad building. Li Jingquan was made its director, and vice minister of railroads Lu Zhengcao was chosen as his number two.[28]

On September 18, Bo Yibo submitted to the central Party the first report on relocating enterprises. According to Bo, if the Party did not "immediately rearrange the layout" of industry, "then as soon as war breaks out, the situation will be worse than at the start of the Soviet Union's anti-fascist war."[29] Bo pointed out that Mao had highlighted the necessity of "building up inland areas" in his 1956 speech on the Ten Great Relationships, but the Party had "wrongly understood the Chairman's directives and engaged in one-sided development of the coast." Now especially defense factories had to be relocated. If immediately moving would "impact the overall economic situation," then a factory, workshop, or piece of equipment could go later. In the meantime, another set of equipment should be made for the Third Front. Bo estimated moving around a hundred enterprises in the next year.

Bo ordered administrators to learn from China's experience with relocating industry during the Korean War and the Soviet Union's during World War II. There had to be precise plans on what would be transferred, "accounting of equipment serial numbers, pictures [of equipment], and solid training of how to disassemble" machinery. Transferred enterprises also had to send cadres to the Third Front to choose factory locations and set up factory buildings and basic infrastructure before enterprises were moved. To save on resources, every effort

[27] Panzhihua shiwei dangshi yanjiu shi bian, *Panzhihua kaifa jianshe da shiji*, 47.

[28] "Zhonggong zhongyang guanyu chengli xinan tielu jianshe zhihui bu deng jigou de jueding," September 11, 1964, in *Zhongguo gongchandang yu sanxian jianshe*, 73.

[29] The quotes in the next three paragraphs are from Bo Yibo, "Guanyu jin, mingnian gongjiao qiye banjia wenti de baoga," September 18, 1964, in *Zhonghua renmin gongheguo jingji dangan ziliao xuanbian (1958–1965), guding zichan touzi yu jianzhu ye juan*, ed. Zhongguo shehui kexue yuan zhongyang dangan bu (Beijing: Zhongguo caijing jingji chubanshe, 2011), 493–495.

should be made to "use abandoned factories and mines" and their buildings, as well as existing water, gas, and power lines.[30] "Equipment should be moved first, and family members should not be brought initially," since there would be inadequate housing and social services.

In a follow-up meeting, Bo Yibo maintained that First Front work units should be responsible for the moving and construction of enterprises, so that the whole process would be quicker. When factories were being relocated, total production would go down, and so other factories should manufacture more materials to make up the shortfall. While Bo thought it was best if the whole relocation process was "done quickly," it should not be done "chaotically." The CCP's new "moving war cry" should also "not lead to forgetting the First Front." Li Fuchun agreed with Bo's recommendations and reiterated that although relocation should be approached "like it was wartime," there "should not be a mass rush to action. There must be ... unified command" and arrangement of local supply lines under the Economic Commission's direction.[31] Vice director of the Planning Commission Gu Zhuoxin echoed Bo and Li's conclusions. He thought that relocating factories was a good idea since, even if no war occurred, the national "layout of industry would still become more reasonable."[32]

Consolidating Centralized Command

On October 10, Li Fuchun, Bo Yibo, and Luo Ruiqing again emphasized the necessity of central oversight when they authorized the first enterprise relocation orders. Practicing what they preached, they stated that after "careful study with the relevant ministries and regions," they were approving the transfer of 109 projects by the end of 1965. In 1964, they only backed moving twenty-nine defense-related projects since most projects "required preparatory work this year."[33] On December 1, the Economic Commission issued formal regulations for all enterprises transferred inland after seeking advice from Shanghai, Tianjin, and central government agencies. "All relocated projects had to be approved by the Party center." None could be ratified by the local government. Both the

[30] For an example, see Du Jiazu, "Xinhua jiqi chang jianshe de qianqian houhou," in *Zhenan xiao sanxian*, ed. Lishui shi zhengxie wenshi ziliao weiyuanhui (Beijing: Zhongguo wenshi chubanshe, 2010), 29.

[31] Li Fuchun, "Zai quanguo jihua huiyi shang de jianghua," 90.

[32] "1964 nian quanguo jihua huiyi 'jihua huiyi qingkuang fanying' di 40 qi," 453.

[33] Li Fuchun, Bo Yibo, and Luo Ruiqing, "Guanyu 1964 nian banchang wenti de qingshi bagao," October 10, 1964, in *Zhongguo gongchandang yu sanxian jianshe*, 94–95.

Planning Commission and the Economic Commission had to sign off on any relocation order.[34]

In February 1965, the State Council consolidated control over the Big Third Front. It ordered all Big Third Front work units to "adopt the Daqing experience and ... have central government agencies take the lead ... and be responsible for the unified direction ... management, and co-ordinated assistance of all provinces, cities, areas, and government offices involved." To oversee operations in the southwest, the State Council converted the Southwest Third Front Preparatory Small Group into the Southwest Third Front Commission, which it instructed to co-operate with central ministries in managing all demands for labor, equipment, and building materials. The State Council gave the Economic Commission supervisory powers over the Southwest Third Front Commission until March 1965, when the Infrastructure Commission was formed and given this authority. The State Council additionally turned the planning groups for Panzhihua Steel and the Chongqing conventional-weapons complex into construction headquarters, and centralized administration of both complexes in their hands.[35]

Other Big Third Front regions followed the same administrative pattern. Both the northwest and south-central China established groups in late 1964 to begin preliminary surveys and planning for the Third Front. In January 1966, the Party center changed the northwest's planning group into the Northwest Third Front Commission. The central Party did the same for south-central China in March 1966. Third Front projects under the jurisdiction of regional commissions, likewise, began with preparatory groups which later became construction headquarters. The next step down in the administrative hierarchy was provincial Third Front committees, followed by municipal and county committees. The latter did not have decision-making authority over Big Third Front endeavors. Their bureaucratic purpose was provisioning projects with local labor, building materials, and daily necessities and keeping their operations secret. As for the Small Third Front, in March 1965 Party leaders concentrated central command over it in the Office of National Defense Industry, which demanded that provinces, cities, prefectures, and counties create special offices to assist with administering projects.[36]

[34] "Guojia jingwei guanyu ban chang gongzuo ji ge juti wenti de guiding," December 1, 1964, in *Zhongguo gongchandang yu sanxian jianshe*, 122.

[35] "Zhonggong zhongyang, guowuyuan guanyu xinan sanxian jianshe tizhi wenti de jueding," February 26, 1965, in *Zhongguo gongchandang yu sanxian jianshe*, 146–147.

[36] Chen, *Sanxian*, 139. Guowuyuan, *Sanxian*, 26. Wang Shangyi. "Tongchuan diqu de sanxianjianshe," in *Shaanxi de sanxian jianshe*, 208–209.

To understand how the above centralized administrative structures recruited labor in practice from cities, let's look at an example from the early days of the coke town of Liupanshui. In mid-1964, the central Party formed an investigation team out of representatives of the Planning Commission and the Coal Ministry and directed them to go to Liupanshui to conduct initial surveys with provincial and local officials. After a month of preliminary research and planning, the Coal Ministry met with Guizhou's Provincial Committee and set out a basic construction plan for the Liupanshui mining area. The Coal Ministry then informed prospecting teams in Beijing, Jilin, Guangdong, Hebei, and Yunnan to rapidly relocate labor and equipment to Liupanshui.[37]

The mobilization of rural labor followed a different pattern. After the Party center approved construction of a Third Front project, it sent orders to channel rural labor into construction brigades or militias. To give one example, in March 1970, the State Council and the Central Military Commission greenlighted building the Xiangfan–Chongqing Railroad. Provincial committees in Hubei, Sichuan, and Shaanxi then commanded the regional military area and provincial military area to mobilize a prescribed amount of labor in the vicinity of the new railroad line. So, for instance, Sichuan province told Nanchong prefecture in 1970 to allocate 50,000 militia members. The local military bureau in conjunction with the People's Armed Forces Office, which was in charge of militia affairs, then set to work filling recruitment quotas.[38]

Formulating Recruitment Criteria

On December 1, 1964, the Economic Commission laid out basic rules about how organizations were supposed to handle Third Front recruitment. These rules would inform subsequent mobilization efforts. The Economic Commission mandated that "the wage levels of First Front labor sent to the Third Front should stay the same," unless the area moved into had higher wage levels, in which case pay should be raised accordingly. The commission additionally informed work units that "it

[37] Huang Keren, "Juezhan Liupanshui, huishi wumeng shan," in *Sanxian fengyun: Zhongguo sanxian jianshe wenxuan Guizhou Liupanshui zhuanji*, ed. Xu Chaolin (Beijing: Dangdai zhongguo chubanshe, 2013), 302.

[38] Liu Xianzhen, "Nanchong minbing shi huizhan xiangyu tielu gaikuang," in *Xiangyu tielu da huizhan: Nanchong minbing shi jishi*, ed. Zhongguo renmin zhengzhi xieshan huiyi nanchong shi weiyuanhui (Nanchong: Nanchong jiaoyu xueyuan yinshua chang, 2004), 1–3, 16. For a similar process in Shaanxi, see "Shaanxi sheng geming weiyuanhui guanyu chengli sheng, zhuan, shi jiben jianshe, zhihuibu jigou de tongzhi (zhaiyao), December 5, 1965, in *Shaanxi de sanxian jianshe*, ed. Zhonggong Shaanxi shengwei dangshi yanjiu shi (Xi'an: Shaanxi renmin chubanshe, 2014), 403.

was best if family members were brought along. If a husband and wife worked at different work units, then they should be transferred" to the same factory or area. If family members did not relocate, they should "still enjoy the same ... welfare benefits" in their place of work. First and Second Front enterprises should also "select outstanding management cadres, technical workers, and production personnel ... to meet the needs of the Third Front and guarantee new factories begin production as soon as possible."[39]

A January 1965 First Machine Building Industry report elaborated on recent central government regulations regarding relocated enterprises.[40] According to the Party center, there had to be

> unified arrangement of technical cadres and managerial cadres and the proportion of cadres to workers had to be balanced overall. The proportion of technical cadres and skilled workers at new enterprises had to not be lower than old enterprises ... All factories that had relocation assignments had to have leading cadres ... head up moving inland ... More leading cadres should relocate and fewer stay behind. Stronger cadres should go, and weaker ones should remain.

Any cadres previously transferred to inland enterprises "in general cannot be sent back. From now on, all job assignments for graduates of junior colleges and technical schools and transferred military officers should give first priority to satisfying the needs of inland construction."

No matter where a Third Front recruit came from, they all had to meet certain physical criteria. Workers "must not be transferred inland" who "had a severe illness, were physically too weak, or could not engage in normal work." All workers also had to "undergo a political review ... to guarantee the purity of cadre teams and labor teams and the security of enterprises." It was forbidden to recruit anyone whose family was "a landlord, rich peasant, counterrevolutionary, bad element, or rightist." Also excluded was anyone whose "immediate family had been suppressed by the Party, had reason to be dissatisfied, was politically suspect, had engaged in major corruption or theft, was a bourgeois element that held an exploitative class position ... or had committed a serious legal violation." With these regulations, the Party center linked eligibility for the Third Front to political reliability. Anyone who was not deemed politically trustworthy could not take part in the Third Front because they were presumed to be antagonistic towards China's socialist enterprise and

[39] "Guojia jingwei guanyu ban chang gongzuo ji ge juti wenti de guiding," December 1, 1964, in *Zhongguo gongchandang yu sanxian jianshe*, 122–123.

[40] All quotes in the next two paragraphs are from Di yi jixie gongye bu, "Guangyu Guanche zhixing 'Zhongyang gongjiao zhengzhibu guanyu zuohao sanxian jianshe de zhengzhi gongzuo de tongzhi' de yijian," January 11, 1965, Sichuan Provincial Archive, p. 5.

liable to disclose "secrets" about the CCP's hidden industrial war machine to its enemies.

In September 1965, the Planning Commission relaxed political qualifications for Third Front recruits according to stipulations set out by Zhou Enlai.[41] Defense enterprises still had to be handled strictly. "As for normal civilian enterprises, standards could be appropriately relaxed ... As long as an individual did not have a serious political problem and had a clear history and good behavior, they could be relocated."[42] Under these new recruitment standards, political reliability was still considered, but someone was not automatically disqualified because of their politically questionable family background. If an individual's personnel file contained a record of good political conduct, then they were eligible for Third Front recruitment.

In the same report, the Planning Commission enumerated some new nonpolitical qualifications. A relocated enterprise had to have every kind of worker required for it to function, and "relocated workers' general skill level had to be higher than the original factory's average." Physical qualifications, on the other hand, were loosened. "Except for workers who are disabled, have a long-term illness, or could not engage in normal work, it was acceptable to pair a stronger with a weaker" worker. Archival sources about the relaxation of recruitment criteria do not state exactly why changes were made. It is likely because of concerns about shortages of skilled labor and politically dependable personnel in the First Front, which I will discuss later in the chapter.

In 1965, the Party also issued important regulations regarding the usage of rural labor. On April 14, the Party center formalized the implementation of the "part-worker–part-peasant labor system" for the Third Front. According to this program, rural residents could be hired as permanent, part-time, or contract workers.[43] In practice, most rural residents were employed as either temporary or contract workers.[44] This policy gave an institutional foundation for hiring rural labor for Third Front construction brigades.

[41] "Gu Mu tongzhi zai banqian gongzuo huiyi de zongjie baogao," September 15, 1965, Sichuan Provincial Archive, p. 8.

[42] All quotes in the next paragraph are from "Quanguo banqian gongzuo huiyi jiyao," September 2, 1965, in *Zhongguo gongchandang yu sanxian jianshe*, 188.

[43] Guowuyuan, *Sanxian*, 23.

[44] "Zhonggong zhongyang pizhuan guanyu 1965 nian gongye jiaotong gongzuo de liang ge wenjian," May 14, 1965, in *Jianguo yilai zhongyao wenxian xuan bian 20*, 313, 318.

Rural militias were the other major source of Third Front labor. They were employed in particularly large numbers during the Third Front's second construction wave between 1969 and 1971. Their rise to prominence was linked to the aftermath of the Cultural Revolution, which wreaked chaos on Third Front mobilization in late 1966.[45] Seeking to re-establish order, the Party center made the PLA's Office of National Defense Industry the highest level of ministerial oversight in 1968.[46] It co-ordinated directing Third Front affairs with the Central Military Commission, the Planning Commission, the Economic Commission, the Construction Commission, and central ministries.[47] Below the central government, the regional military command was granted authority over Third Front activities. Just underneath them were provincial revolutionary committees led by PLA representatives.[48]

Accompanying the further militarization of Third Front organizations in the late 1960s was the mass mobilization of rural militias to, as the Shaanxi Provincial Revolutionary Committee phrased it, "wage shock attacks and rush construction of key projects."[49] The Shaanxi government called up hundreds of thousands of militia members for Third Front construction in 1969 and 1970. Like elsewhere in China, poor and lower-middle peasants were chosen as the leaders of local rural militias because the CCP categorized people of their class background as more loyal to its socialist mission and more antagonistic towards its domestic and foreign opponents.[50] In 1970, the Shaanxi provincial government ordered "administrative organizations headed up by poor and lower-middle peasants in prefectures, counties, and communes participating in Third Front construction ... to form militia divisions, regiments, battalions, companies, and brigades." Prefectures and counties that had "militias

[45] For a more in-depth discussion of the Cultural Revolution's impact on the Third Front, see Chapters 3 and 5 below.

[46] Third Front scholar, Beijing, June 2018.

[47] Guowuyuan, *Sanxian*, 24–25.

[48] Chen, *Sanxian*, 201–202.

[49] Shaanxi sheng geming weiyuanhui, "Guanyu jiaqiang di, xian yi yuan hua lingdao, da da renmin zhanzheng jiakuai sanxian jianshe de tong zhi (caogao) zhaiyao," June 6, 1970, in *Shaanxi de Sanxian jianshe*, 438.

[50] On rules governing militia membership, see Liao Guoliang, Li Shishun, and Xu Yan, *Mao Zedong junshi sixiang fazhan shi*, 526. On the political status of poor and lower-middle peasants, see Ralph Thaxton, *Catastrophe and Contention in Rural China: Mao's Great Leap Forward Famine and the Origins of Righteous Resistance in Da Fo Village* (Cambridge: Cambridge University Press, 2008), 41–43, 327–331. Anita Chan, Richard Madsen, and Jonathan Unger, *Chen Village: The Recent History of a Peasant Community in Mao's China* (Berkeley: University of California Press, 1992), 59, 131. Edward Friedman, Paul G. Pickowicz and Mark Selden, *Revolution, Resistance, and Reform in Village China* (New Haven and London: Yale University Press, 2005), 49.

participating in large battles for key projects" had also to "send responsible cadres ... to organize an on-site headquarters and establish central leadership of the construction site and construction troops."[51]

Explaining Mobilization

Once central and provincial authorities decided on a source of labor, they transmitted documents to local officials informing them that they had to contribute labor to, as the Infrastructure Commission said, "establish a powerful strategic rear and transform the unreasonable industrial imbalance between coastal and inland areas."[52] Ministries, provinces, and cities assigned teams to urban industrial enterprises to inform them about the recruitment process.[53] Prefectural Party committees also organized meetings with county committees and the People's Armed Forces to marshal rural recruits.[54] When a work unit received mobilization orders, it was told to first perform political thought-work "inside the Party and then outside the Party, first with cadres and then workers, and then level by level mobilize workers."[55] At every level of mobilization, recruiters should "take Mao's strategic thought as the guiding principle, teach employees to consider the big picture, resolutely obey the needs of the country, take pride in supporting Third Front construction ... and help solve employees' concrete problems."[56]

When mobilization efforts reached down all the way to specific individuals, mobilization occurred in two main ways. Sometimes an individual would receive a "notification" (*tongxin shu*) that they had been assigned to the Third Front. This was most common with work units that only dispatched a portion of their labor force, military conscripts, or graduates

[51] Shaanxi sheng geming weiyuanhui, "Guanyu jiaqiang di, xian yi yuan hua lingdao, da da renmin zhanzheng jiakuai sanxian jianshe de tong zhi (caogao) zhaiyao," June 6, 1970, in *Shaanxi de Sanxian jianshe*, 438.

[52] Guojia jiben jianshe weiyuanhui, "Guanyu banqian gongzuo de ji xiang guiding (caogao)," July 23, 1965, Sichuan Provincial Archive, p. 1. For example, see Bian Xinghai, "Wo qinli de Xinhua jiqi chang jianshe," in *Zhenan xiao sanxian*, 23–24.

[53] Gu Mu, *Gu Mu Huiyi lu* (Beijing: Zhongyang wenxian chubanshe, 2008), 210–213, 217–219. Gao Yangwen, *Fengyu lichen shi ba xujiu (shang)* (Beijing: Yejin gongye chubanshe, 1998), 368. Qian Min, "Wo qinshen jingli de xinan sanxian jianshe," in *Xin Zhongguo wangshi: Bulu xiezhen*, ed. Quanguo zhengxie wenshi he kexue weiyuanhui (Beijing: Zhongguo wenshi chubanshe, 2011), 33–34.

[54] Jiangjin de gewei zhiyuan xiangyu tielu jianshe bangongshi, "Guanyu di yo pi minbing shang cang de zhiyuan gongzuo zongjie," January 2, 1970, Chongqing Municipal Archive, 1216–28-1, p. 61.

[55] Di yi jixie bu, "Di yi jixue bu guanyu ji ge jixie gongchang banqian qingkuang de baogao," May 15, 1965, Sichuan Provincial Archive, pp. 1–2.

[56] Guojia jiben jianshe weiyuanhui, "Guanyu banqian gongzuo de ji xiang guiding (caogao)," July 23, 1965, Sichuan Provincial Archive, p. 4.

of technical schools or universities who were given a job assignment by a central ministry or provincial bureau.[57] The other principal method of mobilizing labor was that an urban work unit or rural commune would organize an "oath-swearing ceremony" (*fashi hui*) or a "mobilization meeting" (*dongyuan hui*) (such as in Figure 2.1) to explain to local labor what the Third Front was and urge people to register.[58]

At such events, the central government instructed local officials to exhort labor to "enthusiastically throw themselves into the battle of inland construction and think of participating in inland construction as an honor and inland areas as their home." Recruiters, however, should not only play up the benefits of Third Front participation. They should "speak clearly about difficulties, not boast, and not make empty promises."[59] Life would be hard at the Third Front, and the Party center did not seek to hide this fact, perhaps because Party leaders were worried that recruits might behave like urban youth sent to develop inland regions in the late 1950s and early 1960s, of whom 400,000 out of 700,000 fled back home.[60]

Local Third Front administrators were told to call upon workers to "learn from the PLA and the Daqing oilfield and use revolutionary spirit to overcome all difficulties." Work units were also encouraged to "use the Chairman's thought to militarize workers' minds."[61] In accordance with this administrative guidance, factories often had employees read Mao's three classic speeches: "Remember Norman Bethune," "The Foolish Old Man Who Moved the Mountains," and "Serving the People."[62] The last speech stressed that every Chinese had to "work entirely in the people's interests." Struggling to serve the people might result in the ultimate sacrifice. But "to

[57] Nan Qingjie, "Panxian yinxiang," in *Sanxian fengyun: Zhongguo sanxian jianshe wenxuan Guizhou Liupanshui zhuanji*, 466. See also Zhang Xiangzhen, "Xiao xiao heng de gushi," in *Zhengcheng: Qianjin zhong de Jiangxi 9304 chang*, ed. Shi Biao (Shanghai: Shanghai Daxue chubanshe, 2016), 82.

[58] Jiangjin de gewei zhiyuan xiangyu tielu jianshe bangongshi, "Guanyu tongliang xian ji zhiyuan xiangyu tielu jianshe qingkuang jianbao," September 16, 1970, Chongqing Municipal Archive, 1218–28-7, p. 2. Shanghai zhiyuan neidei jianshe gongzuo lingdao xiaozu bangongsh, "Shanghai shi gongchang qiye banqian gongzuo de qingkuang baogao," April 27, 1966, Shanghai Provincial Archive, A38-1–348, p. 15.

[59] "Quanguo banqian gongzuo huiyi jiyao (caogao)," September 4, 1965, Shanghai Provincial Archive, B09-1–602, p. 9.

[60] "Zhongyang pizhuan nongkun bu dangzu guanyu dongyuan qingnian canjia bianjiang she gongzuo qingkuang he jinhou yijian de baogao," in *Xinjiang shengchan jianshe bingtuan shilia xuanji 12*, ed. Xinjiang shengchan jianshe bingtuan shizhi bianzuan weiyuanhui bongtuan dangwei dangshi yanjiushi (Urumqi: Xinjiang renmin chubanshe, 2003), 5, 7.

[61] "Quanguo banqian gongzuo huiyi jiyao (caogao)," p. 15.

[62] Di yi jixie bu, "Di yi jixue bu guanyu ji ge jixie gongchang banqian qungkuang de baogao," May 15, 1965, Sichuan Provincial Archive, pp. 1–2.

Figure 2.1 Mobilizing the First Automobile Works to build the Second Automobile Works in the late 1960s. Source: "'Dongfeng 50 nian lao zhaopian' zhe xie hanjian lao wupian, ni jian guo ma," *Dongfeng qiche weixin*, August 12, 2019, www.10yan.com/2019/0812/623890.shtml

die for the people is weightier than Mount Tai." If someone chose instead to work for China's enemies and "die for the exploiters and oppressors," their death would be "lighter than a feather."[63] Someone who refused a transfer order was thus by implication siding with China's Cold War opponents, and their life was of little significance.

Shanghai propaganda guidelines from 1965 give an in-depth sense of what was supposed to be communicated to urban recruits about the meaning of the Third Front campaign.[64] The guidelines state that China's "industrial battlefront had entered a new stage of development.

[63] Mao Zedong, "Serving the People," September 8, 1944, *Marxists Internet Archive*, www.marxists.org/reference/archive/mao/selected-works/volume-3/mswv3_19.htm, accessed August 22, 2018.

[64] All quotes in the next four paragraphs are from "Dongyuan zhigong zhiyuan neidi jianshe xuanchuan tigang," January 30, 1965, Shanghai Municipal Archive, A38-1–343, pp. 90–97.

The kinds of products and their quality were experiencing a new leap forward." China's advancements in producing machinery, raw materials, and nuclear weapons "illustrated that our techno-scientific level and production capacity have dramatically gone up . . . and our powers of self-reliance have risen." The period of adjustment of the last few years was over, and "industrial and agricultural production are surging ahead." Now the country had to focus on transforming the interior's "backward conditions" and make China into a "great and strong socialist country."

China's current industrial layout was "unreasonable" because before the CCP liberated China, imperialism "concentrated industry in a few coastal cities." The Party had ordered the Third Front campaign "in order to construct an independent and complete industrial base for our country." Since Shanghai was "one of the most important industrial and technoscientific bases in the whole country," it had a responsibility to "fully support inland construction with equipment, technology, and labor power." Recruiters assured people that "we know that to construct a factory . . . it will take a few years." But in the long run developing inland areas would save money since the interior had more raw materials than the coast.

Industrializing inland regions was also necessary because American imperialism was "incessantly plotting to overthrow our socialist system and . . . stage a capitalist restoration." The United States sought either to "eat away at irresolute elements in our country or . . . expand military readiness and wage armed attacks." American imperialism had attempted in the Korean War to "stamp out our new country." China had won that fight, but America still occupied Chinese "territory in Taiwan" and launched commando raids with Chiang Kai-shek in the southeast. Washington had also surrounded China with "several military bases." This all showed that, as Mao had stated, "As long as imperialism exists, there is the possibility of war." It was thus absolutely necessary to "consider military readiness," move industry away from the front lines, and strengthen the Third Front.

Third Front recruits had to carry forward the revolutionary tradition of "being ready to realize one's aspirations anywhere in the country," protect every single corner of the country, and learn from "the revolutionary spirit of the Red Army of . . . undertaking a long and arduous journey and still fighting on." Individual concerns had to be set aside since "personal and national prospects are tightly wound together." Many people might be reluctant to leave family. But which of China's "revolutionary martyrs did not have parents . . . a wife . . . or children?" Picking up on a theme that was also prominent in Chinese political discourse in the early twentieth century, propagandists noted that now the country was like one "big family," and each individual family "a component element."[65] People ought to prioritize "ardently loving our big family's revolutionary mission" and "arduously struggle to build up our country through thrift and hard work."

County officials in Sichuan discussed similar themes when they mobilized rural militias to build the Xiangfan–Chongqing Railroad in 1970. They stressed the significance of "preparing for war and famine and serving the people." They reminded locals of Mao's command to "remain vigilant and defend the motherland" during the Korean War, and they emphasized the significance of preventing "enemy destruction at home and abroad ... and protecting national economic construction." The Third Front was "Chairman Mao's great strategic arrangement," and if "Third Front construction was not done well, then the Chairman would not sleep well." During the building of the Xiangfan–Chongqing Railroad, propagandists added another reason that was not brought up prior to the overthrow of Liu Shaoqi and Deng Xiaoping during the Cultural Revolution. After the Great Leap, "Liu Shaoqi and Deng Xiaoping had wasted three years" during the period of economic adjustment.[66] Now this lost time had to be made up for, and the Third Front had to be constructed soon, so that, as a contemporary *People's Daily* editorial said, Chinese socialism could "smash the aggressive plots of American imperialism, Soviet revisionism, and counterrevolutionaries."[67]

Views of Inland Leaders

Regional leaders digested the Party center's explanations of the Third Front campaign in a number of different ways. Vice director of the Southwest Third Front Commission Cheng Zihua was a strong backer of the campaign. As Cheng noted in his memoirs, "Preparing for war was absolutely necessary" because the United States "had launched a war of aggression against Vietnam at our country's southern door ... [and] the situation at our northern border was very tense" due to rising Soviet hostility. In Cheng's view, the Third Front also helped to rectify "the almost total lack of industry in the interior" before 1949 that had lasted into the 1960s.[68]

65 Susan L. Glosser, *Chinese Visions of Family and State, 1915–1953* (Berkeley: University of California Press, 2003), 164–165, 174, 197–200.

66 Jiangjin de gewei zhiyuan xiangyu tielu jianshe bangongshi, "Guanyu tongliang xian ji zhiyuan xiangyu tielu jianshe qingkuang jianbao," September 16, 1970, Chongqing Municipal Archive, 1218–28-7, p. 3.

67 "Junmin tuanjie ru yi ren, shi kantian xia shei neng di," *Renmin ribao*, September 16, 1970, p. 3.

68 Cheng Zihua, *Cheng Zihua huiyi lu* (Beijing: Jiefangjun chubanshe, 1987), 407–408.

Cheng treated his management of the Third Front campaign as another phase in his decades-long dedication to building Chinese socialism. Cheng had joined the Party at the age of twenty-one in 1927, gone to the Jiangxi Soviet, walked the Long March, and fought against Japan and the GMD. After 1949, he served as the Party secretary of Shanxi, minister of commerce, and vice director of the Planning Commission before being transferred to Third Front work.[69] Cheng's revolutionary career is evident in documents relating to the Third Front, where he and other top leaders refer to each other by their first names, demonstrating their familiarity as lifelong comrades in arms working to construct a socialist China, a bond shown in Figure 2.2 where Cheng Zihua shares a laugh with Deng Xiaoping and Li Jingquan when they came to visit the Third Front town of Panzhihua.[70]

In a September 1964 speech to Party leaders in the Panzhihua Investigation Team, Cheng related the Third Front directly to their collective experience of China's socialist revolution. He asked them "to remember when during the War of Resistance against Japan we pulled out of Yan'an … and we endured lots of difficulties." Nonetheless, they had been able to "completely move out in a single night. During the War to Resist American Aggression and Aid Korea, Shenyang's factories … were also relocated very quickly." Cheng's career as a Party administrator was also on display in his speech. Cheng treated the Third Front as a technical issue. He laid out leadership structures and presented who would hold what position, and he described government administrators and technical experts figuring out how to remake the economic geography of the southwest as a "task" (*renwu*).[71]

A similar bureaucratic approach to Third Front mobilization pervades Cheng's other reports about Third Front construction. This is perhaps seen most clearly in his conduct during the Cultural Revolution. In early 1967, Cheng spent part of his day being struggled against by Red Guards, after which he would go back to work.[72] During this period, Cheng wrote to Mao and Yu Qiuli and updated them on the state of Panzhihua's construction.

[69] Cheng, *Cheng Zihua huiyi*, 7, 46–109, 152–247, 320–407.

[70] "Cheng Zihua xie gei Fuchun bing dangzu de xin," August 5, 1964, in *Panzhihua kaifa*, 130–131. "Xiang Deng Xiaoping zong shuji huibao xinan gangtie gongye fazhan wenti de huiyu jiyao," December 7, 1965, in *Panzhihua kaifa*, 11–12. For a similar attitude from a Third Front administrator in Tianshui in Gansu, see Xu Lanru, *Da Sanxian: Bingong daodan* (Changsha: Hunan jiaoyu chubanshe, 2016), 189–199.

[71] The other three tasks are constructing mines and industry in the Panzhihua region, choosing locations for other steel plants, and building an industrial complex around Chongqing. "Cheng Zihua tongzhi zai Panzhihua diaocha gongzuozu tihui renyuan dahui shang de jianghua jiyao," September 7, 1964, in *Panzhihua kaifa*, 131–132.

[72] "Cheng Zihua tongzhi tan zhongyang guanyu jianshe Panzhihua de youguan qingkaung," December 2, 1985, in *Panzhihua kaifa*, 127. For other examples of this tendency, see Chen Zhiqiang and Ming Decai, eds., *Pujiang fengcai* (Beijing: Tuanjie

Figure 2.2 Cheng Zihua, Li Jingquan, and Deng Xiaoping in Panzhihua in 1965. Source: "'Zhe li de tian du hou!' Jintian, women chongwen Deng Xiaoping dui Panzhihua de shenqing guanhuai," *Panzhihua wang*, August 22, 2018, www.pzhol.com/pzh/2018/150498.html

He discussed the size of the workforce, how much had been invested, how much was built, and projected completion dates for different parts of the industrial complex.[73] An analogous high-modernist view of Third Front mobilization as an issue of economic planning permeates documents by other members of the bureaucracy which refer to the relocation of hundreds of thousands of people or the building of whole new cities as a "task" or "problem" (*wenti*) that administrators had to supervise according to standardized procedures formulated by central government agencies.[74]

Cheng Zihua recalls in his memoirs that Party elites all thought that one standard was central to the Third Front campaign. Economic planners could "not engage in industry and squeeze agriculture" like the Party had done in the past.[75] Sichuan's first Party secretary Li Jingquan held the same view. Like

chubanshe, 2016), 15–16. Zhang Mao, *Raobin zhuanji* (Beijing: Huawen chubanshe, 2003), 215–226.

[73] "Cheng Zihua guanyu Panzhihua gangtie jidi jianshe jinzhan qingkuang xiang zhuxi, zhongyang, bing Qiuli, Gu Mu tongzhi de huibao dian," January 18, 1967, in *Panzhihua kaifa*, 139–140.

[74] For instance, "Guanyu Panzhihua gongye jidi jianshe jinzhan qingkuang de baogao," January 11, 1965, in *Panzhihua kaifa*, 899–900.

[75] Cheng, *Cheng Zihua huiyi*, 412. On a national level, Dali Yang has chronicled Party restraint around grain procument after the Leap. *Calamity*, 71–120.

Cheng Zihua, Li Jingquan enjoyed close personal relationships with members of the Party center and had long followed their orders, most infamously during the Great Leap when he purged "rightist" cadres who resisted fulfilling the campaign's high production targets.[76] According to Party secretary of Sichuan Liao Zhigao, Li and other members of the Sichuan Provincial Committee also had qualms about sending grain out of Sichuan during the Leap. In early 1960, they conveyed their concern to the Party center during a telephone meeting, and vice premier Li Xiannian replied that grain had to be shipped out. If cities had problems, there would be adverse international consequences, and the Soviets would laugh at China. The State Council reiterated over the phone in late 1960 that it was better if problems occurred in Sichuan than in Beijing, Tianjin, or Shanghai.[77] In early 1961, Li Xiannian again called Li Jingquan and commanded him to send grain to the coast. According to the former director of the Construction Commission, He Haoju, Li reluctantly complied.[78]

The Sichuan Provincial Committee warned against the Third Front impacting local agriculture from early on in the campaign. In September 1964, the provincial committee ordered local officials to "think thoroughly about the needs of agricultural and industrial development and reasonably arrange labor" while still "actively supporting Third Front construction."[79] Vice director of the Southwest Third Front Commission Yan Xiufeng gave more detailed instructions at a regional planning meeting in late 1965. Yan asserted, "During the construction phase of a factory ... we should absorb as much local peasant labor power as possible and use a few skilled workers to train [them] ... This way we can greatly decrease the number of skilled construction workers." This method would also reduce enterprises' "welfare burden ... [and] total costs ... increase national accumulation ... cultivate peasant talents ... and raise the income of commune production brigades and peasants."

Yan, however, stated that the Party should not take too much labor away from agriculture. "In the past, when we engaged in construction, we not only did not pay enough attention to ... agriculture, we also ...

76 MacFarquhar, *Origins of the Cultural Revolution*, 200.

77 Liao Zhigao, "Guanyu sichuan diaoliang de huigu yu fansi," in *Dangdai Sichuan yaoshi shilu 1*, ed. Dangdai koushu shi congshu bienweihui (Chengdu: Sichuan renmin chubanshe, 2010), 59.

78 He Haoju, "Wo suo zhidao de sichuan diaoliang," in *Dangdai Sichuan yaoshi shilu 1*, 51.

79 Zhonggong Sichuan shengwei, "Zhonggong Sichuan shengwei pizhuan sheng laodongju fen dangzu 'guanyu sanxian jianshe dangqian jixu laodongli anpai de qingshi baogao'," September 22, 1964, in *Sanxian jianshe zai Sichuan: Mianyang juan*, ed. Zhonggong Mianyang shiwei dangshi yanjiushi (Chengdu: Sichuan sanxian jianshe ziliao congshu bianweihui, 2016), 35.

deprived peasants and damaged agriculture."[80] Yan was the Party secretary of Sichuan during the Great Leap, when, according to historian Cao Shuji, 9.4 million Sichuanese died of famine.[81] Although Yan here talks in code about famine, his meaning was surely transparent to his audience. They should mobilize rural labor to prepare China for war but should not forget about agricultural production as a result.[82]

The failure of the Great Leap also hung over government affairs in northwest China. Representatives from the region talked about the importance of paying due attention to agricultural production during a meeting with the Planning Commission in 1964. On the other hand, they made no mention of the negative impact that moving factories would have on the First Front. Instead, they named medium and small cities in the northwest that would be good locations for Third Front projects.[83] In 1970, the Shaanxi Provincial Revolutionary Committee pressed local cadres to extend appropriate attention to agriculture too, pointing out the necessity of "reasonably arranging agricultural production and farmland infrastructure construction" while carrying out Third Front construction. "In the farming off-season, more labor should be dispatched. In the busy farming season, less labor should be sent." Agricultural labor "should be used sparingly ... and it is strictly forbidden to misuse the rural labor force."[84] The Shaanxi Provincial Committee did not clarify what abusing rural labor concretely meant. Local officials almost surely had their own examples in their heads. Some may have personally seen famine victims during the Great Leap.[85] Others perhaps came across orphans who had fled to Shaanxi from bordering provinces, such as Sichuan, which were harder hit by food shortages.[86]

Party secretary of the South-Central China Commission Li Yiqing also highlighted the importance of not neglecting agriculture in a meeting with the Planning Commission in October 1964, inquiring rhetorically, now

[80] "Yan Xiufeng tongzhi zai xinan diwu jiben jianshe gongzuo huiyi shang de zongjie fayan (yaodian)," December 23, 1965, Sichuan Provincial Archive, pp. 9, 13.

[81] Cao Shuji, "Da Jihuang: 1959–1961 nian de zhongguo renkou," *Zhongguo renkou kexue* 1 (2005), www.yhcw.net/famine/Research/r060628a.html, accessed August 15, 2018.

[82] On the need to talk in code about the famine, see Felix Wemheuer, *Famine Politics in Maoist China and the Soviet Union* (New Haven: Yale University Press, 2014), 99–101.

[83] "1964 nian quanguo jihua huiyi 'jihua huiyi qingkuang fanying' di 99 qi," October 10, 1964, in *Zhonghua renmin gongheguo jingji dangan ziliao xuanbian*, 456–457.

[84] Shaanxi sheng geming weiyuanhui, "Guanyu jiaqiang di, xian yi yuan hua lingdao, da da renmin zhanzheng jiakuai sanxian jianshe de tong zhi (caogao) zhaiyao," June 6, 1970, in *Shaanxi de Sanxian jianshe*, 439.

[85] On famine conditions in Shaanxi during the Great Leap, see Yang Jisheng, *Tombstone: The Great Chinese Famine, 1958–1962* (London: Allen Lane, 2012), 138–140, 414.

[86] On Great Leap orphans, see Xun Zhou, *Forgotten Voices of Mao's Great Famine, 1958–1962: An Oral History* (New Haven: Yale University Press, 2013), 172.

that Third Front construction had begun, "what is agriculture going to do? Weakening it is absolutely not allowed. Because only if agriculture is well taken care of . . . will it be possible to remain committed to fighting a war." Li Yiqing stressed the need for "meticulous thought-work" and addressing "concrete problems related to relocation." There could not be one-size-fits-all solutions to every problem. It was imperative that "different situations are handled differently." Relocation plans had to be well formulated and managed by "reliable Party members." Even though Li Yiqing was from south-central China and his region would thus benefit from the relocation of First Front enterprises, he still urged the Planning Commission to not overlook the development of old cities and factories.[87]

Views of Shanghai Leaders

Shanghai officials' views of the Third Front were more ambivalent than those of inland leaders. In September 1964, the municipal committee declared that since industry and people were heavily concentrated in Shanghai,

> As soon as war breaks out, we will definitely suffer great losses . . . We must have a firm attitude . . . Whatever the Third Front needs, whatever Shanghai can move, it should move. Whatever is wanted, we should move . . . We should move half or even a bit more . . . This is implementing the Party line on how to build socialism.

Factories would have to go to the Big Third Front in "the southwest" and Shanghai's Small Third Front in "Jiangxi and Anhui." Yet even as factories left Shanghai for the Third Front, the city had to still fulfill its "original . . . industrial production assignments."[88]

Shanghai's vice mayor was more reserved about his city's participation in the Third Front in an October 1964 letter to the Planning Commission. After declaring his "full support" for the Third Front, he cautioned against "not fully using the First Front and not paying attention to the technical updating of old factories." He especially disagreed with the CCP's new policy of "not approving any new things being done in the First Front. This will not only be disadvantageous to advancing production . . . it will also be disadvantageous to . . . using new techniques to support Third Front construction," since developing the coast would "increase labor productivity . . . lower production costs . . . and raise revenue."[89]

87 "1964 nian quanguo jihua huiyi 'jihua huiyi qingkuang fanying' di 108 qi," October 11, 1964, in *Zhonghua renmin gongheguo jingji dangan ziliao xuanbian*, 456–457.

88 Shanghai shi weiyuanhui, "Guanyu Shanghai gongchang qiye banjia de baogao (caogao)," September 9, 1964, Shanghai Municipal Archive, A38-1-256, pp. 1–3.

89 "1964 nian quanguo jihua huiyi 'jihua huiyi qingkuang fanying' di 111 qi," October 9, 1964, in *Zhonghua renmin gongheguo jingji dangan ziliao xuanbian*, 456.

In January 1965, the Shanghai Construction Bureau continued to push back against directives to transfer resources to the Third Front. It asked the Construction Ministry to "grant an exemption" and allow it not to fill a request from Chongqing for 1,000 people to assist in developing Sichuan's metallurgy sector since there was "a shortage of workers to complete Shanghai's construction assignments."[90] In March 1965, Marshal Zhu De, Marshal He Long, and secretary of the Central Commission Dong Biwu made known their disagreement with Shanghai's foot dragging during a visit to Third Front projects in Sichuan. They were so shocked with how underdeveloped the province was that they telephoned first secretary of east China and Mao loyalist Ke Qingshi to ask for help. Ke promptly sent a survey team to Sichuan which came up with a plan to send 251 factories and 100,000 people.[91]

Work units lower down in the Shanghai administrative hierarchy nonetheless still tried to block the implementation of relocation orders. In May 1965, Sichuan sent Shanghai requests for equipment. The city replied with a five-page report which listed Sichuan's industrial capabilities and deflected demands for aid by stating that Shanghai was short on industrial equipment. If Sichuan needed some, they "should apply to the relevant department to allocate it."[92] Shanghai officials continued to air complaints during the Cultural Revolution. In October 1966, the Shanghai Municipal Committee pointed out to the First Machine-Building Ministry that it was setting unfulfillable transfer demands. In the previous year, the ministry had ordered the Shanghai Heavy Machinery Factory to give equipment and labor to the Second Heavy Machinery Works in Sichuan. Now it was asking for more machinery for a Shaanxi factory. If the Shanghai Heavy Machinery Factory complied with both orders, it would be unable to accomplish production targets set by the ministry.

Another Shanghai factory was told to give equipment to both the Big Third Front and the Small Third Front. The factory responded that it could not meet both demands and still achieve the ministry's production goals.[93] Six months later, four Shanghai industrial departments made

[90] Shanghai shi jianzhu gongcheng ju, "Guanyu choudiao shigong Liliang zhiyuan sanxian jianshe wenti de qingshi baogao," January 19, 1965, Sichuan Municipal Archive, B119-1-806, pp. 9–10.

[91] Chen, *Sanxian*, 146–147. On Ke Qingshi as a Mao loyalist, see MacFarquhar, *Origins of the Cultural Revolution*, 200, 262.

[92] "Guanyu xinan diqu yanqiu Shanghai gongchang banqian, zhiyuan shebei he jizhu renyuan de baogao," May 7, 1965, Sichuan Municipal Archive, pp. 2–6.

[93] Zhonggong Shanghai shiwei zhiyuan neidi jianshe lingdao xiaozu bangongshi, "Banqian gongzuo qingkuang jianbao 24: 1967 nian zhinei xiangmu anpai Zhong de ji ge maodun," November 5, 1966, Shanghai Municipal Archive, A38-1–355, pp. 218–219.

similar complaints to the municipal revolutionary committee. They had already relocated 154 factories and 21,855 employees to inland areas. Central ministries had demanded the relocation of another 230 factories and 47,760 people in the next two years. If their departments carried out this order, they would be unable to realize production quotas. It was also hard for some factories to relocate because, due to the Cultural Revolution, "Some factories have only temporary authority structures, and revolutionary committees have not yet been established."[94]

Some Shanghai work units persisted in responding slowly to requests to support Third Front construction in the 1970s. By 1974, the Planning Commission had told the Shanghai Department of Instrumentation and Telecommunications to transfer sixty-five projects to the Big Third Front. Through negotiating with relevant ministries, the department had the number decreased to fifty-six, and it had completed over forty transfer assignments. According to the department, the remaining projects had not been finished because of bureaucratic disorganization at the central level and in inland areas. As evidence, the department presented the case of an instrumentation factory that was supposed to relocate to Shaanxi. The First Machine-Building Ministry demanded that the factory move, and the Shaanxi Provincial Revolutionary Committee told the factory to come and select a location. But when factory representatives arrived in Xi'an, "The provincial revolutionary committee did not know what products the factory made," and the local affiliate of the First Machine-Building Ministry had no knowledge of the relocation order.[95]

Urban Concerns about Recruitment

Uncertainties surrounding the Third Font campaign also shaped how urban workers perceived being mobilized. When they registered, they did not how long they would be gone since recruiters usually did not specify when the Third Front campaign would end. It could be a few years, or it could be their whole life. The CCP did tell recruits where they were moving. But people from coastal and northeastern cities were frequently not very familiar with their destination since most were far away from their current place of residence. One Peking University graduate recalled how, when he was issued a transfer order for Panzhihua in 1969, he asked

94 "Quanyu dangqian jiyuan neidi jianshe gongzuo zhong de ji ge jixu jiejue de zhuyao wenti de baogao," June 16, 1967, Shanghai Municipal Archive, B103-4–24. The quote is from p. 6.

95 Shanghai shi yibiao dianxu gongye ju geming weiyuanhui, "Guanyu da sanxian weiqian xiangmu qingshi bao gao," December 29, 1974, Shanghai Municipal Archive, B103-4–549, pp. 9–11.

a local military representative where precisely that was. The military representative obliged him and took out a map out of Sichuan. Unable to find it on the map, he said it was somewhere in the south. The young man was very uneasy about going somewhere that did not even make it onto a map.[96]

The reason why the Peking University military representative could not locate Panzhihua was because it was a national secret that officially did not exist. Recruits transferred from the Guizhou Provincial Advanced College of Commerce in Guiyang encountered a similar situation. They lived in the same province as the Third Front coke town of Liupanshui, but they did not know exactly what it was since Liupanshui was officially referred to as "the Southwest Coal Mine Construction Headquarters." In July 1966, a representative from a Liupanshui work unit came to their school and informed them that they had been assigned to his clandestine work unit where, unbeknownst to them, twenty-two of their colleagues in the Guizhou Provincial Commerce Department had already been sent.[97]

People in Shanghai, who knew about the Third Front, were also not supposed to talk about it publicly. Word eventually got out since hundreds of thousands of Shanghainese were assigned to the Third Front, and factories organized activities to exhort workers to sign up, which locals noticed.[98] The Shanghai Electrical Instrument Factory posted signs all over beseeching workers to "quickly build the Third Front, so that Chairman Mao can sleep well" and entreating "all good people and all good horses to go to the Third Front." The factory cultural bureau held special showings of revolutionary films, and the factory PA system played revolutionary model operas.[99] As shown in Figure 2.3, some factories even encouraged workers to take the official notification from the Shanghai government that "warmly congratulated" a comrade for "having already been gloriously approved to participate in Third Front Construction" and turn it into a large red poster to hang inside their home. In the poster's background was a "double happiness" (*shuang xi*) – a set of characters typically used to signal the joining of two families in marriage. Here, it marked the bureaucratic linking of the individual's life to the Third Front.[100]

Many Shanghainese were not happy about this coupling of the personal and the political. According to a March 1965 report, when many people

[96] Interview with Beijing University graduate, Panzhihua, December 2012.

[97] He Zhaoming, "'Sanxian' yishi." In *Sanxian fengyun: Zhongguo sanxian jianshe wenxuan Guizhou Liupanshui zhuanji*, 421.

[98] Interview with Ni Tongzheng, June 2018.

[99] "Huang Danxian, "Sanxian ren de ru huo suiyue," in *Sanxian fengyun Zhongguo sanxian jianshe wenxuan: Zhongguo sanxian jianshe yanjiuhui*, ed. Zhang Hongchun (Chengdu: Sichuan renmin chubanshe, 2017), 186.

[100] Private communication with Ni Tongzheng, spring 2018.

Figure 2.3 A Third Front notification letter made into a poster. Source: Huo Zhichi, personal communication

"first heard about the relocation of the factory, they were shocked. They didn't eat. They couldn't sleep. Some cried. Some voiced complaints." Some were likely distressed because, according to Mao's command to Bo Yibo, anyone who did not go to the Third Front should be let go and stripped of their Party membership.[101] During factory meetings, "Some asked for big loans. Others asked for big bonuses. Some demanded to bring their rural family members with them."[102] Some people said to factory heads, "Conditions are good in Shanghai, why do we need to move inland?" Others dug their feet in and stated, "The factory can move, but I am not willing to go." Some even questioned the validity of all the talk of war: "We talk a lot about guarding against war, but it doesn't look like war is coming. Moving a lot of people is not worthwhile."[103] Many urban workers were upset about being relocated because they did not want, as the popular 1958 Chinese movie said, to "love the factory as family" (*ai chang ru jia*).[104] They loved family as family, and they felt

[101] Interview with Third Front scholar, spring 2013.

[102] "Guanyu Shanghai wu ge chang neiwang sanxian de gongzuo baogao," March 12, 1965, Shanghai Municipal Archive, A38-1-343, p. 100.

[103] Shanghai shi zhiyuan neidi jianshe gongzuo lingdao xiaozu bangongshi, "Shanghai shi gongchang qiye banian gongzuo de qingkuang baogao," April 4, 1966, Shanghai Municipal Archive, A38-1-349, p. 4.

[104] *Ai chang ru jia*, DVD, directed by Zhao Ming (Shanghai: Shanghai Film Studio, 1958).

coerced when they had to put collective interests over familial affairs. Individuals also thought of their current workplace as their factory and did not want to move and build another one.

When one group of workers in Wuxi in Jiangsu province

> heard the news about moving inland, everyone talked a lot. The most common response was they feared hardship ... and feared leaving their hometown. They only considered matters from the perspective of their individual interests. Some said, "Sichuan is 5,000 *li* from Wuxi. I've never left my hometown." Some wives couldn't stand leaving their husbands. Some kids couldn't stand leaving their parents. After they got to Sichuan ... it would be hard to see friends and family ... Others heard [from acquaintances] that "it was so hot that you can stick flatbread on the wall" [and that] "the mosquitoes were as big as dragonflies."

Others were afraid that they could not get used to eating Sichuan's spicy food.[105]

Shanghai residents were also troubled by what relocation might mean for their loved ones. Some thought that it was unfair that their families had to go to inland when factory leaders were not taking theirs.[106] "Some were afraid that their wife and kids would have a rough time. If they are going to the northwest, they worry about eating coarse grain. If they are going to the southwest, they worry about the heat and humidity ... snakes, and bugs."[107] Some people who were not relocated teased those who were. When a young man from Taiyuan in Shanxi was assigned to a secret airplane production facility in Zunyi, his neighbors mischievously asked, "Guizhou is where in Guiyang?" And they reminded him of the popular saying that in Guizhou, "There are never three sunny days in a row, and there are not three square feet of level land."[108] A seventeen-year-old factory intern from Shenyang in Liaoning had "never heard of Longxi county in Gansu," where she was given a job. So she asked her neighbor what she knew about the place. What she learned made her and her mother very distressed. Her neighbor told her that "Gansu is really poor," and that the local saying about Longxi county was that it had a few big wonders. "Humans and donkeys pull carts together. The rooves of

105 Hongyan jixi chang weiyuanhui, "Huibao jiare tuan zhibu banqian Zhong de gongzuo qingkuang," March 23, 1966, Chongqing Municipal Archive, p. 2. One *li* is approximately half a kilometer.

106 Shanghai shi laodong ju, "Guanyu neiqian zhigong suidai jiashu de qingkuang he yijian baogao," June 21, 1965, Shanghai Municipal Archive, B127-1–865, p. 16.

107 The quotes in the following three paragraphs are from Shi banqian gongzuo zu, "Banqian gongzuo qiangkuang jianbao (10): Liu shen jiashu qingkuang," February 7, 1966, Shanghai Municipal Archive, A38-1–355, pp. 40–42.

108 Sun Tailin, "Nan Wang de guang," in *Zunyi sanxian jianshe qinli ji*, ed. Zunyi shi zhengxie wenshi yu xuexi weiyuanhui (Zunyi: Zunyi shi zhengxie wenshi yu xuexi weiyuanhui, 2013), 249.

houses lean up against hillsides. Women's faces are all black and red from the cold . . . and the noodles are like leather belts."[109]

One geological worker was also not at all pleased when he learned that his survey team was going to be transferred from Anhui to Yunnan. He considered his new work assignment to be a big step down since Yunnan was "poor, barbaric, and backward."[110] Other recruits were apprehensive about moving to the Third Front since not only were most enterprises situated in mountainous areas which were poor and far from any major cities, but also rumor had it that wild animals still roamed there, and some even worried that bandits still lurked. The remoteness of Third Front enterprises provoked additional disquiet about whether recruits would be able to understand local dialects.[111]

Shanghai parents were also "afraid that their children would not be able to go to schools and will have no future, so there are even some people who go [to the Third Front] and leave their children behind."[112] Some workers wanted to see what the "real situation" was at their new work unit and then decide what to do with their family. Other families opted to have one parent stay behind with the children or entrust them to relatives.[113] Some older workers hoped that after a few years they could return to Shanghai to retire. Families with multiple wage earners were concerned about how relocation would affect their household income. Some family members of transferred workers were employed in collective enterprises and were upset to learn that there was no place to reassign them near their spouse's new work assignment. Female textile workers were especially unsatisfied that it was "not possible to find a place for them," since switching to another line of work would lead to a reduction in their wages, and they had no interest in changing to another economic sector.

Another family issue that caused recruits distress was family separation. When some children informed their parents that they had been selected to go to the Third Front, the parents became very upset and refused to let

[109] Bai Fanglai, "Wu hui de qingchun zai Longxi zhanfang," in *Qingchun de huimou: Sanxian jianshe zhe de fendou gushi*, ed. Jiang Xin (Chengdu: Dianzi keji daxue chubanshe, 2012), 62–63.

[110] Zhang Xueliang, ed., *Xinan tongtu: Chengkun tielu sheji shigong yu jianshe tongche* (Changchun: Jilin chuban jituan youxian gongsi, 2010), 32.

[111] Interview with Second Automobile Works worker, Deyang, August 2011. Interview with truck driver, Chongqing, January 2013. Interview with construction worker, Chengdu, December 2012.

[112] All quotes in this paragraph are from Shi banqian gongzuo zu, "Banqian gongzuo qingkuang jianbao (10): Liu shen jiashu qingkuang," February 7, 1966, Shanghai Municipal Archive, A38-1-355, p. 42.

[113] People from other First Front cities also left their children behind or sent them to live with family in the countryside. Cui Shuping, "Nanwang chuangye chuqi," in *Shaanxi de sanxian jianshe*, 205.

them go.[114] Children also worried about whether they could see their parents again. According to Party policy, if someone was unmarried, and their parents were alive, then they were permitted two weeks of paid family leave, not including travel time. On the other hand, if someone was married, and they brought their spouse with them to the Third Front, then they were not granted annual family leave.[115] This is why one man at the Shanghai Power Machinery Factory turned down his wife's plea to go along with him: "If you go, then I will never see my parents again for my whole life." The wife deferred to her husband, but she missed him so much that she suffered "from some mental disorders."[116]

In January 1966, the Shanghai Municipal Committee responded to worker resistance to relocation by allocating on average fourteen RMB per family to celebrate Spring Festival. All workers moving in the next half-year were awarded an additional seven RMB bonus. Many of them "were very touched" by the concern the Party showed them. Some workers felt ashamed that they had not done their job, and they had still been given a bonus.[117] Another area of difficulty was family members who stayed behind in Shanghai. City representatives visited them to check on their status. When they discovered that sixty-one households were suffering economic difficulties, the city decided to give fifteen RMB per family to help them resolve personal issues. Some families reportedly were so happy that they declared, "I will definitely write [relocated employees] and tell them to be very productive in order to repay the Party for caring about me."[118]

In late 1966, some defense factories in Shanghai expressed a quite different concern to the city government. Over the last year, they had strictly followed recruitment criteria and parted with many of their most physically fit and politically reliable workers. Some factories thus "joked that if this situation continues, then our factory is going to become a place to care for the old and weak and a concentration camp" for people with bad political backgrounds. Maintaining production had also become difficult because so much equipment had been shipped off to the Third

[114] "Jiang dinghan, Zhou Xuemei fangtan lu," in *Women renmin chang (shang)*, ed. Jiangxi "xian sanxian" 9333 chang shilu bian (Shanghai: Shanghai renmin chubanshe, 2014), 27–28.

[115] Interview with Ni Tongzheng, Shanghai, June 2018.

[116] Shi banqian gongzuo zu, "Banqian gongzuo qingkuang jianbao (10): Liu shen jiashu qingkuang," February 7, 1966, Shanghai Municipal Archive, A38-1–355, p. 41.

[117] Shi banqian gongzuo zu, "Neiqian gongzuo qingkuang jianbao (8)," January 19, 1966, Shanghai Municipal Archive, A38-1–355, p. 20.

[118] Shi banqian gongzuo zu, "Banqian gongzuo qingkuang jianbao (10): Liu shen jiashu qingkuang," February 7, 1966, Shanghai Municipal Archive, A38-1–355, p. 40.

Front, and many cadres had gone too. To rectify the situation, they suggested that relocation plans be adjusted in the future.[119]

The leadership of another Shanghai factory did not expect any issues with mobilization because most workers were ex-servicemen who "had received a revolutionary education in the army."[120] To rally workers to the Third Front cause, factory leaders called on all employees to be like Wang Jie, a member of the PLA Engineering Corps who died saving militia members during a land mine training exercise in July 1965. The following November, the PLA's *Liberation Daily* praised him as "a loyal soldier of Chairman Mao," and the National Defense Ministry urged all troops to study his diary, in which he had formulated the "two no-fears" spirit of "not fearing hardship and ... not fearing death." Zhou Enlai lauded Wang Jie by saying, "We are building for the people. Don't fear working hard or becoming tired. Be willing to take your youth and give it to the people."[121]

At first, it appeared that all factory employees were being devoted Maoists like Wang Jie. They all registered for the Third Front and wrote "letters declaring their determination to participate in inland construction." Yet once the factory posted the list of recruits, six people demanded to stay in Shanghai. To punish them, the factory did not give them work and did not pay their wages. And yet they still did not budge. What became of this group of recalcitrant factory workers is unclear. Their factory might have dismissed them and canceled their Party membership, as central government policy allowed. Or, perhaps this group of factory labor eventually folded and became part of the Third Front's industrial retreat into China's interior.

Rural Concerns about Recruitment

Most people in the countryside were hired to assist with Third Front construction projects close to their current residence from anywhere from a few days to a few years. There were a few exceptions to this general rule. Regional planners assigned some rural residents permanently to Third Front enterprises. For instance, the Sichuanese city of Yibin transferred three communes to Yunnan to build a natural-gas plant, and the Party

119 Shi banqian gongzuo zu, "Shanghai shi banqian gongzuo qingkuang (caogao)," October 11, 1966, Shanghai Municipal Archive, A38-1–359, p. 51.

120 Shi banqian gongzuo zu, "Banqian gongzuo qingkuang jianbao (12): Meiyou tuchu zhengzhi de yi gen neiqian chang zai sixiang dongyuan gongzuo Zhong de jiaoxun," March 30, 1966, Shanghai Municipal Archive, A38-1–355, p. 64.

121 Bo You, Zhu Chaoquan, and Huang Jiandong, "Wang Jie tongzhi 'yi bu pa ku, er bu pa si' de shiji shi zhe yang xuanchuan chuqu de," *Zhongguo gongchandang xinwen wang*, http://dangshi.people.com.cn/GB/144964/145566/8821579.html, accessed August 19, 2018.

center mobilized rural youth from Henan and Shandong to aid Yunnan with road construction.[122] The PLA also conscripted some rural men and very few women into the Railroad Corps and Infrastructure Corps.[123] Third Front work units hired some local rural youth and veterans too.[124] These groups, however, did not constitute the bulk of rural recruits. Most rural labor was enrolled for a short while in militias or construction brigades to set up infrastructure near their home.

For some rural residents, the fact that Third Front projects were close by was precisely the problem. In 1970, members of the Sha'ping Commune in Jiangjin County in eastern Sichuan expressed no interest in contributing local dried vegetables to workers at a road construction site. They thought that such activities "were not worthwhile," and they "feared that they would suffer losses." The source does not state what losses locals had in mind. It was probably earning less than they thought was a fair price because later on they declared, "Our dried vegetables are supporting Third Front construction . . . It is a way of showing our loyalty to Chairman Mao, so we don't need to worry how much we are earning."[125] Another commune did not allow militias to take part in Third Front work because they would have to distribute work points to them, but the commune was not compensated by the state with extra funds.[126] Neighboring Nanchuan county also encountered local concerns about being underpaid for their services, and so local leaders held special study sessions to criticize "the theory of serving the people leads to losses" (*wei renmin fuwu chi kui lun*) and denounce it along with other "counterrevolutionary revisionist fallacies" advanced by "quisling and traitors," like the "theory of bringing up children to support parents in

122 He, *Sanxian*, 234.

123 Duan Haiyan, ed., *Kule nianhua: Tiedaobing nubing fengcailu* (Beijing: Jiefangjun wenyi chubanshe, 2012). On the Infrastructure Corps, see Liu Jixian, *Zhongguo jiefangjun jiben jianshe gongchengbing shi* (Beijing: Junshi kexue chubanshe, 2015), 3–11. For the Infrastructure Corps in the oil industry, see "Shiyou shiren" Sichuan youqi tian bianweiyui, *Shiyou shiren: Zai Sichuan youqi tian jilu* (Beijing: Shiyou gongye chuban she, 1997). "Shiyou shiren" Changqing youtian bianweiyui, *Shiyou shiren: Zai Changqing youtian jilu* (Beijing: Shiyou gongye chuban she, 1997). For the Infrastructure Corps in the coal sector, see "Junlu qing" bianji weiyuanhui, *Junhun zao: Jijian gongchengbing meitan budui lao zhanyou shidai fengcai* (Beijing: Junlu qing bianji weiyuanhui, 2006). "Junlu qing" bianji weiyuanhui, *Junlu qing: Huiyi zai jijian gongchengbing meitan budui de rizi li* (Beijing: Junlu qing bianji weiyuanhui, 2004).

124 Interview with factory worker, Chengdu, January 2012. Interview with airplane factory worker, Xi'an, 2012.

125 Jiangjin de gewei zhiyuan xiangyu tielu jianshe bangongshi, "Guanyu Jiangbei xian liang lu qu chongfen fadong qunzhong zhiyuan Xiangyu tielu jianshe de qingkuang jianbao," September 17, 1970, Chongqing Municipal Archive, 1216–28-7, p. 22.

126 Di, xian zhiyan bangongshi diaochazu, "Hechuan xian hongguan gongshe si da dui gewei hui banju xiaujian xiangyu tielu minbing jiashu xuexiban de qingkuang baogao," December 24, 1970, Chongqing Municipal Archive, 1216–28-9, pp. 6–7.

their old age" (*yanger fanglao lun*), a theory whose name suggests parental pushback against letting their children work at the Third Front.[127]

Elsewhere in the county, some "class enemies" spoke out against enrolling locals in militias. They claimed that "militias are not going to build railroads. They are being driven to the front to wage a war." Some families became extremely worried and wrote letters to their loved ones and demanded they return right away.[128] Since the CCP at the time regularly employed military language to describe economic endeavors, it might seem odd that parents thought that their children were being mustered for a bona fide war. Yet rural parents had reasons to believe that their children's marching orders were real. The media incessantly talked about American and Soviet threats to socialist China, and rural militias regularly held civil defense drills in which they practiced with rifles and grenades how they would respond to foreign attacks on local areas.[129]

Parental fears were further justified by the fact that some rural militias were not just engaging in war games. According to recent Chinese estimates, the CCP covertly siphoned 320,000 soldiers to Vietnam to fight the United States from 1965 to 1973, and so perhaps some parents had heard rumors of local children being deployed there.[130] Whatever caused parents to have these fears, the fact that some rural parents thought that the local government would falsify their children's actual destination shows that there was substantial distrust towards local officials. This lack of faith in local government organizations was perhaps a manifestation of the broader suspicion that folks in the countryside expressed towards government initiatives after the policy disaster of the Great Leap, highlighted by scholars such as Dali Yang and Ralph Thaxton.[131] Some families in Sichuan may have also been unwilling to offer up their children to defend socialist China in battle, because, as Jeremy Brown has shown, some Sichuanese were shipped off to fight in the Korean War and never returned home.[132]

[127] Nanchuan xian wu yu qu lengshui gongshe canjia xiangyu tielu minbing zhizhan yuan jiashu, "Changxin shu," October 22, 1970, Chongqing Municipal Archive, p. 59.

[128] Jiangjin de gewei, "Guanyu Jiangbei," 23.

[129] Li and Hao, *Wenhua da geming zhong de renmin Jiefangjun*, 259–266. For examples of militias prepping for war during the Cultural Revolution, see Bo Jianwei, "Minbing xunlian gushi," in *Minjiang suiyue*, ed. Lu Zhonghui (Pengzhou: Sichuan huabao she youxian gongsi, 2010), 215–218.

[130] Deng Lifeng, "Yuan yue kangmei shulue," *Dangdai zhongyou shi yanjiu* 1 (2002): 84. For a contemporary account of militia activities, see Hunan renmin chubanshe, ed., *Zheng dang zhandou xiongying: Hunan minbing wei yuanyue kangmei kulian yinggong de shiji* (Changsha: Hunan renmin chubanshe, 1965).

[131] Yang, *Calamity*, 71–120. Thaxton, *Catastrophe and Contention*, 231–267.

[132] Jeremy Brown, "From Resisting Communists to Resisting America: Civil War and Korean War in Southwest China, 1950–1951," in *Dilemmas of Victory: The Early Years*

Parents of girls recruited into railroad militias appear to have also not had confidence in the young men that their daughters worked alongside. Some state agents took it upon themselves to make sure that sexual norms were not transgressed.[133] A leading cadre of one militia troop assigned to construct part of the Zhicheng–Liuzhou Railroad took very seriously the responsibility of looking after the young women that families had entrusted to his management. Prior to even allowing a woman to join a railroad militia, they had to undergo a gynecological exam to check on their sexual status, so that there could be no accusations that they had sexual relations while away from home.[134] This cadre also strictly forbade young men from flirting with women, and he ordered the female battalion instructor charged with looking after women to perform her duty with care, so that girls' parents would have nothing to worry about. The cadre was particularly pleased when he heard that the battalion instructor every day after work sat outside the female tent and made sure that no men bothered them. When the battalion instructor saw a young man glance at their tent, she yelled at the men living nearby to mind their own business and leave the women alone. To limit interactions with men, girls were also not allowed to walk around outside after work.

Male militia members were additionally not permitted to interact with local women. When a piece of paper was found in a tent that said that "I would like to bring a wife back to my hometown," the leading cadre spoke out against this sort of behavior. He was concerned that many local women might want to marry militia men under his command because they came from a more affluent county. If local women married out of local society, then the number of local unmarried men would climb, and relations between locals and railroad workers would sour. The leading cadre admitted during a meeting with county leaders that it was impossible to prevent young people from having "youthful passions," but he still thought it was best to teach them to "think of the big picture" and "to not fall in love . . . for the sake of speeding up Third Front construction."[135]

While railroad cadres policed relations between the sexes at construction sites, some families advised their members against even signing up. One young man's brother-in-law counseled him against serving in a militia on the Xiangfan–Chongqing Railroad because it was "temporary work, and

of the People's Republic of China, eds. Jeremy Brown and Paul G. Pickowicz (Cambridge, MA: Harvard University Press, 2007), 105–129.

133 Emily Honig has dealt with the issue in a broader context. "Socialist Sex: The Cultural Revolution Revisited," *Modern China* 29:2 (2003): 151.

134 Shao Keqiu, "Yansu mian zixiang de zhihui zhang Li Ziying," in *Zhiliu qingchun: Baiwan Zhiliu tielu jianshe zhe da huizhan jishi, 1970–1975*, ed. Yan Jianzi (Changsha, Hunan chubanshe, 2013), 21.

135 Shao Keqiu, "Yansu mian zixiang de zhihui zhang Li Ziying," 18–19.

living conditions would be harsh." He advised him to "wait until later when factories are recruiting," and then he would give his brother-in-law an introduction that would help him become a factory worker. His sister also disapproved of his joining a railroad militia since it would leave his two elderly parents at home alone, and "carrying water and coal would be hard" for them.[136] Other rural residents were concerned about the hardships that working at the Third Front would pose to themselves. Rural cadres in Leshan along the Chengdu–Kunming Railroad were "afraid of mountains ... water ... and flying rocks," caused by explosions to clear the way for the railroad. Other rural residents in the town of Bijie near the Guiyang–Kunming Railroad were not interested in signing up to build it because they had to complete the "busy agricultural season," already had other sources of earning money, and would rather gain cash from "agricultural sidelines."[137]

Support at the Grassroots

Other people were excited about participating in the Third Front, but for reasons that the party-state did not intend. Rural militia members in Jingshan County in Hubei came up with the idea that "Third Front construction would be very pleasant," because it "relied on upper levels" of government which would provide plentiful "resources and funding." Some Third Front recruits thought that resources would be so plentiful that they brought a bag to collect extra goods to bring back home.[138] In eastern Sichuan, militia members were eager to partake in the construction of the Xiangfan–Chongqing Railroad because they could earn more work points than was possible from agricultural work.[139] This is perhaps why one sixteen-year-old rural girl, who gave up school to support her old parents and younger siblings, quickly enrolled in a local militia assigned to build a Third Front road in Hubei.[140]

[136] "Xiangyu tielu si duan Jiangjin minbing shi hechuan xian minbing tuan wu ying shiwu lian fu ban zhang Wang Songbo," August 26, 1970, Chongqing Municipal Archive, 1216–10-80, p. 184.

[137] Sichuan tielu jianshe zhiyuan weiyuanhui, "Xiong Yuzhong tonzhi zai xinan tielu jianshe zhiyuangongzuo huiyi shang de jianghua," September 13, 1965, Sichuan Provincial Archive, A-271, pp. 14–15.

[138] "Jingshan minbing shi, "Jiaohzhi tielu huizhan hubei sheng zhihui bu jian bao 10," October 21, 1969, Hubei Provincial Archive, SZ-139–4-32, p. 21.

[139] Jiangjin de gewei zhiyuan xiangyu tielu jianshe bangongshi, "Guanyu guanche di gewei jun fenqu 'guanyu renzhen zuohao canjia Xiangyu tielu jianshe de minbing jiashu gongzuo de tongzhi' de qingkaung baogao," Chongqing Municipal Archive, 1216–28-1, p. 6.

[140] Zhu Yihai, "Weu xiuzhu Yilian (827) sanxian jianshe gonglu xisheng de Nie Houying shiji," in *Sanxian jianshe zai Yichang*, ed. "Sanxian jianshe zai Yichang" bian weihui (Yichang: Yichang zhengxie wenshi ziliao weiyuanhui, 2016), 198.

A high-school graduate from Pingyao county in Shanxi province came to the Third Front because he wanted a better life too. In his case, ending up at the Third Front was an accident. Word spread in his area that the PLA was forming a special military group, and it was going to be stationed in Beijing. Wanting to leave the provinces for the capital, the young man quickly registered. Only later did he learn that the Party had used "Beijing" as a front to hide the secret character of the military unit. The real destination was an underground nuclear power plant in the mountains of eastern Sichuan which had yet to be built.[141]

According to Jeremy Brown, material motivations were also behind the excitement of a group of sent-down youth from Tianjin who were assigned to a Small Third Front steel plant in rural Hebei, which they had wrongly been told was south of Tianjin, "where all seasons are like spring."[142] A group of soldiers in Sichuan sent to help build the steel town of Panzhihua were, likewise, led to believe that it was like "a second Shanghai" and were enraged when they discovered that it was actually made up of barren mountains.[143] A group of sent-down youth in western Hubei developed positive views of Third Front construction as well when they heard hushed talk about its associated work units. The mystery surrounding the Third Front piqued their curiosity.[144] Probably further stimulating their interest was a desire, common to sent-down youth nationwide, to gain a job in a state-owned enterprise.[145] Former sent-down youth talked about this point during interviews. They had heard about the Third Front from friends and family, and they preferred to be given a position there since it enabled them to retain their urban residency and granted them the widely coveted status of a state-owned enterprise employee.[146]

Hunanese high-school graduate Shen Xiaoyang remembers her classmates registering for less materialistic reasons to serve in a militia slated to build the Hunan–Guizhou Railroad. In early 1971, Shen received notification from the prefecture to attend a meeting. She ran six kilometers to arrive on time, only to discover that several of her former classmates had also been invited. When a prefectural official informed them that they had been called to help construct a railroad that Chairman Mao himself thought was crucial to national defense, they all made the same declaration.

141 Chen Huaiwen, "Nan wang de 8342 'tezhong bing' suiyue," in *Sanxian fengyun Zhongguo sanxian jianshe wenxuan*, 164–165.

142 Brown, *City versus Countryside*, 179.

143 Member of PLA Infrastructure Corps, Panzhihua, December 2012.

144 Peng Leyun, "Shenmi de sanxian," in *Sanxian jianshe zai Yichang*, 266.

145 Bernstein, *Up to the Mountains*, 103, 242–243, 251.

146 Group interview with diesel pump factory workers, Pengzhou, June 2016. Interview with medical worker, Panzhihua, December 2012.

"We will immediately listen to the Party's summons. Wherever the Party points, we will quickly head in that direction. We will never fail to live up to the Party and people's hopes."[147] Other rural youth remember initially not having any idea of what the Third Front was but just being happy to get away from home and the boredom of a lifetime of agricultural work.[148] Later, their excitement grew larger when a military representative came and gave each new militia member a special book filled with quotes by Chairman Mao about the importance of the Third Front. Some recruits felt especially lucky since the Party only allowed people considered politically reliable to go to the Third Front.[149]

In an interview, a couple who were retired employees of the Second Automobile Works, connected their willingness to sign up for the Third Front to their personal experience of China's socialist revolution. When I asked whether they had wanted to come to Hubei and build the Second Automobile Works, the husband replied,

> it is difficult for you young people to understand. Things were different then. We were proud to go to where the Party needed us the most . . . We began participating in the revolution in the 1930s in Shandong and went to the mountains to assist the Party in fighting the Japanese devils . . . Later, we participated in land reform . . . and in the construction of the First Automobile Works.

This couple's view of helping establish the Second Automobile Works was akin to Cheng Zihua's outlook on overseeing Third Front construction in the southwest. Both of them thought of the Third Front as part of their life-spanning devotion to the CCP's program of strengthening China.[150]

According to contemporary documents, many rural families were also supportive of building the Xiangfan–Chongqing Railroad in Sichuan. "Fathers and sons, husbands and wives, and brothers all fought to get first to the railroad line. Parents brought their sons. Wives brought their husbands, and sisters-in-law brought their nephews." Members of one commune declared that "constructing the Xiangfan–Chongqing Railroad

[147] Zhong Xiaoyang, "Xiangqian tiejian nu minbing," in *Tiejian fengbei*, ed. Shaoyang shi zhengxie wenjiao weiti wenshi xuexi wenyuanhui (Beijing: Zhongguo wenshi chubanshe, 2006), 56–57.

[148] Bernstein found similar motivations among sent-down youth. *Up to the Mountains*, 90. For similar tendencies at another Third Front factory, see Wu Xuehui, "Lue guo taozi gou shang kong de liuxing," in *Pujiang jiyi (xia)*, ed. Chen Nianyun and Wu Xuehui (Beijing: Tunajie chubanshe, 2016), 303–304.

[149] Zhou Weizu, "Zai sanxian Zhiliu de na xie rizi li," in *Zhiliu qingchun: Baiwan Zhiliu tielu jianshe zhe da huizhan jishi, 1970–1975*, 116–118.

[150] Director of engine factory at the Second Automobile Works, Shiyan, January 2013. Similar worker sentiments are expressed in Xie Shaopeng, *Xiao sanxian jungong chang de nanwang suiyue* (Jinan: Shandong wenyi chubanshe, 2015), 3–4.

is Mao's directive. We will resolutely implement it. If people are needed, we will give the best people. If materials are needed, we will give our full support."[151] The close correspondence between these statements and the Party's requirement that work units provide the Third Front with "good people and good horses" raises questions about their authenticity. Even if these statements are fabrications, it does not change what officials in inland China did in practice.

Government representatives followed the Party's dictates and mobilized local militias to build the Xiangfan–Chongqing Railroad, mustering roughly 300,000 people in Sichuan, 150,000 people in Shaanxi, and 135,000 in Hubei.[152] One reason why rural officials could probably recruit such large numbers of people was because railroad militias earned a much higher wage than the average rural resident. At the time that the Xiangfan–Chongqing Railroad was built, workers in rural areas earned roughly eleven to fifteen RMB per year in cash.[153] If someone was hired as a railroad militia member, they earned thirty-two RMB per month.[154] Although railroad militia members only pocketed six RMB, and the rest went to the collective, railroad work was still a way to boost household income. Even if individuals were not attracted by the prospect of making more money, some rural officials were surely eager to raise their collective's earnings by enrolling more locals in railroad militias. Even higher monthly wages (37.5 RMB) for militias on the Jiaozuo–Zhicheng Railroad certainly also factored into rural officials channeling a million people into its construction.[155]

Shanghai officials reported more mitigated enthusiasm for the Third Front. At one factory, workers were initially hesitant to enlist in the Third Front campaign. To bring them on board, the factory held study sessions where they taught laborers to "overcome their false sense of security, establish a war-preparedness mindset, and recognize the great significance of speeding up construction of the strategic rear [and] changing the industrial layout" of the country.[156] To reinforce their message, factory officials read

[151] Jiangjin de gewei zhiyuan xiangyu tielu jianshe bangongshi, "Guanyu tongliang xian ji zhiyuan xiangyu tielu jianshe qingkuang jianbao," September 16, 1970, Chongqing Municipal Archive, 1218-28-7, pp. 2, 4.

[152] Zhonghua renmin gongheguo tiedaobu, *Tielu xiujian shiliao, 1963–1980* (Beijing: Zhongguo tiedao chubanshe, 1991), 69.

[153] *Nongye jingji ziliao, 1949–1983* (Beijing: Nong mu yu ye bu jihua si, 1983), 516–17. I thank Jacob Eyferth for this source.

[154] Liu Xianzhen, "Nanchong minbing shi huizhan xiangyu tielu gaikuang," in *Xiangyu tielu da huizhan*, 6.

[155] Qu Deqian and Zheng Zhubin, eds., *Yidai jiang xing: Kong Qingde* (Beijing: Jiefangjun chubanshe, 2001), 478.

[156] All the quotes in this paragraph are from Shanghai shi zhiyuan neidi jianshe gongzuo lingdao xiaozu bangongshi, "Shanghai shi gongchang qiye banian gongzuo de qingkuang baogao," April 4, 1966, Shanghai Municipal Archive, A38-1-349, pp. 4–5.

Mao's three classic speeches and taught them how to handle "the connection between collective and personal interests and establish a revolutionary … holistic view." Afterwards, one worker stated, "Chairman Mao stands tall, sees far, and thinks deeply. I will definitely listen to Chairman Mao and engage in a race against time with imperialism, revisionism, and counterrevolutionaries … and construct an indestructible strategic rear." Another laborer said he felt compelled to go because "I am a great Chinese worker. It is a small matter to sacrifice some personal interest for the sake of China's revolution … and the happiness of future generations." As in rural areas, no matter what motivations lay behind Shanghai workers making these affirmations of support for the Third Front, local officials acted on Party commands coming from above. In total, over 354,900 Shanghainese went to work at the Third Front between 1964 and 1979.[157] Whether a Third Front recruit went of their own accord or because they felt that they had no choice but to submit to CCP orders, every single person selected had to find a way to make a new life out of building a military industrial complex in China's hinterlands.

Leaving for the Third Front was an experience that was stamped firmly in people's memories, as it pulled men and women out of their daily routines and set them on a new life course full of uncertainty. Mobilization orders could not wait to be filled. War was perceived to be coming, and the Chinese state had to respond now. The hurriedness of the relocation process made the experience of going to the Third Front even more intense. Recruits had at most a few months to get ready but more often had only a few weeks or just a few days.[158] Within these compressed time frames, much had to be done. Calculations had to be made about which family members would go and which would remain. Goodbyes had to be said to family and friends, and bags had to be packed.[159] If a whole factory was relocating, then workers had to itemize its contents, pack them onto trucks and trains, and ship them off to their new workplace.[160] If new machinery was needed, then factory leaders sometimes put in requests for specific factories to act as suppliers and placed orders with central ministries.[161] Other times, factories had to

[157] Shanghai shi difangzhi bangongshi, "Shusong jishu rencai jianshe da xiao sanxian," www.shtong.gov.cn/node2/node2245/node4471/node56224/node56232/node56234/userobject1ai42781.html, accessed August 13, 2018.

[158] Wu Xuehui, "Gao yi fei xiao zhuan," in *Pujiang jiyi (xia)*, 278–279. Chen Ziliang, "Shaanxi qiche jianshe yolue," in *Shaanxi de sanxian jianshe*, 147.

[159] Tang Wenbin, "Chuanye jiannan baizhan duo," in *Sanxian zai chunqiu*, ed. Guizhou sheng Anshun shi zhengxie xuanjiao wen wei ti weiyuanhui (Anshun: Guizhou sheng Anshun shi zhengxie xuanjiao wen wei ti weiyuanhui, 2012), 98–99. Liu Fangyin, *Sanxian* (Beijing: Zuojia chubanshe, 2006), 8.

[160] Ye Fuyi, "Yu xingcheng liangju de sheji zhizao guocheng," in *Minjiang suiyue*, 221–223.

[161] Hong Peikun, "Xinhua jiqi chang jianshe qianhou de diandi huiyi," *Zhenan xiao sanxian*, 34.

Figure 2.4 Sending off recruits from Shanghai in July 1968. Source: "Sanxian rensheng," *Zhongguo guojia dili* 2 (2014), www.dili360.com/cng/article/p5350c3d60bc9c49.htm

make new equipment to send inland with recruits.[162] No matter what equipment was required, leading cadres had to go ahead to inland China,

[162] Shanghai shi jingji jihua weiyuanhui, "Guanyu 1965 nian yi fen wei neiqian gongchang shengchan huifu qingkuang de baogao," March 21, 1966, Shanghai Municipal Archive, A38-1–359, p. 6.

Figure 2.5 Workers march to a Third Front project. Source: "Beizhan beihuang: Qiang zhan sanxian," *Zhongguo hangtian kegong*, October 6, 2019, https://kuaibao.qq.com/s/20191006A02U4A00?refer=spider

decide where to locate their new work unit, and arrange for local officials to provide labor and other resources to assist with setting up roads, housing, and other basic infrastructure.[163]

[163] Chen Zhiqiang and Ming Decai, *Pujiang fengcai*, 3–5. "Zhua geming cu shengchan lingdao xiao zu kuada huiyi," September 26, 1968, in *Minjiang suiyue*, 171–173.

When recruits departed for the Third Front, some went alone. They received a government notice that they had been selected to serve at the Third Front, and so they went to purchase a ticket at the train station and began their journey inland. Small groups of workers from a single factory did the same.[164] When larger groups of people were relocated, local leaders typically organized a special event to send them off. If a whole factory was going, then city officials would accompany recruits to the train or bus station and wave goodbye from the platform. As Figure 2.4 shows, in some cases, send-off ceremonies included people playing the piano and giving speeches before trains took recruits away to their new life in the mountains.

Rural areas held similar ceremonies. People gathered in the local meeting area, beat drums and clashed cymbals, and watched as militias packed into truck beds or marched off in columns. Often leading the group was a person holding a Red Flag or picture of Chairman Mao. As rural militias walked out of sight, they often chanted revolutionary songs which affirmed their enthusiasm for completing the missions that Mao and the Party gave them.[165] Memoirs of urban recruits do not recount as much excitement for going to the Third Front. A more common motif is people tearing up, as their train pulled out of the station and steamed towards an unknown future in a remote part of China.[166]

[164] Ma Yunxiang, "Min ji wang xifeng lai, juanke jinri huihuang," in *Sanxian suiyue*, ed. Ma Yunxiang (Chengdu: "Sanxian suiyue" bianwei bianji, 2017), 3–11. Wang Wenying, "Nanyi yangue de jiyi," in *Zhengcheng: Qianjin zhong de Jiangxi 9304 chang*, 60.

[165] Deng Peng. "Tiejian jiqing suiyue," in *Tiejin fengbei*, 209–211. Wang Tingshun, "Ji Nanching xian shi minbing tuan di wu ying Xiangyu tielu huizhan," in *Xiangyu tielu da huizhan*, 49.

[166] Jiang Rong, "Wo de qingchun zai Longxi jixie bosa," in *Qingchun de huimou*, 143. Wang Chongde, "Bai yi tianshi zhinei ji," in *Zunyi sanxian jianshe*, 160–161.

3 Concentrating Forces to Wage Wars of Annihilation

When the Chinese Communist Party mobilized workers for the Third Front campaign, it gave them one central objective: construct a heavy-industrial base in the interior, so that socialist China could withstand a war with the United States or the Soviet Union. This chapter examines the Maoist approach to development underlying the building of the Third Front's heavy-industrial apparatus. The Party summed up its developmental strategy with a maxim derived from Mao's military thought – "concentrate forces to wage wars of annihilation."[1] Where Mao's original idea pertained to armed forces engaged in actual battles, the CCP's latter-day adaptation was a militarized formula for achieving rapid development.

In this chapter, I explore different ways that the Communist Party militarized the building of the Third Front. One way was by stressing learning from how the Red Army overcame resource shortages during its battles against the GMD and the Japanese through a strategy of self-reliance.[2] On a national level, self-reliance translated into central planners pooling scarce skilled labor and industrial equipment from all over the country and funneling it to Third Front construction sites.[3] On a local level, self-reliance consisted of government authorities from the provincial level down marshaling labor, handicrafts, and construction materials for big battles to build industrial infrastructure.

The CCP leadership additionally militarized the Third Front by connecting the future industrial geography of China to Cold War security threats. Central Party leaders determined that the PLA could neither

[1] A classic Party statement of this economic strategy is Zhonggong zhongyang pizhuan guojia jingji dangzu, "Guanyu jizhong liliang zai jingji jianshe shang da jianmie zhande baogao," February 6, 1965, in *Jianguo yilai zhongyao wenxian xuan bian 20*, ed. Zhonggong zhongyang wenxian yanjiu shi bian (Beijing: Zhongguo wenxian chubanshe, 1998), 56–61. For the original military version, see Mao Zedong, *Mao Zedong xuanji di si juan* (Beijing: Renmin chubanshe, 1991), 212–214, 218.

[2] Schmalzer, *Red Revolution*, 36.

[3] For the use of a similar strategy for the development of China's nuclear weapons programs, see Lewis and Xue, *China Builds the Bomb*. Evan A. Feigenbaum, *China's Techno-warriors: National Security and Strategic Competition from the Nuclear to the Information Age* (Stanford: Stanford University Press, 2003). For a discussion of self-reliance at national, regional, and local levels, see Riskin, *China's Political Economy*, 204–212.

control China's skies nor stop a land invasion, and so they forbade placing Third Front projects in large cities, in border areas, or along the coast. As with Maoist developmental strategy, the Party leadership found security in the military techniques elaborated in its former revolutionary base areas and required Third Front planners to scatter and hide projects in the mountains. This policy resulted not only in the core of Chinese industrial development in the late 1960s and early 1970s being almost completely obscured from public view. Major industrial projects were also completed without any public mention. CCP leaders not only tied the location of Third Front projects to Cold War military pressures; they also linked the pace of Third Front construction to the temperature of Chinese tensions with the United States and the Soviet Union.

Judging a great-power war to be just around the corner, central planners mandated that the builders of the Third Front, in Mao's words, "engage in a race against time with American imperialism and Soviet revisionism."[4] The resultant work style was a variety of what E.P. Thompson has named task-oriented time in which clock time and the regular eight-hour workday no longer regulated how long laborers stayed on the job to finish a given task.[5] Instead, the Party encouraged people to live according to a hardy work ethic and behave like wartime soldiers.[6] They should channel all their time into accomplishing their assigned "missions" (*renwu*) as fast as possible, so that the Third Front would be completed before China had to fight off an invading enemy force. In the rush to construct the Third Front, some people died. The Party depicted their passing as timeless contributions to the building of Chinese socialism and its defense against hostiles.

The Third Front was militarized in one final way when Mao Zedong launched the Cultural Revolution in 1966.[7] Historians have long debated why Mao began the Cultural Revolution. Some have argued that Mao undertook the Cultural Revolution to enhance his own personal

[4] Mao Zedong, "Zai tingqu changyuan guihua shexiang huibao shi de zhishi," January 23, 1965, in *Panzhihua kaifa*, 7.

[5] Thompson, "Time, Work-Discipline, and Industrial Capitalism," 59–61.

[6] For a discussion of this trend at a national level, see Cheng, *Creating the "New Man,"* 93–97.

[7] The extensive literature on the Cultural Revolution has shown that many factors were behind how it started and played out. I am only examining here how it affected the Third Front. Some representative works on the Cultural Revolution are Lynn T. White III, *Policies of Chaos: The Organizational Causes of Violence in China's Cultural Revolution* (Princeton: Princeton University Press, 1989). Elizabeth J. Perry and Li Xun, *Proletarian Power: Shanghai in the Cultural Revolution* (Boulder: Westview Press, 1997). MacFarquhar and Schoenhals, *Mao's Last Revolution*. Andrew Walder, *Fractured Rebellion: The Beijing Red Guard Movement* (Cambridge, MA: Harvard University Press, 2012).

authority.[8] Others have presented Mao's actions as the result of an ideological conflict between Mao and political leaders over how the CCP should pursue the construction of socialism in China.[9] As Joel Andreas has pointed out, "There is ... no necessary contradiction between explanations that emphasize personal power and those that stress ideology," since "Mao's vision of a Communist future was inseparably linked with a conception of his personal role in leading the people."[10]

In the context of the Third Front, what was particularly consequential was Mao's call at the start of the Cultural Revolution for his loyal followers "to struggle against and overthrow those persons in authority who," like Soviet revisionists, were "taking the capitalist road" and granting bureaucratic elites and technical workers power over socialist construction in China.[11] With this political maneuver, Mao turned fighting against Cold War adversaries into a domestic affair.[12] With the inauguration of the Cultural Revolution, the Chinese people not only had to be ready to repel American imperialists or Soviet revisionists in battle. They also had to combat internal enemies who were conspiring to bring China over to the capitalist side in the Cold War. At the top of the party-state, Liu Shaoqi and Deng Xiaoping were castigated as "capitalist roaders" and pushed out of power.[13] Similar fates befell administrators and technical personnel all the way down to the grassroots of individual work units, causing the Chinese economy and Third Front construction to stall.[14]

As Daniel Leese, Guobin Yang, and Alessandro Russo have noted, the Cultural Revolution also led to people deploying Maoist ideas in factional struggles to achieve a variety of aims.[15] At some Third Front work units, rebel groups asserted that local leaders were capitalist roaders and

[8] Jing Huang, *Factionalism in Chinese Communist Politics* (Cambridge: Cambridge University Press, 2000), 267. Jung Chang and John Halliday, *Mao: The Unknown Story* (New York: Anchor Books, 2005), 503–527.

[9] Lowell Dittmer, *China's Continuous Revolution: The Post-Liberation Epoch, 1949–1981* (Berkeley: University of California Press, 1987), 77–107. Meisner, *Mao's China*, 312–315.

[10] Andreas, *Rise of the Red Engineers*, 89.

[11] MacFarquhar and Schoenhals, *Mao's Last Revolution*, 92.

[12] A similar point is made in Walder, "Cultural Revolution Radicalism," 41–61. Li and Xia, *Mao and the Sino-Soviet Split*, 99–103, 233–243.

[13] MacFarquhar and Schoenhals, *Mao's Last Revolution*, 467, 470.

[14] Wu Li, ed., *Zhonghua renmin gongheguo jingji shi* (Beijing: Zhongguo jingji shi, 1999), 683.

[15] Alessandro Russo, "The Probable Defeat: Preliminary Notes on the Chinese Cultural Revolution," *positions: asia critique* 6 (1998): 179–202. Guobin Yang, "Mao Quotations in Factional Battles and Their Afterlives: Episodes from Chongqing," in *Mao's Little Red Book: A Global History*, ed. Alexander C. Cook (Cambridge: Cambridge University Press, 2014), 61–75. Daniel Leese, *Mao Cult: Rhetoric and Ritual in China's Cultural Revolution* (Cambridge: Cambridge University Press, 2011), 151–173.

toppled them, making construction work impossible. At other work units, people blamed poor working and living conditions on capitalist roaders and demanded that they be improved.[16] Shanghai officials, meanwhile, averred that they could not send more recruits inland because capitalist roaders had previously implemented faulty relocation policies. The central Party, on the other hand, proclaimed that it was the fault of capitalist roaders that Third Front construction had halted and branded anyone who did not go back to work as colluding with China's enemies.

The Party center made the restoration of worker discipline into a matter of national security when it appeared in 1969 that the Soviet Union might take border skirmishes at Zhenbao Island as a pretext for launching a large-scale attack on China. Here again central Party officials referred to the danger that capitalist roaders posed to Chinese socialism as a way to reaffirm political order, saying that the best way for China to defeat capitalist roaders was for labor to concentrate on war preparations. With this turn towards military readiness, the Third Front campaign picked back up. The conspiratorial politics of the Cultural Revolution, however, did not go away. People who promoted technical expertise or slower development were still denounced as traitors to the socialist cause, while people who advocated building projects as briskly as possible were lauded as defenders of the Maoist developmental way.

Planning the Third Front

The earliest central planning of the Third Front campaign centered on the southwest.[17] In mid-June 1964, Zhou Enlai organized an investigation team in response to Mao's repeated calls to prime the national economy for war. Zhou ordered it to start preparations for the Chengdu–Kunming Railroad and industrial complexes around Panzhihua, Liupanshui, and Chongqing. The investigation team met for the first time on June 23 in Chengdu. Present at the meeting were provincial leaders in the southwest, vice directors of fourteen central ministries, and technical experts. Totaling 360 people, the team established groups to handle work relating to coal, metallurgy, railroads, defense industries, transportation, labor, agriculture, forestry, geology, electricity, overall planning, and the regional layout of industry.

Before the investigation team began conducting regional surveys, its leader, Cheng Zihua, organized study sessions of Mao and Zhou Enlai's

16 For a similar economistic trend among Shanghai workers, see Perry and Li, *Proletarian Power*, 4–5, 97–117.

17 The information in the next two paragraphs is from Dan, "Sui Cheng Zihua," 16, 19.

comments on the Third Front in order to ram home to everyone how important their endeavor was. Cheng also had everyone discuss Mao's texts "On Practice," "On Contradiction," and "Opposing Book Worship" in order to unify their thinking. The investigation team then packed into jeeps and headed up winding dirt mountain roads for over 500 kilometers until they reached Panzhihua along the banks of the Jinsha river. Along the way, the survey team made several stops to inspect potential sites for the Chengdu–Kunming Railroad and other Third Front projects.

In late July 1964, the investigation team met in Xichang and finalized their report to the Party center on how to develop the southwest. They suggested three possible locations for the Panzhihua steel plant: Xichang, Leshan, and Nongnongping – a mountainside in Panzhihua. Xichang was subsequently eliminated because it had too many earthquakes and lacked water and coal. First Party secretary of Sichuan Li Jingquan was in favor of a mountainous area near Leshan because it had more flatland, and its proximity to Chengdu would make supply lines easier to maintain. Cheng Zihua thought Nongnongping was a better location. Iron and coal mines were right next door. The Jinsha river could provide water. The Chengdu–Kunming Railroad could solve transportation needs, and the surrounding mountains could serve as a security blanket, whereas Leshan was exposed to the prying eyes of enemy aircraft.[18] On February 5, 1965, Mao met with Li Fuchun and Bo Yibo to discuss the site of the Panzhihua steel factory. Mao sided with Cheng Zihua's view that Nongnongping was the best choice since it had coal and iron on site.[19]

In July 1964, debate also broke out about the speed of railroad construction. Over the previous months, the Transportation Ministry, Railroad Ministry, and Railroad Corps had charted out plans for railroads between Chengdu and Kunming, Kunming and Guiyang, and Guiyang and Chongqing.[20] According to Hao Zhaojian, the chief engineer of a railroad design institute, his colleagues were hesitant to follow the Party center's order to quickly build railroads. They had taken part in the big wave of railroad building in the southwest during the Great Leap, and it had been a very "traumatic" (*chuang shang*) experience. Hao does

[18] Cheng Zihua, "Panzhihua gangtie jidi shangma qianhou," in *Dangdai Sichuan yaoshi shilu 2*, ed. Dangdai koushu shi congshu bienweihui (Chengdu: Sichuan renmin chubanshe, 2010), 19–21.

[19] Zhonggong Panzhihua shiwei dangshi yanjiushi, *Liu zai da liegu de jiyi* (Chengdu: Sichuan cishu chubanshe, 2003), 107–108. Zhonggong Panzhihua shiwei dangshi yanjiushi, *Panzhihua kaifa jianshe shi dashiji* (Chengdu: Chengdu keji daxue chubanshe, 1998), 58.

[20] Zhonggong Panzhihua shiwei dangshi yanjiu shi bian, *Panzhihua kaifa jianshe da shiji*, 42–43.

not say why this was the case. However, railroad workers likely suffered from famine given the large numbers of workers deployed and the remoteness of many construction sites.[21]

Railroad work units thought it was possible to soon finish the Sichuan–Guizhou Railroad since it was almost done, and they were amenable to a tight schedule for the Guiyang–Kunming Line. They pushed back against the idea that the 1,000-kilometer-long Chengdu–Kunming Railroad could be completed by 1970 since the mountainous topography required almost constant tunnels and bridges for 400 kilometers. Hao Zhaojian recalls other members of the investigation team "laying siege" to the railroad group and pressuring them to accept a faster construction timeline.[22] The railroad group stood their ground, and the ministry's final report to the Party center projected completing the Chengdu–Kunming Railroad "by 1972 and struggling to have it done by 1971."[23] On September 13, Li Fuchun overrode the railroad group's suggestion and demanded that the Chengdu–Kunming Line be finished by 1969.[24]

The investigation team was more united about what to construct elsewhere in the southwest. Over the previous two months, the Coal Ministry and Guizhou province had surveyed Liupanshui's coal mines. The Ministry of Power and Water Resources had studied where to place thermal and hydroelectric plants in the southwest, and the Defense Ministry had examined potential locations for military factories.[25] Based on their findings, the investigation team proposed building the following projects: the Panzhihua complex; a coal complex centered on Liupanshui; a weapons complex scattered over twenty counties around Chongqing; several power plants and an electrical grid for the southwest; and an aerospace complex in Zunyi, an airplane complex in Anshun, and an electronics complex in Duyun.[26] On August 24, Li Fuchun and Bo

21 For an overview of the building of the Chengdu–Kunming Railroad during the Great Leap, see Zhonghua renmin gongheguo tiedaobu, *Tielu xiujian shiliao, 1949–1962* (Beijing: Zhongguo tiedao chubanshe, 1991), 97–101.

22 Hao Zhaojian, "Ta bian qing shan," in *Sanxian jianshe tao fengbei*, ed. Nie Ronggui (Chengdu: Sichuan renmin chubanshe, 1999), 109–110.

23 Lu Zhengcao, "Guanyu jiasu xiujian chengkun deng xinan tielu de baogao," August 11, 1964, in *Zhongguo gongchandang yu sanxian jianshe*, 58.

24 Li Fuchun, "Guanyu jingji gongzuo he jihua gongzuo gei Mao Zedong de huibao xin," September 12, 1964, in *Zhongguo gongchandang yu sanxian jianshe*, 82.

25 Guizhou sheng Liupanshui shi, *Liupanshui sanxian*, 64. Panzhihua diaocha gongzuo zu, "Yi Panzhihua wei zhongxin de dianli gongye guihua," August 5, 1964, in *Panzhihua kaifa*, 455–457.

26 Zhong Ziyun, "Xichang huiyi ji Liupanshui kuangqu kaifa de huiyi," in *Sanxian fengyun: Zhongguo sanxian jianshe wenxuan Guizhou Liupanshui zhuanji*, ed. Xu Chaolin (Beijing: Dangdai zhongguo chubanshe, 2013), 24. Yu Chaolin, "Sanxian jianshe yu Guizhou gongye tixi de xingcheng," in *Sanxian fengyun: Zhongguo sanxian jianshe wenxuan Guizhou Liupanshui zhuanji*, 95. Chen Puru, "Shidai de jucece, lishi de gongxian," in *Sanxian*

Yibo backed the Panzhihua investigation team's report and signed off on the implementation of their recommendations.[27]

On September 21, Li Fuchun formulated the Third Front campaign's overarching aims at a national planning meeting.[28] Li declared that the Third Front campaign aimed to establish "a comprehensive strategic rear industrial complex . . . in the southwest and northwest as well as in western Hunan, Hubei, and Henan."[29] Li projected taking seven to eight years to construct an industrial complex in southern Sichuan dedicated to "metallurgy, chemicals, and energy that relied on raw materials from Panzhihua." He envisioned taking three years to establish another industrial complex between Chongqing and western Hubei that "can manufacture conventional weapons and essential machinery with Chongqing Steel as the main provider of raw materials." A final "comprehensive industrial complex" had to be built in the northwest in "five to six years" which "could produce conventional weapons and essential machinery" and would "rely on Jiuquan Steel for raw materials." Li Fuchun did not lay out any concrete plans for Third Front projects in Hunan or Henan. Nor did he elaborate on plans to industrialize the northwest and Hubei beyond the complexes set up around Jiuquan and Chongqing.

While Li Fuchun and Bo Yibo headed up efforts to plan the development of basic industry in the Third Front, chief of staff Luo Ruiqing took the lead on planning for the defense sector. On September 3, 1964, Luo told a gathering of military leaders to spread all new industrial projects out in secret mountain locations. Shortly after, vice director of the National Defense Industry Office Zhao Erlu took a two-and-a-half-month excursion with central ministry representatives to scope out potential locations for military factories in the mountains of inland China. After reviewing 1,499 sites, the group designated 682 as suitable for Third Front ventures. The chosen sites were in southern Gansu; northern and southern Shaanxi; Ningxia; Sichuan; Guizhou; northeast Yunnan; and the western halves of Hubei, Hunan, and Guangxi.

When Luo Ruiqing reported the group's findings to Mao in early 1965, Luo praised the group for searching out sites that were "near mountains, in ravines, and far from existing cities." Luo recommended investing 13.3 billion RMB over the next seven years to build 495 projects. The

jianshe jingshen tao fengbei shang ce, ed. Zhongguo renmin zhengzhi xieshang huiyi Guizhou sheng zhengxie wenshi zi liao weiyuanhui (Guiyang: Guizhou sheng zhengxie wenshi zi liao weiyuanhui, 1995), 2.

27 Li Fuchun and Bo Yibo, "Guanyu jianshe Panzhihua gangtie jidi," 76.

28 Chen, *Sanxian*, 125. He, *Sanxian*, 7.

29 Quotes in this paragraph are from Li Fuchun, "Zai quanguo jihua huiyi shang de jianghua," September 21, 1964, in *Zhongguo gongchandang yu sanxian*, 88–90.

plan included one new nuclear base, four missile facilities, six airplane complexes, one tank manufacturing base, four shipbuilding complexes, eight wireless-electronics bases, and multiple arms production facilities. On March 21, the Party center approved Luo's proposal and instructed central ministries to construct this new arsenal of Chinese socialism.[30]

All these projects were in the Big Third Front. Luo Ruiqing additionally oversaw planning the construction of light-arms manufacturers in every province, or what Mao called the Small Third Front. In October 1964, Luo commanded provinces and large cities to draw up plans for modest-sized military industrial complexes in their mountainous hinterlands and submit them to the Party center. Based on their recommendations, Luo suggested to Mao on February 5, 1965, that the Party invest 260 million RMB over three years in fourteen new arms bases. Luo noted that the areas selected "were for the most part … revolutionary base areas during the War of Resistance against Japan and the Chinese Civil War."[31]

It is possible that Luo mentioned this fact because Mao had said that the Small Third Front should be built where revolutionary base areas had previously been located. Or it could be that this is another case of what Roderick MacFarquhar and Michael Schoenhals have called "working toward the Chairman," where officials promoted policies that they thought would find Mao's favor.[32] Either way, the overlapping of the Small Third Front's industrial geography with the CCP's revolutionary history struck a chord with the central Party, which instructed ministries and provinces to construct the Small Third Front on March 8, 1965.

When the Economic Commission explained how the Party would build all these new projects, it too drew links to the Party's revolutionary past. According to the commission, central planners had to take an approach to socialist industrialization inspired by Chairman Mao's military strategy of concentrating the best forces, completely surrounding the enemy, and striving for total annihilation. Just like in war, central planners had to "choose the proper target to attack" and "concentrate forces to wage wars of annihilation" for only a select number of projects.[33] To ensure

[30] The quote is from Luo Ruiqing, "Guanyu guofang gongye zai er sanxian di qu xinjian xiangmu buju fangan de baogao," February 20, 1965, in *Zhongguo gongchandang yu sanxian jianshe*, 144–145. Chen, *Sanxian*, 139.

[31] Luo Ruiqing, "Xiang zhongyang tichu de 'guanyu anpai yi er xian sheng shi houfag jianshe de baogao' de yijain," February 7, 1965, in *Zhongguo gongchandang yu sanxian jianshe*, 139–140.

[32] MacFarquhar and Schoenhals, *Mao's Last Revolution*, 47.

[33] All quotes in this paragraph are from Guojia jingji weiyuanhui dangzu, "Guanyu jizhong liliang zai jingji jianshe shang da jianmie zhan de baogao," January 17, 1965, in *Jianguo yilai zhongyao wenxian xuan bian 20*, 58–60.

construction endeavors were well co-ordinated, every project also had to have a "battle headquarters." The project's top leader had to be a vice minister or provincial department director who worked with other ministerial and provincial leaders on preparing and executing a unified "battle plan." To assist with completing the battle plans of Third Front projects, the Central Secretariat formed the Infrastructure Corps on February 21, 1966. The Secretariat filled its ranks by taking 300,000 people from construction teams at industrial work units around the country and transferring authority over them to the Central Military Commission and the Infrastructure Commission. By the time the Third Front campaign wound down in the late 1970s, the Infrastructure Corps's rolls increased to 502,000 soldiers.[34]

Waging War for Base 61

One place where the Infrastructure Corps went was Base 61.[35] On September 9, 1964, the Ministry of National Defense's Fifth Research Institute informed its employees about the Third Front campaign and told them that the State Council had commanded the aerospace sector to build a new facility called Base 61 in northern Guizhou. The second branch of their institute had been chosen to serve as the leading enterprise. Like other work units given this mission, they were "responsible for completing three tasks" (*sanbao yi di*). They had to provide labor and supplies, manage construction, and ensure the fulfillment of the state's production plans.[36] Wasting no time, the next day a group of workers went to Guiyang to meet with members of the Guizhou Provincial Committee and Guiyang Military Area, as well as representatives of the Shanghai Second Electrotechnical Bureau and the Second, Third, Fourth, and Fifth Machine-Building Ministries.[37] Together this group of ministerial and provincial leaders drafted an itinerary of mountainous places to survey in northern Guizhou that could possibly serve as the site of Base 61. Thus began for the builders of Base 61 what one Third Front memoir has called the "era of insomnia" in which people engaged in nearly constant work.[38]

[34] Liu, *Zhongguo jiefangjun*, 8–9. [35] Liu, *Zhongguo jiefangjun*, 91.

[36] The information in the next three paragraphs, unless otherwise noted, comes from Zhu Shide and Wang Jianxue, "Hangtian jungong jueqi zai qianbei shenshan," in *Zunyi sanxian jianshe*, 26–31. For other examples of projects pursuing these three tasks, see Zhou Mingzhang, "Dongbei yu zhiyuan sanxian chengshi fazhan," *Kaifang shidai* 2 (2018), www.opentimes.cn/Abstract/9417.html, accessed July 15, 2018.

[37] Zunyi shi defang zhi bianzuan weiyuanhui bangongshi, ed., *Zunyi shi sanxian jianshe zhi* (Beijing: Zhongguo wenshi chubanshe, 2016), 202.

[38] Tan Chengjian, *Shimian shidai* (Beijing: Xin xing chubanshe, 2012).

Base 61's survey group drove and hiked through the mountains of thirty counties for two months "carrying luggage and dry food on their backs." Due to almost incessant fog and rain, the group often had to trudge through muddy ground. To quench their thirst, they "drank from mountain streams." To satiate their hunger, they "munched on cold *mantou*." When it got dark, they set up camp. For "many comrades it was their first time in a high plateau . . . and they could not get used to the local climate." Some became sick, and yet they still walked onwards and performed daily surveys. At the end of their trek, they chose over a hundred spots for further consideration. Base 61's construction headquarters whittled acceptable sites down to forty-two and sent four groups to perform in-depth inspections for forty days.[39]

The inspection team then submitted their findings to the Fifth Machine-Building Ministry for review. Their plan proposed hiring 33,460 people to build twenty-two separate work units in the mountains around Zunyi. The ministry agreed and authorized waging a battle to build Base 61. To conceal the base's identity, it was publicly referred to as Kaishan.[40] A local military leader suggested putting a power plant in a very deep cave as an additional safety measure. After performing a feasibility study, the idea was abandoned.[41]

Although Base 61's power plant was not placed underground, its leadership decided that all important factory workshops had to be hidden in caves. Aboveground factory buildings had also to be made to look like local buildings, so that if enemy forces flew over, they would not see a factory, much less a producer of high-tech aerospace equipment.[42] To help build this secret military industrial complex, the Party center sent construction workers and survey and design personnel from all over China. They came from Sichuan, Shanghai, Fujian, and Guiyang. Altogether, labor rolls totaled 20,000 people.[43]

In line with the Third Front policy of local self-reliance, families at first lodged in the homes of rural residents, and single men lived in tents.[44]

[39] Chen Li, "Daihao 61: Ji du fengyu ji du chunqiu," in *Chong zuo sanxian lu: Wo guo hangtian sanxian jidi jianshe biqin*, ed. Zhongguo hangtian bao bian (Beijing: Zhongguo yuhang chubanshe, 2016), 17. A *mantou* is a steamed bun.

[40] Zunyi shi defang zhi bianzuan weiyuanhui bangongshi, *Zunyi shi sanxian jianshe zhi*, 203, 205.

[41] Wang Shaoyan, "Da sanxian qu," in *Chong zuo sanxian lu*, 3. For another detailed treatment of the process involved in choosing a factory location, see Zhou Yongkang, "Choujian 011 jidi chuqi gongzuo qingkuang de huiyi," in *Sanxian chunqiu*, 30–43.

[42] Wang Xin, "061 jidi jianshe huigu," in *Zunyi sanxian jianshe*, 21.

[43] Shi Xiaobo, "Zunyi de sanxian jianshe," in *Sanxian jianshe zai huichuan: Huichuan qu wenshi ziliao 4*, ed. Zhengxie Zunyi shi huichuan qu weiyuanhui (Chengdu: Zhengxie Zunyi shi huichuan qu weiyuanhui, 2010), 8–9.

[44] Zhao Yuanxing, "Wanshi kaitou nan," in *Sanxian jianshe zai huichuan*, 34.

When tents ran out, workers set up grass sheds which leaked when it rained and were bone-chillingly cold in winter. Recruits from coastal big cities found it hard to adapt to the rainy weather and walking every day on muddy roads in muddy pants.[45] Food was sparse and of low quality. However, as Judith Farquhar has remarked in a different context, fatigue heightened the taste buds and made meals taste "particularly extraordinary" to some people.[46] To increase the local food supply, workers applied the Party's maxim to "make use of local resources" (*jiudi qucai*) and scoured rivers for finless eels, fish, and shrimp. Others foraged for wild mushrooms and lilies. Some asked their family to send vegetable seeds from home and planted gardens near their living area.

Before beginning construction, project leaders held an "oath-swearing ceremony" (*fashi hui*) in which everyone declared their determination to soon provide Base 61 with what in the bureaucratic parlance of the time were called "the three connections and one level" (*santong yiping*) – that is, water, power, and transportation lines, and flatland.[47] To assist with setting up power lines, the Zunyi government transferred 200 factory workers to Base 61, who acquired electricity transformers from a local production brigade and repurposed them to set up a small electrical grid. The Zunyi government also assigned trucks to Base 61 "to constantly shuttle in" bricks, tiles, gravel, and rocks, "both day and night."[48]

Workers remember bringing every day to the battlefield their "weapons: long knives [to cut down plants], a water bottle, an antidote for snakebites, garlic, *mantou*, and pickled vegetables." Laborers additionally carried what they called the "three treasures" of people working in Guizhou's wet climate: "rain clothes, rainboots, and a big cotton-padded jacket." As workers trudged through muddy construction sites, they saw large slogans, plastered all over, reminding them that their hardships were part of socialist China's "race against time with American imperialism" and that they had to "make strenuous efforts, strive for first place, and construct the Big Third Front in a more, faster, better, and more economical way."[49]

[45] An Hongchun, "Tianyi dian gongchang banqian jishi," in *Zunyi sanxian jianshe*, 62–63.

[46] Judith Farquhar has remarked on the link between hunger and enhanced taste buds in Maoist China in *Appetites: Food and Sex in Post-socialist China* (Durham, NC: Duke University Press, 2002), 131.

[47] Other examples of the "three connections and one level" policy can be found in Zhonggong Panzhihua shiwei dangshi yanjiu shi, *Liu zai da liegu de jiyi (qingshao nian ban)* (Chengdu: Sichuan cishu chubanshe, 2003), 56–75.

[48] An Hongchun, "Difang zhengfu zhiyuan tianyi chang jishi," in *Zunyi sanxian jianshe*, 182.

[49] Zhu and Wang, "Hangtian jungong jueqi zai qianbei shenshan," 28. Feng Daoqian, "Shanghai lu de bianqian," in *Zunyi sanxian jianshe*, 94–95.

One way that workers did this was by making up for a dearth of trucks with their own muscle power. When supply shipments arrived on site or at the train station a few kilometers away, project leaders would "organize labor power . . . to carry in goods. No matter if it was day or night, windy or raining, everyone vied with each other and rushed to load and unload goods." When trucks "were lacking, goods were carried on shoulders, including . . . all sorts of machine tool equipment."[50] Not wanting to appear weaker than men, women hoisted bags of cement onto their shoulders and lugged them to the construction site.[51] As during the Great Leap, the construction process continued at night.[52] Technical workers retreated inside to plan the next day's work and make blueprints for tasks yet to come. Lacking electricity, they "lit candles and kerosene lamps" and hid under mosquito nets, while workers continuing construction work outside used torches and watched out for bugs, whose bites numbed the skin and left large welts.

Older workers connected the rigors of their intense work schedule to the high drama of the Party's revolutionary wars, remarking, "We are living just like we did in wartime." Young workers, meanwhile, referenced the popular Soviet film *How the Steel was Tempered* and said, "We have seen here the work style of the old Eighth Route Army. This really is the forge of the revolution, and we have found the best place to temper ourselves."[53] Some workers did not live to tell the tale of the time they spent building the Third Front. The parents of a nineteen-year-old were particularly miserable when they learned of their only son's passing. At his funeral, local officials likely eulogized his death in a way similar to how his coworkers remember, as "giving his precious life while selflessly working" to construct the Third Front.[54] Memorials erected for members of the Railroads Corps who died making the Chengdu–Kunming Railroad made comparable declarations. Cenotaphs proclaimed that they were "martyrs" who "made a heroic sacrifice" and "gave their life to the revolution."[55]

50 An Hongchun, "Tianyi dian gongchang banqian jishi," in *Zunyi sanxian jianshe*, 63.

51 For a similar phenomenon during the Great Leap, see Kimberley Ens-Manning, "The Gendered Politics of Woman-Work: Re-thinking Radicalism in the Great Leap Forward," *Modern China* 32:3 (2006): 349–384.

52 Hershatter, *Gender of Memory*, 241.

53 Zhu and Wang, "Hangtian jungong jueqi zai qianbei shenshan," 29. David Pietz has analyzed the linking of the revolution's past with present-day industrial construction in his book *The Yellow River: The Problem of Water in Modern China* (Cambridge, MA: Harvard University Press, 2015), 218.

54 Zhu and Wang, "Hangtian jungong ueqi zai qianbei shenshan," 31.

55 For the memorial quotes, see this website by a former Railroad Corps member: "Chengkun tielu shang de tie er ju de lieshi linyuan," April 21, 2014, 2018, http://blog.sina.com.cn/s/blog_8812919f0101fry0.html, accessed September 5, 2018.

Building the Chengdu–Kunming Railroad

The Chengdu–Kunming Railroad is the deadliest Third Front project on record. On average two people died for every kilometer of track.[56] The Chengdu–Kunming Railroad is also one of the most celebrated Third Front projects in China. Like the ten great monuments built in Beijing to commemorate the tenth anniversary of the founding of the People's Republic of China, the Chengdu–Kunming Railroad was a grand testament to the Communist Party's technical ability to remake the Chinese landscape in their own image.[57] Rising from an altitude of 500 meters on the Chengdu plain to 2,280 meters at its highest point, the line snakes through the mountains between Sichuan and Yunnan for over 700 kilometers, literally passing through mountains 427 times. The line has a large bridge every 1.7 kilometers and crosses rivers over eighty times. In total, bridges and tunnels make up over 40 percent of the line. Despite the technical complexity of constructing the Chengdu–Kunming Railroad, when it was completed in 1970 the Party made no public announcement because it was a Third Front project and had to be kept hidden from China's Cold War foes in the United States and the Soviet Union.[58]

The Party conceived of building the Chengdu–Kunming Railroad as part of a giant battle to fill out the railroad infrastructure of southwest China. In the words of the Southwest Railroad Construction Headquarters, which was in charge of building the line, "Completing the Sichuan–Guizhou Railroad is in order to fight another battle on the Guiyang–Kunming Railroad. Once victory is achieved on the Guiyang–Kunming line, only then can we shorten the battlefront and concentrate forces for a decisive battle for the Chengdu–Kunming Railroad."[59] Mao kicked off this regional developmental campaign in August 1964 with a statement that railroad workers repeatedly heard: "The Chengdu–Kunming line must be built quickly."[60] This proclamation was shouted over megaphones, written up in construction site newspapers, and scrawled on big-character posters alongside tunnels.[61]

[56] Xie Xinhua, "Gaoyuan zhi lu," in *Tiedaobing bu liao qing*, ed. Song Shaoming (Beijing: Jiefangjun wenyi chubanshe, 2002), 387–388.

[57] Hung, *Mao's New World*, 51.

[58] Tiedaobing shanhou gongzuo lingdao xiaozu, *Zhongguo renmin jiefangjun tiedao bing jianshi* (Beijing: 1986), 144–145. The Party only publicized its construction in 1974. "Chengkun tielu shenglu jianshe tongche," *Renmin ribao*, March 23, 1974.

[59] Zeng Juan, ed., *Jianshe houfang: Quanguo sanxian jianshe xianqi gaochao* (Changchun: Jilin chuban jituan youxian zeren gongsi, 2010), 46–47.

[60] Zhongguo renmin Jiefangjun zong zi 520 budui zhengzhi, ed., *Zhandou zai Chengkun xian* (n.l.: Zhongguo renmin Jiefangjun zong zi 520 budui zhengzhi, 1970). Mao Zedong, "Zai zhongyang shuji chu huiyi shang de chahua," August 1964, in *Panzhihua kaifa*, 7.

[61] Zeng, *Jianshe houfang*, 40.

The first task that Third Front labor had to accomplish was performing geological surveys. In October 1964, the vice minister of railroads, Lu Zhengcao, chaired a meeting about this matter with the Southwest Third Front Railroad Construction Headquarters. At the meeting, it was decided that the Geology Ministry would transfer survey teams from seven provinces and assign each of them to conduct research on a specific portion of the Chengdu–Kunming Railroad. The members of a team dispatched to the Jinsha river knew about the area from Mao Zedong's poem "The Long March," which chronicled how the Red Army's "fearless" trek through "ten thousand crags and torrents" passed "the steep cliffs lapped by the waters of the Jinsha river" onward to the "cold iron chains" of the Luding Bridge where the Red Army famously pulled up the planks of the bridge while crossing it during a firefight with the Guomindang in the 1930s.[62]

When the geological team arrived at the Jinsha river, they encountered adversity too. Alpine winds whipped dust into the air, knocked over tents, and made each step a challenge, as workers hiked through steep mountains for days with their supplies on their backs. Some mountains were not easily passable on foot, and so survey teams had to go down freezing river rapids in flimsy wooden boats that sometimes flipped. Some people fell into the river and never came back up. Others were left with memories of just narrowly escaping death. At night, survey teams packed like sardines into tents and slept on the ground. Since wolves roamed the mountains in packs, some survey teams tended a bonfire all night and guarded their camp in shifts.[63]

The head of one geological survey team said to his coworkers that their new assignment was an "honor." Mao was "not sleeping well" because the Third Front was not built, and so "when we are on site, we will also never sleep." They would work nonstop. Constructing the Chengdu–Kunming Railroad was particularly meaningful because China's former Cold War friend-turned-militarized-enemy – the Soviet Union – "had said it was impossible to build the Chengdu–Kunming Railroad ... We don't believe that. We are going to build it ourselves."[64]

62 Mao Zedong, "The Long March," October 1935, *Marxists Internet Archive*, www.marxists.org/reference/archive/mao/selected-works/poems/poems15.htm, accessed September 5, 2018. In the late 1970s, Deng Xiaoping said that the battle at the Luding Bridge was actually small, and the Party played it up for propaganda purposes. This was not known in China when the Chengdu–Kunming Railroad was being built. Zbigniew Brzezinski, "America and the New Asia," March 9, 2005, Asia-Pacific Research Center Stanford Institute for International Studies, https://web.archive.org/web/20060917015112/http://iis-db.stanford.edu/evnts/4110/Brzezinski_New_Asia_03_2005.pdf.

63 Zhang, *Xinan tongtu*, 33–38. Cheng, *Cheng Zihua huiyi*, 414.

64 The information in this paragraph is from Zhang, *Xinan tongtu*, 26–30. The quotes are on page 28.

While geological personnel undertook surveys, the Southwest Railroad Construction Headquarters contacted cities, prefectures, and counties along the future route of the Chengdu–Kunming Line and commanded them to provide food, daily essentials, and building materials.[65] This was no easy task. Between late 1964 and early 1966, over 350,000 people went into the mountainous borderlands between Sichuan and Yunnan to construct the Chengdu–Kunming line.[66] The sudden influx of people into isolated, sparsely populated areas created huge logistical problems. In Sichuan, severe shortages of trucks developed. According to the provincial government, Sichuan had 5,276 trucks, and Third Front projects required 3,000 trucks. Yet regular economic affairs alone already needed 4,000 vehicles.[67] To lighten the load of supply lines, work units were told to "adapt to local conditions" (*yindi zhiyi*) and "make use of local resources" (*jiudi qucai*).[68]

In accordance with the CCP's localization policy, counties with Third Front projects transferred to them any abandoned buildings.[69] In addition, "local cadres and the masses were mobilized" to let railroad workers "rent or borrow existing public . . . and private housing" that was currently being used.[70] So that less building materials could be trucked in, and production costs could be lowered, housing for workers and railroad buildings were made out of local tree branches, wild grasses, and rammed earth. During the agricultural slack season, rural residents also set up kilns to produce bricks and tiles, and they chopped down firewood.

Feeding and clothing railroad workers was another pressing issue. The provincial government again reduced the need to freight in materials by leaning on counties near railroads. Special areas were set up to produce vegetables for railroad labor, and prices were raised to stimulate local production. Peasants skilled at vegetable growing were brought in to tend

65 Sichuan sheng zhiyuan tielu jianshe weiyuanhui, "Guanyu zhiyuan chengkun tielu jianshe gongzuo qingkuang de baogao," December 30, 1964, Sichuan Provincial Archive, p. 1.

66 Tiedaobing shanhou, *Zhongguo renmin jiefangjun tiedao bing jianshi*, 146.

67 Sichuan sheng tielu jianshe zhiyuan weiyuanhui, "Guanyu zhiyuan chengkun tielu gongzuo qingkuang de baogao," October 13, 1965, Sichuan Provincial Archive, A-270, pp. 1–4, 7–8.

68 Zhonghua renmin gongheguo jiatong bu zhongguo renmin Jiefangjun zong canmo bu, "Guanyu jiaqiang jiaotong beizhan de zhishi," July 16, 1965, Sichuan Provincial Archive, p. 1.

69 Sichuan sheng zhiyuan tielu jianshe weiyuanhui, "Guanyu zhiyuan chengkun tielu jianshe gongzuo qingkuang de baogao," December 30, 1964, Sichuan Provincial Archive, pp. 1–2. Gu Mu, *Gu Mu Huiyi lu*, 211.

70 Unless otherwise noted, the information in the next two paragraphs comes from Sichuan sheng tielu jianshe zhiyuan weiyuanhui, "Guanyu zhiyuan chengkun tielu gongzuo qingkuang de baogao," October 13, 1965, Sichuan Provincial Archive, A-270, pp. 1–4, 7–8.

farms at construction sites, and counties were contracted to provide grain, cooking oil, coal, peanuts, meat, cigarettes, liquor, cotton cloth, clothes, blankets, towels, sleeping mats, and coal. Local officials had to gather up tools and cart them off to construction sites too. They requisitioned "hand-woven baskets, rice carts, shoulder poles, and bamboo rope."[71] Local areas were also encouraged to manufacture materials normally furnished by the central government, such as cement, iron, and steel. Only when provinces could not fill the resource demands of railroad construction were they supposed to ask for assistance from central ministries.[72]

The Party center, however, had no intention of relying entirely on resources within the southwest to build the Chengdu–Kunming Railroad. As with the establishment of Base 61, the Party's policy was to take work units which had technical labor and industrial machinery and make them responsible for completing a Third Front project. The Chengdu–Kunming Railroad was much too large for any one work unit to handle alone, and so the Railroad Ministry divided the line up into sections and granted railroad work units from around the country a supervisory role over different sections. The lead work units were five Railroad Corps divisions (132,000 people) and three engineering bureaus, and an electrical engineering team from the Railroad Ministry (33,000 people).[73] These more capital-rich work units trucked in a panoply of industrial resources. They brought tons and tons of cement and iron. They shipped in gas generators, electrical cables, explosives, hand tools, tracks, pre-made bridge sections, and mechanical hoists.[74] The machine that railroad workers remember the most is the pneumatic drill. To hollow out a tunnel, a drill operator had to press hard against it to counteract constant recoil. After drilling away for hours, a laborer's hearing was muted, and their body felt as if it had morphed into jelly.[75]

To drill six tunnels near Leshan in Sichuan province, the Railroad Ministry transferred a railroad engineering department from northern

[71] Sichuan sheng zhiyuan tielu jianshe weiyuanhui, "Guanyu zhiyuan chengkun tielu jianshe gongzuo qingkuang de baogao," December 30, 1964, Sichuan Provincial Archive, p. 4.

[72] On the Third Front policy of localization, see Zhu, *Zhongguo xiandai gongye shi*, 471–472. Sigrid Schmalzer has chronicled a similar trend in scientific farming. Schmalzer, *Red Revolution*, 141–145.

[73] Tiedaobing shanhou, *Tiedao bing jianshi*, 90. Zhonggong Sichuan shengwei dangshi yanjiu shi, ed. *Zhongguo gongchandang sichuan lishi dashi ji (1950–1978)* (Chengdu: Sichuan renmin chubanshe, 2000), 260.

[74] The Infrastructure Corps played a similar role in other industrial sectors. For a history of their activities, see Liu, *Zhongguo jiefangjun*, 237–473.

[75] Interview with Railroad Corps member, Panzhihua, December 2012. Interview with railroad militia member, Xi'an, January 2013.

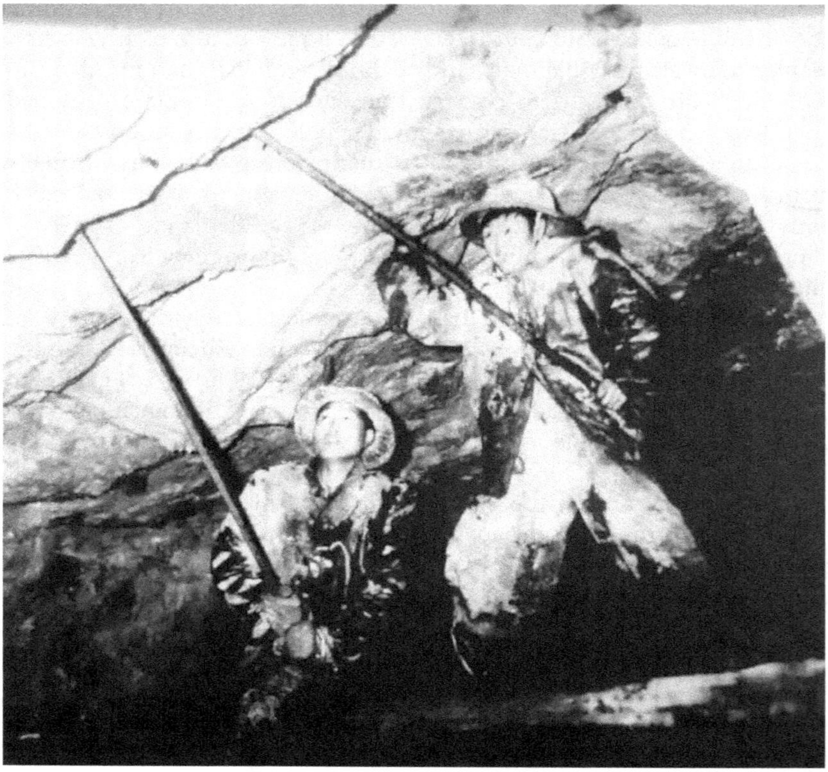

Figure 3.1 Drilling a tunnel for the Chengdu–Kunming Railroad in the late 1960s. Source: "Leshan dahe xiagu tiedaobing bowuguan," *Sohu .com*, September 12, 2018, www.sohu.com/a/253416199_100223122

China. When workers arrived at their designated location, not only were they short on food and clothing, they also lacked qualified technicians and proper equipment because they "had not built a tunnel in many years." Having no place to stay, they decided to live inside a partially built tunnel.[76] Cadres motivated disheartened workers by holding a meeting about the "great strategic importance of building our motherland's great southwest" and discussing how railroad construction contributed to China's struggles against the United States in Southeast Asia.

76 The quotes in this paragraph are from "Suidao shigong zhong sixaing zhengzhi gongzuo de ji dian zuo fa," October 14, 1965, Sichuan Provincial Archive, pp. 20–21.

At the end of the meeting, workers made declarations that connected their hard work to their devotion to Chairman Mao. Laborers swore "to finish the ... [tunnel] ahead of schedule, so that Mao could sleep well." Workers also linked their usage of "pneumatic drills" to China's broader fights in the global Cold War, depicting "the rocks" they bore holes in as "American wolves" and the lengthening of the tunnel as contributing to "the people of Vietnam's war" with the United States.[77] Until the tunnel was finished, laborers should "forget about time ... and material rewards, continue to work when they were sick" or lightly injured, and "willingly delay marriage." Neither fear of death, loss of sleep, nor being away from family should deter them from working hard. All their temporal concerns had to be subordinate to pushing Third Front construction forward.

Halfway through the team's allotted time to finish the tunnel, the project's leadership received a call reiterating the need to stay on schedule. Yet at that point in time only half of the tunnel was built. To push labor to work even more, propaganda personnel again highlighted the links between local development and Chinese aid for Vietnam. Vice minister of railroads Lu Zhengcao and director of the Southwest Third Front Commission Li Jingquan also came and offered words of encouragement. Nonetheless, some workers still harbored "five fears: ... hardships ... injury and death ... their income being lowered ... no one being around to protect their wife and kids, and ... when they finished their five-year contract, not being sent home." After a botched explosion killed people, some laborers refused to go to the construction site and pretended to be sick. Some "even openly asked to resign and go home."[78]

Project leaders responded with study sessions in which they encouraged workers "to creatively study and apply" (*huo xue huo yong*) Mao's works to their daily lives.[79] As prescribed in Mao's speech "Serving the People," one worker declared that his death at work "would be weightier than Mount Tai."[80] The kitchen squad took the same speech and made it into a reason to guarantee that workers ate dumplings while building a two-hundred-meter-long tunnel. Other cadres complained that "the new equipment" they had received was of "poor quality" and that they "had never built" a tunnel before, so it would be "very hard for them to

[77] For other examples of the linking of local struggles to the Cold War, see Shapiro, *Mao's War*, 142–145, 163.

[78] The quotes in the next two paragraphs are from "Suidao shigong zhong sixaing zhengzhi gongzuo de ji dian zuofa," October 14, 1965, Sichuan Provincial Archive, pp. 22–23.

[79] For examples of this practice before the Cultural Revolution, see Ho, *Curating Revolution*, Chapter 4. Ho chronicles a similar trend in the ways that people engaged with Mao-era exhibitions.

[80] The quotes in this paragraph are from "Suidao shigong zhong sixaing zhengzhi gongzuo de ji dian zuo fa," October 14, 1965, Sichuan Provincial Archive, p. 24.

do." Leaders organized another study session of Mao's story "Who Says Chicken Feathers Cannot Fly in the Sky." Workers again took inspiration from Mao's writings. One laborer referenced the Soviet claim that the Chengdu–Kunming Railroad was too technically complicated to build and asserted that "what foreigners cannot accomplish we definitely will get done." Another nameless Third Front recruit linked his ardor at work to national struggles to win respect through international sports competitions, declaring that he "would attack building a hundred meters" like three-time world table tennis champion "Zhuang Zedong plays ping pong and fights for the motherland."[81]

Through the labor of hundreds of thousands of other anonymous workers, construction of the Chengdu–Kunming Railroad moved along at a fast clip from late 1964 into the first half of 1966. The central Party was so pleased that nearly half of the line had already been completed that it shortened the projected finish date from July 1, 1969, to a year earlier.[82] This optimistic prediction was not realized. Instead, the unexpected occurred. Mao inaugurated the Cultural Revolution, factional struggles exploded, and the Party's campaign to industrially protect China against the perils of the Cold War fell apart due to attacks on domestic enemies.

Contradictory Campaigns to Defend Socialism

Mao Zedong conceived of both the Third Front and the Cultural Revolution as ways to defend Chinese socialism from danger. In the case of the Third Front, Mao ordered central planners to build industrial enterprises in covert inland locations, so that China's industrial base was less vulnerable to sudden attack by the United States or the Soviet Union. Central planners complied with Mao's commands, and they portrayed every advancement in the Third Front campaign not just as developing inland regions but also as military victories over China's Cold War competitors.

The Cultural Revolution, on the other hand, cast doubt on the political loyalties of all bureaucratic and technical personnel. China's rivals in the Cold War were purportedly no longer lurking just beyond the PRC's borders. They had already penetrated into the Chinese body politic and found "hidden enemies and traitors within Chinese intellectual circles and within the Party," who, as Andrew Walder has said, sought to "overthrow Communist political power and restore capitalism."[83] Attempts to

[81] For the history of sports and national prestige in China, see Guoqi Xu, *Olympic Dreams: China and Sports, 1895–2008* (Cambridge, MA: Harvard University Press, 2008).

[82] Zhonghua renmin gongheguo tiedaobu, *Tielu xiujian*, 91.

[83] Walder, "Cultural Revolution Radicalism," 41.

stage a capitalist revival with Soviet assistance had supposedly even been committed at the very top by "China's Khrushchev" – Liu Shaoqi.[84]

In the heated political atmosphere of the Cultural Revolution, no administrator or technical expert was free from suspicion. Anyone could secretly be a "capitalist roader" who was willing to collaborate with hostile foreign forces and undermine China's march towards socialist modernity.[85] Such was the conspiratorial Cold War logic of the Cultural Revolution. In making this statement, I do not intend to claim that the politics of the Cultural Revolution are reducible to surreptitious plotting. As we will see below, Maoist notions were employed in factional conflicts to attain multiple different objectives. By highlighting the conspiratorial character of Cultural Revolution politics, I also do not aim to assert that Mao's striking out against his colleagues was a hollow power play devoid of ideological content.

Mao's conflicts with Party leaders, such as Deng Xiaoping and Liu Shaoqi, were based on disagreements over the direction that the Chinese revolution should take, with Mao pushing back against practices that he viewed as leading towards a capitalist resurgence in China, just like he had done in the lead-up to the Third Front campaign.[86] Similar to the rollout of the Third Front, international tensions played an integral part in the initiation and course of the Cultural Revolution. Growing military clashes between the United States and Chinese-backed North Vietnamese troops helped to make credible concerns about foreigners seeking out Chinese Benedict Arnolds.[87] Soviet leaders added further fuel to fears of a fifth column when they authorized editorials and Mandarin-language radio broadcasts into China which declared that the Soviet Union would assist any "genuine communists" who overthrew Mao and halted "his erroneous course."[88]

Assaults during the Cultural Revolution on bureaucratic organizations and technical expertise directly clashed with the construction of the Third Front. Building a large industrial base depended on the effective operation of top-down administrative structures. Central ministries had to be able to transmit orders to specific work units who in turn had to be able to

[84] Garver, *China's Quest*, 278.

[85] For an in-depth study of the deadly consequences of concerns about foreign infiltration during the Cultural Revolution, see Tan Hecheng, *The Killing Wind: A Chinese County's Descent into Madness during the Cultural Revolution* (Oxford: Oxford University Press, 2017).

[86] Benjamin I. Schwartz, "The Reign of Virtue: Some Broad Perspectives on Leader and Party in the Cultural Revolution," *China Quarterly* 35 (1968): 7, 13–14. Tang Tsou, "The Cultural Revolution and the Chinese Political System," *China Quarterly* 38 (1969): 63–78.

[87] Chen, *Mao's China*, 240. [88] Garver, *China's Quest*, 278.

count on supplies from upper levels of government and other companies. Technical and scientific personnel, likewise, had to be able to utilize their skills and knowledge to solve complex engineering problems. The political fault lines of the Cultural Revolution undercut both the work of technical personnel and the basic functioning of every level of government, as they laid open to question the political dependability of every technician and administrator.[89]

The contradictory goals of the Cultural Revolution and Third Front campaigns became quickly apparent in May 1966 when Red Guards began to depose administrators responsible for directing Third Front construction. One major exception was Premier Zhou Enlai, who weathered the many storms of the Cultural Revolution. As Roderick MacFarquhar and Michael Schoenhals have observed, Zhou Enlai "used almost every public occasion to call desperately for the insulation of the economy from the Cultural Revolution."[90] The policy Zhou tried to push was for workers to "grasp revolution and promote production," with Zhou's emphasis being primarily on the latter. According to this policy, the Party center mandated that "Third Front construction projects, whether they are already built or are still under construction, are all national secrets," and so they "cannot be entered at will" by groups involved in the Cultural Revolution.[91] The State Council, which was under Zhou's direction, also notified all Third Front work units that they should maintain an eight-hour workday, that Red Guards were not allowed into their work units, and that they did not have to permit big-character posters or the free airing of views. Third Front work units should instead concentrate on the developmental missions they were assigned because of their military importance.[92]

At a national planning meeting in December 1966, an unnamed central Party official again reiterated the significance of building the Third Front, and he depicted the campaign as a success thus far. According to him, "Many major projects' construction times were around half of what they took in the past," and China's "industrial layout" had already undergone

89 For a broader discussion of the contradictions between Mao's developmental and revolutionary goals, see Riskin, *China's Political Economy*, 201–204. Rebecca E. Karl, *Mao Zedong and China in the Twentieth-Century World: A Concise History* (Durham, NC: Duke University Press, 2010), 83–84.

90 MacFarquhar and Schoenhals, *Mao's Last Revolution*, 141.

91 "Zhonggong zhongyang guanyu zhua geming cu shengchan de tongzhi," September 14, 1966, in *Wenge da geming yanjiu ziliao shang ce*, ed. Zhongguo renmin jiefangjun guofang daxue dangshi dangjian zhenggong jiaoyan shi (Beijing: Zhongguo renmin jiefangjun guofang daxue dangshi dangjian zhenggong jiaoyan shi, 1988), 115.

92 Zhonggong Sichuan shengwei dangshi yanjiu shi, *Zhongguo gongchandang sichuan lishi*, 296. Liu Jinxiang, "Guanyu sanxian jianshe de yi duan huiyi," in *Zunyi sanxian jianshe*, 78.

a "big change."[93] In the next few years, First Front work units were going to continue to be relocated to the Third Front, and laborers were going to "work hard to speed up Big and Small Third Front Construction's new industrial bases and the building of railroad lines." At the same time, people in China had to "concentrate forces" on a very different political mission – "attacking the handful of people in authority taking the capitalist road . . . and digging up the roots of revisionism."

Some Third Front work units were insulated from Cultural Revolution struggles against capitalist roaders and revisionists. Party secretary of the Shaanxi Provincial Infrastructure Committee Ren Jun recounts a few cases in his memoirs. His own work unit at first came under heavy attack. Rebel forces shot it up with artillery and occupied it for a month because they thought that its lack of big-character posters proved that it was not taking the Cultural Revolution seriously. The Shaanxi Provincial Military Area then dispatched soldiers to protect the Infrastructure Committee, so that it could shield the Third Front from the Cultural Revolution. In response, the committee sent inspection teams to Third Front work units to check their status.

Ren Jun visited a missile launching test center with no big-character posters or criticism sessions. When nearby rebels demanded entry, Ren did not say no. He dared the rebel group to come in and risk revealing classified activities to China's foes. The rebels backed down and left. Ren Jun saw another example of a Third Front work unit muting factional conflicts at a physics institute in Hanzhong. Local rebels had labeled famed theoretical physicist Zhou Peiyuan a "capitalist roader," and so a struggle session was held against him. During the session, Zhou was never beaten or forced to assume awkward positions, as often occurred in other struggles sessions.[94] He was allowed to sit comfortably in a wicker chair, and after the session was over, people went back to construction work.[95] Rebel groups' restrained criticism of Zhou Peiyuan fits with a larger pattern demonstrated by Evan Feigenbaum of work units tied closely to national security experiencing less disruption during the Cultural Revolution because of protection by central officials.[96]

This trend, nevertheless, had its limits. Some Third Front work units took very seriously stamping out the perceived threat that capitalist

93 The quotes in this paragraph are from "Zai quanguo jihua gongye jiaotong huiyi shang de jianghua (jilu gao)," December 23, 1966, Sichuan Provincial Archive, pp. 2–4, 6.

94 For examples of violent struggle sessions, see Yang Su, *Collective Killings in Rural China during the Cultural Revolution* (New York: Cambridge University Press, 2011), 102, 133, 164, 173.

95 Ren Jun, "Wo suo jingli de Shaanxi sanxian jianshe," in *Sanxian fengyun Zhongguo sanxian jianshe wenxuan: Zhongguo sanxian jianshe yanjiuhui*, 74–76.

96 Feigenbaum, *China's Techno-warriors*, 72.

roaders and revisionism posed to Chinese socialism. In Sichuan, provincial officials noticed that "some cadres didn't dare support" senior cadres because they "feared that someone would label them a rightist or conservative" and that they would become an object of attack.[97] Others worried that if cadres that they had criticized in the past regained authority, they would take revenge and target them as counterrevolutionaries.[98] At a military factory in Guangyuan, rebels severely beat a longtime cadre for being a "traitor" to China's socialist endeavor. In spite of being assaulted, the cadre still wanted to help build socialism and hoped that one day the CCP would allow him to again serve the revolution.[99]

On the Chengdu–Kunming Railroad, the labor force split into opposing factions. Battles at first were very fierce, as the Railroad Corps had a large cache of weapons which they used against each other. After a few armed battles, nearly all workers left construction sites.[100] Laborers also ran away from factional struggles at Small Third Front construction sites in Shanxi and Liaoning.[101] In Yunnan, the Provincial Military Control Commission sent in troops to escort to Kunming a group of Shandong recruits who wanted to return home. When troops arrived, a rival faction opened fire. In the ensuing skirmishes, 104 people were killed.[102]

At Base 61 in Guizhou, recruits recently arrived from Shanghai complained that they had been lied to about inland construction and demanded that they be permitted to go back home to participate in the Cultural Revolution. Big-character posters then appeared all over the factory calling for the "overthrow of capitalist roaders" and "oaths to protect Mao's revolutionary line." People who sought to continue building the factory walked around the construction site looking dejected, while their coworkers struggled against people presumed to be "capitalist roaders" and "spies working for foreign agents (*nei jian*)."[103] Some cadres at Base 61 escaped attacks by committing suicide. In Guiyang, a regional official in charge of Base 61 slipped town and disappeared. Rebel groups,

97 On the dangers of acquiring a bad political label, see White, *Policies of Chaos*, 318.

98 "Sichuan sheng zhua geming cu shengchan gongye jiatong jijian huiyi di16 qi," March 16, 1967, Sichuan Provincial Archive, p. 2.

99 Yang Xiaohong, "Zhuiyi wo de fuqin: 308 chang keyansuo suochang er san shi," in *Sanxian fengyun Zhongguo sanxian jianshe wenxuan*, 130. Ning Wang has found a similar trend among some people labeled as rightists in the Anti-Rightist Campaign; see *Banished to the Great Northern Wilderness*, 4, 9, 19, 95, 99.

100 Zhonghua renmin gongheguo tiedaobu, *Tielu xiujian*, 91. Gu Xiu, *Licheng huiwang* (Shanghai: Shanghai wenyi chubanshe, 2006), 143. Interview with Railroad Corps member, Panzhihua, December 2012.

101 "Guowuyuan guofang gongye bangongshi xiao sanxian jianshe huibao tigang," February 6, 1968, in *Zhongguo gongchandang yu sanxian jianshe*, 239.

102 Chen, *Sanxian*, 187.

103 Feng Daoqian, "Shanghai lu de bianqian," in *Zunyi sanxian jianshe*, 95.

meanwhile, made Base 61 more revolutionary by changing the name of the main thoroughfare of the factory complex from "Youth Road" to "Anti-imperialism Road" and later to "Jinggangshan Road" after the CCP's former base area in Jiangxi.[104]

At Base 61's titanium factory, leaders were accused of being capitalist roaders and were regularly criticized in struggle sessions. The vice director of the factory, nonetheless, still held weekly meetings with other leaders, though he did not have the heart to give them additional work because being constantly struggled against had imprinted a dead look in their eyes.[105] At another Base 61 factory, all the cadres were toppled but one. He tried to maintain production by claiming that he supported local rebels who controlled the factory's oil depot. When he went to recoup the rewards of his political allegiance and collect oil, local rebels rebuffed his advances. They thought he was an impostor, and so they threw a grenade at him and called in rebel groups from other work units to assist with a nighttime inspection of the homes of suspected capitalist roaders in order to find and seize all their weapons.[106]

Elsewhere in Guizhou, the director of Shuicheng Steel, Tao Xicheng, was at first able to prevent rebel factions from forming on site. Construction efforts were still impaired because factional battles had broken out at Shuicheng Steel's parent company – Anshan Steel – whose assistance played a leading role in building efforts. In June 1967, Red Guards came from Anshan Steel and began to help set up a rebel group to criticize local capitalist roaders. Tao Xicheng persuaded them to leave by saying that if the Third Front was not built, then Mao would not sleep well.

Anshan rebel groups then sent incendiary leaflets to Shuicheng Steel. Tao locked them up and forbade anyone to read them. Tao, however, was unsure how to move forward with Shuicheng Steel's construction because communication lines had broken down, and the factory was no longer receiving central directives. Tao thus decided to fly to Beijing to speak directly with Party leaders. They were already under attack themselves, and so Tao went back to Shuicheng Steel. Since his departure, rebel groups had sprouted up. They quickly seized and beat Tao when they

104 Liu Jinxiang, "Gaunyu sanxian jianshe de yi duan huiyi," in *Zunyi sanxian jianshe*, 79–80. For examples of this trend elsewhere in China, see Paul A. Cohen, "The Contested Past: The Boxers as History and Myth," *Journal of Asian Studies* 51:1 (1992): 100.

105 Chen Jihong and Li Tianhui, "Shanguang de tai zhu," in *Zunyi sanxian jianshe*, 128.

106 Wang Zhongxiu, "Chongman haoqing de shi nian," in *Zunyi sanxian jianshe*, 133–134. The seizing of another faction's weapons is also chronicled in Tan Hecheng, *Killing Wind*, 363, 371.

learned of his return. Tao tried to continue to work at night. Yet he eventually died from his wounds.[107]

The Third Front and Cultural Revolution in Shanghai

Many Shanghai recruits tried to escape from working at the Third Front during the Cultural Revolution. According to historian Chen Donglin, 20,000 Shanghainese fled the Third Front in January 1967 and demanded not to be shipped back.[108] On February 7, the State Council ordered all recruits to stay at their new work unit and take up the "extremely honorable and great task" of industrializing inland regions and "act like model workers ... and put into practice Chairman Mao's policy of grasping revolution and promoting production."[109] Giving yet another twist to the Cultural Revolution idea that "capitalist roaders in positions of authority" were seeking to subvert China's socialist revolution, the Party center claimed that capitalist roaders at Third Front work units had "hoodwinked" workers and their families into returning to their original work unit.

The State Council allowed that if laborers were dissatisfied, they could write letters or put up big-character posters. "If it was absolutely necessary, they could send a small number of representatives" to take part in the Cultural Revolution at their original workplace. Any people who had already left should "quickly return inland." No First Front enterprises should give returnees work, and "capitalist roaders" who had convinced people to decamp from the Third Front should be "struggled against in mass criticism sessions" or "punished according to the law" if their conduct was particularly "vile."

This central Party directive gives relatively little information about why workers were departing from the Third Front. A report written the following November by Shanghai's First Mechanical Engineering Department sheds some light on this topic. According to the department, some people had raided the archives of Third Front work units and discovered that their name had been switched for someone else's on relocation rolls, and so they went back to Shanghai to rectify the situation. More people bolted from the Third Front because, as one worker said,

[107] Shuigang xuanchuan bu, "Gaoyuan fei tie qi: Sanxian xian gongchen," in *Wei wei wu meng shan youyou xiang siqing: Liupanshui shi sanxian jianshe zhe koushu shi*, ed. Zhonggong Liupanshui shiwei danshi yanjiu shi (Beijing: Zhongyang wenxian chubanshe, 2016), 22–23. Guizhou sheng Liupanshui shi, *Liupanshui sanxian*, 133.

[108] Chen, *Sanxian*, 188, 190.

[109] The quotes in the next two paragraphs are from Zhonggong zhongyang Guowuyuan, "Guanyu zhiyuan neidi yu bianjiang de zhigong ying jiudi canjia wenhua da geming de jingji tongzhi," February 17, 1967, in *Wenge da geming yanjiu ziliao shang ce*, Zhongguo renmin jiefangjun guofang daxue dangshi dangjian zhenggong jiaoyan shi, 312.

"Inland construction had split up my family," and fights in inland areas "had made it difficult" to stay clear of violence.[110] In some cases, families in Shanghai heard about armed struggles in the interior and sent "fake telegrams" about an imaginary "medical crisis" that required their prompt return home.

When Third Front recruits arrived back in Shanghai, some linked up with rebel groups and beat up senior cadres. Short on food, some returnees stole foodstuffs from their former work unit. To avoid problems, some factories took proactive measures. They declared that returnees had "no right to speak" because they were "deserters." Other factories "hung up posters at the front gate," saying returnees "are not welcome, will not be received, and are not allowed to enter into the factory." If returnees wanted their issues resolved, they would have to speak with higher authorities.

Eventually Shanghai factories gathered returnees to study central Party directives which stated that "the more difficult a place, the more someone should want to go there. Only then is someone a good comrade." While some returnees were supposedly convinced by Party propaganda, some still insisted on being given "work, food, clothing, and housing" in Shanghai. Others were willing to go back to the Third Front as long as they still had work; fights in the interior were over, and their "life and possessions" were safe. Others demanded better medical care and schools. Shanghai factories responded and contacted Third Front work units to ensure that if returnees came back, not only would they not be attacked as capitalist roaders, but also living standards would be improved. After these measures were taken, almost all returnees headed back to the Third Front. While some probably did so in response to policy improvements, others certainly did so because the military gathered workers up and forced them to go back.[111]

One reason why the Shanghai government wanted people to move back to the Third Front was that Shanghai was still receiving orders to ship out new recruits. In June 1967, Shanghai's First Mechanical Engineering Department claimed that relocation had stopped because the city's leadership had embraced "the reactionary capitalist line" of Liu Shaoqi, Deng Xiaoping, and Bo Yibo and had "conspired to damage Third Front Construction and block the transfer of personnel, equipment, and materials."[112] There is reason to doubt that the First Mechanical

[110] The quotes in the next two paragraphs are from "Guanyu dongyuan fanhu zhinei zhigong hui neidi de gongzuo huibao," November 10, 1967, Shanghai Municipal Archive, B103-4-24, pp. 19–21.

[111] Interview with Chinese scholar, Beijing, June 2018.

[112] The information in the next paragraph is also from Shanghai shi di yi jidian ju Yixian zhihui bu, "Guanyu dangqian zhiyuan neidi jianshe gongzuo Zhong ji ge ji xuyao jiejue

Engineering Department's primary concern was the political misconduct of central and local officials who had recently been ousted from power.

It seems more likely that the First Mechanical Engineering Department was using the idea that capitalist roaders were undermining Mao's vision of Chinese socialism in order to engage in their own foot dragging. Shanghai's First Mechanical Engineering Department had plenty of reasons to slow down labor transfers to the Third Front. By its own omission, there were already insufficient resources to provide to relocated enterprises, and past transfers had made it very difficult to fulfill production targets. Likely seeking to tie the whole relocation issue up in bureaucratic knots, the department asked the city government to contact the Planning Commission for further instructions and furnish more trained personnel and resources before additional relocations took place.

Reasserting Order and Reviving the Third Front

In late 1967, the Party center deployed the PLA to violently suppress political factions nationwide and form revolutionary committees directed by military officers. By the end of 1968, every province had a military-led revolutionary committee. Factional struggles, nevertheless, continued to produce political strife and economic disarray.[113] As part of the central Party's push to reassert political order, it tried to resuscitate the Third Front campaign. Between March and May 1968, the State Council held a series of meetings with central government agencies and provincial leaders to discuss the building of the Small Third Front.[114] After these meetings, the Planning Commission and the State Council's National Defense Industry Office issued a report which again drew on the notion that capitalist roaders in China posed an insider threat.

In their hands, the idea that capitalist plots were brewing in China became a justification for re-establishing centralized control over the Small Third Front. The report claimed that since the beginning of the Cultural Revolution, "a handful of capitalist roaders" had "incited violent struggles, stoked the black wind of economism, and damaged production and construction."[115] To overcome these problems, what needed to be

de zhuyao wenti de baogao," June 16, 1967, Shanghai Municipal Archive, B-103-4-4, pp. 2–5. The quotes are on pages 2, 3.

113 MacFarquhar and Schoenhals, *Mao's Last Revolution*, 239–240, 245–246. Andrew G. Walder, "Rebellion and Repression in China, 1966–1971," *Social Science History* 38:3–4 (2014): 518–523.

114 Guowuyuan, *Sanxian jianshe*, 375.

115 "Guojia jiwei, guowuyuan guofang gongban guanyu xiao sanxian defang jungong jianshe ji ge wenti de qingshibaogao," June 20, 1968, in *Zhongguo gongchandang yu sanxian jianshe*, 235.

Figure 3.2 Establishing a revolutionary committee in Panzhihua in 1968. Source: "Panzhihua lao zhaopian," *Panzhihua yishu zaixian*, http://pzhsyol.com/col.jsp?id=149

done was for provinces, cities, and central planning agencies to work together on devising and executing a plan for Small Third Front construction for the next three years.[116] This policy recommendation did not lead to a revival of the Third Front campaign.

Central Party efforts to revitalize construction of the Third Front only succeeded after border fights erupted in 1969 between China and the

[116] "Guowuyuan guofang gongye bangongshi xiao sanxian jianshe huibao tigang," February 6, 1968, in *Zhongguo gongchandang yu sanxian jianshe*, 239.

Soviet Union at Zhenbao Island.[117] Chinese leaders perceived the Sino-Soviet border conflict to be part of a wider pattern of Soviet aggression in the global Cold War. Foremost amongst Chinese concerns was the Soviet invasion of Czechoslovakia in 1968 to suppress political groups which the Kremlin thought threatened the international socialist movement. Beijing was apprehensive that Moscow might see the domestic turmoil of the Cultural Revolution as a reason to undertake a similar military action in China. Chinese fears of war intensified when Beijing learned that Moscow was asking East European states how they would respond to nuclear attacks on the PRC.[118]

At the time of the Zhenbao incident, the Planning Commission was holding its first major meeting since the start of the Cultural Revolution. Worried that the conflict at Zhenbao Island might morph into a Soviet invasion, Mao ordered every county to form militia units, so that Soviet forces would encounter informal military personnel everywhere.[119] The Planning Commission additionally mandated that economic work in 1969 must focus on "vigorously strengthening defense industry, basic industry, and the construction of inland industry."[120] In preparation for battle, the Construction Commission commanded every region on May 30 to re-establish a Third Front Commission to implement the Party center's plans, approve the location of projects, and co-ordinate the supply of local resources.[121]

In July, the Party center's determination to restart the Third Front campaign became intertwined with the PLA's efforts to enforce political discipline and destroy the factions that had emerged during the Cultural Revolution.[122] On July 23, the central Party ordered all factions to immediately stop armed conflicts and turn in their weapons.[123] Not entirely effective, the Party center made a similar order on August 28 which demanded all Chinese unite behind Chairman's Mao directive to "increase vigilance, defend the fatherland, and prepare to wage war." Anyone who did not promptly return to work and prevented China from "making full preparations to resist a war of invasion" would be

[117] Chen, *Mao's China*, 240. [118] Garver, *China's Quest*, 278, 282.

[119] Zheng Qian, "Zhonggong jiu da qianhou quanguo de zhanbei gongzuo," in *Zhonggong dangshi ziliao 41*, ed. Zhonggong zhongyang dangshi yanjiushi (Beijing: Zhonggong dangshi chubanshe, 1992), 209–210.

[120] Chen, *Sanxian*, 200. [121] Chen, *Sanxian*, 201.

[122] On the wider repression of factions, see Walder, "Rebellion and Repression in China." Andrew G. Walder and Yang Su, "The Cultural Revolution in the Countryside: Scope, Timing and Human Impact," *China Quarterly* 173 (2003): 74–99.

[123] "Zhongguo gongchandang zhongyang weiyuanhui bugao," July 23, 1969, in *Wenge da geming yanjiu ziliao zhong ce*, 356–357. Zheng, "Zhonggong jiu da qianhou quanguo de zhanbei gongzuo," 215–216.

viewed as engaging in "splittist activities" (*fenlie huodong*) that stood in the way of making China into "a military stronghold to bury imperialism, revisionism, and counterrevolutionaries."[124] Following the issuance of these two directives, revolutionary committees across the country worked with the PLA to quash factions in order to guarantee that China could produce enough materiel for a Sino-Soviet war that seemed to CCP leaders to be just around the corner.[125]

While the central Party tried to overcome domestic conflicts and ready the country for war, Zhou Enlai endeavored on the international front to cool tensions between China and the Soviet Union. At Zhou's request, Soviet premier Alexei Kosygin made a brief stop at the Beijing airport to talk with him on September 11. They agreed to peacefully settle the boundary dispute and gradually remove troops from the border. Chinese leaders, nonetheless, still acted as if the Soviets might soon carry out an invasion or nuclear attack.

On September 27, minister of national defense Lin Biao called for "using a war-fighting perspective" in all circumstances.[126] A few days later in his National Day address, Lin warned that "American imperialism and Soviet revisionism . . . were vainly planning a war of invasion," and so "the whole nation had to . . . strengthen war preparations and be ready at any moment to annihilate any enemy that dares to invade."[127] Although Lin Biao reminded the country that the American threat had not gone away, the central Party's main concern was the one-million-strong Soviet force camped on China's northern border. Just in case Soviet troops decided to move south into Chinese territory, 940,000 PLA troops were sent to wartime positions.[128]

At the same time that the Defense Ministry placed the country on a war footing, the central Party continued to try to put an end to factional conflicts. In October 1969, the Party began to shift their attention partially away from repressing factions to redirecting people's energies towards war-preparedness. Work units organized study sessions in which they read Mao's writings on war and national discipline. Laborers also practiced military drills and took part in campaigns to store grain, build military roads, set up emergency supply networks, form fire brigades, maintain public order, and make air-raid shelters.[129]

124 "Zhongguo gongchandang zhongyang weiyuanhui mingling," August 28, 1969, in *Wenge da geming yanjiu ziliao zhong ce*, 365–367.
125 Zheng, "Zhonggong jiu da qianhou quanguo de zhanbei gongzuo," 216–217.
126 Zheng, "Zhonggong jiu da qianhou quanguo de zhanbei gongzuo," 212.
127 "Lin Biao zai qingzhu zhonghua renmin gongheguo er shi zhounian dahui shang de hianghua," October 1, 1969, in *Wenge da geming yanjiu ziliao zhong ce*, 380–381.
128 Garver, *China's Quest*, 283–285.
129 Zheng, "Zhonggong jiu da qianhou quanguo de zhanbei gongzuo," 221–224.

By 1971, Chinese had excavated enough civil defense structures to house underground around 60 percent of the country's urban population. Cities were also evacuated, and subterranean escape routes were dug.[130] In Beijing, a network of tunnels was formed for central leaders to secretly go inland undetected.[131]

So that the CCP would have a larger industrial base to fall back on, the central Party threw Third Front construction into high gear.[132] State expenditures on national defense grew so much that their share of the state budget (40 percent) exceeded that of the Korean War (33 percent).[133] Leading the charge to expand China's defense capabilities was a group of military leaders commonly referred to as the Lin Biao clique.[134] They asserted their authority through the Central Military Commission's Administrative Group, which wrested control over the defense sector away from the State Council led by Zhou Enlai. The group's core goal was to create an independent and complete military industrial complex. They wanted six big military industrial complexes in the northeast and Big Third Front provinces in addition to four small military industrial complexes in the Small Third Front in Xinjiang, Anhui, Shandong, and the Fujian–Jiangxi borderlands. In these areas, the Lin Biao clique ordered the construction of a large number of facilities to produce transport planes, helicopters, and rocket launchers.[135]

To supervise the growth of military industry, the Central Military Commission's Administrative Group set up four small groups to handle affairs related to aerospace, electronics, weapons, and shipbuilding.[136] Leader of the aerospace group deputy chief of the General Staff Wu Faxian directed funds into developing long-range bombers and aircraft carriers, although China did not have the technology to build either. He also greenlighted building thirty-five projects which had absolutely no plans. In 1969, Wu visited an exhibition of the J-6 III fighter jet. Impressed by its performance, he demanded that a local factory "from now on produce this kind of plane." When aerospace personnel protested that the J-6 III was still undergoing tests, and designs had not yet been finalized, Wu declared "the design is now finalized; go back, and produce it immediately."[137]

[130] Li Ke and Hao Shengzhang, *Wenhua da geming zhong de renmin Jiefangjun*, 252–253.
[131] Covell Meyskens, "Third Front Railroad and Industrial Modernity in Late Maoist China," *Twentieth-Century China* 40:3 (2015): 243.
[132] Chen, "Sanxian jianshe," 16. Li and Hao, *Wenhua da geming zhong de renmin Jiefangjun*, 258.
[133] Chen, *Sanxian*, 235. Li, *Modern Chinese Army*, 112.
[134] The group consisted of Lin's wife Ye Qun, chief of staff Huang Yongsheng, deputy chief of the General Staff Wu Faxian, General Li Zuopeng, and General Qiu Huizuo.
[135] Chen, *Sanxian*, 225, 227. [136] Chen, *Sanxian*, 223. [137] Chen, *Sanxian*, 225–228.

Other members of the Lin Biao clique sought to boost Chinese military capacity by other means. Director of the PLA General Logistics Department Qiu Huizuo suggested investing 12 billion RMB in conventional weapons production. This amount was twice what the CCP had spent on weaponry in the past two decades. The vice minister in charge of manufacturing conventional weapons, Zhang Liankui, spoke out against Qiu's proposal. Qiu silenced him by accusing him of being a rightist. In another incident, Lin Biao's son, Lin Liguo, saw in a foreign movie a plane that could land vertically. Fascinated by it, he told the PLA to figure out how to make one even though China's regular fighter jets were still under development.[138] General Li Zuopeng exercised his technological imagination too. He demanded that a combat ship have a special radar system that could detect a wide range of atmospheric elements despite the fact that the radar system required an antenna that was 3,000 meters wide and thirty meters tall.[139]

Around the same time, Lin Biao decided that the location of China's nuclear weapons program did not sufficiently conform with the Third Front policy of placing work units in "mountainous, dispersed, hidden" locations. To fix the situation, Lin Biao recommended packing up nuclear facilities in Jiuquan and Baotou and moving them via train to northern Sichuan. Officials in the Second Machine-Building Ministry, which was in charge of China's nuclear program, were against Lin Biao's idea because they knew that everywhere the train went would be contaminated with nuclear pollution. They did not dare to directly resist an order from Lin Biao, so instead they drew up a plan for what would happen if China's nuclear program was relocated. When Zhou Enlai got wind of Lin Biao's idea, he blocked its implementation. In other instances, the Lin Biao clique's adamant insistence on dividing up Third Front projects yielded rather unique geographic results. In Shanxi, the military spread a tank production facility out over a 120-kilometer area connected by 100 kilometers of railroads. The high cost associated with this project led some workers to joke that they weren't waging a "people's war" (*renmin zhanzheng*) to defend China through industrial development but a "people's money war" (*renmin bi zhanzheng*) which absorbed exorbitant amounts of national currency.[140]

Militarizing the Power of the Three Gorges

Alongside the Lin Biao clique's drive to reinforce Chinese military power, the Ministry of Water Resources and Power undertook a big campaign to

[138] Interview with Chinese Scholar, Beijing, June 2018. [139] Chen, *Sanxian*, 228.
[140] Chen, *Sanxian*, 231–232.

boost electricity production in the Third Front. In June 1970, the ministry inaugurated the campaign by denouncing as "traitors" pre-Cultural Revolution personnel who had promoted a "counterrevolutionary revisionist line" and imposed a "dictatorship of foreign tenets" on China's power sector. They had gone against Maoist developmental methods and "suppressed the masses," advocated slow growth rates, and believed that "without technology it is impossible to get anything done." The power sector had now to take up "our country's … high-speed developmental way" and double electrical output by 1972. This "new great leap forward" could be realized by acting on Maoist principles, "rousing the enthusiasm" of the masses, and "making the most out of [domestic] potential."[141]

The largest electricity project that the ministry pursued at the time was a dam in the Three Gorges region of the Yangzi river. In March 1969, governor of Hubei province Zhang Tixue put forward the idea of building the Three Gorges Dam to the vice heads of the Ministry of Water Resources and Power, Qian Zhengying and Wang Yingxian. Qian and Wang endorsed Zhang's proposal, much to his delight. On a visit to Hubei in May, Mao met with Zhang and discussed the Three Gorges Dam. Mao poured cold water on Zhang's enthusiasm. With Sino-Soviet tensions intensifying, Mao thought, "Right now is a time to prepare for war. It is inadvisable to consider this … If a basin of water fell on your head, would you be scared?"[142]

Not deterred, Zhang looked for other options. A member of the Yangzi Commission suggested the Gezhouba Dam. Like the Three Gorges Dam, it would churn out mammoth amounts of energy, but it was a low dam, and so the consequences of its bombing would be less disastrous than the elimination of the Three Gorges high dam. Hubei leaders quickly composed a report and proposed to the Party center constructing Gezhouba in order to "speed up socialist construction and solve" the electricity demands "of Third Front construction in western Hunan, western Hubei, and eastern Sichuan."[143]

141 "Quanguo Dianli gongye zengchan jieyue huiyi jiyao," June 21, 1970, in *Xin zhongguo dianli gongye fazhan shilue*, ed. Li Daigeng (Beijing: Qiye guanli chubanshe, 1984), 201, 203.

142 Zhonggong zhongyang dangshi yanjiu shi Zhonggong Hubei sheng Yichang shi weiyuanhui, Zhonggong Hubei shengwei dangshi yanjiushi, *Zhongguo gongchandang yu Changjiang sanxia gongcheng* (Beijing: Zhonggong dangshi chubanshe, 2007), 12.

143 Wuhan junqu Hubei sheng geming weiyuanhui, "Guanyu Xingjian Yichang Changjiang Gezhouba shuili shuniu gongcheng de qingshi baogao," October 30, 1970, in *Sanxia gongcheng shiliao xuanbian 1918–2015*, ed. Sanxia gongcheng shiliao xuanbian bianzuan weiyuanhui (Wuhan: Sanxia gongcheng shiliao xuanbian bianzuan weiyuanhui, 2015), 217.

Zhou Enlai arranged to talk about the Three Gorges project at a national planning meeting in February 1970. Cultural Revolution struggles had landed the former head of the Yangzi River Commission Lin Yishan in an informal prison in Wuhan. Wanting to know his opinion, Zhou had Hubei military leaders secure his release. At the meeting, Lin learned to his great surprise that Zhang Tixue and other Hubei officials were pushing to build the Three Gorges Dam while Mao was still alive even though designs and construction plans were still not fully fleshed out.[144] In October 1970, Hubei leaders reported their ideas to the State Council. During the meeting, Zhang Tixue made a military pledge to Zhou Enlai and other Party leaders present. "If there was a problem with the Gezhouba Dam, then take my head and hang it from Tiananmen."[145]

Despite his apparent ardor for Gezhouba, Zhang still preferred the Three Gorges Dam, and so he visited Mao in December. Mao started out by chastising Zhang for hurting so many with his past failed dams.[146] He then tempered his criticism and said that on the other hand, Zhang did have experience and his partner – commander of the Wuhan Military Region Zeng Siyu – was not bad at fighting battles. And yet, Mao still wondered whether they were ready for the Yangzi river's first dam. Zhang responded with a famous Mao quote in which he praised learning by doing. Mao complimented him for having guts.

Zhang then discussed how a decade of preparations had already occurred, and how the dam would realize Mao's 1956 poem "Swimming," in which he mused that one day "walls of stone will stand upstream . . . to hold back . . . the clouds and rain till a smooth lake rises in the narrow gorges," a feat which would cause the legendary goddess of the Three Gorges "to marvel at a world so changed."[147] Mao was not swayed and rejected their proposal because they did not have adequate funds, designs, scientific information, or construction plans. Also, if an atomic bomb hit the Three Gorges Dam, it could cause flooding all the way to Shanghai. At that point, Zhang began pressing his case for the Gezhouba Dam, stating that he had brought experts to Gezhouba to research it, and

144 Hubei sheng weiyuanhui xuexi wenshi ziliao weiyuanhui, *Hubei sheng wenshi ziliao, Volume 42* (Wuhan: Hubei sheng chubanshe, 1993), 32.

145 Zhonggong zhongyang dangshi yanjiu shi, *Zhongguo gongchandang yu changjiang*, 12.

146 Mao was probably referring to the Danjiangkou Dam, the construction of which was directed by Zhang Tixue during the Great Leap, and which yielded many problems. Wei Tingjing, "Hanjiang Danjiangkou shuili shuniu gongcheng guihua sheji zhong ruogan zhongda wenti de huigu," in *Hubei wenshi ziliao zong, Volume 41*, ed. Hubei sheng weiyuanhui xuexi wenshi ziliao weiyuanhui (Wuhan: Hubei renmin chubanshe, 1992), 31–35.

147 Mao Zedong, "Swimming," 1956, *Marxists Internet Archive*, www.marxists.org/reference/archive/mao/selected-works/poems/poems23.htm, accessed 27 March 2017.

they were ready to move ahead. Mao gave permission and told them to talk with Zhou Enlai and co-operate with the relevant ministries.[148]

Meanwhile, Zhou Enlai asked director of the Yangzi River Commission Lin Yishan to draw up a position paper in which he assessed the Three Gorges and Gezhouba dam proposals. In November 1970, the State Council held a meeting on the different options. Lin Yishan argued that the Three Gorges Dam should be built first because Gezhouba would cause the water level to rise twenty meters and make erecting the Three Gorges Dam more difficult and expensive.[149] There were also not adequate plans for Gezhouba. The Party's intention had always been to build the Three Gorges Dam, and so engineers had made designs. Only since 1969 had there been much work on Gezhouba, and these efforts had yet to yield formal designs. In spite of Lin's criticisms, the State Council provisionally approved the construction of Gezhouba.[150]

Zhou Enlai, however, thought Lin's position paper was "a powerful opinion," and so he submitted it to Mao along with the Gezhouba plan, his own letter, and a report which depicted Gezhouba as realizing the ideal immortalized in Mao's poem "Swimming." In addition, Gezhouba would fulfill electricity demand, stimulate river transport, and overcome Yangzi river floods. As a low dam, it posed less of a security challenge, and planning was based on a decade of geographic research and dam modeling experiments for the Three Gorges project, so the past twenty years of mistakes in dam building could be avoided, and adjustments could be made during construction.[151]

Mao read the Gezhouba file on his seventy-seventh birthday, December 26, 1970, and despite the fact that there were insufficient designs, he gave it his imprimatur with the caveat that later revisions should be made as appropriate.[152] The Party center distributed the Gezhouba file to central ministries and regional officials in Central China and told them to "mobilize the masses to wage a big people's war" to construct the Gezhouba Dam. Since such a large dam would be a prime target, the project's leaders had to develop "reliable measures" to prevent its destruction "from harming downstream areas." Designs for the dam had also to be made "on site within the next year and submitted ... to the Construction Commission to review and

148 Hubei sheng weiyuanhui, *Hubei sheng wenshi ziliao, Volume 42*, 10–17.
149 Zhonggong zhongyang dangshi yanjiu shi, *Zhongguo gongchandang yu changjiang*, 12.
150 Hubei sheng weiyuanhui, *Hubei sheng wenshi ziliao, Volume 42*, 20, 33–34, 54.
151 Hubei sheng weiyuanhui, *Hubei sheng wenshi ziliao di si shi er*, 4.
152 Hubei sheng weiyuanhui, *Hubei sheng wenshi ziliao di si shi er*, 34.

approve." If any problems occurred, they should be ready to "make adjustments."[153]

Hubei provincial leaders then made a choice that would mar the first attempt to build the Gezhouba Dam. They did not wait for designs to be finished to start building the dam. This decision set off of a tidal wave of activity, as the Central Military Commission sent in Unit 61 of the Infrastructure Corps, and the Hubei provincial government mobilized 100,000 militia members and implemented a policy known as "the three simultaneities" (*san bian*) in which survey, design, and construction work were carried out simultaneously. As work on the dam began, technicians expressed concern to Gezhouba's leadership about a lack of anti-silting plans. They also criticized project leaders for allowing workers to pour concrete without waiting for it to cool and stop expanding. Technical personnel warned that if nothing was done, the dam would eventually crack. Project leaders excoriated technical personnel as capitalist roaders who were betraying Maoist developmental methods.[154]

After a few months, Gezhouba rose above the Yangzi river. There was one big problem. Its innards were like a honeycomb because concrete had not cooled properly.[155] When Zhou Enlai learned about the situation, he convened a meeting with project leaders and yelled at them, "If the Yangzi river has troubles, this isn't just going to affect one person ... It's going to be a problem for the entire country and the entire Party." Zhou also censured Gezhouba's leaders for "not controlling the temperature" of concrete. Zhou admitted that the Party center had agreed to "start [the project] very quickly." But Mao had told them to alter designs if they had any problems. "Now we must revise designs ... We cannot wait any longer."[156] In 1974, after designs were completed, construction work started up again, and Gezhouba began to generate electricity in 1979.

Chinese historians regularly portray Zhou Enlai's involvement in the construction of the Gezhouba Dam as an example of his serving as a bulwark of reason against political extremists. According to this narrative, Zhou stood up to Hubei leaders who were building Gezhouba too

153 "Zhonggong zhongyang dui xingjian Gezhouba de pifu ji zhongyao pishi," December 25, 1970, in *Sanxia gongcheng shiliao xuanbian 1918–2015*, 221–222.

154 Hubei sheng weiyuanhui, *Hubei sheng wenshi ziliao, Volume 42*, 34, 75–79. "Zheng Zhen huiyi lu: Zai Gezhouba gongcheng zhihuibu," *China Gezhouba Group Company*, September 6, 2009, www.cggc.ceec.net.cn/art/2015/9/6/art_7369_388024.html, accessed June 7, 2017. Liu, *Zhongguo jiefangjun*, 348.

155 Hubei sheng weiyuanhui, *Hubei sheng wenshi ziliao, Volume 42*, 69.

156 "Zhou Enlai zai Gezhouba gongcheng jishu weiyuanhui shang de jianghua," November 8–21, 1972, in *Sanxia gongcheng shiliao xuanbian 1918–2015*, 237–238.

Figure 3.3 Building the Gezhouba Dam in 1970. Source: "Dujia Changjian le wanli changjiang di yi ba Gezhouba shuili shuniu gongcheng," China Energy Engineering Group Co., Ltd, February 28, 2014, group.ceec.net.cn/art/2014/2/28/art_738_13.html

fast, and in the process he prevented the dam from failing.[157] While this interpretation adds to Zhou's saintly image in China, it leaves out important information. As Gao Wenqian has illustrated in his biography of Zhou, his survival atop the Chinese party-state was due to his ability to sense which way the political winds were blowing and deflect criticism away from himself towards others.[158]

Zhou's involvement in the Gezhouba Dam corresponds with this larger trend. When Gezhouba developed structural problems, Zhou recognized he was partially at fault but placed blame mainly on Hubei leaders. Yet Zhou Enlai bore just as much responsibility for Gezhouba's issues as did people like Zhang Tixue. Zhang did not have the authority to start the Gezhouba Dam project. He had to gain Zhou's approval. Nor did Zhang

[157] See, for instance, Yang Xingzheng and Han Qijie, eds., *Yichang: Shuidian zhi du* (Wuhan: Hubei renmin chubanshe, 2005), 68. Zhonggong zhongyang dangshi yanjiu shi, *Zhongguo gongchandang yu changjiang*, 12–13.

[158] Gao Wenqian, *Zhou Enlai: The Last Perfect Revolutionary* (New York: Hachette, 2008).

decide on his own how quickly to build Gezhouba. It was Zhou, Mao, and other central Party leaders who authorized accelerating the Third Front campaign to meet pressing security concerns, and who endorsed labeling people in favor of decelerating building efforts as capitalist traitors.

Rushing Railroad Construction

In addition to rushing the building of the Gezhouba Dam, the Party center hastened the construction of railroads in the Third Front. Of utmost importance to the campaign was the completion of the Chengdu–Kunming Railroad. Factional conflicts were still raging in the region, and so Zhou Enlai summoned Sichuanese leaders to Beijing in November 1969 and told them to disband armed factions, attack counterrevolutionaries, and consolidate political control in revolutionary committees, so that they could supervise Third Front projects and "guarantee that Panzhihua Steel smelted iron, and that the whole line of the Chengdu–Kunming Railroad was connected by July 1, 1970."[159] This goal was accomplished by ordering a large infrastructure-building battle. The Metallurgy Ministry assigned 15,000 more people to Panzhihua, and the Southwest Railroad Construction Headquarters mustered 700,000 people to work on the Chengdu–Kunming Railroad.[160]

Another railroad project undertaken as part of the Third Front campaign was the Jiaozuo–Zhicheng Railroad linking Henan and Hubei provinces. In June 1969, Mao visited Wuhan and told the commander of the Wuhan Military Region, Zeng Siyu, to begin work on the line because the Soviet Union and the United States where sticking their hands into everything, and the CCP had no way of telling when they would start a war with China. At present, the Beijing–Guangzhou Railroad was the only line connecting China's north and south. If it was bombarded, rail traffic between the north and south would break down. So that this did not happen, the Party had to build the Jiaozuo–Zhicheng Railroad as quickly as possible.[161]

Zhou Enlai appointed as the head of the project assistant commanding officer of the Wuhan Military Area Kong Qingde. When Zhou asked him to direct the project, Kong replied that he did not "know how to build railroads." He only knew "how to tear railroads up" from his time fighting Japan and the GMD. When Zhou told Kong that Mao "would not sleep

159 Zhonggong Sichuan shengwei dangshi yanjiu shi, *Zhongguo gongchandang sichuan lishi*, 351–353. The quote is on page 353.
160 Chao Lihua, "Yunnan sanxian jianshe de lishi yanjiu," in *Zhongguo gongchandang yu sanxian*, 464. Chen, *Sanxian*, 205.
161 Qu and Zheng, *Yidai jiang xing*, 473.

well" until the Jiaozuo–Zhicheng Railroad was built because the line was key to China's national security, Kong swiftly agreed to oversee the project.[162] Drawing on Mao's thinking on how to handle difficult situations, Kong said he would learn from practice how to build a railroad. Kong then stood up, gave a military salute, and swore to Zhou Enlai, "I will definitely complete the mission you have given and let Chairman Mao sleep well."[163]

In mid-August, the Railroad Ministry convened a preparatory meeting in Beijing with the provincial leaders of Henan and Hubei. Attendees agreed that because of foreign military hostility they should shorten the construction time from the end of 1971 to the end of 1970. Kong Qingde argued for waging a huge people's war in which the majority of work was done by rural workers during the slack season between autumn planting and the spring harvest. His colleagues concurred and ordered construction to commence on November 1. This gave less than three months to plan a 753-kilometer railroad.[164]

Upon returning to Wuhan, Kong Qingde held a meeting with representatives from counties along the projected route of the Jiaozuo–Zhicheng Railroad. Kong informed them that the line was now going to be built and that a battle headquarters had been approved with him as the director. Each county had to establish sub-headquarters for each section of the railroad. Kong suggested mobilizing a million workers for a big people's war, like during the Chinese Civil War and the war against Japan. Some people questioned whether this was possible. During the Huaihai campaign in the Chinese Civil War, the Party only mustered 600,000 people. Kong maintained that it was necessary to break free from convention and quicken the pace of construction.[165] In the end, Kong, who was known to speak like a "cannon" (*dapao*), won the argument, and Henan and Hubei called up 1.15 million rural militia members to build the Jiaozuo–Zhicheng Railroad.[166] The Party center drew as well on technical forces from around the nation and dispatched 36,000 technicians employed by the Railroad Ministry in different parts of China.[167]

In conjunction with the Jiaozuo–Zhicheng Railroad, the Party center endorsed constructing three other interprovincial lines in central China – the Zhicheng–Liuzhou, Hunan–Guizhou, and Xiangfan–Chongqing

162 Yan Jianzi, ed., *Zhiliu qingchun zhiliu zhi ge* (Changsha: Hunan renmin chubanshe, 2013), 669–670.
163 Qu and Zheng, *Yidai jiang xing*, 474.
164 Zhonghua renmin gongheguo tiedaobu, *Tielu xiujian*, 60.
165 Qu and Zheng, *Yidai jiang xing*, 476–478.
166 Zhang Wei, "'Tiezui jiangjun': Kong Qingde de baisue rensheng," *Changchun shiwei dangxiao xuebao*, June 2015: 45–48.
167 Zhonghua renmin gongheguo tiedaobu, *Tielu xiujian*, 62.

Figure 3.4 Making baskets for workers on the Shaanxi Southern Railroad in the early 1970s. Source: "Xiujian Yang'an tielu," *Hanzhong shi dangan ju*, November 15, 2012, daj.hanzhong.gov.cn/nry2014.jsp?urltype=news.NewsContentUrl&wbnewsid=11726&wbtreeid=11311

railroads – along with the building of a railroad through southern Shaanxi. A total of roughly three million militia members took part in building these lines.[168] Every single railroad undertaken had a codename to hide its identity from outsiders due to its links with national defense. For instance, the headquarters that ran the Zhicheng–Liuzhou and Hunan–Guizhou railroads was called 920, while the sub-headquarters for the Guangxi section was named 9202, and the sub-headquarters for the Hunan section was number 9201.[169]

When militias reached their clandestine worksite, they came to a place which the Party had turned into the battlefield of a developmental proxy

[168] Zhang Xuejun, "Yi qu 'xiuliu lianren' de Zhuang ge," in *Zhiliu suiyue: Zhiliu tiejian Changsha fenzhi zhiqing tu wenji 1972–1975*, ed. Yan Jianzi (Changsha: Hunan renmin chubanshe, 2008), 13. Zhonghua renmin gongheguo tiedaobu, *Tielu xiujian*, 69.

[169] Li Boyang, "Xiangqian tielu da huizhan," in *Zhiliu qingchun zhiliu zhi ge*, 15. Chen Jianxiang, "Languang de tiejian zhi lu," in *Tie jian fengbei*, ed. Liu Weiyao (Beijing: Zhongguo wenshi chubanshe, 2006), 2.

war against China's Cold War enemies. All over the place construction troops were engaged in manual labor. They were laying roads, surveying mountains, and trudging through forests. The environment was also painted red with communist flags, and Party sayings were displayed everywhere. Some signs called on workers to "engage in a race against time with American imperialism, Soviet revisionism, and counterrevolutionaries." Other signs declared labor's determination to "build the railroad well, so that Chairman Mao can sleep well."[170] In practice, railroad workers paid more attention to speeding up construction than they did to quality control.

Construction brigades held regular study sessions which associated taking a more measured pace with disgraced Party leaders – Liu Shaoqi and Deng Xiaoping. According to Chairman Mao, Liu and Deng had "held up" Chinese economic development for "three years" after the Great Leap. This lost time had to "be taken back. Even finishing [the Third Front] one hour earlier would be better."[171] As a report from a militia regiment on the Jiaozuo–Zhicheng Railroad explained, workers could not follow the ideas of "the contemptible Liu [Shaoqi]," who had advocated taking a "step-by-step" approach to development and thought that "slow work leads to skilled work."[172] Laborers had to "stamp" Mao's ideas about Third Front construction into their "brains" and "struggle to make the most of every minute and every second" (*zhengfen duomiao*). Every worker had to "wake up before dawn ... and work energetically," so that socialist China could sooner "eradicate American imperialism and Soviet revisionism."

Militia members had also to remain vigilant. China's opponents were not only abroad. There were "traitors and fifth columnists" on the home front who did not adhere to Mao's idea that China should "break free from foreign frameworks and walk its own road to industrial development." Instead, they supported Liu Shaoqi's "comprador philosophy," which, like Soviet revisionism, prioritized technical expertise and industrial machinery in the developmental process. To ensure that China stayed on a Maoist path to socialist industrial modernity and relied on

[170] Deng Peng, "Tiejian jiqing suiyue," in *Tiejian fengbei*, 212. For an example of similar slogans being pasted at construction sites, see Fang Guangming, "Sanxian jianshe de shi," in *Sanxian chunqiu*, 249.

[171] The quote is from "Mao zhuxi dui sanxian jianshe de zhongyao zhishi" (undated). Ao Yaohuan, "Liang shang sanxian dang 'minbing': Xiaxiang shenghuo zhuiyi," *Jiu san xueshe Hunan sheng weiyuanhui*, http://hn93.gov.cn/shownews.asp?id=4222, accessed September 21, 2017.

[172] The quotes in the next three paragraphs are from Neixiang minbing tuan, "Mao zhuxi sanxian jianshe de guanghui zhishi shi jiaoshi huizhan de jingshen yuanzidan," in *Mao zhuxi renmin zhanzheng guanghui sixiang de shengli: Jiaozhi tielu huizhan Henan sheng zhihuibu di si minbing shi dianxing cailiao* (Nanyang: Jiaozhi tielu huizhan di si minbing shi zhenggoong zu, 1970), 17–19.

what resources they had at hand, the militia regiment struggled against turncoats in their own ranks.

Afterwards, when they were building the foundation for a bridge over a river, they did not consult designs, they just "began work immediately." When they were pouring concrete for the bridge's pillars, "they didn't make a model," they kept adding concrete. "When there weren't enough rubber shoes and gloves, everyone worked bare-handed and barefoot." When sandstone was lacking, project leaders launched a "people's war" in which workers continued "construction while hustling in materials and practicing self-reliance." It appears that being self-sufficient in this context meant using dirt in bridge pillars since workers had to fix a pillar that began to "collapse" due to dirt "falling down in pieces." Not fazed by construction problems, workers "recited Mao's directives on the Third Front," jumped into the ice-cold river, and repaired the pillar, even as their "hands became numb, feet froze, and clothes became sopping wet."

Figure 3.5 Female commandos haul rocks on the Shaanxi Southern Railroad in the early 1970s. Source: "Xiujian Yang'an tielu," *Hanzhong shi dangan ju*, November 15, 2012, daj.hanzhong.gov.cn/nry2014.jsp?urltype=news.NewsContentUrl&wbnewsid=11726&wbtreeid=11311

This incident was not an isolated one. Except for the Chengdu–Kunming Railroad, all Third Front railroads built between 1969 and 1971 had significant construction problems. This was just as true of the Hunan–Guizhou Railroad as it was the Zhicheng–Liuzhou and Jiaozuo–Zhicheng lines. All three projects were officially finished in the early 1970s. However, they were not fully operational until the late 1970s because project administrators cut corners in a dash to expand China's railroads before foreigners attacked. When people spoke up in favor of being less hurried and undertaking more extensive planning, they often ran into the same political response as did critics of the Gezhouba Dam. Their policy proposals were censured in line with Cultural Revolution discourse as being counterrevolutionary, and they were accused of aiding and abetting China's enemies in the global Cold War.[173] For the millions of workers recruited into the Third Front campaign, one principle of Maoist development deeply affected their everyday lives both before and after the Cultural Revolution began – the Party's assertion that the defense of Chinese socialism depended on putting rapid industrialization ahead of labor's livelihood.

[173] For the Zhicheng–Liuzhou Railroad, see, for instance, Li Boyang, "Xiangqian tielu da huizhan," in *Zhiliu qingchun zhiliu zhi ge*, 20. Luo Zisong, "Zhiliu tielu huizhan jishi," in *Zhiliu qingchun zhiliu zhi ge*, 421. Ding Yimou, "Zhiliu tiejian huigu," in *Zhiliu qingchun zhiliu zhi ge*, 386.

4 Produce First and Consume Later

As the first light of dawn creeped over the mountaintops, a group of men woke up in canvas tents along the muddy banks of the Jinsha river. Just a few days before, these men had opened their eyes to a very different situation. They had been residents of Chongqing, had jobs at the local steel plant, and lived in its apartment blocks. Then one day they were informed that Chairman Mao had decided that the mineral wealth of Panzhihua in southern Sichuan must be developed to ready China for a looming war with the United States or the Soviet Union. The Metallurgy Ministry had tasked Chongqing's steel factory with dispatching a team to collect iron samples for testing, and they had been selected to join the collection team. A short while after, they had set out to begin their new job assignment at the Third Front. When some of them awoke that morning in Panzhihua, they felt crestfallen that all they could see were barren mountains surrounding them on all sides. Others were eager to get to work on the many tasks that lay ahead.[1] No matter how people responded to being sent to Panzhihua, everyone knew what the CCP expected them to think and feel about living in a militarized industrial town.

Third Front recruits were supposed to see Panzhihua as a special place. Mao himself had ordered the city's creation, and he considered its founding so important that he told the central Party that until it was built he would "not sleep well a single day."[2] If central leaders "didn't build Panzhihua," then Mao would "ride a donkey [there] and hold a meeting" to found it himself.[3] So that Chairman Mao could be at ease, and China could be militarily prepared for war with the United States or the Soviet Union, Third Front recruits had to "produce first and consume later" (*xian shengchan hou shenghuo*) and "work hard" (*jianku*

[1] Li Yujian, "Zai Panzhihua jianshe shang xia xia de yi mao renmen," in *Jianshe Panzhihua de ren*, ed. Zhonggong sichuan shengwei dangshi gongzuo weiyuanhui (Chengdu: Chengdu keji daxue chubanshe, 1987), 87–89, 96.

[2] Mao Zedong, "Dui 'sanwu' guihua de zhishi," August 1964, in *Panzhihua kaifa*, 7.

[3] Zheng Sheng, *Zhanlüe tiaozheng: Sanxian jianshe juece yu sheji gongcheng* (Changchun: Jilin chubanshe jituan youxian zeren gongsi, 2010), 62.

fendou) to industrialize the interior.[4] Regardless of what personal hardships people experienced, they had to defer consumption and familial considerations and concentrate on raising industrial production. It was a matter of national security that Third Fronters kept their priorities in line with the CCP's, since foreign enemies were at China's gates, and they could break them down at any moment.

Vice director of the Planning Commission Bo Yibo explained in very concrete terms what prioritizing production meant when he consulted with Panzhihua leaders in October 1964. Bo maintained that giving precedence to production did not mean undertaking policies similar to the Great Leap in which many people did not have "grain to eat." The Party "must not make this mistake again."[5] Yet the CCP must also not make the mistake of modeling itself after its Cold War enemy – the Soviet Union – and construct "multistory buildings ... cultural areas ... and service areas." China should emulate the Maoist way of building socialism developed at the Daqing oilfield and enforce a regime of austerity, so that more resources could go into heavy industry. Director of the Planning Commission Li Fuchun stated in even plainer Chinese what material life at Panzhihua was supposed to be like – "dig a hole for a toilet," and "all that are needed" for housing are "canvas tents." Historian of the Daqing oilfield Hou Li has called the resultant style of urban formation "industrialization without urbanization."[6]

In this chapter, I engage in an intensive investigation of everyday life in Panzhihua and how people experienced basic human activities, such as eating, working, and making families. I show that some people viewed life in Panzhihua in ways that were not in tune with Maoist expectations. Although urban recruits understood that as employees of state-owned enterprises they were privileged compared to many people in China, they still wished they could move to someplace higher up in socialist China's hierarchy of urban places. Many also looked forward to their next annual leave when they could see family faraway while hoping even more that they would one day be permanently reunited in a better-off city. In the meantime, parents tried to ensure that children had a better life than their own. Rural recruits pined as well for the day when the CCP did not require them to think of serving socialism first and being concerned with family matters as a distant second. On the other hand, rural recruits

4 Guowuyuan, *Sanxian*, 228. Interview with manager of China Construction Bank, November 2012.

5 The quotes in this paragraph are from Panzhihua linshi gonzuo zu, "Li Fuchun, Bo Yibo tongzhi 1964 nian 11 yue 1 ri zai renhe tingqu Panzhihua ge jianshe zu huibao shi de jianghua jiyao," November 2, 1964, in *Panzhihua kaifa*, 17–18.

6 Hou, *Building for Oil*, 4, 94.

saw a permanent job in a Panzhihua state-owned enterprise as a socioeconomic elevator up into China's urban stratum.

Despite these divergences from Maoist norms, Maoist standards still significantly shaped the daily affairs of people involved in Panzhihua's construction because the Party ran the city in accordance with them. Central ministries directed flows of resources towards activities related to production and restricted investment in consumption. Some people were discontent with the resultant asperity of the quotidian in Panzhihua but still worked long hours and took pride in advancing China's industrialization. Other people did not take issue with material scarcity and gauged personal difficulties to be part of placing the good of the collective above that of the individual. Yet even the most ardent Maoists complained that living in Panzhihua was boring because there was very little to do but work.

Party officials commended people who aligned their conduct with the dictates of the Maoist state. The government, however, never praised Third Fronters nationally no matter how much they reproduced Maoist principles in their daily life, and how hard they worked to realize Party objectives. In this regard, the Third Front was distinctly different than other big industrial projects which the Communist Party routinely lionized in the press as signs that socialist industrial modernity was progressing in China. The government never showered public compliments on the Third Front because the central Party deemed its invisibility a necessary component of China's defense in the global Cold War.

Going to the Third Front

Central and provincial officials marshaled hundreds of thousands of people to build Panzhihua. To direct activities at Panzhihua Steel, the Metallurgy Ministry transferred around 40,000 people from top steel enterprises in Wuhan, Chongqing, and Anshan, while Sichuan and Yunnan provinces shipped in around 20,000 young rural men to perform labor-intensive tasks.[7] Leading coal companies from Fushun, Benxi, and Fuxin were charged with heading up local mines, and tens of thousands of young rural males manned their front lines.[8] The PLA dispatched the Railroad Corps Fifth Division to lay railroads and the

[7] Panzhihua gangtie jituan gongsi, *Pangang zhi, 1964–1986* (Beijing: Kexue chubanshe, 1994), 55, 258.

[8] Zhonggong Panzhihua shi dangshi yanjiushi, ed., *Panzhihua kaifa jianshe shi wenxian ziliao xuanbian* (Panzhihua: Zhonggong Panzhihhua shiwei dangshi yanjiushi bian, 2000), 451–460, 482–491, 493–494, 498–501.

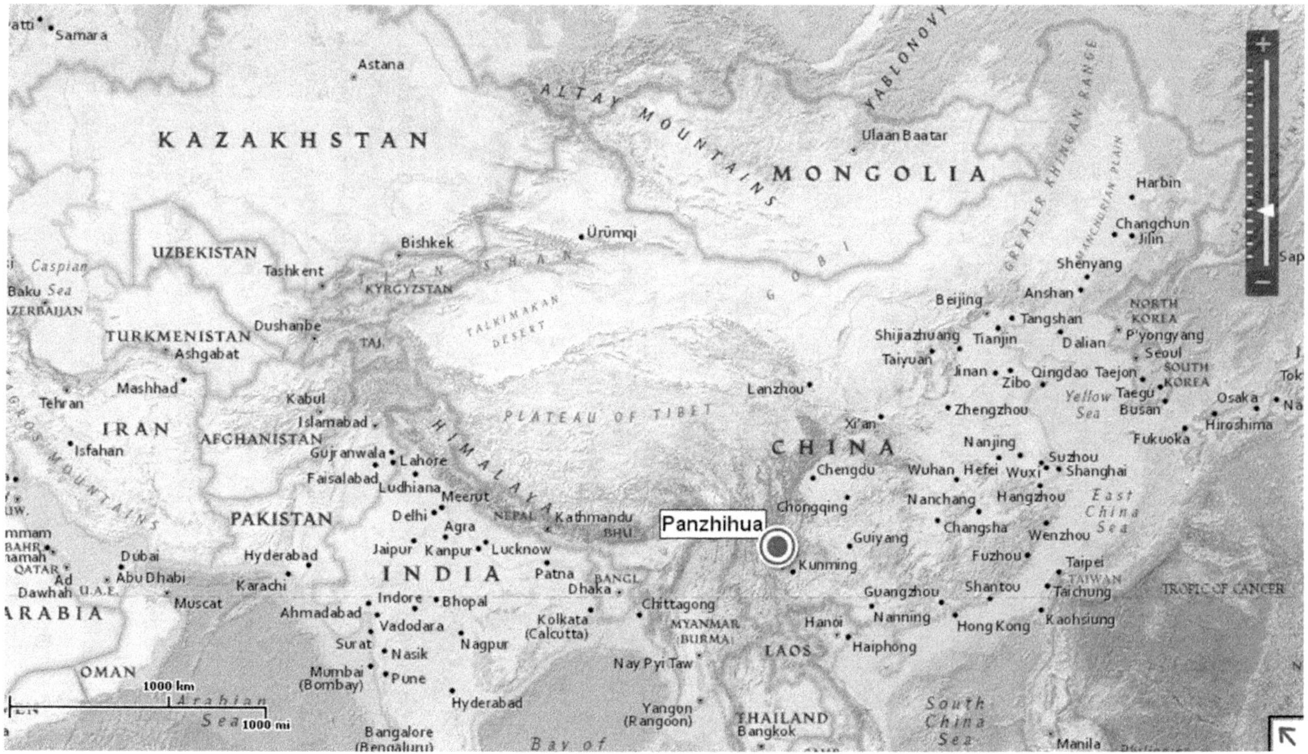

Map 4.1 Map showing the location of Panzhihua in China

Infrastructure Corps Unit 851 to build roads.[9] To handle social services, Chengdu, Kunming, and Chongqing reassigned people to work units in Panzhihua.[10]

People sent to build Panzhihua remember the experience vividly. Almost everyone can recollect the exact month, if not the precise day, when they "entered Panzhihua."[11] If someone was from a nearby village or small town, then they marched with other recruits over mountains into Panzhihua, or they took a short ride in a truck. Their trip rarely lasted more than a day.[12] For people from large cities along the coast and in the northeast, coming to Panzhihua was a long-drawn-out process which made them deeply aware how far into the hinterlands the Party was sending them. They were used to working at "big enterprises" and living in cities that had running water, "flat roads, high-rises, electric lights, telephones," movie theaters, and performance centers.[13] When they moved to Panzhihua, they had to leave all of these modern amenities behind.

Recruits first had to travel a day and half by train to Kunming or Chengdu, where Panzhihua officials had set up relay stations charged with shuttling in supplies of people and other resources.[14] Once people arrived in Chengdu or Kunming, their mode of transportation changed. Since the Chengdu–Kunming Railroad had not yet been built, recruits packed into the back of Liberation trucks and took either a three-day ride from Kunming or a five-day ride from Chengdu, as in Figure 4.1. Their journey was made even more harrowing by the fact that they were sometimes so crammed into a truck bed that they were forced to stand for hours as their truck bobbed along rugged roads.[15]

As people ascended into the towering mountains of southern Sichuan, many passengers first stared at their surroundings in awe. They had always lived on China's plains, and they had never seen such high peaks. After a day of driving on steep alpine roads, their awe frequently morphed into shock. Many had never slept outside, and so the impromptu campsites

[9] Liu, *Zhongguo jiefangjun*, 381–383. Tiedaobing shanhou, *Tiedao bing jianshi*, 160–161.
[10] Zheng Xucai, "Panzhihua shi chuqi de shangye huigu," in *Liu zai da liegu*, 229–235. Wang Shilin, "Panzhihua chuqi liangshi gongzuo de huigu," in *Liu zai da liegu*, 340–344.
[11] Ma Guoguang, "Tieren shi de shijia yuan: Hu Yanguang," in *Jianshe Panzhihua*, 176.
[12] Interview with woman from Huaping county, December 2012. Interview with woman from Miyi county, December 2012.
[13] Li Yujian, "Zai Panzhihua jianshe shang xia xia de yi mao renmen," in *Jianshe Panzhihua*, 92.
[14] Yejin gongye bu, "Guanyu chengli Chengdu, Guiyang, Kunming zhuanzhan de tongzhi," April 15, 1964, in *Panzhihua kaifa*, 842.
[15] Interview with Peking University graduate, Panzhihua, December 2012.

Figure 4.1 A Liberation truck transporting labor to the Third Front. Source: Zhang Quanjing, "Mao Zedong yu sanxian jianshe: yi ge weida de zhanlue juece," *Shijie shehui zhuyi yanjiu* 1 (2016), www.cwzg.cn/history/201808/43717.html

they pitched nightly along dusty roadsides only heightened their sense of how far into the middle of nowhere the Communist Party was sending them, perhaps for the rest of their lives. Their daily diet of rice porridge, usually accompanied with no more than seaweed or pickled vegetables, further lessened their taste for moving to the Third Front.[16]

One of the first people to go to Panzhihua was vice director of the Southwest Third Front Commission Cheng Zihua. In his memoirs, Cheng recalls thinking that Panzhihua's "lofty mountains and steep hills" were an "ideal" location for "a strategic rear" because "enemy infantry couldn't reach there," and "Airplanes would have difficulties bombarding it."[17] The first time Cheng went to Panzhihua in mid-1964, there were only eight households. Cheng asked a local man about conditions in the area. He replied that food and clothing were scarce. It was hot and dry all year, and local residents often drank muddy water from the Jinsha river. It was impossible to raise animals because wild

[16] Interview with Peking University graduate, Panzhihua, December 2012.
[17] Cheng, *Cheng Zihua huiyi*, 426.

wolves ate them. A wolf had even on one occasion seized a young boy, and almost dragged him into the mountains. Luckily, local residents had beaten back the wolf, and the boy was saved.

When Cheng's guide told him that, according to local rumors, there were tigers in the area, Cheng declared, "What is there to be scared of? Isn't waging war dangerous? Isn't it best to still rush ahead?" Nonetheless, Cheng still had his team carry a submachine gun in case they stumbled on a tiger.[18] Another survey team was paralyzed with dread when they came across a leopard during a trek through the mountains.[19] The animal that most people feared running into was the wolf.[20] Another cause of anxiety among early recruits was traversing the Jinsha river. Cheng Zihua made an example of how people ought to address this worry when a group of thirteen vice ministers came to Panzhihua. Some vice ministers were against the idea of crossing the river by boat because some vessels had recently capsized, but Cheng convinced the group to hop aboard.[21]

Early recruits were also distressed about the presence of nearly 700 lepers in the area. Locals told recruits that if a chicken ate the spit of a leper, and a human consumed that chicken's eggs, then they could contract leprosy. To dispel these rumors, Cheng Zihua telephoned the minister of health, who promptly sent medical experts to explain that the rumors had no scientific basis.[22] Perhaps because worries about leprosy were not quelled, Panzhihua officials decided to relocate all lepers to a special hospice outside the area.[23]

In addition to fears of wild animals and disease, new arrivals in Panzhihua were disturbed by the mammoth task ahead of them. Some recruits from a Changsha design institute were at a loss as to how they were going to complete the "honorable mission" the Party had given them of designing local iron mines. They were fresh out of school and "didn't have enough experience" to design a "large complex mine according to a tight schedule and high standards."[24] A Tongji University graduate also felt intense dismay when he first set foot in Panzhihua. Before coming, he had heard that Panzhihua was a Third Front project and that talented

18 Dan, "Sui Cheng Zihua," 16–17.

19 Wumingde and Pang Zaiyuan, "Shenjing de shiming," in *Jianshe Panzhihua*, 236.

20 Zhang Chun, "Zhengjiu tehu bing de hao yisheng," in *Jianshe Panzhihua*, 210.

21 "Cheng Zihua tongzhi tan zhongyang guanyu jianshe Panzhihua de youguan qingkuang," in *Panzhihua Wenshi ziliao di 7 qi*, 72.

22 Cheng, *Cheng Zihua huiyi*, 415.

23 "Panzhihua gongye jidi yiyuan sheji renwu shu he ji ge juti wenti de jianyi," September 25, 1964, in *Panzhihua kaifa*, 536. Zhang Chun, "Zhengjiu tehu bing de hao yisheng," in *Jianshe Panzhihua*, 212.

24 Changsha heise jinshu kuangshan sheji yuan zhengzhi bu, "Wei geming er sheji," December 18, 1965, Sichuan Provincial Archive, p. 2.

people were in short supply. His parents and friends had tried to convince him to stay in Shanghai, but he insisted on going and "making a career for himself."

Conditions in Panzhihua "were far worse" than he "had imagined." There were just desolate, isolated mountains, and everyone lived in canvas tents. Determined to keep a positive outlook, he told himself that Panzhihua "had ample room to show his abilities."[25] A worker sent to help build local mines maintained a similar attitude. He had lived his whole life on China's plains and found it difficult to adjust to the local alpine climate. The air was dry and thin and made it challenging for him to breathe. Yet he did not let despair consume him. Hardships only made him more determined to overcome them.[26]

Work Is Struggle

One special group that went to Panzhihua was central Party leaders.[27] Unlike other Third Front participants, they did not have to take a truck ride for several days to reach Panzhihua. Due to their political status and power, they could requisition one of China's few airplanes and fly over the bumpy mountain road leading to Panzhihua all the way to the nearby town of Xichang. Unlike other people involved in the Third Front, central Party leaders only stayed in Panzhihua for at most a few days before boarding another plane out of town. During their brief time in Panzhihua, top leaders checked on the city's progress and issued directives about how to push forward its construction.

In late October 1964, Bo Yibo and Li Fuchun took a plane to Panzhihua to consult with its lead planning group. At that time, it was still not possible to reach Panzhihua by car, and so Bo and Li hazarded a boat trip across the rapids of the Jinsha river. Bo and Li then did what Mao threatened he would do a few months earlier if the Party leadership did not build Panzhihua: they rode donkeys around and held meetings.[28] Knowing that constructing Panzhihua would require much equipment,

[25] Wang Jimin, "Jiaota shidi Yong pan gaofeng," in *Jianshe Panzhihua*, 334–335.

[26] Han Tiesuo, "Ba xinxie qing zhu zai jianzhu ye shang," in *Jianshe Panzhihua*, 270.

[27] "Dang he guojia lingdao ren shicha Panzhihua jianjie," in *Panzhihua Wenshi ziliao di 7 qi*, ed. Panzhihua shi zhengxie wenshi ziliao wenyuanhui (Panzhihua: Panzhihua shi danganju, 1992), 1–2. "Xu Chi wang yejin bu lingdao bing dangwei huibao Deng Xiaoping deng lingdao tongzhi dao Xichang, Panzhihua jiancha gongzuo shi de zhishi," December 19, 1965, in *Panzhihua kaifa*, 12. Well-known visitors included Deng Xiaoping, Peng Zhen, He Long, Peng Dehuai, Guo Moruo, Chen Boda, Li Fuchun, Bo Yibo, Yu Qiuli, and Gu Mu.

[28] "Cheng Zihua tongzhi tan zhongyang 'guanyu jianshe Panzhihua de youguan qingkuang'," in *Panzhihua Wenshi ziliao di 7 qi*, 70–71.

Bo told local leaders to get in touch with him if they lacked any supplies. Workers could not just rely on their own bodies in construction battles, or, as Bo said in the militarized language of the day, "guerillas could not only have long spears and big knives. They had to have some small arms."[29]

Bo Yibo and Li Fuchun also stressed that there had to be a centralized group that directed wars of annihilation to construct the various pieces of the city.[30] Local leaders followed Bo and Li's instructions and organized battle after battle to build Panzhihua. Laborers' efforts were focused on completing three large missions – producing iron, steel, and steel products. In order to achieve these long-term goals, the Party first ordered labor to open up local coal and iron mines, construct a power plant and a cement factory, lay roads and railroads, and build mud huts for residences.[31] In line with the CCP's policy of giving production top billing, all but one of these aims was tied to building industrial infrastructure. Only the order to make mud huts was related to living arrangements. Yet even this policy was designed to reduce investment in non-production-related activities.

For Panzhihua to be productive, it had to acquire a road network that connected local mines and factories. The Panzhihua government began a battle to achieve that planning goal in January 1965 and assigned leading cadres the role of battle commander. They "went on site and drove [lower ranking] cadres to … distribute drinking water, handout food, give out tools and building materials … divvy up labor assignments, handle thought work, guarantee safety, check the quality [of construction work], and ensure the improvement of technical operations."[32]

Laborers on the "front line" became caught up in a whirlwind of work too. In some cases, no industrial equipment was present, and so cadres "relied completely on labor power to dig and fill in holes" in roads. One labor brigade, that had to "excavate a twelve-meter high boulder, lacked confidence in the beginning and quarreled … and dawdled on the job." To shore up worker confidence, the local Party branch organized a study session and had everyone talk about Chairman Mao's saying "What is work? Work is struggle." Propaganda workers also came up with the motivational slogan "Hardship is honorable. Tenaciousness is the path to victory." After this

[29] "Li Fuchun, Bo Yibo tongzhi 1964 nian 11 yue 1 ri zai renhe tingqu Panzhihua ge jianshe zu huibao shi de jianghua jiyao," November 2, 1964, in *Panzhihua kaifa*, 17.
[30] "Li Fuchun, Bo Yibo tongzhi 1964 nian 11 yue 1 ri zai renhe tingqu Panzhihua ge jianshe zu huibao shi de jianghua jiyao," November 2, 1964, in *Panzhihua kaifa*, 18.
[31] Zhonggong Panzhihua shiwei dangshi yanjiu shi, *Liu zai da liegu de jiyi (qingshao ban)*, 77.
[32] The quotes in this paragraph are from "Panzhihua diqu linshi gongzuozu jiaotong zu qingkuang jianbao," January 20, 1965, in *Panzhihua kaifa*, 686.

study session, workers "did not leave the front line" for the next two days. To encourage labor, local leaders "went all-out with . . . propaganda encouragement work." Propaganda teams went around the construction site with megaphones and "praised good workers and good deeds ... generated congratulatory letters, and bulletins of good news." Cultural troupes staged performances at building sites and played "flower drum songs and rhythmic comic talk accompanied by bamboo clappers" about the progress of local construction work.[33]

Vice premier Peng Zhen came in February 1966 to see the victories of the construction battles that workers were fighting and give advice on how to press forward. Knowing that it was common for people to be told to make nearly every single second of the day into work time, Peng cautioned local leaders that people "cannot always work. You must pay attention to balancing sleep and work. They must be allowed to sleep eight hours."[34] The following day, as pictured in Figure 4.2, Peng met for dinner with labor models who drove industrial equipment up narrow mountain roads into Panzhihua. The irony was that their habit of "not sleeping and eating" in order to accomplish deliveries quickly exemplified the will to ceaseless work that Peng had just cautioned against.[35] While the drivers that Peng Zhen had a meal with had finished their delivery runs in record times, 141 people engaged in their line of work died between 1966 and 1969 when their truck either flipped or fell off a cliff.[36]

During Peng's dinner with local truck drivers, he praised their work ethic and said that "the battle" in Panzhihua

> was very important for the entire national economy and changing the layout of the whole country. What you are doing here is a victory for preparatory work to defeat American imperialism and a victory for preparing to fight [Soviet] revisionism. You are contributing to the socialist construction of our motherland.

The local press paid more attention to Peng's praise for people speeding up economic development than to his reminder that workers needed to get enough sleep, stating in a news article that Peng's visit had emboldened workers to "use the greatest determination, the fastest pace . . . and

[33] Wu Xuechang, "Panzhihua jianshe chuqi gonghui huodong he gongren yundong de huigu," in *Panzhihua gongren yundong shiliao xuanbian*, ed. Panzhihua shi zong gonghui shiliao yanjiushi (Panzhihua: Panzhihua shi gong yun shi ziliao yanjiushi, 1991), 27.

[34] "Xhu Chi guanyu Peng Zhen deng dao Panzhihua shicha de qingkuang baogao," June 19, 1966, in *Panzhihua kaifa*, 25.

[35] Zhonggong Panzhihua shiwei dangshi yanjiu shi, *Liu zai da liegu de jiyi (qingshao nian ban)*, 84.

[36] Xie Xinhua, "Gaoyuan zhi lu," in *Tiedaobing bu liao qing*, ed. Song Shaoming (Beijing: Jiefangjun wenyi chubanshe, 2002), 387–388.

Figure 4.2 Peng Zhen dines with local workers in 1966. Source: "Panzhihua lao zhaopian," *Panzhihua yishu zaixian*, http://pzhsyol.com/col.jsp?id=149

the lowest cost to ... exceed assigned quotas and complete the mission Chairman Mao has given us."[37]

At the time of Peng Zhen's visit, Panzhihua was in the midst of a big battle involving 80,000 people to construct basic infrastructure.[38] A summative report in late 1966 updated the Party center on recent developments. According to the report, the city council held an "all-out-war oath-swearing ceremony" attended by 10,000 people to stimulate

[37] "Qinqie de guanhuai, juda de guwu Peng Zhen tongzhi dao wo shi shicha jiejian jiu ge wu ha jiti biaobing daibiao he ba chuangjiang, liu jin hua," March 3, 1966, in *Panzhihua kaifa*, 26.

[38] Zhonggong Panzhihua shiwei dangshi yanjiu shi, *Liu zai da liegu de jiyi (qingshao nian ban)*, 77.

labor enthusiasm.[39] At the ceremony, city leaders laid out the operational plan for building Panzhihua, divided local labor into different groups, and ordered them to compete against each other to complete certain tasks within a given timeframe. After finishing a task, work units held meetings in which more productive laborers were praised for their hard work. Afterwards, another labor competition was started to accomplish another work task.

To further enhance worker morale, city officials instructed construction teams to "educate all laborers about war-preparedness" and instill in them a "deep animosity towards American imperialism." Like their compatriots in other parts of China, laborers were encouraged to always carry their copy of the *Quotations of Chairman Mao*, so that if they encountered problems at work, they could consult it, "militarize themselves," and figure out a way ahead.[40] If a worker for some reason did not have a copy of the *Quotations*, local leaders made sure that they could still read Mao's ideas throughout the day. Mao quotes were written on blackboards at work sites and living areas, so that whenever a laborer "lifts their head they see a quote" that boosts their determination to "always forge ahead."

Housing, Food, and Cultural Activities

While Panzhihua officials gave much thought to assuring that laborers were immersed in Mao's writings, they devoted very little attention to worker housing. This was in stark contrast to items linked with production. Detailed plans were drawn up for developing local mines, factories, railroads, roads, forests, banking, and communication networks. Residential areas, on the other hand, scarcely appear in available planning documents. There are just a few comments about the size of the labor force, the amount of living space they would require, and anticipated costs.[41] The Panzhihua government, however, never made an overall plan for residential areas, and so housing was scattered all over the place.[42]

[39] The quotes in the next two paragraphs are from Panzhihua tequ dangwei, "Panzhihua jidi jianshe da huizhan 1966 nian shang ban nian gongzuo baogao," July 20, 1966, in *Panzhihua kaifa*, 610–612.

[40] On the constant carrying of the *Quotations* in other parts of China, see Leese, *Mao Cult*, 211–212.

[41] Panzhihua diaocha gongzuo zu jianshe buju zu, "Panzhihua diqu gongye jianshe buju de guihua fangan," August 12, 1964, in *Panzhihua kaifa*, 494–496. Panzhihua tequ dangwei, "Guanyu Panzhihua deqi minyong jianzhu biaozhun caoan de qingshi," June 24, 1965, in *Panzhihua kaifa*, 602–603.

[42] Yejin gongye bu Panzhihua gangtie gongsi, *Pangang shengchan jiansheshi* (Panzhihua: Yejin gongye bu Panzhihua gangtie gongsi, 1983), 31.

Although Panzhihua's leaders did not provide a clear road map for local housing development, they did stipulate what sort of housing work units were allowed. All residences had to implement the rammed-earth spirit of the Daqing oilfield. According to this policy, workers were supposed to either live in canvas tents (as in Figure 4.3) or gather local dirt and make it into mud huts, like labor had at Daqing. The local newspaper maintained that this housing policy was beneficial because it enabled the city government to "take limited investment funds, building materials, transport capacity, and building power and concentrate them on production-related construction." With fewer resources going into housing, "the speed of building could be greatly increased, and China could seize the initiative and win its struggle for time with [American] imperialism and [Soviet] revisionism."

Figure 4.3 Canvas tent lodging in Panzhihua. Source: "Panzhihua lao zhaopian," *Panzhihua yishu zaixian*, http://pzhsyol.com/col.jsp?id=149

Workers came up with a more hard-knocks "jingle" (*shun kou liu*) to sum up the stern existence that resulted from the Party repressing consumption for the sake of accelerating Third Front construction. "During the daytime, steel bars press down on our shoulders, and at night, we press down on hard beds."[43] From dawn to dusk, workers carried heavy loads around construction sites, frequently suffering nosebleeds precipitated by the hot and arid local atmosphere. After work, they retired to mud huts or canvas tents where they slept on wooden beds or handwoven mats.[44]

Some tents and rammed-earth structures were small and only housed a few people. Others accommodated dozens of workers. Most residences were arranged like barracks and had only rows of beds. Some dwellings had tables and chairs for performing office work. Yet even top industrial designers lived in tents and slept in bunk beds. In their tents, there was no real division between workspace and living space. The two blurred together as rows of desks were crammed into the middle of the room while bunk beds were squashed right behind them along tent walls. Some workers did not have a desk in the center of the tent, and so they stuffed small wooden desks onto their bunks.[45]

Most people preferred living in mud huts over tents, not because they were any less cramped, but because they were cool in the summer and warm in the winter, whereas tents were the exact opposite. They had terrible ventilation and frequently smelled rank.[46] The last condition was in part because Panzhihua initially had no running water, so people fetched water from the river in a basin and filtered out silt with alum. Many workers suffered diarrhea and contracted hepatitis from drinking dirty water.[47] Due to the river's rapids, bathing in it was not safe. Some people still tried and drowned. Most people went for the less risky option of collecting water in a basin and washing off in front of their residence.[48]

Gradually, work units laid pipes from the river up the mountainside, set up public faucets, and pitched tents for showers. The city also built a water-processing plant in 1966 along with two power stations. Factories and mines had priority access. Only some residences obtained filtered water and electricity. Other people had to still gather water from

43 Feng Hua, "Ni cong liegu zoulai," *Zhongguo shijiu ye jituan youxian gongsi*, June 7, 2016, www.19mcc.com.cn/Sinfo.aspx?t=23&ContentId=3739, accessed June 13, 2017.
44 Zeng, *Jianshe houfang*, 25. Han Tiesuo, "Ba xinxie qing zhu zai jianzhu ye shang," in *Jianshe Panzhihua*, 269–270.
45 Yejin gongye bu Panzhihua, *Pangang shengchan*, 23, 50.
46 Interview with Peking University graduate, Panzhihua, November 2012.
47 Zeng, *Jianshe houfang*, 25.
48 Interview with local historian, Panzhihua, November 2012.

the Jinsha river or small streams.[49] Even if someone lived in a building with running water and electricity, water and power outages were still frequent occurrences, and workers still had to mix water with alum in the rainy season when the river became packed with sludge.[50]

Obtaining water was especially an issue for the many workers who were assigned to complete tasks, such as road construction or digging a mining shaft, in areas far from any water source. This is why workers referred to a water bottle as one of the "four treasures" that they always brought with them wherever they went. The other three precious items were a towel to wash up, a straw hat to block out the sun, and a walking stick for long hikes in the mountains to existing construction sites and to survey the locations of future ones.[51]

Survey teams regularly carried their own food. One team assigned to collect iron samples at a mine ran out of water on a trek in the blistering heat. Their throats were parched. Their lips had been scorched to cracking. Their noses were bleeding, and all they had to eat was old dry *mantou*. The leader of the group fought back tears and said that they must get over hardships like he had in the People's Volunteer Army during the Korean War at the Battle of Triangle Hill in which China had prevented American troops from advancing but at the cost of an estimated 19,000 lives.[52]

Work units with fixed locations set up makeshift kitchens in which, as a popular "ditty" (*shun kou liu*) stated, "Three rocks held up a pot." Since the Party sought to keep labor engaged in productive activities, cooking staff often brought meals to construction sites. Only when projects were nearing completion did work units typically build designated eating areas. Even then many workers ate standing up or squatting down since work units only gradually allotted funds for tables and wooden stools.[53]

Third Front administrators took several measures to supply Panzhihua with food. All work units were supposed to "carry forward the spirit of the Nanniwan" revolutionary base area in southern Shaanxi and "go into the mountains, reclaim land, grow vegetables, and raise pigs ... and chickens."[54] City officials also relocated villagers from the nearby town of Xichang to Panzhihua, drew up contracts with communes in the vicinity, and founded a grain and vegetable farm across the Jinsha river

49 Wang Du, "Ta ping kan ke cheng da dao: Fenzhan 'san tong yi ping' jian mie zhan," in *Liu zai da liegu*, 237–240.

50 Panzhihua gangtie, *Pangang zhi*, 520. 51 Dan, "Sui Cheng Zihua," 19.

52 Pangang lanjian tiekuang xuanchuan ke, "Jianshe jianbing," in *Liu zai da liegu*, 196–197. Casualty statistics are from Walter G. Hermes, *Truce Tent and Fighting Front* (Washington, DC: Center of Military History, United States Army, 1992), 318.

53 Panzhihua gangtie, *Pangang zhi*, 508–509, 511. Interview with steelworker, Panzhihua, November 2012.

54 Yejin gongye bu Panzhihua, *Pangang shengchan*, 51.

from Panzhihua Steel.[55] The Sichuanese provincial government additionally brought in a hundred vegetable-growing households from the Chengdu plain to plant high-yield grain seeds and educate locals about the best available agricultural techniques.[56]

Despite these special measures, local food output was still inadequate to provide for labor's nutritional needs, and so the bulk of the local diet had to come from far away. To deal with this and other supply issues, central planners formed a trucking company in 1964 out of transport work units from Anhui, Beijing, Shanghai, and Shandong. Central planners gave the company 1,500 trucks.[57] That might not sound like a lot. But all of Guangxi province had only 5,000 trucks in 1965 while Panzhihua was granted about a third of the same number for its own use.[58] Likely because 1,500 trucks were such a large order, work units supplying them delayed shipments, such that by the end of 1965 only 500 trucks had arrived in town.[59] Nonetheless, in the late 1960s, truck drivers still carried in 170,000 tons of equipment.[60]

In spite of the Party's efforts to furnish Panzhihua with food, fresh produce was still frequently lacking, and meat and fish were delicacies rarely enjoyed more than once a month. For the most part, people's diet consisted of coarse grains, dried seaweed, and pickled vegetables. Some urban recruits recalled with disgust having to endure this bland regimen for years.[61] Some people remembered sometimes being so famished after a long day's work that they scarfed down food.[62] Two men from the countryside said that they were not bothered by their sparse diet since they had become accustomed to the culinary austerity of rural life.[63]

One aspect of life in Panzhihua that was hard for laborers to adjust to was the absence of anything to do expect work. Some people came up with ditties to describe their daily routine. During the day, we "go to work and fight with rocks. After work, we walk along the road concerning

[55] Panzhihua diaocha gongzuo zu laodong zu, "Guanyu laodong gongzi guihua de chubu yijian," August 5, 1964, in *Panzhihua kaifa*, 491. "Panzhihua diqu gongye jianshe buju de guihua fangan," August 12, 1964, in *Panzhihua kaifa*, 495.

[56] Panzhihua gangtie, *Pangang zhi*, 506. [57] Panzhihua gangtie, *Pangang zhi*, 32.

[58] Guangxi zhuangzu zizhi qu difangzhi bianzuan weiyuanhui, *Guangxi sheng jiaotong zhi* (Nanning: Guangxi renmin chubanshe, 1993), 148.

[59] Panzhihua jianshe zhihui bu, "Guanyu jixu xiezhu wancheng Panzhihua gongye qu jianshe wuzi he shenghuowuzi de yunshu renwu de qingshi," December 26, 1965, in *Panzhihua kaifa*, 495.

[60] Gu, *Licheng*, 143.

[61] Interview with transportation construction worker, Panzhihua, November 2012. Interview with steelworker, November 2012.

[62] Han Guobin, *Jiannan de Pangang suiyue* (Panzhihua: Zhonggong Panzhihua shiwei dangshi yanjiu shi, 1995), 5. Interview with Ni Tongzheng, Shanghai, June 2018.

[63] Interview with coal miner, Panzhihua, November 2012. Interview with PLA construction worker, Panzhihua, December 2012.

ourselves with love affairs." Another expression was "During the daytime is a barrel of laughs. At night, we miss home." City officials were aware that many workers were homesick and discontented with the paucity of local cultural activities. To liven up life in Panzhihua, the city government expanded the number of cultural venues and events.

The city organized sports competitions, and laborers made ping-pong tables and basketball hoops. The city cultural bureau also quintupled the number of places where people could gather and listen to the radio to learn about local happenings as well as international and national affairs. The number of mobile film projection teams was increased as well, jumping from fifteen to sixty-eight. Every night projection teams went to a different part of town and held open-air showings. Screenings were so frequent that every night it was possible for someone to watch a film if they walked to a neighboring work unit. Some workers liked seeing movies so much that they watched three or four a week.[64]

In addition to increasing film showings, the city government recruited forty young people from high schools attached to performing-arts centers in Chengdu and formed them into the Panzhihua War Drum Cultural Troupe. The troupe was dispatched all over the city to give performances. It went to construction sites, agricultural fields, and the mouths of mine shafts. Since the troupe did not have its own truck, its members had to go on long mountain hikes, carrying all the way their instruments, costumes, props, clothes, and soap for cleaning up. Treks were particularly long to coal mines which were dozens of kilometers away. At construction sites, the cultural troupe also washed workers' laundry and mended their clothes.[65]

Some work units established their own cultural troupes. Their performance repertoire was similar to that of other local cultural troupes in the 1960s and 1970s.[66] On some occasions, troupes gave performances of nationally known songs, dance routines, and Jiang Qing's model operas. In other instances, troupes created songs and dances about local labor models, the completion of big projects, and the wonders of the rammed-earth spirit in local housing. So that locals did not have to wait for a performance to hear music, Panzhihua's cultural bureau established

[64] Wu Xuechang, "Panzhihua jianshe chuqi gonghui huodong he gongren yundong de huigu," in *Panzhihua gongren*, 37.

[65] Wang Daoyi, "Ding jiao tu tai wu balei," in *Liu zai da liegu*, 291. Le Huaqiao, "Zhangu wengong tuan chengzhang zhuangda de lichen," in *Panzhihua shi zhi, Volume 2*, ed. Panzhihua shi zhi bangongshi (Panzhihua: Panzhihua shi panzhihua shizhi zazhi shi, 1987), 20.

[66] For a history of the performing arts at the time, see Paul Clark, *The Chinese Cultural Revolution: A History* (Cambridge: Cambridge University Press, 2008), 157–201.

cultural centers in canvas tents around the city and furnished them with musical instruments.[67]

Single Men, Families, and Children

One reason why Panzhihua's government paid attention to creating a local cultural life was the city's severe gender imbalance. In 1966, the workforce was 95 percent male. Women were so few in town in part because most investment went into heavy industry, which employed mainly men.[68] This demographic fact meant that for many single men an assignment to Panzhihua was equivalent to a long-term sentence to celibacy. When interviewees discussed the deficit of local women, they often brought up local mines where there were almost no women at all, and so miners had sex with goats and gawked at women in cultural troupes when they came to perform.[69] The regularity with which these stories were told to me suggests a fair amount of social anxiety about a man's inability to find a sexual partner, to say nothing of a girlfriend or wife. Another consequence of a shortage of women was sexual violence. When I asked a former policeman which crimes were most common in Panzhihua in the 1960s and 1970s, he said "rape," an offense that Emily Honig has pointed out existed among sent-down youth too.[70]

In Panzhihua, not only were there very few single women, but there were not many married women either. Rural kin were not allowed to move to the city since they did not possess urban residency permits, and the Panzhihua City Council "strictly restrict[ed] urban workers' family members" from becoming registered residents because "the city council [thought] that for the next few years worker energy and material resources should be concentrated on construction." In addition, work units were advised to "make every effort" to send back to their official place of residence "any family members that ... came to [Panzhihua] without

67 Le Huaqiao, "Zhangu wengong tuan chengzhang zhuangda de lichen," in *Panzhihua shi zhi, Volume 2*, 20–21. Interview with cultural troupe member, November 2012. Han, *Jiannan*, 6.

68 Panzhihua shi chengxiang jianshe weiyuanhui, ed., *Panzhihua shi chengshi jianshe zhi* (Panzhihua: Panzhihua shi chengjian bianzuan weiyuanhui, 1995), 8–10. Wu Xuechang, "Panzhihua jianshe chuqi gonghui huodong he gongren yundong de huigu," in *Panzhihua gongren*, 28.

69 Interviews with construction worker, steelworker, and local historian, Panzhihua, November 2012. Interview with group of Railroad Corps members, December 2012.

70 Interview with Panzhihua policeman, December 2012. This was an issue at other Third Front factories. Interview with Third Front scholar, Shanghai, June 2018. Honig, "Socialist Sex."

authorization."[71] Family members were especially absent in mining areas where local officials stipulated that couples could comprise only 1 percent of workers.[72]

Aware that family separation dragged down worker morale, the city government sought to relocate some spouses to Panzhihua. Preference was given to the wives of cadres. The City Personnel Committee permitted giving them jobs in Panzhihua "when conditions allowed." If there were open positions for "medical personnel, teachers, or accountants," wives could take these posts as long as they were urban residents, had a good political background, were physically healthy, and could temporarily leave their children behind.[73] Some urban family members were also moved to nearby villages along the future route of the Chengdu–Kunming Railroad until Panzhihua Steel made iron in 1970.[74] Prior to that point, the CCP only provided on-site housing to single individuals and couples who were both employed at a work unit.[75]

Some recruits from big cities were not dissatisfied with this restrictive policy. One such individual was a man named Qi Wei, who willingly responded to the CCP's call to head up Panzhihua's coal mines even though he had to leave his family behind in Yunnan. He had already done so before to work at other mines during his career. When Qi Wei became afflicted with cancer, the Party offered to take care of him at a top hospital on the coast. He refused and continued to work long days. Qi eventually became so sick that he agreed to go to a local hospital. Even on his deathbed, Qi could not stop being a socialist workaholic.[76] He still demanded regular reports about the local coal industry, so he could help with any problems.[77]

An old veteran from Chengdu, Ma Kerang, viewed leaving his family in a different but similar ideological light. He originally did not want to go to Panzhihua when his commanding officer suddenly suggested that he

[71] Zhonggong dukou shiwei, "Guanyu dangqian jiashu ruhu wenti de tongzhi," December 5, 1966, in *Panzhihua kaifa*, 633.

[72] Dukou shi zhihui bu, "Guanyu Baoding kuangqu chengshi guihua zhong de renkou he danshen sushi wenti de yijian," October 21, 1965, in *Panzhihua kaifa*, 790.

[73] Dukou shi renwei, "Guanyu zhubu de you jihu de anzhi ganbu airen jin Dukou gongzuo wenti de tongzhi," November 24, 1966, in *Panzhihua kaifa*, 632–633.

[74] A similar policy was instituted for Third Front projects in Hubei. Hubei sheng geming weiyuanhui jihua weiyuanhui, "Sanxian diqu qianjian chang zhigong jiahsu anzhi qingkuang," September 16, 1972, Hubei Provincial Archive, S-843-5-447, pp. 40–42.

[75] Panzhihua gangtie, *Pangang zhi*, 515.

[76] For a childhood memoir about a workaholic Third Front father, see "Huiyi wo de bab Liu Qingmo," in *Pujiang jiyi (xia)*, 283–286.

[77] Liu Xiaoping and Yi Bangquan, "Duomei baotie: Longdong huizhan jishi," in *Liu zai da liegu*, 345–350, 375–382. Wen Jilong and Chen Ligao, "Yiwang qiangshan: Qi Wei shiji jieshao," in *Liu zai da liegu*, 345–350, 375–382.

work on setting up local militias because his elderly mother, wife, and four children all relied on his salary and help around the house. Eventually, he came around to thinking of going to Panzhihua as part of his duty as a soldier to serve the nation, and he resolved to "obey his orders." Before departing for Panzhihua, he bought food and clothing for his family and sent them back to his hometown.

The next day he rode a truck to Panzhihua with other men tasked with directing local militia activities. Many of them had "disappointment, worry, and unhappiness ... written all over their faces" when they first saw the secluded mountainous hinterland where they were going to live out the next phase of their life. As for Ma Kerang, he "did not care much" about the harshness of life in Panzhihua since he had become inured to suffering during his time as a soldier. As a military man, what concerned him the most was fulfilling his mission to establish Panzhihua's militias.[78]

Some couples chose a different path than Ma Kerang and did not split up their family. They came to Panzhihua with their children, and the city assisted in providing schooling for them, recruiting a 100 high-school graduates from Chengdu and Chongqing. The Sichuan provincial government also assigned twenty graduates of education institutes and 200 graduates of junior colleges to be local teachers.[79] Panzhihua Steel set up its own schooling arrangements. Factory administrators decided that there were not enough children to warrant independent primary or secondary schools, and so they took classes in nearby villages and other work units in town.

Younger children went to on-site nurseries and kindergartens. Over 90 percent were inside the residences of families or single workers, and family members made up more than 80 percent of their staff. As these numbers show, a significant portion of childcare work was performed by family members and done in family homes. Some parents could not rely on others to watch their children since their workshop had no childcare services, and so parents brought children to their workplace. Some mothers even carried their baby on their back around construction sites.[80]

Lauding Labor within Cold War Limits

All the work that people undertook to build Panzhihua produced a milestone in the city's history on June 29, 1970. On that day, the first puddle of iron sloshed out of the blast furnace of Panzhihua Steel. On July 2, the city government held a ceremony with 50,000 people to celebrate this

78 Pei Ming, "Panzhihua minbing de chuangjian zhe," in *Jianshe Panzhihua*, 121–124.
79 Chen Dazhi, "Jiaoshi duiwu laiyuan kaocha," in *Panzhihua shi zhi, Volume 2*, 36–37.
80 Panzhihua gangtie, *Pangang zhi*, 469, 488, 491. Han, *Jiannan*, 9–10. Insufficient childcare was a common problem at Third Front work units; see Guowuyuan, *Sanxian*, 228.

Figure 4.4 A mass meeting to celebrate the smelting of iron in 1970. Source: "Panzhihua lao zhaopian," *Panzhihua yishu zaixian*, http://pzhsyol.com/col.jsp?id=149

momentous step forward (depicted in Figure 4.4). The central Party sent deputy chief of staff Wu Faxian to congratulate the people of Panzhihua on their landmark accomplishment. Also in attendance were ministerial, regional, and local leaders, along with tens of thousands of workers.[81] To mark the occasion, a stage was built with a large poster of Chairman Mao hanging in the background. In front of the stage, rows and rows of people sat on the ground as far as the eye could see. Amidst this sea of labor, a big-character poster rose up ten feet into the air declaring that "Panzhihua producing iron on July 1 is a great victory of Mao Zedong thought."[82]

[81] Zhonggong Panzhihua shiwei dangshi yanjiushi, *Panzhihua kaifa jianshe da shiji*, 146–147.

[82] The quotes in the next paragraph are also from "Duo shuo Pan gang yi hao gaolu qi yi chu tie, cuo!" *Panzhihua shi dangan guan xinxi wang*, September 30, 2016, www.pzhda.gov.cn/xxgk/daldpzh/620464.shtml, accessed June 23, 2017.

Workers showed their personal devotion to Maoism by carrying their copy of the *Quotations of Chairman Mao*, as they sat and listened to congratulatory letters from work units around the country. Among them was a telegram from the Metallurgy Ministry which praised the production of iron at Panzhihua Steel as an emblem of Maoist China's policy of self-reliance. Chinese workers had "self-designed" the factory, "self-manufactured equipment, and independently constructed" a new steel town. This was only the second time since the establishment of the PRC in 1949 that Chinese labor had built a large steel plant. The first time was Wuhan Steel, and it had been completed with Soviet aid. When Wuhan Steel made iron in 1958, the Party feted this monument to the powers of national planning by publishing worker poems and speeches from Party leaders.[83]

When Panzhihua smelted iron for the first time, the national media were completely silent. There were no radio broadcasts or newspaper articles that sang paeans to Panzhihua workers. Nor were there pictures of Party leaders pressing the flesh and honoring local labor models for all that they had done to advance socialism. None of this was possible with Panzhihua or any other Third Front project because they were top secret. The covert nature of the Third Front affected the meanings that Panzhihua could acquire in socialist China. Neither Panzhihua nor the workers who built it had any place in Chinese public discourse since the Third Front was kept out of popular consciousness in order to ensure that it could protect China from the dangers of the Cold War.[84]

Panzhihua workers could never have their personal achievements raised up and made into labor models for people elsewhere in China to emulate no matter how much they exemplified Maoist attitudes and values in their daily affairs. Nor was it possible for Panzhihua to become a model of how to build a Maoist city. In this regard, Panzhihua was unlike its Stalinist double – the Magnitogorsk steel plant – which the Soviet Union established in the 1930s in the Ural mountains in preparation for war with Western capitalist states. Magnitogorsk was known to the outside world, and it was constructed on an open plain with little concern about being seen by enemy aircraft.[85] Panzhihua, on the other hand, was a product of the age of aerial warfare and nuclear weapons in which states presumed that if foreign forces could see something from the sky, then it was susceptible to attack. This is why the Communist Party

[83] "Xiang jingai de Wugang zhuhe," *Renmin ribao*, September 14, 1958. "Mao zhuxi zai Wugang," *Renmin ribao*, September 29, 1958.

[84] For another Cold War example of the linking of secrecy and national security, see Joseph Masco, *The Nuclear Borderlands: The Manhattan Project in Post-Cold War New Mexico* (Princeton: Princeton University Press, 2006).

[85] On Magnitogorsk, see Kotkin, *Magnetic Mountain*.

did not allow the media to treat Panzhihua or any other Third Front endeavors as monuments to the progress of Chinese socialism.[86]

To maintain the Third Front's safety, laborers were given a special "subsidy to keep secrets" (*baomi fei*). Third Front participants were also required to engage in extra work to make industrial enterprises fit in the mountainous locales that the central Party judged to be more secure.[87] Panzhihua Steel is one example of how project designers handled the problems of building factories in areas with a scarcity of flatland. Situated on a slope, workers carved out of the mountainside two large man-made steps and divided one big step into six small steps and another into twelve small steps, so that Panzhihua Steel had the even foundation that was necessary for a steel plant to be operational.[88]

Panzhihua Steel's placement on a mountainside created transportation problems too. A steel factory in a flat location often depends on an internal railroad system to move items around. Panzhihua's managers decided against trying to engineer a railroad network for a factory compressed onto a mountainside. Instead, technical personnel created a system of cables to connect different parts of the factory complex. Nowadays, the Panzhihua city government depicts this last invention as evidence of Chinese technological ingenuity.[89] At the time it was constructed nobody outside Panzhihua knew about this triumph of technical skill because the central Party considered public praise of the Third Front campaign to be militarily perilous.

The Privileged Hardship of Third Front Labor

As for Panzhihua workers, some worried about the hazards that local industrialization posed to their safety. According to interviewees, one economic step forward that caused particular problems was the firing up of the steel plant. Not only did its employees have to work long hours inside the blazing confines of steel workshops. The factory also emitted into the hot atmosphere a steady stream of embers. When mixed with the arid winds that frequently tunneled through Panzhihua's narrow valley, sparks ignited holocausts that leveled tent encampments and seared memories of burning homes into local history. To cope with the

86 On celebrations of industry in the Soviet Union, see Richard Stites, *Revolutionary Dreams: Utopian Vision and Experimental Life in the Russian Revolution* (Oxford: Oxford University Press, 1989), 145–164.

87 For an example of this practice in the aerospace industry, see Zhang, *Sanxian jianshe tao fengbei*, 321–330.

88 Shen Zhongfan, "'Xiangya weidiao' shi de Pangang sheji," in *Liu zai da liegu*, 125–135.

89 Ge Hong, "Panzhihua: Zhongguo suodao de yaolan," in *Liu zai da liegu*, 260–264.

ever-present danger of fire, people stored valuables underground. Panzhihua Steel's machinery also released a perpetual drone every hour of the day. The insomniac groaning of industrial equipment penetrated the thin dirt and canvas walls of nearby residences and gnawed waking hours out of people's sleep.[90]

With the arrival of local industry also came extensive pollution that endangered local public health. Coal miners suffered from asthma and pneumoconiosis since their work units provided them with little protection from harmful aerosols.[91] In addition, the city government did not establish adequate waste management systems, and so fecal matter and industrial pollutants from factories and mines flowed into the local water supply, causing Panzhihua residents to contract chronic stomach ailments.[92] As Judith Shapiro has illustrated, the government was aware of this environment of illness, but it did not immediately remedy the situation.[93] Only in the early 1970s did the city government build formal human waste management systems. As for industrial pollutants, the government only significantly reduced the toxicity of local air and water in the mid-1980s.[94]

The many hardships that people faced living in Panzhihua raise the question of whether anyone ever tried to leave. According to a 1971 report, some people did flee Panzhihua. At a work unit with 4,400 employees, a little over 160 people had abandoned their post for more than a year. Yet there were also over 2,000 people who had moved from villages to live with family in Panzhihua and had refused to go back to the countryside. The city told work units to fill vacated posts with rural family members who had rebuffed government attempts to make them leave.[95] This shows that foot dragging was useful not only as a rural survival strategy, as Ralph Thaxton has demonstrated in his study of Da Fo village, but also sometimes as a way to climb up Maoist China's socioeconomic hierarchy out of the countryside and into the city.[96]

When I asked interviewees whether they had thought about running away from Panzhihua, they did not mention people who skipped town.

[90] Interview with steelworker, Panzhihua, November 2012.

[91] Panzhihua shi weisheng zhi bianzuan weiyuanhui, *Panzhihua shi weisheng zhi* (Beijing: Minzu chubanshe, 2004), 76–78.

[92] Yin Guangqiang, "Sanshi nian mojian zhe 'heilong'," in *Liu zai da liegu*, 333–335. Panzhihua shi weisheng bianzuan, *Panzhihua shi weisheng zhi*, 100.

[93] Shapiro, *Mao's War*, 154–157.

[94] Yin, "San shi nian mojian zhe 'heilong'," 336–337.

[95] Zhongguo renmin jiefangjun Sichuan sheng Dukou shi gongan jiguan junshi guanzhi weiyuanhui, "Guanyu zuo hao 1971 niandu renkou tongji gongzuo de qingshi," October 26, 1971, in *Panzhihua kaifa*, 634.

[96] Thaxton, *Catastrophe and Contention*, 158–160.

They said that they had no choice but to stay and work. The Party had sent them to Panzhihua, and there was no way to leave. Receiving an official transfer was nearly impossible and to flee was highly risky. If someone moved without official approval, they would lose their membership in an urban work unit and all the associated benefits.[97] Interviewee responses point to the fact that a single-minded focus on the austerity of life in Panzhihua overlooks the privileged status of its residents.

Nearly all Panzhihua work units were state-owned enterprises which provided permanent employees with an array of social services. While Panzhihua residents certainly did not enjoy as high living standards as employees at established state-owned enterprises in centrally located cities, they still benefited from a far more robust welfare net than people in rural areas. Panzhihua residents all had guaranteed food, housing, schools, and medical services, and central planners gave the city and its work units funds for paved roads, electricity, running water, and trucks. The Maoist state never looked after the material life of rural inhabitants so intently. Rural areas had to rely overwhelmingly on local resources to fund their activities.[98] In short, while life at the Third Front was hard, it was a privileged hardship compared to conditions in the countryside.

Workers in Panzhihua had access to an array of material resources. In the 1970s, the province helped expand local educational facilities by assigning 200 university graduates to teaching positions in Panzhihua. The city government also set up local training programs to increase teaching staff.[99] Panzhihua Steel bolstered educational programs as well. In 1970, the factory established an elementary school and a middle school. Since there were not enough children of high-school age, they attended courses with junior-high students until 1973. Panzhihua Steel also sent sixteen people to Chengdu for six months of teacher training. Upon returning, they took charge of schools and instituted local teacher-training programs.[100]

To look after the health of workers and their families, the Panzhihua city government established a hospital in 1965. As locals like to say of the city's population in general, hospital employees "came from all over the

[97] Interview with Peking University graduate worker, Panzhihua, November 2012. Interview with construction worker couple, Chengdu, January 2013.

[98] For a structural analysis of this point, see Vivienne Shue, *The Reach of the State: Sketches of the Chinese Body Politic* (Stanford: Stanford University Press, 1988), 132–147. For socioeconomic analyses of what the urban–rural divide meant in material terms, see Jacob Eyferth, "Women's Work and the Politics of Homespun in Socialist China, 1948–1980," *International Review of Social History* 55:4 (2012): 1–27. Brown, *City versus Countryside*.

[99] Chen Dazhi, "Jiaoshi duiwu laiyuan kaocha," in *Panzhihua shi zhi, Volume 2*, 37.

[100] Panzhihua gangtie, *Pangang zhi*, 474, 477, 469–470.

place" (*laizi simian bafang*). Personnel were shipped in from Shanghai, Tianjin, Shenyang, Chengdu, and Chongqing. Since Panzhihua work units were spread out at a number of different construction sites, hospital administrators decided that it was best not to have patients solely come to them. Instead, they followed a strategy similar to the barefoot doctor teams formed to handle the medical needs of rural China. Mobile teams circulated between construction sites and provided basic medical services.[101]

Panzhihua Steel also built a hospital in 1970. Between 1971 and 1978, Panzhihua Steel invested a half-million RMB in this facility, and it created separate pediatric, gynecological, and ENT wards.[102] To care for the sick and injured, the factory recruited medical personnel from hospitals around the country, and it sent over 100 people to receive training at hospitals in northeast China. By 1978, Panzhihua Steel had one medical worker for every fifty-six workers. This ratio was sixty-one times more than the average in rural areas.[103]

Panzhihua residents were also monetarily advantaged compared to rural inhabitants who on average earned about eleven to fifteen RMB per year.[104] It is unclear exactly how much Panzhihua residents were paid since local gazetteers do not contain this information. It was almost surely over 550 RMB per annum because no industrial sector had a lower wage at the time.[105] Data are available for Panzhihua Steel where salaries averaged 638.75 RMB per year between 1970 and 1977.[106] This amount was twenty-three RMB lower than the national average for metallurgical workers.[107]

Based on the factory gazetteers of thirty Third Front work units, it appears that Panzhihua Steel is an outlier when it comes to how much workers earned compared to people in similar positions elsewhere in China. Over three-fourths of the factories that I have examined had wages above the national norm for their industrial sector, suggesting

[101] Li Xingyou, "Shi zhongxin yiyuan jin xi tan," in *Liu zai da liegu*, 287. Interview with medical worker, Panzhihua, December 2012. For a history of barefoot doctors, see Xiaoping Fang, *Barefoot Doctors and Western Medicine in China* (Rochester, NY: University of Rochester Press, 2012).

[102] Panzhihua gangtie, *Pangang zhi*, 264, 488–489, 491, 496.

[103] Panzhihua gangtie, *Pangang zhi*, 264, 496. Zhonghua renmin gongheguo guojia tongji ju, "1978," www.stats.gov.cn/tjsj/tjgb/ndtjgb/qgndtjgb/200203/t20020331_29991.html, accessed June 23, 2017. "1949–1978 nian weisheng yiliao de chuantong 'Zhongguo moshi'," *Zhongguo xinwen wang*, September 30, 2009, www.china.com.cn/news/zhuanti/09dlms/2009-09/30/content_18636976.htm, accessed June 23, 2017.

[104] Zhongguo shehui kexue yuan nongye jingji yanjiu suo, *Nongye jingji ziliao, 1949–1983* (Beijing: Nongye yuye bu shuichan ju, 1983), 516–517. I thank Jacob Eyferth for making me aware of this source.

[105] Guojia tongji ju, *Zhongguo laodong*, 159–160.

[106] Yejin gongye bu Panzhihua, *Pangang shengchan*, 174.

[107] Guojia tongji ju, *Zhongguo laodong*, 159.

that central ministries gave Third Front workers higher salaries, perhaps to compensate for their remote location.[108]

Whether this was the case or not, employees in Panzhihua also received subsidies on top of their base wage. Every month, a Panzhihua worker was eligible to receive fifteen subsides. They obtained six RMB for meals and 2.5 RMB for grain. A family was entitled to three RMB for each dependent, whereas people without dependents were granted 1.5 RMB. The Party offered additional subsidies to buy coal, pay for vaccinations, and cover heating costs in the winter. If someone had to work after 11 p.m., their meal was reimbursed too.[109]

Worker Discontent, Satisfaction, and Divertissement

In spite of their relative affluence, Panzhihua residents that I interviewed did not talk about their life as one of privilege. They typically characterized life in Panzhihua as "hard" (*jianku*) and "crude" (*jianlou*). The same words appeared in the contemporary Party slogans "work hard" (*jianku fendou*) and "crude and simple living" (*yin lou jiu jian*). The first slogan referred to how people at the time were supposed to approach their job, and the second slogan encapsulated what the Communist Party considered to be normal living standards at the Third Front. Interviewees occasionally turned on their heads the Party's prescribed words for describing their work and living conditions. Official discourse was not wrong about the rudimentary character of life at the Third Front. Nor was it incorrect that people engaged in labor that was long, tiring, and physically painful. But their lives were just that – hard.[110]

Just because people viewed their work lives as difficult, however, did not mean that they thought of their labor as only arduous. When Third Front recruits arrived in Panzhihua, local managers assigned them physically demanding tasks, but in the end the hardships people endured produced one very notable result. Third Fronters had built a new "steel town" (*gangtie cheng*) in a place that had once been a "wasteland" (*bu mao zhi di*).[111] Although many people in

[108] Guojia tongji ju, *Zhongguo laodong*, 159–160. For a list of factory gazetteers consulted, see the Bibliography. Remote areas frequently had higher wages; see Lardy, *Economic Growth*, 114.

[109] Sichuan sheng Panzhihua shi bianzuan weiyuanhui, ed., *Panzhihua shi zhi* (Chengdu: Sichuan kexue jishu chubanshe, 1994), 751.

[110] Interview with steelworker, Panzhihua, November 2012. Interview with railroad worker, Panzhihua, December 2012. Interview with construction worker, Chengdu, January 2013.

[111] Interview with teacher, Panzhihua, November 2012. Interview with steelworker, Panzhihua, November 2012. Interview with Peking University graduate, Panzhihua, November 2012.

Figure 4.5 Reading the Little Red Book at Panzhihua Steel in the early 1970s. Source: "Panzhihua lao zhaopian," *Panzhihua yishu zaixian*, http://pzhsyol.com/col.jsp?id=149

Panzhihua today feel a sense of accomplishment for taking part in the creation of a new industrial city, how people perceived this developmental objective at the time was varied.

When a retired veteran from Anhui went to Panzhihua, some of his colleagues were always thinking up ways to be allowed to go back home. He, on the other hand, came to see Panzhihua as his "second hometown" and took performing his job as a truck driver well as his duty. He recalls, "Whenever my truck had problems, I always was in a bad mood." His colleagues told him to have his truck fixed at a local garage since it was "dirty" and "tiring" work. He opted to repair the truck on his own because he thought it was his responsibility to make sure that "the truck the country gave him realized its full potential."[112]

A recruit from Anshan Steel, Han Guobin felt honored to have the opportunity to even come to Panzhihua. He recalls "brimming with joy" (*xin hua nu fang*) when he was informed in 1968 that he was being transferred to Panzhihua Steel.[113] He had grown up studying Mao Zedong thought and was eager to serve the Party in whatever way he could.[114] A few years earlier he had applied to work at a Third Front steel plant in Liupanshui. To his disappointment, he had not been selected.[115] Han Guobin additionally thought himself lucky to have arrived in Panzhihua in 1968 because when people originally came in 1965, there was no water, electricity, or roads. Panzhihua was also less impacted by the Cultural Revolution, which enabled workers to "realize the strategic mission" that Chairman Mao had given them of developing inland China.[116]

A Peking university graduate I interviewed also found meaning in taking part in China's struggle to build a steel town in a remote mountainous area. He, however, did not hold an entirely positive view of Panzhihua. When he first entered town, he was disappointed that the local labor department appointed him to a housing construction team because his position had nothing to do with his years of training in the hard sciences. Nonetheless, he still tried to become skilled at constructing rammed-earth buildings.

Later, he was given a managerial position at a new chemical factory. Although he was not a chemical expert, he still found more of a sense of self-worth as a factory administrator than as a manual laborer. One day, this man invited me to his house to talk after dinner and showed me the blueprints he had come up with for the factory with his coworkers. He had never designed a factory before, and so he felt a special sense of accomplishment that he and his colleagues had been able to figure out how to make a functioning chemical plant.[117]

He also noted that he was lucky to have been given a job assignment in Panzhihua. Some of his classmates had not been so fortunate. They were sent to the countryside, and the skills they had learned in school had gone to waste for over a decade.[118] Liu knew all too well the impact that

[112] Shi Zongchen, "Pingfan zhong shanguan," in *Jianshe Panzhihua*, 170–173. The quotes are on pages 171, 173.
[113] Han, *Jiannan*, 1.
[114] For a similar trend among other members of this generation, see Chan, *Children of Mao*. Schmalzer, *Red Revolution*, 155–180.
[115] Han, *Jiannan*, 2. [116] Han, *Jiannan*, 5–6.
[117] Interview with Peking University graduate, Panzhihua, December 2012.
[118] For similar views among sent-down youth, see Bernstein, *Up to the Mountains*, 91, 96–98. Bonnin, *Lost Generation*, 248–257.

rustification could have on a person. His younger sister was sent to a village after graduating from high school, and she was very unhappy with her lot. Trying to help her out, he secured her a transfer to a job at Panzhihua. She could not adjust to life there. Fearing that she would never be allowed to leave, she committed suicide.[119]

Another university graduate held a bleak view of Panzhihua. He was posted to a coal mine for several years. Day after day he descended underground and dug up coal. From his experience as a coal miner, he had not developed a devout attachment to socialism. He had learned that there was no difference between socialism and Buddhism because socialism provided people with so little that they came to accept that it was pointless to want anything at all.[120] This man's point of view can be seen as a damning condemnation of the austerity of life at the Third Front. And yet, if we only pay attention to his negative viewpoint, we overlook an important part of his attitude towards work. Although he was displeased with his job assignment, he did not completely refuse to work. He still did as he was told and mined coal.

One of the local leaders calling the shots for people like him was a man named Gu Xiu. Gu was a lifetime revolutionary. He had started doing revolutionary work for the CCP at seventeen during the Chinese Civil War, and he had subsequently risen up the Party's military arm, serving in the Korean War and the Railroad Corps before coming mayor of Panzhihua in early 1970. Prior to being transferred to Panzhihua, Gu Xiu had already been engaged in Third Front affairs, taking part in the building of the Guiyang–Kunming and Chengdu–Kunming railroads. When Gu assumed the mayorship of Panzhihua, Zhou Enlai gave him one central task – produce iron by July 1, 1970.[121] At the time, many people thought Zhou's order was impossible to fulfill because of supply shortages. Some people doubted Zhou's proclamation so much that they said, "If iron is made by July 1, then I will drink it."[122]

Gu Xiu was of a different mind. He thought Zhou's deadline was feasible if labor was mass-mobilized, and so the city government founded a battle headquarters. During the battle, work units did not observe regular work hours. People did not to go to work and then afterwards go back to their residence. They lived and ate at the construction site.

[119] Interview with Peking University graduate, Panzhihua, November 2012. For suicides among people deported from cities, see Brown, *City versus Countryside*, 157–158. For suicide among sent-down youth, see Bonnin, *Lost Generation*, 357–358.

[120] Interview with coal miner, Chengdu, February 2013.

[121] Xu Chi, "Zhou Enlai lingdao women jianshe Panzhihua," *Renmin wang*, March 15, 2018, http://zhouenlai.people.cn/n1/2018/0315/c409117-29869164.html, accessed October 4, 2018.

[122] Gu, *Licheng*, 143.

Some people came up with a motivational expression to describe their commitment to realizing their mission. "We don't miss dad, don't miss mom, don't miss the kids, and don't miss home. Our whole heart is concentrated on building Panzhihua. Until we make molten iron, we won't go home."[123] Some of the workers that used this expression were probably mouthing the words and did in fact ache for their family. Nevertheless, some of them did not go to the hospital when they got a serious illness. Others delayed taking leave to visit family and pushed back their wedding date. One work unit even soldiered on when an earthquake damaged their hometown.[124]

Coal miners had to work especially hard because factional struggles at Liupanshui had paralyzed operations at the mine that the Infrastructure Corps was supposed to construct to provide Panzhihua with coking coal.[125] To make up for this deficiency, workers in Panzhihua went into overdrive to finish building a local coal mine. Panzhihua Steel had also to rush through preparations to manufacture coke out of local coal. Normally, it took seventy-two days to complete this task. The coking plant proposed completing it in sixty-two. Mayor Gu Xiu said coking coal had to be made in forty-five days, and it was. The State Construction Commission organized five special truck brigades to ship in over two million tons of supplies. Skilled workers were brought together to solve technical difficulties, and the line between technical and manual laborer partially blurred, as both partook in the backbreaking work of installing heavy equipment by hand.[126]

As we have seen, Third Front laborers had a variety of different responses to the hard work ethic that the Party expected them to embody in their daily endeavors. There was, however, one aspect of life in Panzhihua that all workers enjoyed. Nearly every single night, a free movie was shown at a work unit somewhere in the city. Many interviewees would visibly light up with happiness when they discussed watching films. When I questioned people about which films they liked the most, many spoke with disdain of Jiang Qing's model operas, which they disliked having to watch again and again and again. People particularly found pleasure in the North Korean film *The Flower Girl* because the film was not political. It was just a love story, and the female lead was attractive.[127]

123 Liu Maocai and Xue Shicheng, eds., *Pangang: Zhongguo gangtie gongye de jiao'ao* (Chongqing: Chongqing chubanshe, 1994), 108–109.

124 Yejin gongye bu Panzhihua, *Pangang shengchan*, 60.

125 Liu, *Zhongguo jiefangjun*, 21–24, 286–292.

126 Yejin gongye bu Panzhihua, *Pangang shengchan*, 61–63.

127 Interview with steelworker, Panzhihua, November 2012. Interview with truck driver, Chongqing, January 2013. This film was popular in other Third Front locations for similar reasons. Interview with Zizhong factory worker, December 2012.

Regular film screenings gave people some release from the daily toil of work. Yet many people still thought life in Panzhihua was "monotonous" (*dandiao*) and "dull" (*kuzao*). Some people found especially boring the constant reading of Mao's "three classic speeches," which they compared to the bland diet of "steamed beans and dried turnip stew" that they had no choice but to eat day after day after day.[128] Panzhihua Steel tried to deal with the dullness of everyday life in Mao's town by increasing the number of mobile film projection teams and organizing military games and ping-pong and soccer tournaments. Nonetheless, many people still complained that cultural life in Panzhihua was "boring." [129]

Family Matters amid Scarcity

Another source of constant complaints among Third Front workers was the absence of family members. Aware of this thorn in the side of workers' *esprit de corps*, central Party leaders drew up special policies for people whose family members did not reside with them. Each worker who was unmarried or lived separately from their spouse, was permitted twelve days of paid family leave per year, and their workplace subsidized travel expenses. The impact of this policy on Panzhihua Steel was significant. In 1975, it had slightly more than 41,000 employees. Over half lived separately from their spouse. Over four-fifths of their partners resided in rural areas elsewhere in Sichuan, and family visits annually cost the factory over four million RMB. On average, every worker took sixty days of family vacation per year. This meant that on any given day around a tenth of employees were on vacation.

Panzhihua Steel wanted workers to spend more time engaged in productive activities. So in 1972 it began a concerted push to relocate rural family members to local areas. Restrictions on rural–urban migration made it impossible to grant them urban residency and positions at the factory. Still wanting to bring in family members, administrators expanded rural farms under their control and populated them with employee kin. Panzhihua Steel also furnished some urban family members with service-sector jobs. Spouses and children served as barbers, cobblers, cleaners, and tailors. They ran canteens and worked at shops selling food and daily necessities.[130]

128 Liu, *Zuihou de guizu*, 66.

129 Yejin gongye bu Panzhihua, *Pangang shengchan*, 172–174.

130 Panzhihua gangtie, *Pangang zhi*, 508–510, 556, 560–565. Analogous issues with family leave existed at other Third Front factories; see Hubei sheng geming weiyuanhui. "Sanxian diqu qianjian chang zhigong jiashu anzhi qingkuang," September 16, 1972, Hubei Provincial Archive, S843-5-447, pp. 40–42. Chen, *Toleration*, 121–123.

To handle the influx of worker kin, Panzhihua Steel constructed more housing for dual-income couples and newly arriving families in 1970. Some families acquired rooms in new four-story electrified brick buildings in which only two households had to share a bathroom. Others obtained spots in new tents and rammed-earth huts. In 1972, Panzhihua Steel put up brick dormitories for single workers, which were equipped with group bathrooms and electric lights. Panzhihua Steel likely undertook this measure because over 75 percent of single people still lived in mud huts and tents in 1971.[131]

Better housing did not much change the conjugal life of single men. Panzhihua was still a heavy-industrial town, and so the CCP transferred few women into its ranks. Many of the city's women were nurses. Medical facilities thus became a place for men to go in their leisure time to catch a glimpse of a female and occasionally even flirt. Most rural recruits had no chance of courting a nurse since medical personnel came from cities, and urbane women did not usually want their betrothed to be a country bumpkin with minimal education and a low-paying job performing manual labor.[132]

On the contrary, a man's status as a city resident generally improved their prospects on rural marriage markets. This was the case for both urban recruits and rural folk who acquired urban residency and became SOE employees. Many rural women viewed marrying an urban male as a way of bettering their socioeconomic position since urbanites had a higher quality of life. Not all rural women took this view. Some could not approve of living separately from their husbands.[133] Rural men also yearned to be with family. Yet as one interviewee wryly noted, while life in Panzhihua was hard, the countryside was much worse. As proof he recounted how, when he returned to his village in the northeast, he brought a bag of grain for his family who lived in a grain-producing region.[134] Husbands also sent remittances to family left behind, a material advantage which sweetened the strains of long-term separation.[135]

131 Panzhihua gangtie, *Pangang zhi*, 512, 515.

132 Interview with steelworker, Panzhihua, November 2012. Interview with local historian, November 2012.

133 Interview with local historian, Panzhihua, November 2012. Interview with bridge builder, Panzhihua, December 2012. This trend was a feature of social life in other Third Front factories. Interview with Chengdu factory worker, Chengdu, February 2013. Interview with factory workers, Pengzhou, June 2016. Chen, *Toleration*, 90.

134 Interview with coal miner, Panzhihua, November 2012.

135 Interview with construction worker, Panzhihua, November 2012.

Families living together in Panzhihua, on the other hand, started to worry about their children's future even before they born. When one man's wife became pregnant, he worried that the barebones regimen that the local populace subsisted on would negatively affect his unborn child's fetal development. To ensure that his wife had adequate nutrition, he walked a few miles to purchase eggs from local farmers. Buying goods directly from farmers was illegal because of CCP views of private markets as "remnants of capitalism" (*ziben zhuyi weiba*), but he did not care. Ensuring his wife and baby had adequate nutrition was more important.[136]

After a child was born, families still had to figure out how to feed them formula or breast milk. Providing infants with adequate quantities of either was no simple matter. Working women had busy schedules which made it not always feasible for a child to be breast-fed. Panzhihua's stocks of formula, however, were invariably inadequate. Shortages of formula in Panzhihua and at other Third Front projects became such a big issue that in 1972 vice director of the Economic Commission Gu Mu told central ministries that they had to address this issue.[137] His order appears to have been ineffective because when parents in Panzhihua heard people were making trips to large cities, they would ask them to buy formula in large quantities along with other consumer goods locally in short supply.[138]

When someone went to Shanghai, parents asked them to buy shoes, dress shirts, sewing machines, and bicycles. Travelers often received purchase requests from many people, and so when Third Fronters went shopping in Shanghai, they often did not just buy one pair of shoes or a single shirt. They bought whole shelffuls. Going back to Panzhihua loaded with goodies, people dashed onto trains so that they could pack their cargo bags into overhead bins. Meanwhile, back in Panzhihua, friends, family, and coworkers were eagerly waiting for them to return from afar with cherished consumer items.[139] Children especially coveted receiving Shanghai candies.[140]

Children who grew up in Panzhihua did not remember thinking much about the material hardships of everyday life. They recalled a tight-knit community in which neighboring families frequently socialized with each other, and children regularly played together outside. They had attended

136 Interview with Peking University graduate, Panzhihua, November 2012.

137 "Shiyan shi huibao shi Gu Mu tongzhi de jianghua," July 10, 1974, Hubei Provincial Archive, S843-5-447, pp. 46–47.

138 Interview with couple from Shanghai, December 2012.

139 Interview with couple from Shanghai, December 2012. Interview with group of Third Front children, Panzhihua, November 2012.

140 Interview with nurse, Panzhihua, December 2012.

Figure 4.6 Panzhihua elementary school in a tent. Source: "Panzhihua lao zhaopian," *Panzhihua yishu zaixian*, http://pzhsyol.com/col.jsp?id=149

tent schools and resided in tent homes. Yet they had not complained about there being a scarcity of goods since they had not known anything else. However, as they became older, the children of urban recruits became aware that their parents thought it would be best if they did not make a home for themselves at the Third Front.[141]

Parents were especially anxious about their children's education. The Communist Party had told them to forgo their own livelihood to construct Panzhihua, and they had done so. Yet they hoped that their children would not share their same geographic fate. Even though the CCP suspended university entrance exams for most of the 1970s, some parents still dreamed that their children might go to college in a less

[141] Interview with group of Third Front children, Panzhihua, November 2012. For other positive childhood experiences of the Third Front, see Deng Yuxia, "Yueliang zai bailianhua ban de yunduo li chuanxing," in *Pujiang wenyun*, ed. Wu Hantao and Li Hebang (Beijing: Tuanjie chubanshe, Beijing, 2016), 167–170. For young people with similar memories of the Cultural Revolution, see Zhong Xueping and Wang Zheng, eds., *Some of Us: Chinese Women Growing Up in the Mao Era* (New Brunswick: Rutgers University Press, 2001).

insular part of China. So that their children acquired a good education, some parents took time out of their busy work schedules to run schools at their work units. Others taught courses in areas in which they had varying degrees of competence since there was a shortage of trained teaching staff. Urban recruits were willing to turn their after-work hours into even more labor time because of how the Party's decision to strengthen China's industrial defenses had affected their own biography. They had given their lives to building Panzhihua, but they did not want to also sacrifice their children's future to the Third Front.[142] Yet even people who regularly had finding a way for their family to leave Panzhihua on their minds were not completely against the Third Front cause. Like many of their coworkers, they still often derived a sense of self-worth from overcoming adversity and constructing a new steel town that helped to develop China's hinterlands.

[142] Interview with local historian, Panzhihua, November 2012. Interview with medical worker, Panzhihua, December 2012. Interview with Peking University graduate, Panzhihua, November 2012.

5 Industrial Development amid Cold War Insecurity

The Third Front campaign was just as much an experiment in economic engineering as it was an effort to produce a population that accepted Maoist behavioral norms. As with Third Front social engineering, the CCP's drive to industrially develop the country's interior generated mixed results. The directing of more funding towards inland regions meant that there were fewer resources available for coastal development and improving living standards. The Third Front policy of investing in mountainous areas also pulled resources away from urban development. Although contemporary campaigns – such as the sent-down-youth movement and the Cultural Revolution – also contributed to lower rates of urbanization, coastal growth, and consumption, the Third Front was surely an important factor given its large resource demands. A more direct line can be drawn between the Cultural Revolution and the Third Front's high cost, as widespread factional fights delayed construction projects. It is clear as well that total expenditures on the Third Front were elevated due to the Party's security requirement that all projects must be spread out in the mountains and some even had to be concealed underground.

Given the level of resources devoted to the Third Front campaign, it might seem plausible that the Party could have better developed inland China through a different policy platform. There is, however, no indication in presently available sources that CCP leaders examined any policy other than the Third Front that would have led to similar levels of inland development. The only economic alternative that the Party center put forward was the preliminary draft of the Third Five Year Plan, and it prioritized coastal industrialization. If the Party had maintained this initial policy platform, China's seaboard would have likely become more developed, but the Chinese interior would have probably fallen economically further behind. This argument is in no way meant to serve as an apology for the problems of the Third Front campaign. The Third Front had many shortcomings, which I present in the first two sections of this chapter. My point is, rather, historical. Of the policy options on the table at the time, the Third Front was the sole course of action that made industrializing inland China into a priority.

In the latter sections of this chapter, I discuss the Third Front's contributions to the industrial development of the Chinese interior. I concentrate my analysis on what Astrid Kander and her colleagues have argued are the three main development blocks that form the basis of industrial modernity. The first development block depends on coal for energy, and iron goods are its main product. The basic elements of the coal development block consist not only of coal and iron mines but also railroads which shuttle materials to factories that manufacture and use iron. The second development block is centered on oil products whose increased availability is historically linked to the growth of the automotive industry, road networks, and the petrochemical sector. The third development block encompasses industries related to electricity generation, such as hydropower, electronics, and electrical grids.[1]

By helping to build up these three development blocks in inland China, the Third Front led to three additional economic consequences. It sped up the circulation of regional resources, advanced the integration of the interior into countrywide networks, and reinforced the CCP's ambition to re-engineer the economic geography of large expanses of territory. Before I proceed to the body of the chapter, first a brief word on its scope. I do not attempt to provide here a full assessment of the Third Front's economic effects. I only aim to address the issues laid out above. I leave the numerical heavy lifting to another scholar who, unlike me, is trained in cliometrics.

Depressed Growth and Problematic Projects

Between 1965 and 1980, China spent 20.52 billion RMB on 1,100 Third Front projects. This funding resulted in 1,945 industrial enterprises and scientific research institutes.[2] Percentage-wise, expenditures were highest between 1965 and 1970 when the Third Front accounted for 52 percent of the capital construction budget (4.8 billion RMB). Between 1971 and 1975, the Third Front's share of capital construction investment declined but stayed high at 41 percent (seven billion RMB). Between 1975 and 1980, the Third Front's portion of national financing continued its downward slide to 33 percent (78.8 billion RMB).[3]

[1] Kander, Malanima, and Warde, *Power to the People*, 134, 287.

[2] Guofang ke gong wei sanxian tiaozheng xiediao zhongxin, "Sanxian jianshe tiaozheng gaizao gongzuo zongjie," December 3, 2003, in *Sanxian jianshe tiaozheng gaizao zongjie wenji*, ed. Guofang ke gong wei sanxian tiaozheng xiediao zhongxin (Beijing: Guofang ke gong wei sanxian tiaozheng xiediao zhongxin, 2006), 28. Chen Pu, "Sanxian jianhse zhanlue yu xibu mengxiang," in Sanxian jianshe zongheng tan, ed., *Sichuan sheng zhonggong dangshi xuehui* (Chengdu: Sichuan renmin chebuanshe, 2015), 10.

[3] Zhao, *Zhonghua renmin gongheguo jingji shi*, 183, 188.

Chinese historians Xu Youwei and Chen Xi have asserted that there is a correlation between investment in the Third Front and the depression of coastal industrialization. The growth rate of industrial output in coastal areas decreased from 17.5 percent between 1962 and 1965 to 11.7 percent between 1966 and 1970, dropping even farther between 1971 and 1975 to 5.1 percent. The allocation of more resources to inland China particularly affected Shanghai. Its share of China's industrial output value declined from 18.1 percent in 1965 to 12.9 percent in 1978.[4] Shanghai's lower rate of industrial growth was accompanied by reduced urbanization. Yet Shanghai did not just grow less. Its population contracted by 6.75 percent between 1965 and 1975. Shanghai was not the only place that experienced depressed urbanization. All of China did in the late 1960s and the 1970s. Nationwide, urban China shrank by 0.6 percent between 1965 and 1975. Coastal provinces were even more impacted, dwindling by 1.4 percent. Inland provinces were affected less. But urban areas still diminished by an average of 0.75 percent.[5]

Very high rates of investment in heavy industry also pushed down government spending on raising standards of living. In total, funding for producer goods between 1966 and 1975 took up 83 percent of the capital construction budget. Housing, on the other hand, obtained less than 5 percent. Social services received less than 3 percent, and urban utilities acquired less 2 percent. These were the lowest rates of investment in lifting living standards of the entire Mao period, even lower than during the Great Leap, which were a few percentage points higher.[6] As Nicholas Lardy has shown, large expenditures on heavy industry did not translate into better wages for workers since almost all financing went to capital construction and boosting production.[7] In fact, average annual wages for SOE workers declined from 636 RMB in 1966 to 605 RMB in 1976, and annual consumption of basic goods – such as grain, meat, and vegetable oil – all stagnated.[8]

It would be imprudent to attribute national patterns of urbanization, industrial growth, and consumption solely to the Third Front since at roughly the same time the CCP carried out the sent-down-youth movement, which shifted 13 million urban youngsters to the countryside, and

[4] Xu Youwei and Chen Xi, "Sanxian jianshe dui zhongguo gongye jingji ji chengshe hua de yingxiang," in *Xiao sanxian jianshe yanjiu luntan*, ed. Xu Youwei and Chen Donglin (Shanghai: Shanghai daxue chubanshe, 2015), 74–76.

[5] Xu and Chen, "Sanxian jianshe dui zhongguo gongye jingji ji chengshe hua de yingxiang," 68–69.

[6] Zhao, *Zhonghua renmin gongheguo jingji shi 1967–1984*, 192.

[7] Lardy, *Economic Growth*, 88, 174.

[8] Sun Jian, *Zhonghua renmin gongheguo jingji shi: 1949–90 niandai chu* (Beijing: Zhongguo renmin daxue chubanshe, 1992), 388. Also see Naughton, *Chinese Economy*, 80–81.

the Cultural Revolution, which impacted economic activities nationwide, especially between 1966 and 1969.[9] That said, there is strong evidence that the Third Front was a major cause. Investment in capital construction along the coast was 12 percent less than during the First Five Year Plan, whereas funding for the Third Front grew and accounted for roughly two-fifths of China's capital construction budget.[10] There is thus little reason to doubt that the Third Front was a significant cause of the coast's economic contraction and reduced urbanization. The allocation of so many resources towards building up heavy industry in the Third Front also surely contributed to reduced consumption throughout China. The Third Front campaign certainly influenced Shanghai's development too, because 354,900 residents were sent to the Third Front between 1964 and 1979. If every single one of these people was an industrial worker, this would mean that around a quarter of Shanghai's industrial labor force in 1964 was assigned to the Third Front.[11] We know this was not the case since some people who were transferred to the Third Front worked in social services. However, this only means that the Third Front's impact on Shanghai's development was not just confined to industry.

Investment in the Third Front also created problems for inland China. In 1984, the State Council issued a report on the status of Third Front enterprises. According to its findings, 48 percent could be considered successful since they had marketable products and favorable prospects. The framing of this statistic gives a positive spin to the Third Front's economic consequences by highlighting its achievements. Looked at from the other side, this number means that over half of Third Front enterprises were a failure. Of these, 7 percent suffered from severe problems, such as flash floods, mudslides, and a lack of water supply. Other work units were located deep inside caves, which led to elevated rates of endemic disease and issues with land subsidence. A few enterprises were even exposed to radioactive pollution. The State Council classified 145 out of 1,945 work units as having acute problems. Of these, 121 were judged salvageable and relocated.[12] The rest were abandoned and left to decay like other military ruins of the global Cold War.[13]

[9] Bernstein, *Up to the Mountains*, 2. Naughton, *Chinese Economy*, 75.

[10] Zhu, *Zhongguo xiandai gongye shi*, 481–482.

[11] Shanghai shi difangzhi bangongshi, "Shusong jishu rencai jianshe da xiao sanxian," www.shtong.gov.cn/node2/node2245/node4471/node56224/node56232/node56234/userobject1ai42781.html, accessed August 13, 2018.

[12] Zhu, *Zhongguo xiandai gongye shi*, 489. Interview with Third Front scholar, Beijing, 2013.

[13] For examples in the United States, see Tom Vanderbilt, *Survival City: Adventures among the Ruins of Atomic America* (Chicago: The University of Chicago Press, 2010).

Historian Chen Donglin estimates that around 18 percent of Third Front expenditures were wasted on failed projects.[14] Unfortunately, Chen does not clarify how he came up with this number. This statistic is still rather stunning. It means that China spent 36.9 billion RMB on industrial endeavors later deemed not worth further developing. This quantity is roughly equal to CCP investment in capital construction for all China in 1964 and 1965.[15] Two whole years of national funding were thus expended on projects that economic planners later found of no use. Government investments in industry had not always performed so poorly in Mao's China.

During the First Five Year Plan, every RMB spent on capital construction added about 0.76 RMB to national revenue in both inland and coastal China. During the Third Front campaign, the return rate plunged to 0.31 RMB for inland China, while coastal areas remained higher at 0.66 RMB. The Third Front campaign performed particularly badly between 1966 and 1968 when the factional strife of the Cultural Revolution was most intense. In 1966, Third Front labor finished only 70 percent of originally planned work. In 1967, completion rates plummeted to 47 percent. In 1968, they fell again to 35 percent. In 1969, the central Party resuscitated the Third Front campaign in the face of skirmishes on the Sino-Soviet border. Building efforts, however, still experienced considerable issues. Between 1971 and 1975, the project completion rate rose to 68 percent. While this rate was better than the Third Front campaign's nadir of 35 percent in 1968, it was still low.[16]

Third Front Development and International Insecurity

Construction delays were one factor that pushed up building costs for the Third Front. Another factor was the central Party's determination that projects must be dispersed in covert mountain locations because China's military could not defend the nation's airspace against the perceived threat of attacks by the United States or the Soviet Union. If projects had been placed in more central locations, they could have drawn on existing infrastructure. There would have been much less need to lay new transport, water, power, and communications lines. It might still have been necessary to construct factory buildings, but it would have not been required to lug materials out into the boondocks to build what Third

[14] Chen, *Sanxian*, 430.

[15] Guojia tongji ju, *Zhongguo tongji nianjian 1983* (Beijing: Zhongguo tongji chubanshe, 1983), 323.

[16] Ma Quanshan, *Xin Zhongguo gongye jingji shi, 1966–1978* (Beijing: Jingji guanli chubanshe, 1998), 282–283.

Fronters often still refer to as their work unit's "little society" (*xiao shehui*). To understand more clearly what Third Fronters are talking about, let us look at an example.

In 1965, the East China Bureau decided to build Factory 9334 in the same area that had housed the Jiangxi Soviet in the 1930s. The precise site chosen was in a dense forest deep in the mountains forty-five kilometers from the nearest county town. Since there was little flatland, the factory complex was split into pieces. Each piece was placed either in a big valley that wrapped around a mountain or in one of two side valleys. In addition to setting up regular factory buildings, a small power plant and local electrical grid were built for the factory. A residential area was constructed a kilometer away which had shops and a school, nursery, bank, post office, assembly hall, bathing house, medical clinic, and canteen.[17] Factory leaders also allocated a few trucks to drive workers over 100 kilometers to the Nanchang train station, so that they could go on work trips and visit relatives.[18]

Regular supply lines for Third Front factories could be very long, too. In some instances, factories in the southwest made parts for coastal assembling plants. Other factories depended on supplies coming from the coast. For instance, the parts of some naval vessels were mainly produced in coastal work units which relied on assembling plants over 1,000 kilometers away in the mountains around Chongqing in Sichuan and Yichang in Hubei. After boats were put to together, they had to travel all the way back down the Yangzi to the coast to be tested and deployed.[19] Shipbuilding was made even more complicated by the fact that some production facilities were put in caves to keep them safe.[20]

The CCP's policy of placing factories in caves lifted construction costs. In total, twenty Third Front power plants were built inside subterranean complexes. In the least costly case, building expenses were ten times more than a comparable power plant aboveground. In the priciest case, financial outlays were almost thirty times more.[21] Available sources do not indicate how many Third Front factories were located in caves. Sources do detail why they were very pricey. Not only did workers have to excavate enough space to fit a factory; they also had to structurally reinforce

17 Zhang Xiaohua, "Huiyi Jiangxi xiao sanxian jianshe," in *Xiao sanxian jianshe yanjiu luntan*, 127.

18 Cheng Yulong, "Jiangxi xiao sanxian jianshe guangming jixie chang (9334 chang)," in *Xiao sanxian jianshe yanjiu luntan*, 158. Fu Rushan, "Wode Jiangxi xiao sanxian huiyi," in *Xiao sanxian jianshe yanjiu luntan*, 139–140.

19 Guowuyuan, *Sanxian*, 158–159, 226–227.

20 Interview with grandson of naval officer, Chicago, 2011.

21 Li Daigeng, ed., *Xin Zhongguo dianli gongye fazhan shilue* (Beijing: Qiye guanli chubanshe, 1984), 221–223.

caverns and make tunnels to divert exhaust, so that enemy planes flying overhead would not know a factory's precise location. Workers also dug out ventilation ducts to reduce humidity. It was hard to generate a strong enough draft to keep caves dry, and so industrial equipment frequently rusted in the moist air.[22] The CCP's order to locate enterprises near mountains led to other water-related problems. When it rained, valleys flooded, and mudslides flowed into factory complexes. A common solution to flooding was erecting stone or concrete walls to prevent landslides and making ditches to channel rainwater away from factory buildings and living areas.[23]

Additional time and energy went into choosing the geographic placement of Third Front projects. Take the well-documented case of the Second Automobile Works. Ministerial and provincial officials drove around in jeeps for a year inspecting sites in Hunan, Sichuan, Guizhou, Hubei, and Shaanxi.[24] They moved around so much that the Second Automobile Works became known as a "briefcase company" (*pibao gongsi*), named after the case full of documents that project leaders carried around during their search for a suitable location.[25] After extensive investigations, the survey team recommended the small town of Shiyan along the Han river in northwest Hubei. The Planning Commission rejected the proposal because nearby mountains did not conceal the factory enough. Practicing the art of bureaucratic resistance, project leaders undertook two more surveys and again recommended Shiyan. The Planning Commission approved their plan the second time around.

However, the precise layout of the Second Automobile Works remained an open question since the approved plan designated an eighty-six-kilometer area. One group of administrators advocated spreading the factory out on both sides of the Han river. Another group pushed for the river's west side, where mountains were higher. Still another group argued that workshops should be made to resemble a village, and

22 Li Daigeng, *Xin Zhongguo dianli gongye*, 221. Chen, *Sanxian*, 431. For examples from the northwest, see Zhongguo dianli shi zhi bianji weiyuanhui, *Zhonghua renmin gongheguo dianli gongye shi xibei juan* (Beiing: Zhongguo dianli chubanshe, 2001), 67–71.

23 Interview with car body factory worker, Shiyan, January 2012. Interview with oil pump factory worker, Pengzhou, June 2016. For an example of flooding at the Second Automobile Works, see Tushifang tuan, wu qi mucai chang, zong zhihui bu baodaozu, "He shan you wo chong anpai," in *Baogao wenxue ji*, ed. Er qi jianshe zong zhihuibu (Shiyan: Erqi jianshe zong zhihuibu, 1972), 257–270.

24 Li Xueshi, "Xuanze erqi changzhi de huiyi," in *Jiqi suiyue: Jinian Dongfeng qiche gongsi jianshe 35 zhou nian*, ed. Dongfeng qiche gongsi li tuixiu renyuan guanli chu (Beijing: Zhongguo shehui chubanshe, 2004), 43–49.

25 "'Di er qiche zhizao changzhi' bianzuan weiyuanhui," *Di er qiche zhizao changzhi 1969–1983*, 8.

buildings should be no bigger than 1,000 square meters. Since the whole factory complex needed a million square meters of building space, this proposal would have required a thousand separate buildings. A leader of China's car industry, Meng Shaonong, thought this idea was preposterous, telling his colleagues at a meeting that its supporters must "have never seen a factory." After a long debate, project leaders decided to construct thirty-four separate sub-factories.[26] Each one had its own air-raid shelter. If every civil defense facility in Shiyan was combined in one single location, they would have been big enough to hold ten football fields.[27]

While these security precautions took extra time and money, provincial military leaders still emphasized speeding up construction since war could erupt at any moment, and the military needed more transport vehicles. One strategy that provincial leaders promoted was reducing the use of scarce materials which the Second Automobile Works would have to wait to obtain. Officials decided that instead of holding off on construction until cement shipments arrived, they should implement the Maoist principle of local self-reliance, make factory buildings out of rammed earth, and in some cases even forgo walls and just put up pillars. Technicians protested that dirt structures would not be able to withstand the vibrations of heavy machinery. The elements would corrode equipment, and peasants would walk into wall-less workshops and steal factory materials. Local leaders accused technical personnel of lacking revolutionary commitment and decried their portrayal of peasants as thieves. Workers then mashed mud together and made factory buildings. A short while later, machinery was installed and rusted in the moist open air. When machines started up, factory walls rocked and cracked. But before that even happened, tools began to disappear from workshops.[28]

The Party center's militarized drive to speed up industrialization also deeply impacted the construction of Third Front railroads. Hurrying to make them operational, workers did not follow regular planning methods and first perform geological surveys, then make designs, and finally begin construction. They did all three at the same time. The resultant railroads had to undergo years of costly refurbishing. Take the Jiaozuo–Zhiliu Railroad. The Party held a ceremony to celebrate its completion in 1970. Yet it was only rideable in 1978. The Beijing–Yuanping, Zhicheng–Liuzhou, Hunan–Guizhou, and Xiangfan–Chongqing

[26] Zhang Guodian, "Qunzhong yu liangdao xiang jiehe de chengguo," in *Erqi jianchang shiliao di yi ji* (Shiyan: Erqi changzhi bianji sh, 1982), 5–8.

[27] "'Di er qiche zhizao changzhi' bianzuan weiyuanhui," *Di er qiche zhizao changzhi 1969–1983*, 429.

[28] Chen Zutao, *Wode qiche shengya* (Beijing: Renmin chubanshe, 2005), 166–167.

railroads all had the same problem. They were structurally unsound, and though they were all officially "built" in the early 1970s, they were not usable until the end of the decade, after designs had been remade, bridges reconstructed, drainage systems refurbished, and mountainsides reinforced.[29]

It is difficult to evaluate how Third Front projects' many problems would have affected Chinese combat operations if the Soviets or the Americans had waged war on China. In the event that fighting had erupted in the early 1970s, Third Front industries would have probably been of limited use since many projects were not operational until the mid-1970s. On the other hand, a completely functional industrial base was not the CCP's immediate goal. This was especially true in the late 1960s when the Soviet Union seemed to be on the brink of invading northern China and launching not just one but several nuclear strikes on major cities. Faced with the perceived threat of a large-scale war against an adversary that the Party center estimated it could only defeat in a protracted struggle, the CCP leadership charged Third Front workers with building a secure industrial base as quickly as possible with any materials that they could find on hand.

When the CCP pursued this defense-centered developmental strategy, it did so at a time when intense government emphasis on security concerns was the norm among China's chief competitors in the Cold War – the United States and the Soviet Union. Moscow and Washington were both channeling huge sums into building up their air forces and nuclear arsenals, acquiring aircraft and nuclear missiles with intercontinental range and incredibly destructive firepower. When the Third Front campaign was undertaken, China did not have the technological or financial capacity to compete in the international effort to obtain ever more powerful nuclear weapons and airplanes. All China could do was acquire a modest air force and nuclear weapons that could strike the Soviet Far East and America's allies in Asia.

Beijing never had the ability to shape Washington or Moscow's strategic calculus when it came to carrying out nuclear attacks on China, since the CCP did not have an intercontinental ballistic missile with which it could retaliate in kind. Nor did China have a navy that could protect its long coastline. The only geographic realm in which China could compete with American or Soviet military power was on the ground. Third Front industry was spatially designed to bolster China's relative strength in

[29] Li Boyang, "Xiangqian tielu da huizhan," in *Zhiliu qingchun zhiliu zhi ge*, 20. Luo Zisong, "Zhiliu tielu huizhan jishi," in *Zhiliu qingchun zhiliu zhi ge*, 421. Ding Yimou, "Zhiliu tiejian huigu," in *Zhiliu qingchun zhiliu zhi ge*, 386. Zhonghua renmin gongheguo tiedaobu, *Tielu xiujian shiliao, 1963–1980*, 31–35, 69–71, 75–76, 85–87, 176–177.

conducting land-based warfare and to build on the CCP's experience waging guerilla warfare, all while working to boost the technological capabilities of China's industrial defense apparatus.

It is anyone's guess what contributions the Third Front would have made to upholding Chinese security in the event that a Sino-Soviet or Sino-American war had broken out. What is certain is that the Third Front was not abnormal for its time. It was part of a Cold War military pattern, seen in both the Soviet Union and the United States, of governments funneling massive levels of resources into maintaining national security. This trend included efforts to possess military capabilities with which they could outdo their adversaries but also was behind military support for foreign allies whose security was viewed as linked to Soviet or American interests, which led to actions such as America's involvement in Vietnam and Soviet intervention in Afghanistan. When viewed from this perspective, the Third Front was not an anomaly, but was rather akin to a series of weighty military policies executed by China's Cold War rivals in response to perceived major threats to their national security. Thus, while we might be tempted to conclude that the Third Front was an irrational excessive response to Soviet and American military pressures, we miss the global dynamics underpinning the Third Front campaign if our line of reasoning stops there, since the Third Front was mirroring the much broader geopolitical irrationality of the Cold War, in which oversized responses to security threats were a global norm.

Industrializing the Interior

While we cannot know for sure how Third Front industries would have fared in battle, we can assess the CCP's efforts to remold the economy of inland China by comparing regional conditions at the beginning of the Third Front and at its end. One notable difference is that regional output of coal, oil, and electricity all grew. The expansion of inland China's energy base did not immediately translate into a big increase in per capita use of hydrocarbons. As Vaclav Smil has illustrated, most people in China at the conclusion of the Mao era did not rely on oil, electricity, or coal to carry out their daily economic activities. They still largely depended on the energy that came from plant life, animals, and human muscles.[30] That said, by increasing regional energy stocks, the Third Front campaign advanced the entrenchment of an industrial economy in inland China. For the Third Front not only raised regional energy supplies, it also augmented downstream

[30] Vaclav Smil, *China's Past, China's Future: Energy, Food, Environment* (London: Routledge, 2004), 10–14.

economic sectors – such as metallurgy, machine building, and railroads – whose operations required the further production of oil, coal, and electricity. In what follows, I present the growth of industries sustained by these three energy sources. Unless otherwise stated all statistics provided are for 1964 to 1980.

The Coal Development Block

Prior to the commencement of the Third Front, the CCP invested mainly in coal mines in north China and the northeast because that is where the largest known coal deposits were and that is where the core of the coal industry had historically been located.[31] The Third Front brought about a significant change in the coal industry's regional focus.[32] The Planning Commission reoriented the Coal Ministry's attention towards southern China for three reasons. The Party leadership wanted to reduce southern dependence on northern coal and decrease the burden that coal shipments placed on train lines heading southwards. The central Party wanted bigger stocks of energy to be at its disposal for any future war and was worried about the loss of coalfields in the north in a battle with the Soviets. Lastly, the initiation of many Third Front projects in southern China rapidly increased regional demand for coal.[33]

Third Front planners gave special consideration to the southwest. In August 1964, the State Council backed the formation of the Southwest Coal Construction Headquarters and placed it under the direction of the Coal Ministry.[34] The Coal Construction Headquarters concentrated its energies on building the coke town of Liupanshui and opening coal mines near Panzhihua and on the outskirts of Chongqing.[35] The Coal Ministry additionally assisted the provincial governments of Hubei, Hunan, and Jiangxi with developing local coal mines.[36] The Coal Ministry also launched battles to mine coalfields in the northwest and established the Helan Mountain Mining Company in 1965 to oversee regional operations. The Helan Mountain Mining Company directed initiatives to expand coal production at the large coalfield it was named after in Ningxia as well as at other sites in Qinghai and Gansu. The ministry set

[31] Tim Wright, The Political Economy of the Chinese Coal Industry: Black Gold and Blood-Stained Coal (London: Routledge, 2012), 20–21.

[32] Chen, *Sanxian*, 307.

[33] Meitan gongye shigaobianyan zu, *Zhongguo meitan gongye: Er shi ba nian shigao 1949–1976* (Beijing, 2001), 317.

[34] Chen, *Sanxian*, 307. [35] He, *Sanxian*, 124–125, 189.

[36] He, *Sanxian*, 310. Meitan gongye, *Zhongguo meitan gongye*, 317–318.

Table 5.1 *Growth of coal development block in Third Front areas, 1964–1980**

Industrial good	Output in 1964 (10,000 tons)	Output in 1980 (10,000 tons)	Percentage of national output in 1964	Percentage of national output in 1980	Percent increase in production volume
Unwashed coal	8,475	30,727	39.5	49.5	262
Washed coal	222.3	1,339.3	15.1	25.8	502.5
Iron ore	242.4	2,518	9.1	22.4	938.8
Iron	179.6	1,180.7	19.9	31.8	547.4
Steel	182.6	3,712	18.9	29.4	497.6
Steel products	100.3	746.1	14.5	27.5	643.9
Nonferrous metals	9.87	62.65	9.87	50.4	534.8

* Guowuyuan sanxian jianshe tiaozheng gaizao guihua bangong shi sanxian jianshe bianxie zu, *Sanxian jianshe* (Beijing, 1991), 90, 122.

up a separate company to head up work on mines in the Weibei region of Shaanxi.[37]

By 1980, the Coal Ministry had invested 13 billion RMB in the Third Front and built 465 new mineshafts. Regional production of coal had tripled and increased its share of national output by 10 percent to almost half.[38] The southwest and northwest regions transformed from coal importers to exporters, and mines in Guizhou and Sichuan supplied coal to users throughout southern China. Hubei, Hunan, and Jiangxi, on the other hand, remained dependent on coal from northern China.[39] Southern demands for coal would grow even larger in later years in part because at the same time as central planners invested in the coal industry, they boosted regional production of iron and steel.[40]

The Metallurgy Ministry devoted 14.6 billion RMB to building new steel production facilities in inland China and another 4.89 billion RMB to improving existing steel plants in Chongqing and Wuhan.[41] To supervise regional activities, the ministry formed one construction headquarters in the northwest and another in the southwest. They supervised the building of thirteen new steel complexes.[42] The biggest new steel factories were

37 Chen, *Sanxian*, 310. 38 Guowuyuan, *Sanxian*, 71, 88, 90.
39 Meitan gongye, *Zhongguo meitan gongye*, 314. 40 Chen, *Sanxian*, 252–254.
41 Guowuyuan, *Sanxian*, 104, 121. 42 Chen, *Sanxian*, 253.

Panzhihua Steel and Changcheng Steel in Sichuan, Shuicheng Steel in Guizhou, Wuyang Steel in Henan, Jiuquan Steel in Gansu, Wulai Steel in Shandong, and Shaoguan Steel in Guangdong.[43] The Ministry of Metallurgy also established a facility to manufacture large amounts of rolled steel in Wuhan. By 1980, regional production of iron and steel had sextupled, and the share of the national total of each rose by 10 percent. Roughly comparable growth occurred in regional output of iron and steel products, while mining of iron ore vaulted upwards 938 percent, and regional production of nonferrous metals skyrocketed 40 percent to about half of national output.[44]

Central planners also administered the growth of the industrial sector that historically has absorbed tons of iron products – railroads.[45] The Railroad Ministry earmarked 20.9 billion RMB to build railroads in inland China. Some funds went into constructing 8,046 kilometers of new tracks and electrifying 3,298 kilometers of new and existing lines. The ministry further augmented regional railroads by laying 3,800 kilometers of additional tracks on existent lines and expanding fifteen railroad hubs in provincial capitals and sub-provincial cities. Overall, regional rail rose from around a fifth of the nation's stock to over a third, and regional freight traffic quintupled. Anticipating growth in regional railroad use, the ministry increased production of boxcars, catapulting the regional share of national output from only 1 percent to slightly above half.[46]

The centerpiece of Third Front railroad construction was ten new interprovincial lines. In the southwest, railroads linked all provincial capitals for the first time with the building of the Guiyang–Kunming and Chengdu–Kunming lines. The Hunan–Guizhou and Xiangfan–Chongqing railroads finally connected every province in central and western China and doubled routes between the two regions from two to four. Further reinforcing links between China's coast and the interior, central planners double-tracked the Shijiazhuang–Taiyuan and Beijing–Baotou railroads and constructed the Qinghai–Tibet Railroad's eastern portion. The Party center also approved giving a second track to a mainstay of traffic between eastern and western China – the Longhai Railroad. As for the country's north–south axis, the Beijing–Liuzhou Railroad became the second line to traverse the country from north to south, and the southern portion of the Beijing–Guangzhou line gained a second track. The Party additionally constructed the Southern Xinjiang Railroad and a railroad across southern Shaanxi.[47]

[43] Guowuyuan, *Sanxian*, 104. [44] Guowuyuan, *Sanxian*, 122.

[45] Nicholas Crafts and C.K. Harley, "Output Growth and the Industrial Revolution: A Restatement of the Crafts–Harley View," *Economic History Review* 45 (1992): 703–730.

[46] Guowuyuan, *Sanxian*, 40–41, 55–57.

[47] Guowuyuan, *Sanxian*, 40–50, 55–57. Zhonghua renmin gongheguo tiedaobu, *Tielu xiujian shiliao, 1963–1980*, 114–120.

Vice premier Li Xiannian explained well the economic rationale behind Third Front railroads during a meeting about constructing the Hunan–Guizhou Railroad in 1970. According to Li, "the southwest . . . had a big stomach" that was rich in resources, but its development was stunted because its "neck was too narrow," and so resources from other regions could not easily reach or move around the southwest. The Hunan–Guizhou line would aid in resolving this infrastructural problem since it would enable more resources to circulate within the southwest as well as be transported in from the rest of the country.[48] After Li Xiannian made these comments, nearly a million workers became involved in building the Hunan–Guizhou line. Construction efforts did not proceed smoothly. The State Council initially set a completion date of 1973.[49] In the end, it took nearly a decade. However, once the line went into service in the late 1970s, it became the principal railroad of western Hunan. Other interprovincial railroads built as part of the Third Front also still serve as major arteries of railroad traffic in the Chinese interior.

The Oil Development Block

During the Third Front campaign, central planners also advanced the growth of the oil industry in the interior, assigning 18.2 billion RMB to its development. The Oil Ministry drilled twenty-nine oilfields and thirty-two natural-gas fields, raising regional production of oil and gas 812 percent and 612 percent respectively.[50] The ministry devoted much of its attention to four large endeavors. The biggest natural-gas project was in Sichuan at Luzhou.[51] The ministry also established the Jianghan oilfield in Hubei, the Central Plains oilfield in Henan, and the Changqing oilfield in the Shaanxi–Gansu–Ningxia basin, and it expanded production at existing oilfields in Qinghai and Gansu.[52] Oil refining capacity was lifted 660 percent, and the number of oil tankers in circulation increased.[53] Regional production of chemical fibers additionally shot up from nil to 16 percent of the national total, and nylon output rose from 6.5 percent to 15 percent.[54]

48 Zhang Xueliang, *Pieshan zaolu: Xiangqian tielu sheji shigong yu jianshe tongche* (Shengyang: Jilin chuban jituan youxianzerengongsi, 2010), 11–12.

49 "Guowuyuan zhongyang junwei pizhuan Xiangqian Zhilu tielu jianshe huiyi jiyao," February 25, 1970.

50 Guowuyuan, *Sanxian*, 84, 99.

51 Guowuyuan, *Sanxian*, 87. Chen, *Sanxian*, 313.

52 Guowuyuan, *Sanxian*, 84–86.

53 Guowuyuan, *Sanxian*, 84. Sichuan sheng defang zhi bianzuan weiyuanhui, ed., *Sichuan shengzhi shiyou tianranqi gongye zhi* (Chengdu: Sichuan renmin chubanshe, 1997), 128–129, 154–155, 194. Shaanxi sheng defang zhi bianzuan weiyuanhui, *Shaanxi shengzhi shiyou huaxue gongye zhi* (Xi'an: Shaanxi renmin chubanshe, 1991), 42.

54 Guowuyuan, *Sanxian*, 206.

Table 5.2 *Growth of oil development block in Third Front areas, 1964–1980**

Industrial good	Output in 1964	Output in 1980	Percentage of national output in 1964	Percentage of national output in 1980	Percent increase in production volume
Crude oil	605,700 tons	5,607,000 tons	7.4	5.29	826
Oil refining capacity	1,908,000 tons	14,420,000 tons	16.45	15.36	656
Natural gas	900 million m^3	6.41 billion m^3	58.21	44.92	612
Trucks	13**	51,090	0	23	392,900
Internal combustion engines	875,800 horsepower***	4,580,400 horsepower	31.45	18.04	423
Mail motorcycles	0	7,400	0	37.5	-
Heavy-duty tires	92,000	2,454,000	4	21.4	2,567.4
Chemical fertilizers	307,500 tons	5,017,500 tons	30.5	40.7	1,531.7
Synthetic fibers	840 tons	72,700 tons	2.63	16.14	8,554

* Guowuyuan, *Sanxian*, 67–68, 134, 187–188.
** This statistic is for 1965–1980.
*** This statistic is for 1965–1980.

Unlike with coal, raising regional output of oil and gas did not lead to inland provinces producing a bigger portion of China's total supply since the Daqing oilfield in Heilongjiang and the Shengli oilfield in Shandong were so much larger than Third Front oilfields.[55] This meant that the regional automotive industry established during the Third Front was from the beginning reliant on outside sources of petroleum, a dependency that would only become bigger as the number of automobiles on regional roads rose, and the amount of weight they carried grew.

Economic planners centered inland China's new automobile industry on three large factories: the Second Automobile Works in Hubei, the Sichuan Automobile Factory near Chongqing, and the Shaanxi Heavy Duty Automobile Factory. In accordance with the productivist predisposition of the Maoist state, none of these factories manufactured cars for individual use. They produced heavy-duty trucks designed to move lots and lots of

[55] On the development of the Daqing and Shengli oilfields, see Liang Hua and Liu Jinyi, eds., *Zhongguo shiyou tongshi, 1949–1978* (Beijing Zhongguo shihua chubanshe, 2003), 201–238.

freight.[56] By 1980, there were significantly more trucks coming out of inland China that could do just that. Regional production climbed from almost nothing to just a little under a quarter of national output. Regional manufacturing of small tractors, meanwhile, rose from 12 percent of national output to 28 percent, and production of internal combustion engines quadrupled. A new tire industry was founded that made a quarter of China's supply. A new bicycle industry was formed that produced 8 percent of the nation's stock, and facilities were built to produce parts for cars and tractors.[57]

As more motor vehicles came into use in inland China, the Transportation Ministry supervised the extension of regional roads. In total, the ministry funneled 28.9 billon RMB into building 227,900 kilometers of roads. By 1980, roads suitable for motor vehicles reached 95 percent of small towns, and 73 percent of roads were paved and usable in all weather.[58] Regional road freight increased by 62 percent. To service trucks traveling along new roads, more gas stations were established; mechanics were trained, and repair shops opened their doors.[59]

The Post and Telecommunications Ministry took advantage of new roads and added postal routes, quadrupling their total length and doubling inland China's proportion of national postal routes to 44 percent. The growth in postal routes was in large part due to the rise of postal motorcycles delivering mail to destinations far and near, as inland China's fleet of postal motorcycles leaped from nothing to almost two-fifths of the national stock. With more postal vehicles plying roadways, regional letter traffic doubled to about 700 million letters per year.[60]

The Electricity Development Block

While the Post and Telecommunications Ministry handled sending more mail around inland China, the Power and Water Resources Ministry enhanced the transmission of electricity, expending 18.5 billion RMB

[56] For an overview of the Chinese automobile industry at the time, see Zhongguo qiche gongye shi bianshen weiyuanhui, ed., *Zhongguo qiche gongye shi, 1901–1990* (Beijing: Renmin jiaotong chubanshe, 1996), 110–125.

[57] Guowuyuan, *Sanxian*, 134, 188, 198. "Hubeisheng zhi gongye zhigao shiyou" bianzuan weiyuanhui, ed., *Hubei shengzhi gongye zhigao shiyou* (Jianghan: Hubei renmin chubanshe, 1990), 188–190.

[58] Guowuyuan, *Sanxian*, 49–50, 60–61.

[59] Guowuyuan, *Sanxian*, 59, 61, 63. Sichuan sheng defang zhi bianzuan weiyuanhui, *Sichuan shengzhi shiyou tianranqi gongye zhi*, 182–185. Hubei shengzhi gongye zhigao shiyou bianzuan weiyuanhui, *Hubei shengzhi gongye zhigao shiyou*, 217–218, 224–225.

[60] Guojia tongji ju guomin jingji zonghe tongji si, *Xin zhongguo 50 nian tongji ziliao huibian* (Beijing: Zhongguo tongji chubanshe, 1999), 558, 583, 716, 741, 785, 835, 859. Guowuyuan, *Sanxian*, 40, 67–68, 93.

on power generation.[61] By 1980, most inland provinces produced ten times more electricity than in 1964. The only exceptions were Yunnan and Shaanxi where electricity output quintupled. In total, the Power and Water Resources Ministry added sixty-four power plants to inland China's energy sector. Their output contributed roughly twenty-four Hoover Dams (102 billion kWh) to annual electricity production, and the region's share of the national electricity supply rose to 10 percent.

Forty-six thermal plants were established. Some were put in provincial capitals like Chengdu and Guiyang. Others went to sub-provincial cities – such as Xuanwei in Guizhou, Jiangyou in Sichuan, or Hancheng in Shaanxi – which obtained a number of Third Front enterprises with large energy requirements. The hydroelectric sector, meanwhile, gained eighteen power stations. Total hydroelectric capacity skyrocketed 1,624 percent to 10.56 million kilowatts, and regional production capacity tripled to three-fifths of national output. The biggest dams were Gezhouba and Danjiangkou in Hubei, Liujiaxia in Gansu, Wujiang river in Guizhou, Fengtan in Hunan, and Longyangxia in Qinghai. As power stations pumped out more energy, regional power lines were extended in length, gaining 49,847 kilometers of high-transmission cables. A portion of these new power lines went into forging interprovincial electrical grids that serviced all major cities in southwest, northwest, and south-central China.[62]

Some power lines went to the defense industry, which came to produce over half of Chinese military hardware.[63] Four billion RMB was funneled to the arms industry. The largest complexes were scattered around Chongqing and in the west of Hubei, Henan, and Hunan. As with other defense-sector projects, the Infrastructure Corps was responsible for much of their construction.[64] The work units they built produced all sorts of small firearms along with heavy artillery, grenades, missiles, and motorcycles. Their combined output by 1980 accounted for two-thirds of Chinese arms production.[65] At the time of the Third Front campaign, nearly all new airplane facilities were constructed in inland China. Prior to that point, there were very few airplane work units in the region. After the government spent three billion RMB on the airplane sector, regional production capacity jumped to about two-thirds of China's output. The biggest projects were a transport plane base in Hanzhong in Shaanxi,

[61] Guowuyuan, *Sanxian*, 93.
[62] Guowuyuan, *Sanxian*, 76–81, 94–95. Chen, *Sanxian*, 285.
[63] He, *Sanxian jianshe*, 24.
[64] For Infrastructure Corps's involvement in defense sector projects, see Liu, *Zhongguo jiefangjun*, 456–473.
[65] Guowuyuan, *Sanxian*, 150–151.

a helicopter base near Jingdezhen in Jiangxi, and two fighter jet facilities in northern Guizhou and Sichuan.[66] In the late 1960s and early 1970s, almost all new aerospace work units were built in the Third Front. Projects in northern Guizhou, Sichuan, southern Shaanxi, and western Henan were allotted 2.3 billion RMB.[67] Emphasis was especially placed on the study and production of long-range missiles. Major accomplishments included the launch of China's first satellite in 1970, the expansion of the Jiuquan Satellite Launch Facility in Gansu, and the construction of

Table 5.3 *Growth of electricity development block in Third Front areas, 1965–1980**

Industrial good	Output in 1964	Output in 1980	Percentage of national output in 1964	Percentage of national output in 1980	Percent increase in production volume
Electricity	13.4 billion kWh	102 billion kWh	24.1	34.0	661.19
Electricity generating equipment	2.03 kW	127.4 kW	2.97	30.38	4,919
Forging equipment	7,028	25,254	–	–	259
Metal cutting tools	53,254	159,550	–	–	200
Mining equipment	80,360,000 tons**	459,000,000 tons	20	28.2	471
Machine tools	6,191***	38,820	15.6	25.5	527
Sewing machines	38,100	1,341,000	3.73	17.47	3,419
Postal routes	556,700 km	2,093,100 km	15.9	44.2	276
Telegraph lines	2,711	3,514	39	38.4	29.6
Radio	38,600	4,542,800	4.93	15.12	11,669
Television	0	320,190	0	12.9	–
Telephone	478,000	1,326,100	23	31.7	177
Long-distance telephone lines	4,109	8,330	41.5	37.8	102.7
Cement	5,671,700 tons	32,990,000 tons	33.2	38	481.7
Sheet glass	15,000 boxes	6,730,000 boxes	0.2	27.9	44,766.7

* Guowuyuan, *Sanxian*, 68, 139, 167, 187–188, 199.
** This statistic is for 1965–1980.
*** This statistic is for 1965–1980.

66 Chen, *Sanxian*, 290–294. 67 Guowuyuan, *Sanxian*, 148.

the Xichang Satellite Launch Facility in Sichuan and the Taiyuan Satellite Launch Center in Shanxi.[68]

An additional 3.6 billion RMB was spent on building an integrated nuclear sector in Sichuan with facilities for uranium mining and processing as well as making nuclear bombs, missiles, and plants.[69] As for the electronics sector, it received about 2.6 billion RMB for new factories and research institutes. Another 2.7 billion RMB was allocated to improving the technical capabilities of existing factories.[70] By 1980, inland China had over half of China's electronics personnel and manufacturing capacity. The most significant electronics facilities were established at Chengdu and Mianyang in Sichuan, at Baoji and Xianyang in Shaanxi, and at Duyun and Zunyi in Guizhou.[71] The best-known Third Front electronics factory today is Changhong Electric in Mianyang, which was an important contributor to regional production of televisions rising from nothing to 32 percent of the national supply.[72]

Another sector dependent on electricity that saw considerable growth was building materials. Regional production of sheet glass rose from nearly nothing to 27.9 percent of the national total, and output of cement went up 481 percent.[73] One place with substantial industrial development was the Sichuanese city of Deyang – home to the Second Heavy Machinery Works – which was a major factor behind rising regional output of mining equipment and machine tools. Deyang was also home to the Dongfang Electric Machinery Company, which was principally responsible for regional production of electrical generators, jumping from zero to a quarter of the national supply.[74]

While electrical generators brought power to more places, new communication lines brought in more information. By 1980, telecommunication networks connected every provincial capital with every large town under its jurisdiction, and the number of telephones in use nearly tripled. Telegraph lines grew at a slower pace than telephones, increasing only 29 percent, whereas long-distance telephone lines rose 102 percent. Radio infrastructure expanded even more quickly than telephonic. Regional production of radios soared 11,668 percent. Radio transmitters

[68] Chen, *Sanxian*, 296–297. Zhang Quanjing, "Sanxian jianshe de juda chengjiu," *Yan'an wenxue* 5 (2019), at http://m.fx361.com/news/2019/1021/5869276.html, accessed January 3, 2020.

[69] Guowuyuan, *Sanxian*, 142–143.

[70] Chen, *Sanxian*, 281. Guowuyuan, *Sanxian*, 154.

[71] Chen, *Sanxian*, 281.

[72] "Zhe xiang Zhongguo shi shang kongqian de zhanlue gongcheng yingxiang shenyuan dangxia nianqing ren que shao you suowen," *CCTV*, http://m.news.cctv.com/2018/02/18/ARTI8vJWX4PEzFAAJub9qi64180218.shtml, accessed November 7, 2018.

[73] Guowuyuan, *Sanxian*, 139.

[74] Guowuyuan, *Sanxian*, 173–175, 182–188. Chen, *Sanxian*, 266–268, 283–284.

rose 534 percent, and the Post and Telecommunications Ministry set up four radio stations in Shanxi, Shaanxi, Hubei, and Sichuan that could send and receive information internationally.[75]

Standardization, Acceleration, and State Power

As inland China's industrial base became larger, so did its industrial labor force, increasing by a total of 246 percent. More industrial workers meant more state-owned enterprises, which went up by 5 percent to 36 percent of the national stock.[76] Inland China also acquired more research institutes, trade schools, and places of higher education.[77] One consequence of the expansion of industrial, educational, and research infrastructure was the standardization of regional affairs. The main vector of standardization was central ministries which oversaw all Big Third Front projects and extended the reach of the state into inland regions.

Take, for example, the activities of the Railroad Ministry. When it established the Chengdu–Kunming Railroad, it did not just lay tracks, put up bridges, and dig tunnels. The ministry also built up administrative infrastructure to support heightened volumes of traffic. The ministry increased staffing at the region's main railroad bureau in Chengdu, and it founded a sub-bureau in the middle of the line in Xichang. The ministry also ordered workers to construct over 100 new train stations. Each new station had departments responsible for handling railroad affairs according to standard rules of procedure. There were regulations about how to handle financial transactions, statistics collection, shipping procedures, and ticket fares.[78]

Adherence to rules instituted by the Railroad Ministry in Beijing was definitely uneven. Just because a ministerial regulation existed did not mean that all work units subordinate to its conditions acted accordingly. As Eddy U's work has illustrated, bureaucrats in Mao's China routinely bent or overlooked rules due to staff shortages or conflicting administrative interests.[79] Nevertheless, even though individual staff flexibly implemented rules, the Third Front campaign still increased the lines of authority that ran from the Railroad Ministry into inland provinces, and centrally mandated rules still defined the range of practices that ministerial work units were officially allowed to engage in when managing resources under their authority.

[75] Guowuyuan, *Sanxian*, 53–54, 68. [76] Guowuyuan, *Sanxian*, 33–35.

[77] Guowuyuan, *Sanxian*, 37–39.

[78] Zhonghua renmin gongheguo tiedaobu, *Tielu xiujian shiliao, 1963–1980*, 89–93. Chengdu tielu fenju "Xichang tielu fen ju zhi" bianweihui, *Xichang tielu fen ju zhi, 1970–1998* (Chengdu: Chengdu tielu fenju Xichang tielu fenju, 2001), 102, 168, 176, 179, 182, 191 .

[79] Eddy U, *Disorganizing China: Counter-bureaucracy and the Decline of Socialism* (Stanford: Stanford University Press, 2007).

Table 5.4 *Increases in industrial labor and industrial companies in Third Front areas, 1965–1980**

Industrial sector	Labor size in 1980	Percentage increase	Number of companies in 1980	Percentage increase
Machine building	1,600,000	396	2,223	100.81
Steel	792,000	100	1,077	898.4
Nonferrous metals	413,400	139	945	483
Oil and gas	NA	NA	110	323
Coal	1,580,000	213.1	1,171	117
Chemicals	861,500	1305.4		
Defense	1,400,000	315	868	463
Aerospace	87,000	590	144	1,800
Shipbuilding	110,000	562	67	570
Light industry	NA	NA	81,807	172.5

* Guowuyuan, *Sanxian*, 89, 100, 122, 129, 133, 164–165, 183–184, 197.

Table 5.5 *Increases in research and educational infrastructure in Third Front areas, 1964–1980**

Research and educational sector	Number of institutes in 1980	Percentage increase	Number of employees	Percentage increase
Research institutes	1,503	197	218,100	136
Higher education	340	172	278,456	215
Trade schools	1,294	122	151,919	193

* Guowuyuan, *Sanxian*, 37–39.

Like Third Front railroads, new factories were also subject to ministerial directives that determined their budget, suppliers, product line, and production schedules, and the purchasers of their goods.[80] To ensure laborers knew regular operating procedures, ministries required participation in training sessions and furnished labor with handbooks that presented correct work practices for someone in their industrial sector. Handbooks set out rules for a wide range of activities.[81] There were rules

[80] Yejin gongye bu Changcheng gang chang si fen chang chang zhi bianji weiyuanhui bangongshi, *Changcheng gangtie chang si fen chang zhi, 1965–1985* (Jiangyou: Yejin gongye bu Changcheng gang chang si fen chang chang zhi bangongshi, 1988), 384–385, 388–389, 392, 396–397.

[81] On the use of handbooks in Mao-era exhibits, see Ho, *Curating Revolution*, 21, 23–24, 362.

about wage scales, safety policies, and evaluating worker performance. Other manuals distributed to technicians gave technical explanations of how to operate different machinery and manufacture different industrial products, such as car parts out of various kinds of steel.[82]

Central authorities also regularly sent down directives that described how work units ought to run various economic campaigns.[83] The standardization of regional economic activities according to campaign demands sometimes impeded the production process. For instance, in the late 1960s, the Party center pushed a policy of "spending less money and doing more things" (*shao huaqian duo banshi*). Changcheng Steel in Sichuan responded to this policy by eliminating the roof over one factory workshop and not erecting a wall around the factory complex. These design decisions harmed the production process. The perpetually wet air of the Chengdu plain corroded equipment, and nearby peasants went into workshops and disrupted factory affairs. Some factory equipment also frequently broke down because manufacturers paid more attention to total output than to quality control.[84]

On the other hand, production at Changcheng Steel would never have been possible if the Metallurgy Ministry had not furnished it with technically trained personnel and standardized industrial hardware. One key piece of equipment that central ministries allotted to Third Front enterprises was trucks which brought in supplies to isolated locations and carried out finished products. When trucks transported materials to Third Front projects, they were also supposed to abide by the rules of the road set by the Transportation Ministry. Regulations covered topics such as correct hand signals, licensing procedures, speed limits, how to handle accidents, and who could take certain types of automobiles.[85]

With the building of more roads and railroads in inland China, regional transit times dropped. The frequency of scheduled trips increased, and passenger traffic on new bus lines and railroads came to adhere to centrally set timetables.[86] For instance, prior to the construction of the Chengdu–Kunming Railroad, a truck ride from Chengdu to Kunming

[82] See, for example, *Di yi jixie bu di er jichuang lingbujian biaozhun shouce* (Beijing: Beijing shi xiatu chang, 1971).

[83] For how this practice worked in the journalism field, see Michael Schoenhals, *Doing Things with Words in Chinese Politics: Five Studies* (Berkeley: Institute of East Asian Studies, University of California, Berkeley, 1992).

[84] Yejin gongye bu Changcheng gang chang si fen chang chang zhi bianji weiyuanhui bangongshi, *Changcheng gangtie chang si fen chang zhi*. For efficiency problems more generally, see Riskin, *China's Political Economy*, 278–279.

[85] For a presentation of traffic rules, see *Chengshi yu gonglu guanli guize* (Beijing: Renmin jiaotong chubanshe, 1972).

[86] Chengdu tielu ju, *Quanguo tielu luke lieche shikebiao* (Chengdu: Chengdu tielu ju, 1975).

required about eight days. After the completion of the Chengdu–Kunming line, it took around eighteen hours. While this new journey was still not short, it was less than a tenth of the previous travel time. Thanks to the advent of rail, it was also possible to take trips between Chengdu and Kunming several times a day.[87] The growth of road networks made it possible to travel faster to even more locations since the total length of new roads was over twenty-seven times greater than that of railroads.

Inland China's expanded communication infrastructure additionally enhanced the integration of the region into nationwide information networks. On new postal routes and telephone lines, more messages reached more places in less time according to nationwide prices and procedures set by the Ministry of Post and Telecommunications.[88] Key users of inland China's augmented communication networks were central government agencies which principally relied on long-distance channels to interact with Third Front work units scattered around the country. Trucks and motorcycles were the main carriers of government orders and reports to Third Front projects. They transported Party documents, newspapers, magazines, and mobile film projection teams, while telephone lines allowed more on-the-spot communication between local and central and provincial authorities. Third Front projects were also linked into national media through a PA system managed by the local cultural department.[89] Every Third Front work unit tuned in twice a day to listen to the Central Radio's digest of domestic and foreign events, so that they saw their own efforts to industrialize inland regions as part of the Chinese people's broader struggle to develop the nation and win the Cold War.[90]

Third Front participants all over China heard national radio broadcasts, whether someone was a top leader in an office in Beijing or a manual laborer at a remote construction site. Uniting all these people was a vision of economic development as a vital national affair that required a centrally directed bureaucracy with administrative branches spanning the whole country. All domestic economic actors were also assumed to take building socialist industrial modernity in China as their primary goal. When it came to big economic initiatives like the Third Front, the necessity of

[87] Interview with steelworker, Panzhihua, 2011.

[88] "Zhongguo youpiao shi" di ba juan bianweihui, *Zhongguo youpiao shi, di ba juan* (1965–1978) (Beijing: Shangwu yin shuguan, 2000).

[89] Interview with diesel pump factory worker, Pengzhou, June 2016.

[90] Interview with cultural worker, Pengzhou, June 2016. Xu Xiaoling, "Shangou li de guangbo zhan," in *Women renmin chang xia: Jiangxi "xiao sanxian" 9333 chang shilu*, ed. Mao Xiaobing (Shanghai: Shanghai renmin chubanshe, 2014), 726–727.

maintaining unified governmental control had been driven home for CCP leaders during the Great Leap. Worried about again putting too much strain on the countryside, Party leaders built on the Daqing model of industrial development and granted central government agencies supervision over Cold War China's hinterland war machine.

Party efforts to keep the Third Front secure from international threats drove up construction costs. Particularly important in this regard was the administrative rule that Third Front projects be placed in "mountainous, dispersed, hidden" locations. Special surveys had to be taken to find the most fitting site for an enterprise, and wherever administrators selected, it was always expensive to outfit each Third Front project with its own "little society" of extensive welfare services. Pushing expenses even further upward was the necessity of laying additional transportation, power, communication, and water lines to maintain production at factories scattered over large areas.

In late 1966, the entire Third Front campaign was inundated with problems when the Cultural Revolution placed in question the political trustworthiness of every technician and administrator and upended the top-down approach to national development that stood at the core of the Third Front campaign. Even when Third Front construction was brought back online due to the 1969 Sino-Soviet border conflict, projects were still plagued with issues, as administrators goaded workers to charge ahead with constructing projects despite the fact that designs were not fully elaborated, and necessary building materials were unavailable. If someone suggested acting otherwise, they were playing with political fire and could easily be attacked as a "capitalist roader" or "revionist" working for the other side in the Cold War.

It is hard to predict with great accuracy how the problems that afflicted Third Front industries would have impacted their performance if they had been called on to supply China with war materiel. It is likely that the CCP leadership would have tried to suppress the causes of construction difficulties, boost industrial production, and increase the relocation of industrial enterprises to inland provinces. But this is just an informed guess based on what the Party did in anticipation of an international conflict during the Third Front campaign. We can chart out with more confidence how the Third Front industrialized inland China.

During the Third Front campaign, the three large development blocks that make up modern industrial societies became more deeply embedded in the economy of inland China. Production of the principal sources of industrial energy – coal, oil, and electricity – all increased. Economic sectors dependent on their power also experienced notable growth with rises in the manufacture of key industrial materials – such as steel, petrochemicals, and cement – as well as of basic industrial machinery – such as automobiles, mining equipment, and power tools. Ten new interprovincial railroads also linked up hundreds of new locations, and new road networks and communication and power lines reached many more places. More research would be required to determine all the effects that the incorporation of so many localities into broader transport networks had on economic activities at the local and national level. The same goes for the consequences of electrification, increased industrial output, and the extension of communication systems. In this chapter, I have emphasized only a few important outcomes.

Due to the construction of more railroads and roads, distance became less tyrannical, as trucks, trains, motorcycles, and bicycles moved more passengers and freight to more locales at accelerated rates. This enlarged circulation of people and goods was in part made possible by rising regional production of automobiles, hydrocarbons, and electricity. In some instances, such as electricity and natural gas, inland China began to become a source of power for the coast. In other instances, such as oil and coal, regional energy supplies could not keep pace with rising demand, and so they had to be shipped in from other regions to make up for local shortfalls.[91] Over time, this situation only intensified as regional resource needs exceeded local and even national capacity.[92]

While telecommunication networks increased considerably less than transportation routes, the doubling of postal routes compressed the time it took to send messages between different locations and made it possible to reach more remote areas by mail. Growth in postal routes had another significant consequence. It enhanced the reach of central and provincial officials into local society. Mail carriers shuttled government directives downwards to individual work units and carried local responses and requests back up to higher levels of government. Through this back-and-forth transfer of information, regional economic activities became more standardized, as local areas aligned their conduct with rules and regulations sent down from above.

The effects of government-led standardization were at times incredibly destructive, most notably when, during the Cultural Revolution, officials distributed Party orders to remove from positions of authority anyone suspected of being sympathetic to China's Cold War foes. However,

[91] Zhang Xueliang, ed., *Xi qi dong shu* (Changchun: Jilin chuban jituan youxian zeren gongsi, 2010). Zhang Xueliang, ed., *Fazhan dongle: Xi dian dong song gongcheng jianshe* (Changchun: Jilin chuban jituan youxian zeren gongsi, 2010).

[92] On China's dependence on foreign resources, see Elizabeth C. Economy, *By All Means Necessary: How China's Resource Quest Is Changing the World* (Oxford: Oxford University Press, 2014).

Party-led standardization of inland China could also produce huge bursts of economic activity which augmented industrial infrastructure. Here again the governmental formulas guiding regional development were sometimes very damaging; especially problematic was the race-to-the-finish mentality that led to an inattention to quality control and ironically slowed the completion of projects. Governmental rules were also behind the subordination of efforts to industrialize inland China to Cold War security concerns, which resulted in the production of a costly economic geography of fear. Perhaps Beijing's defensive developmental response to American and Soviet hostility was too much.[93] But was it any more disproportionate than the United States' and the Soviet Union's military response to the perceived threat of nuclear war or to each other's activities in the Third World? Such was the excessive rationality of the global Cold War, where outsized militarized reactions to the danger of capitalist or communist expansion turned into a norm of international statecraft.[94]

[93] Naughton, "The Third Front," 381.
[94] On this point, see Westad, *Global Cold War*; Paul Thomas Chamberlin, *The Cold War's Killing Fields: Rethinking the Long Peace* (New York: Harper Collins, 2018).

Epilogue: The Demilitarization of Chinese Socialism

On February 21, 1972, Richard Nixon became the first American president to visit the People's Republic of China. The roots of this momentous event can be traced back to the late 1960s when both Beijing and Washington re-examined their geopolitical role in the Cold War. On the American side, Nixon sought to extricate the United States from the military quagmire in Vietnam and work towards improved relations with China.[1] Nixon's opening towards China could have failed, were it not for Mao's decision in 1969 to counter mounting Soviet aggression by forging a better relationship with the United States.[2] After years of preparation, Nixon came to China, and Washington and Beijing issued the Shanghai Communiqué. Its contents signaled a historic transformation in how China and the United States characterized each other.

Gone were Chinese proclamations that history's arrow ineluctably pointed towards, as Lin Biao said, "capitalism and imperialism ... heading for their doom and socialism and communism ... marching to victory."[3] The communiqué instead stated that socialist and capitalist states "should conduct their relations" based on the principles of "equality ... mutual benefit ... and peaceful coexistence." If, for some reason, "international disputes" happened between China and the United States, they should be resolved "without resorting to the use or threat of force."[4] After Beijing and Washington declared support for peacefully resolving international disagreements, neither one immediately stopped backing their allies in Vietnam. However, by 1975, they

[1] Evelyn Goh, *Constructing the U.S. Rapprochement with China, 1961–1974: From "Red Menace" to "Tacit Ally"* (Cambridge: Cambridge University Press, 2004), 107, 122.

[2] Chen, *Mao's China*, 239–241, 245–249. The quote is from page 246.

[3] Lin Biao, *Long Live the Victory of People's War*, September 2, 1965, *Marxists Internet Archive*, www.marxists.org/reference/archive/lin-biao/1965/09/peoples_war/ch08.htm, accessed November 21, 2017.

[4] "Joint Statement Following Discussions with Leaders of the People's Republic of China," February 27, 1972, *Foreign Relations of the United States*, https://history.state.gov/historicaldocuments/frus1969-76v17/d203, accessed November 10, 2017.

had both ended their aggression towards each other, not just in Vietnam but all over the world.[5]

As Chinese foreign affairs became uncoupled from militarily pushing back against the exercise of American power abroad, the CCP began to demilitarize its approach to national development. The Planning Commission took an important step in this direction in August 1972 when it recommended that the First and Second Fronts should no longer take supporting the Third Front as "their primary task." They should only treat assisting the Third Front as an "important task." In November, the Planning Commission sounded off again against excessive funding for the Third Front, which had led to the neglect of heavy industry in the First and Second Fronts and underinvestment in agriculture and light industry.[6] Despite the Planning Commission's complaints about China's economic priorities, the Party center only took concerted action to change them at a Work Conference in May 1973.

At the meeting, the Third Front lost its status as the most important economic objective, and central planners resolved to no longer militarize the nation's industrial geography and base the location of new projects on whether enemy bombers could likely see and strike them. In line with this policy decision, state investment was directed away from inland China towards the coast and the northeast, and heavy industry was demoted from its top spot in economic planning and replaced by agriculture and light industry.[7] In accordance with China's new attention to increasing consumer goods, when the Party center allocated $4.3 billion to buy foreign equipment in 1973, they gave precedence to purchasing machinery to produce fertilizer and synthetic fibers.[8]

Most imported machinery was given to companies in the First and Second Fronts. Central planners justified this policy choice by stating that if "foreign counties sent technical experts" to aid with installing and maintaining equipment, "it would be difficult to keep secret Third Front construction." While this may have been true, it is significant that planners did not criticize relying on foreigners from capitalist countries to set up and run equipment and also made no mention of the ease with which foreign forces could attack coastal areas. Instead, they made an efficiency-based argument and asserted that the coast was the best place to locate new equipment because it "had a better industrial base" which could help "imported equipment to become productive faster."[9] To further facilitate

[5] McMahon, *Limits of Empire*, 74–75, 166–169, 180. Khoo, *Collateral Damage*, 100–102, 141.

[6] Chen, *Sanxian*, 242. [7] Ma, *Xin zhongguo*, 109, [8] Ma, *Xin zhongguo*, 110–111.

[9] Chen, *Sanxian*, 240.

coastal economic growth, central planners directed funding towards enhancing port facilities.[10]

Although Mao approved of investing more in the coast and cultivating more friendly relations with the United States, he still wanted Beijing to keep a distance from Washington and opposed Henry Kissinger's suggestion in 1973 that China and the United States form a military alliance against the Soviet Union.[11] Up to Mao's death in 1976, Chinese leaders continued to publicly denounce the United States as capitalist "oppressors." However, they stopped militarily supporting revolutionary anti-imperialist groups and provided economic assistance to the developing world instead.[12] On the domestic front, Mao also wavered between calling for the continuation of revolutionary activities and attacks on Soviet revisionism and bourgeois capitalism *and* supporting reforms that favored development and downsizing the military.[13]

After Mao passed away, it only took a few months for Deng Xiaoping to marshal his extensive contacts among senior leaders and regain top posts in the party-state.[14] Upon taking power, Deng, unlike Mao, did not hesitate to firm up ties between Beijing and Washington. He encouraged more contacts with the United States and normalized relations with China's former Cold War enemy in January 1979.[15] Deng then traveled to the United States and inked agreements to increase cultural, educational, and techno-scientific exchanges. During Deng's visit, Sino-American military relations changed, too.[16] Marking a shift in Chinese nuclear strategy, Deng informed US national security adviser Zbigniew Brzezinski that Beijing was not afraid of a Sino-Soviet war because China had nuclear weapons, which could level major Soviet cities. Deng also let President Jimmy Carter know

[10] Ma, *Xin zhongguo*, 518. Wang Jian, "Su Yu dajiang yu Tianjin gang san qi jiangang gongcheng," *Gonghui xinxi*, April 10, 2015, 43–45.

[11] Chen Donglin, "Zhou Enlai zui jiannan de shike: 1973 nian 'pi zhou' fengbo kaoshu," in *Ershi yi shiji Zhou Enlai yanjiu de xin shiye*, ed. Xu Xing (Beijing: Zhongyang wenxian chubanshe, 2008), 731–743. For an in-depth treatment of Mao's wavering approach to foreign policy in the 1970s, see Yang Kuisong and Yafeng Xia, "Vacillating between Revolution and Détente: Mao's Changing Psyche and Policy toward the United States, 1969–1976," *Diplomatic History* 34 (2010): 395–423.

[12] Chen Jian, "China's Changing Policies towards the Third World and the End of the Global Cold War," in *The End of the Cold War: New Perspectives on Regional Conflicts*, eds. Artemy Kalinovsky and Sergey Radchenko (London: Routledge, 2011), 105–107, 110–111. The quote is on page 107. Friedman, *Shadow Cold War*, 215–221.

[13] For a detailed treatment of this period, see Frederick C. Teiwes and Warren Sun, *The End of the Maoist Era: Chinese Politics during the Twilight of the Cultural Revolution, 1972–1976* (Armonk: M.E. Sharpe, 2007).

[14] Meisner, *Mao's China*, 437. Pantsov and Levine, *Deng*, 325–328. Tanner, *China*, 237.

[15] Ezra F. Vogel, *Deng Xiaoping and the Transformation of China* (Cambridge, MA: Harvard University Press, 2013), 311–348.

[16] Pantsov and Levine, *Deng*, 347.

that China was planning on going to war with Vietnam.[17] With these diplomatic gestures, Deng signaled not only that China and America were both opposed to the Soviet Union. Beijing was also willing to discuss secret war plans with its new capitalist friend across the Pacific.

Deng also spoke with Carter about China's intention to attack Vietnam because he was more worried about the prospect of a Sino-Soviet War than his comments about China's nuclear capabilities let on. The Soviet Union still had hundreds of thousands of troops on China's northern border, as well as missiles and airplanes, which could inflict a massive retaliatory strike on China if it ever carried out a nuclear attack on Soviet territory.[18] Making China even more vulnerable was the fact that Moscow was a close ally of Hanoi. Deng thus sought to gain assurances from Carter that the United States would back China up in the event that the Soviets came to Vietnam's defense. While Washington did not make a formal statement in Beijing's favor, it did send a series of messages to the Kremlin, which indicated that if the Soviet Union acted militarily, then the United States would intervene on China's side.[19]

A month after Deng returned from Washington, the PRC fought a war with socialist Vietnam.[20] Chinese forces fared very badly, losing 25,000 troops in the one month it took for the most intense battles to ignite and peter out.[21] Prior to the Sino-Vietnamese War, Deng had already begun engaging in military reforms, shrinking the PLA by 900,000 to 5.2 million. After hostilities subsided, Deng used China's poor performance to override resistance from military leaders to more reforms.[22] Further legitimizing this policy shift was the Soviet Union's lack of response to China's assault on Vietnam, which significantly reduced concern in Beijing about Moscow using its formidable military might against China. As John Garver has noted, "So too did the fact that Soviet forces were bogged down in an expanding war in Afghanistan."[23]

[17] Pantsov and Levine, *Deng*, 348. For a detailed treatment of Chinese nuclear policy from the late 1970s, see Lei Liu, "'Dog-Beating Stick': General Zhang Aiping's Contribution to the Modernisation of China's Nuclear Force and Strategy since 1977," *Cold War History* 1 (2018): 485–501.

[18] Allen S. Whiting, "Sino-Soviet Relations: What Next?" *Annals of the American Academy of Political and Social Science* 476 (1984): 145.

[19] Garver, *China's Quest*, 400.

[20] For a recent history of the Sino-Vietnam War, see Xiaoming Zhang, *Deng Xiaoping's Long War: The Military Conflict between China and Vietnam, 1979–1991* (Chapel Hill: University of North Carolina Press, 2015).

[21] Garver, *China's Quest*, 385–386.

[22] David C. Gompert, Hans Binnendijk, and Bonny Lin, *Blinders, Blunders, and Wars: What America and China Can Learn* (Santa Monica: RAND Corporation, 2014), 125–126. Vogel, *Deng Xiaoping*, 525–526.

[23] Garver, *China's Quest*, 429.

If the Soviet Union nonetheless still chose to attack China, Deng made clear to the Central Military Commission in 1979 that he intended for the United States to play a significant role in China's defense strategy, saying that if a large-scale war broke out, China should rely on American military support. There was, though, no need for China to formalize its alliance with the United States or purchase lots of foreign military equipment because "at least for ten years there will not be a big war in the world," and so China did not "need to prepare all things." It just needed "to pick a small number of projects and focus on them."[24] Assured of China's international security, Deng and his colleagues decreased expenditure on national defense from 4.6 percent of GNP in 1979 to 1.4 percent in 1991.[25]

As the likelihood of a great-power war faded into the background, the CCP ceased depicting taking up arms and defending the country in battle as the responsibility of every citizen. In the unlikely event that war occurred, the PLA would be adequate to protect the nation. Judging the PLA to be even too large for China's shrinking security needs, the Party discharged a million soldiers in the early 1980s and placed more emphasis on professionalism.[26] In the post-Mao era, the Party's use of militias underwent a dramatic transformation, too. The entire nation was no longer viewed as a gigantic reserve of guerilla fighters that had to be ever-ready to wage a protracted people's war against a foreign invasion. No longer worried about a major assault on Chinese territory, the CCP required only a small number of people to serve in militias, and it did not demand that they engage in regular military drills and prepare to fight off international enemies. Militias were instead charged with maintaining domestic law and order.[27]

In addition to ending militia involvement in military affairs, the Party discontinued their usage in economic endeavors. Never facing a major international security crisis, CCP leaders did not issue orders to mobilize millions of people into militias for large militaristic campaigns to construct industrial infrastructure as fast as possible in anticipation of a massive battle between China and its Cold War rivals. Secure with China's geopolitical position, the Party leadership also disbanded the Railroad Corps and the Infrastructure Corps, which had previously operated as the capital-intensive core of high-speed industrialization drives. In

[24] Deng Xiaoping, "Jungong shengchan yao weixiao guimo zhua zhongdian," March 19, 1979, in *Zhongguo gongchandang yu sanxian jianshe*, 282.

[25] Vogel, *Deng Xiaoping*, 540–541. [26] Li, *Modern Chinese Army*, 246–248.

[27] Perry, *Patrolling the Revolution*, 275–302.

total, roughly 400,000 railroad soldiers and 500,000 infrastructure soldiers were demobilized in the early 1980s.[28]

With the abandonment of big militarized industrialization campaigns, the CCP gave up its policy of treating consumer austerity as a necessary feature of building socialist industrial modernity in China. The government also no longer denounced material incentives and asserted that their use was a revisionist or bourgeois practice that generated social stratification and made people value their individual interests more than the collective project of making China into a socialist industrial nation.[29] In what Deng Xiaoping significantly called China's new era of "peace and development," building Chinese socialism was no longer equated with a flat social structure. Nor was it associated with material asceticism for the sake of expanding China's industrial base and strengthening its defense apparatus.

The advancement of Chinese socialism was instead identified with rising standards of living, and material incentives were viewed as a way to achieve this goal by increasing labor productivity, stimulating efficiency, enhancing quality control, and promoting innovation in response to market signals.[30] Central to the accomplishment of these aims was a new understanding of science and technology's role in national development. No longer were technicians, scientists, and administrators accused of being capitalist roaders or supporters of Soviet revisionism because they did not follow the Maoist developmental way of mass-mobilizing labor and locally available supplies and instead stressed the importance of bureaucratic control, technical expertise, industrial equipment, and machine-made goods.

In the post-Mao era, the CCP came to a quite different assessment of the developmental role of scientists, technicians, and administrators. They were lauded for their scientific, technical, and managerial abilities, as the Party turned away from the Maoist critique of the dangers of giving technicians and bureaucrats too much authority and affirmed a strong technocracy as the best way to lead socialist China towards higher living standards.[31] It was they – the technocrats – who were designated the

[28] Liu, *Zhongguo jiefangjun jiben jianshe*, 645–648. Tiedaobing shanhou, *Tiedao bing jianshi*, 118–120. Zhang Zheng and Bao Yongjuan, "Xin shiqu wo jun di yi ci da caijun yi qi lishi yingxiang," *Dangshi Wenyuan*, June 2008: 24–25.

[29] Dwight H. Perkins, "Reforming China's Economic System," *Journal of Economic Literature* 26:2 (June 1988): 626.

[30] For a general overview of these changes, see Naughton, *Chinese Economy*, 88–109.

[31] Denis Fred Simon and Merle Goldman, eds., *Science and Technology in Post-Mao China* (Cambridge, MA: Harvard University Press, 1989). Andreas, *Rise of the Red Engineers*, 233–248. For a study of post-Mao praise for scientists, see Schmalzer, *Green Revolution*, 47–72.

stewards of national industrialization. It was they, too, who were charged with overseeing the importation of technology from Japan, Western Europe, and the United States and administering the gradual opening up of Chinese markets to foreign trade. This recoupling of the Chinese economy with the international capitalist order was made possible by Beijing's decision to bury the anticapitalist hatchet that the Party had swung so forcefully during the Mao era and instead extend a hand across the Pacific and befriend Washington.[32]

As part of this reorientation away from the political prerogatives of Mao's China, the CCP shut down a number of Third Front projects. Between 1979 and 1983, central planners canceled 134 projects.[33] Another 120 projects were "closed down, halted, merged, transformed, or moved" between 1986 and 1990.[34] The State Council instituted special policies to assist labor at remaining Third Front enterprises. Most significant of all for families that had one foot in the countryside was a policy that allowed anyone who had worked for more than eight years at the Third Front to transfer their spouse and children to their work unit even if they were registered as rural residents.[35] This special provision was especially important because Deng and his colleagues did not do away with the urban favoritism of Mao's China. They maintained the Mao-era practice of granting cities more resources and treating rural residents as second-class citizens.[36] Many Third Fronters were, however, still discontent with having to live in urban areas that were in "difficult" (*jianku*) parts of the country. To ease their worries, central ministries invested more in Third Front housing, hospitals, cultural activities, and schools.[37]

To aid Third Front children with their studies, teaching staff were dispatched from defense institutes and technical schools to Third Front work units. Once children finished their secondary studies, they were given preferential treatment on the newly revived national college entrance examinations.[38] Wages were also raised for all

[32] Li, *Modern Chinese Army*, 245–247. Liu Huaqiu, "Deng Xiaoping guoji zhanlüe sixiang lunyao," *Dang de wenxian*, March 2007: 23–31, 46. Dwight H. Perkins, "The Centrally Planned Economy, 1949–1984," in *The Routledge Handbook of the Chinese Economy*, ed. Gregory C. Chow and Dwight H. Perkins, 51–52. London: Routledge, 2015.

[33] Guowuyuan, *Sanxian*, 230–231.

[34] Mel Gurtov, "Swords into Market Shares: China's Conversion of Military Industry to Civilian Production," *China Quarterly* 134 (1993): 213–241.

[35] Guowuyuan, *Sanxian*, 232.

[36] Dorothy J. Solinger, "China's Floating Population," in *The Paradox of China's Post-Mao Reforms*, eds. Merle Goldman and Roderick MacFarquhar (Cambridge, MA: Harvard University Press, 1999), 220–240.

[37] Guowuyuan, *Sanxian*, 231.

[38] Guowuyuan zhongyang junwei pizhuan guofang ke gongwei, jiaoyu bu, "Guanyu jiefang guofang keji gongye sanxian he banyuan jianku diqu jiaoyu gongzuo ruogan wenti de

technical personnel at the Third Front and all high-school and college graduates sent there.[39] Despite state assistance to Third Front enterprises, a number of employees were not satisfied with the special privileges that the central government afforded them. On average, 30 percent of technicians opted in the 1980s to "jump into the sea" (*xiahai*) of emerging markets and find better jobs on the coast or in bigger cities in the interior. At some work units, more than half of technical personnel left the Third Front to improve their own and their family's life trajectory.[40] Rural recruits, on the other hand, were often inclined to hold on to their post in a state-owned enterprise since they typically occupied a company's lower ranks, and their less refined skill set tended to be better compensated in the public sector.[41]

Whether workers decamped from the Third Front or stayed at their posts, Third Front labor collectively built economic infrastructure that endowed inland China with the building blocks of industrial modernity and fastened the region more firmly into the national economy. While China might have possibly developed more if the CCP had devoted more attention to coastal growth, following this alternative economic path would have most probably resulted in a bigger economic gap between the coast and inland regions, since the Party leadership devised no policy at the time that promoted both coastal and inland development. The only policy that advocated industrializing the interior was the Third Front campaign. In making these statements, I have no intention of painting the Third Front as a success story, not least because it was not only an economic phenomenon.

The Third Front campaign also produced trying human experiences, which eroded support for the CCP's attempt to cultivate acceptance of Maoist norms. Most painful of all for many Third Front participants was family separation. Sometimes, estrangement from loved ones only lasted as long as it took to build a nearby road. Yet even then parents still anxiously waited for their children's return and worried about whether they would be hurt. Other times, families had to endure for over a decade the pains of being apart from those they held dear. Urban families who lived together did not necessarily count themselves as more fortunate since they still had to figure out a way to cobble together schooling for their children, and many ached for the day when they could get away from China's hinterlands and move back to larger cities with better material conditions. Many technicians also resented having their skills and

baogao de tongzhi," October 11, 1983, in *Zhongguo gongchandang yu sanxian jianshe*, 284–285.

39 Guowuyuan, *Sanxian*, 232. 40 Guowuyuan, *Sanxian*, 242.

41 Group interview with workers at diesel pump factory, Pengzhou, June 2016.

education downplayed and criticized, and they longed to be able to put them to good use.

The Chinese Communist Party tried to valorize Maoist economic strategy and its prioritization of mass mobilization and speed over technical expertise. Project administrators also regularly extolled the benefits of building the Third Front in the underdeveloped interior. They held gatherings at which people read Party proclamations, and cultural workers performed plays and sang songs that celebrated the accomplishments of local labor. The government even furnished Third Fronters with higher wages and wide-ranging welfare guarantees. Nevertheless, the CCP was never able to overcome the bedrock of familial relations, the impetus of the educated and the technically skilled to employ their know-how, and popular preferences to live in better-off centrally located cities. Rural residents viewed Third Front work more favorably than did urbanites. Yet even they prized their family leave time, and their attraction to the Third Front was often rooted in materialistic aspirations that contradicted the Party's struggle to fashion a Maoist subject that was unmoved by material concerns.

Some Third Front participants definitely did not identify with Maoist norms. But there were others who saw their own life aims in the Party's projects and made it their mission to achieve them. Even though some people disagreed with the Maoist tenets underlying the Third Front campaign, they still strove to make the best of their circumstances. Some even came to see value in living and working at the Third Front. Despite participant dissent, the Third Front campaign's chief developmental objective was still fulfilled. A multitude of projects were built that more deeply rooted an industrial economy in inland regions. In this regard, the Third Front campaign could be considered an economic success – although this conclusion is mitigated by the fact that roughly half of Third Front projects were found to be economically unviable and were consigned to the dustbin of history.

Nor were the projects that remained operational free from problems. Increases in regional steel production and railroad traffic came with greater demands for coal. Regional automobile manufacturing expanded, and with its growth came greater demands for petroleum. Heightened regional demands for coal and oil have resulted in extensive mining, leaving barren industrial landscapes once their resources were exhausted. And the legacy of these projects includes carbon emissions and a growing profusion of industrial waste, two troubling phenomena which both show no signs of abating.[42] The hydropower stations that were constructed

[42] Judith Shapiro, *China's Environmental Challenges* (Cambridge: Polity Press, 2012), 4–5, 46–50.

during the Third Front have helped fuel regional development, but have also served as the basis of latter-day plans to dam and transform the ecology of more rivers in order to satiate the ever-growing appetite for energy.[43]

The Chinese Communist Party has thus far responded to higher resource requirements in much the way it did during the Third Front campaign. It has taken a paternalist approach to national development and assigned centralized state-led institutions the monumental task of redesigning the social and economic geography of the Chinese nation. This technocratic tendency was a driving force behind the development of coastal regions and the construction of special economic zones in the 1980s.[44] Later, when it became apparent in the 1990s that the Party's coastal strategy had led to the Chinese interior trailing behind developmentally, the central government launched the Open the West campaign to rectify widening economic divides.[45] Failing to alleviate regional disparities, in 2013 President Xi Jinping initiated the even more ambitious Belt and Road initiative.[46] The geopolitical and environmental impact of this mammoth developmental project to build industrial infrastructure throughout Eurasia now presents one of the great questions of the post-Cold War era.

[43] On post-Mao dam building, see Bryan Tilt, *Dams and Development in China: The Moral Economy of Water and Power* (New York: Columbia University Press, 2015).

[44] On the coastal developmental strategy, see Dali Yang, "Patterns of China's Regional Development Strategy," *China Quarterly* 122 (1990): 241–257. On Shenzhen, see Mary Ann O'Donnell, "Heroes of the Special Zone: Modeling Reform and Its Limits," in *Learning from Shenzhen: China's Post-Mao Experiment from Special Zone to Model City*, eds. Mary O'Donnell, Winnie Wong, and Jonathan Bach (Chicago: The University of Chicago Press, 2017), 39–64.

[45] David S.G. Goodman, ed., *China's Campaign to "Open Up the West": National, Provincial and Local Perspectives* (Cambridge: Cambridge University Press, 2004).

[46] For an overview of the Belt and Road initiative, see Tom Miller, *China's Asian Dream: Empire Building along the New Silk Road* (London: Zed Books, 2017).

Appendix: Third Front Demographics

Total Numbers

According to my research, around 3.9 million urban workers took part in the Third Front campaign between 1964 and 1980.[1] Another 11.1 million recruits came from rural areas. All participants in the Third Front were not workers. Some were family members. To arrive at the total number of people involved in the Third Front, it is thus necessary to include family members. Most rural recruits were temporary workers, and so I do not include their family members in population estimates. Some Third Front projects employed people from the countryside as permanent workers, but their rural families were not allowed to move to the Third Front because of Party restrictions on rural–urban migration.

At present, insufficient data are available to arrive at the exact number of family members that took part in the Third Front campaign. Nor is it possible to calculate precisely how many family members came to the Third Front as workers. It is, however, feasible to make a general estimate of the number of family members. One method is to draw on contemporary demographic trends. According to historical demographer Zeng Yi, the average urban family in China between 1964 and 1982 had four people.[2] This time period is roughly the same as the Third Front campaign. So, if Third Front work units followed national trends, then 17 million urban residents took part. This number is likely too large for at least two reasons. First, it supposes that all urban participants had a spouse and two children, which memoirs and interviews show was not usually the case. Some workers arrived as singles. Others were married without children, and other delayed marriage and having children until conditions improved at the Third Front. Second, the above guesstimate assumes that when an urban family was assigned to the Third Front, only one member was transferred

[1] Materials used to calculate these demographic estimates are listed in the bibliography under "Sources for Demographic Calculations."

[2] Zeng Yi, *Family Dynamics in China: A Life Table Analysis* (Madison: University of Wisconsin Press, 1991), 36.

as a worker. But some families had many members sent as laborers, and the Communist Party made a concerted attempt to find work for spouses when they came on site.[3]

A more accurate estimate is derivable from Third Front factory gazetteers, which occasionally list the number of employees as well as the number of children attending factory schools.[4] Based on this information, I have established that the number of children was typically around 30 percent of the number of employees, which means that about 1.17 million family members took part in the Third Front. Based on the above ratio of a little over three workers to every child, the total number of urban participants was about 5.08 million. Combining this approximation with the previously stated 11.1 million rural recruits, the total number of people involved in the Third Front between 1964 and 1980 was about 16.3 million.

Table A.1 *Total Third Front population: rural and urban, 1964–1978*

Source	Population
Rural	11,233,287
Urban	3,909,805
Urban family	1,172,941
Total	16,316,033

Table A.2 *Labor participation by province and source, 1964–1980**

Province	Source	Population
Fujian	Relocated within Fujian	6,137
	Relocated to Fujian	1,046
Total		7,183
Gansu	Lanzhou Chemical Industry Company	33,000
	Northeast Research Institutes	3,365
	Jiuquan Iron and Steel Company	Transferred Beijing technical personnel: 8,130 Total: 25,000

[3] Han, *Jiannan*, 9–10. Interview with Guizhou airplane factory couple, Shiyan, January 2013.

[4] For a complete list of the factory gazetteers consulted, see the Bibliography.

Table A.2 *(cont.)*

Province	Source	Population
	Northwestern Aluminum Fabrication Plant	45,000
	Liujiaxia Hydroelectric Power Station	7,000 Hui minority militias
	Oil prospecting	52,400
	Coal	5,510
	Demobilized soldiers	20,600
	Jinchang Nonferrous Metal Plant	30,000
Total		261,095
Guangxi	Nuclear	3,202
	Aerospace	2,194
	Military electronics	5,223
	Shipbuilding	4,500
	Arms industry	8,671
	Railroads	447,000
	Waterways	6,000
	Roads	34,600
	Steel	5,000
	Coal	Engineers and technicians: 6,000 Rural militias: 180,000
Total		697,890
Guizhou	Shuicheng Steel	Rural militias: 30,000 Anshan Steel: 6,603 Guiyang construction troops: 2,000
	Liupanshui coal complex	100,000
	Aerospace, airplanes, and electronics	relocated: 100,000
	Metallurgy (excluding Liupanshui)	10,000
	Hydroelectric	7,000
	Railroads	893,000
		Total: 987,206
Hebei	Small Third Front	16,539
Heilongjiang	Big Third Front	16,096
	Small Third Front	216 factories split up and 76 new factories built
Henan	Military factories	80,000
	Railroad	460,000
	Steel	86,000
	Glass	1,000
	Power plant	6,000
Total		633,000
Hubei	Second Automobile Works	100,000
	Shipbuilding base	50,000 (includes family)

Table A.2 *(cont.)*

Province	Source	Population
	Zigui county rural militias	44,900
	Zaoyang county demobilized soldiers	1,063
	Jianghan oil fields	128,900
	Gezhouba Dam	100,000
	Danjiangkou Hydropower Station	4,496
	Huanglong Hydropower Station	8,000
	Hubei Pharmaceutical Company	2,400
	Xiangyang Axle Factory	6,278
	Jiangshan Machine-Building Factory	6,506
	Chinese Opto-electronic Factory	4,200
	Textiles	15,000
	Wuhan Steel project	100,000
	Railroads	965,000
	Military factories	104,000
	Railroads	836,800
Total		2,477,543
Hunan	Railroad	1,090,200
	Third Front industrial labor (excluding Huaihua)	86,000
	Huaihua city	300,000
Total		1,476,200
Jilin		112,700 (includes family)
Liaoning	Labor	99,800
	Family	156,600
Total		255,800
		32 projects
Ningxia	Relocated to Ningxia	19,715
Shaanxi	Hydropower	Rural militias: 6,500
	Coal	550
	Railroads	1,365,900
	Roads	Rural militias: 82,100
	Hanzhong industrial base	Relocated industrial labor including family: 400,000
		Locally hired industrial labor: 21,519
		PLA support: 25,000
		Local construction troops: 15,000
		Nationwide construction corps: 30,000
		Rural militias: 11,000
	Baoji industrial base	47,500
	Xi'an electronics base	18,000(includes family)
Total		2,023,069
Shandong	Small Third Front	Light industry: 1,948

Table A.2 *(cont.)*

Province	Source	Population
		Machine building: 3,855
		Construction workers: 4,000
		Railroad rural militias: 75,000
		Agricultural industry: 30,000
		Arsenals: 100,000 (includes family)
		Metallurgy: 27,987
Total		242,790
Shanghai	**Small Third Front**	
	Jiangxi factory complexes and institutes	17,813
	Anhui factory complexes and institutes	56,474
	Fuel and raw materials base	80,000
	Big Third Front	234,400
Total		388,687
Jiangxi		256,500
Shanxi	Railroads	192,000
	Military factories and research institutes	43,300
	Electronics	23,617
Total		258,917
Sichuan	Panzhihua Steel and Coal Enterprises	373,639
	Chongqing complex	500,000
	Deyang Power Station Equipment Enterprises	28,000
	Deyang Second Heavy Machinery Works	15,500
	Sichuan Heavy Duty Truck Factory	5,300
	Jiangyou Enterprises	45,480
	Chengdu	Electronics: 38,849
		Aircraft: 3,000
		by the year 2000: 128,400
	Railroad	1,050,000
	Leshan Factories and mines	30,000
	Guangyuan	Electronics: 20,000
	Southern Sichuan: Luzhou, Zigong, Yibin, Neijiang	Factory complexes and institutes: 114,156 (includes family)
		Rural militias: 86,108
		Construction companies: 36,237
	Mianyang	80,000
Total		2,426,269
Yunnan	Relocated to Yunnan	117,000

Table A.2 *(cont.)*

Province	Source	Population
	Military road construction	1,000,000
	Forestry	31,710
	Shipping materials to Vietnam	Militias: 817,000
	Shipbuilding	3,055
	Railroads	300,000
Total		2,237,055
Zhejiang	Small Third Front	Chongqing and Hangzhou technical personnel 10,000
	Lower and middle peasants	8,000
	Basic construction troops	13,000
Total		31,000

* All numbers do not include family members unless otherwise noted.

Table A.3 *Railroad labor by line and source*

Railroad	Source	Population
Chengdu–Kunming Railroad	Railroad Corps	400,000
	Guizhou, Yunnan, and Sichuan militias	300,000
Total		700,000
Chongqing–Guiyang and Guiyang–Kunming	Railroad Corps	230,000
	Sichuan and Guizhou militias	190,000
Total		420,000
Beijing–Yuanping	Railroad Corps	60,000
	Beijing, Hebei, Shanxi militias	70,000
Total		130,000
Hunan–Guizhou	Guizhou militias	280,000
	Hunan militias	500,000
	Guizhou railroad workers	80,000
	Hunan provincial office workers	17,000
	Hunan railroad offices	26,5000
	Hunan military cadres	1,600
Total		905,100
Xiangfan–Chongqing	Sichuan militias	300,000
	Shaanxi militias	400,000
	Shaanxi junior high-school graduates	25,000
	Hubei militias	135,000
	Railroad Corps	240,000

Table A.3 *(cont.)*

Railroad	Source	Population
Total		965,000
Yangpingguan–Ankang	Railroad Corps	70,000
	Shaanxi militias	400,000
	Shaanxi additional labor of unclear source	130,000
Total		600,000
Xi'an–Baoji	Shaanxi militias	70,000
	Xi'an Railroad Administration	3,000
Total		73,000
Xi'an–Hancheng	Railroad Corps	2,600
	Shaanxi militias	200,000
	Shaanxi additional support labor	60,300
	Shaanxi Railroad offices	5,000
Total		267,900
Taiyuan–Jiaozuo		Numbers not found
Jiaozuo–Zhicheng	Henan militias	600,000
	Hubei militias	406,100
	Railroad workers	368,600
Total		910,000
Zhicheng–Liuzhou	Hunan militias	500,000
	Guangxi militias	400,000
	Hunan provincial office workers	17,000
	Hunan railroad offices	26,5000
	Hunan military cadres	1,600
Total		945,100
Qinghai–Tibet (Western portion)	Railroad Corps	62,000 (same divisions as earlier)
	Mechanic and truck brigades	57,000
Total		119,000
Xinjiang Southern	Ürümqi Railroad Administration	2,000
	Ürümqi militias	1,000
	Xinjiang Production and Construction Corps	16,500
	Railroad Corps	64,500 (same divisions)
Total		84,000
Tai'an–Zibo (Shandong)	Rural militias	75,000
Gansu branch lines	Lines	
	Jiajing branch line	12,000
	Baibao branch line	Lanzhou Railroad Administration: 3,000 Gansu militias: 23,000
	Mt. Wangjia branch line	Gansu militias: 2,000

Table A.3 *(cont.)*

Railroad	Source	Population
Wanyuan–Baisha		10,000
Panxi		73,000
Weijia–Anlu	Militias	60,000
Yaqiaoling–Guanzhuang	Militias	100,000

Bibliography

Archives

Beijing Municipal Archive
Hubei Provincial Archive
Shanghai Municipal Archive
Sichuan Provincial Archive

Published Primary Sources in Chinese

Bai Chaode, ed. *Tianshui wenshi ziliao di shi san ji*. Tianshui: Tianshui zhenzgxie wenshi ziliao weiyuanhui, 2008.

Beijing di yi jixie chang, ed. *Jixue gongren qiuxiao shouce*. Beijing: Jixie gongye chubanshe, 1971.

Chen Donglin, ed. *Zhongguo gongchandang yu sanxian jianshe*. Beijing: Dangdai zhongguo chubanshe, 2015.

Chengdu tielu ju. *Quanguo tielu luke lieche shikebiao*. Chengdu: Chengdu tielu ju, 1975.

Di yi jixie bu di er jichuang lingbujian biaozhun shouce. Beijing: Beijing shi xiatu chang, 1971.

Dukou meitan zhihuibu. *Gongye xue daqing jingyan jiaoliu dahui cailiao huibian*. Dukou: Dukou meitan zhihuibu, 1972.

Dukoushi. *Dukou gongye xuexi daqing huiyi*. Dukou: Dukou shiwei, 1977.

Dukoushi weisheng fangyizhan. *Weishieng fangyi ziliao huibian*. Dukoushi: Dukoushi weisheng fangyizhan, 1980.

Erqi jianchang shiliao, Volumes 1–4. Shiyan: Erqi changzhi bianji sh, 1982–1984.

Erqi jianshe zong zhihuibu. *Baogao wenxue ji*. Shiyan: Erqi jianshe zong zhihuibu, 1972.

"Fandui Meiguo qinlue Yuenan de langchao xi juan ge zhuyao chengshi: Quanguo yi qian duo wan ren shiwei youxing" *Renmin ribao*, August 10, 1964.

Guofang daxue di er bian yanjiushi "Xu Xiangqian zhuan" bianxiezu, ed. *Xu Xiangqian junshi wenxuan*. Beijing: Jiefangjun chubanshe, 1993.

Guofang ke gong wei sanxian tiaozheng xiediao zhongxin. *Sanxian jianshe tiaozheng gaizao zongjie wenji*. Beijing: Guofang ke gong wei sanxian tiaozheng xiediao zhongxin, 2006.

Hubei sheng zhiliu yaguan tielu huizhan zhihuibu zhenggongzu huibian. *Zhenggong jianbao*, 1971.

Hunan renmin chubanshe. *Zheng dang zhandou xiongying: Hunan minbing wei yuanyue kangmei kulian yinggong de shiji*. Changsha: Hunan renmin chubanshe, 1965.

Jiaotong bu. *Xiangqian tielu shigongjishu huibian*. Guiyang: Jiaotongbu dier tielu gonchengju shigongchu, 1974.

"Junmin tuanjie ru yi ren, shi kantian xia shei neng di," *Renmin ribao*, September 16, 1970.

"Lei Feng shi de minbing Zhang Xianzhong," *Renmin ribao*, January 13, 1978.

Mao Zedong. *Mao Zedong xuanji, Volumes 1–4*. Renmin chubanshe, 1991.

Mao Zedong dui sanxian jianshe de youguan zhishi.

Mao zhuxi renmin zhanzheng guanghui sixiang de shengli: Jiaozhi tielu huizhan Henan sheng zhihuibu di si minbing shi dianxing cailiao. Nanyang: Jiaozhi tiely huizhan di si minbing shi zhenggoong zu, 1970.

Meitan gongye gandalei jianzhu diaocha zu. *Xinan diwu gandalei jianzhu ziliao xuanbian: Jianzhuu buzhi*, 1968.

Nanyang shi minbing tuan. "Zuigao zhishi: Maozedong sixiang fang guangmang, 'gandalei' jianqi dzhan fang," 1970.

Panzhihua shi wenhuaju. *Panzhihua ribao*. Panzhihua: Panzhihua shi wenhuaju, 1965–1980.

Panzhihua wenyi. Panzhihua: Panzhihua shi wenhuaju, 1970–1980.

Panzhihua shi zong gonghui shiliao yanjiushi. *Panzhihua gongren yundong shiliao xuanbian*. Panzhihua: Panzhihua shi zong gonghui shiliao yanjiushi, 1991.

"Quanguo dou yao xuexi Jiefangjun," *Renmin ribao*, February 1, 1964.

"Quanguo gedi jin sibai wan ren youxing," *Renmin ribao*, January 16, 1964.

Sanxia gongcheng shiliao xuanbian bianzuan weiyuanhui. *Sanxia gongcheng shiliao xuanbian 1918–2015*. Wuhan: Sanxia gongcheng shiliao xuanbian bianzuan weiyuanhui, 2015.

Shanxi sheng geming weiyuanhui, *Qingdui yida sanfan xuexi wenjian*. Taiyuan: Shanxi sheng renmin chubanshe, 1972.

Tiedaobu. *Chengkuntielu beiduan shigongjishu zongjie*, 1975.

Tiedaobu di si sheji yuan. *Tiedao sheji shouce: Qiaohan*. Beijing: Renmin tiedao chubanshe, 1965.

Tiedaobu jiben jianshe zong ju. *Tielu shigong jishu zhouce*. Beijing: Renmin tiedao chubanshe, 1965.

"Xiang jingai de Wugang zhuhe," *Renmin ribao*, September 14, 1958. "Mao zhuxi zai Wugang," *Renmin ribao*, September 29, 1958.

"Xuxin xuexi jiefangjun quanli zhiyuan Jiefangjun gedi renmin reqing weiwen yingxiong zidi bing," *Renmin ribao*, January 18, 1966.

Ye Jianying. *Ye Jianying junshi wenxian*. Beijing: Jiefangjun chubanshe, 1997.

"Yinjie di san ge wu nian jihua de di yi nian: Yi jiu liu liu nian yuandan xiansi," *Renmin ribao*, January 1, 1966.

Yunyang diqu cheliang linli suo. *Chengshi yu gonglu jiaotong guanli guihua wenjian huibian*. Yunyang, 1972.

Zhang Quanjing. "Sanxian jianshe de juda chengjiu." *Yan'an wenxue* 5 (2019), at http://m.fx361.com/news/2019/1021/5869276.html. Accessed January 3, 2020.

"Zhe li de tian du hou: Jintian, women chongwen Deng Xiaoping dui Panzhihua de shenqing guanhuai," *Panzhihua wang*, August 22, 2018. www.zhelirenhe.com/news/488.html. Accessed January 1, 2019.

Zhonggong Deyang shiwei dangshi yanjiushi, ed. *Sanxian jianshe zai Sichuan: Deyang juan Volumes 1–3*. Chengdu: Sichuan sanxian jianshe ziliao congshu bianweihui, 2016.

Zhonggong Luzhou shiwei dangshi yanjiushi, ed. *Sanxian jianshe zai Sichuan: Luzhou juan*. Chengdu: Sichuan sanxian jianshe ziliao congshu bianweihui, 2016.

Zhonggong Mianyang shiwei dangshi yanjiushi, ed. *Sanxian jianshe zai Sichuan: Mianyang juan*. Chengdu: Sichuan sanxian jianshe ziliao congshu bianweihui, 2016.

Zhonggong Panzhihua shi dangshi yanjiushi. *Panzhihua kaifa jianshe shi wenxian ziliao xuanbian*. Panzhihua: Zhonggong Panzhihhua shiwei dangshi yanjiushi bian, 2000.

Panzhihua kaifa jianshe shiliao zhaibian, 1964–2000. Panzhihua: Zhonggong Panzhihua shiwei dangshi yanjiushi bian, 2000.

Zhonggong Shaanxi shengwei dangshi yanjiu shi. *Shaanxi de sanxian jianshe*. Xi'an: Shaanxi renmin chubanshe, 2014.

Zhonggong Zigong shiwei dangshi yanjiushi. *Sanxian jianshe zai Sichuan: Zigong juan*. Chengdu: Sichuan sanxian jianshe ziliao congshu bianweihui, 2016.

Zhonggong zhongyang dangshi yanjiu shi Zhonggong Hubei sheng Yichang shi weiyuanhui, Zhonggong Hubei shengwei dangshi yanjiushi bian, *Zhongguo gongchandang yu Changjiang sanxia gongcheng*. Beijing: Zhonggong dangshi chubanshe, 2007.

Zhonggong zhongyang wenxian yanjiu shi. *Jianguo yilai Mao Zedong wengao, Volumes 11–13*. Beijing: Zhongyang chubanshe, 1996.

Jianguo yilai zhongyao wenxian xuan bian, Volumes 11, 16–20. Beijing: Zhongguo wenxian chubanshe, 1992–1998.

Zhongguo renmin jiefangjun guofang daxue dangshi dangjian zhenggong jiaoyan shi. *Wenge da geming yanjiu ziliao, Volumes 1–3*. Beijing: Zhongguo renmin jiefangjun guofang daxue dangshi dangjian zhenggong jiaoyan shi, 1988.

Zhongguo renmin Jiefangjun zong zi 520 budui zhengzhi, ed., *Zhandou zai Chengkun xian*. N.l.: Zhongguo renmin Jiefangjun zong zi 520 budui zhengzhi, 1970.

Zhongguo shehui kexueyuan. *Zhonghua renmin gongheguo jingji dangan ziliao xuanbian (1958–1965)*. Beijing: Zhongguo caizheng jingji chubanshe, 2011.

Memoirs in Chinese

Bo Yibo. *Ruogan zhong da juece yu shijian de huigu*. Beijing: Zhonggong zhongyang dangxiao chubanshe, 1991.

Chen Gang. *Sanxian de rizi: Wode 1966–1979*. Hong Kong: Wong Sart Limited, 2009.

Chen Nianyun and Wu Xuehui, eds. *Pujiang jiyi (shang, xia)*. Beijing: Tuanjie chubanshe, 2016.

Chen Puru, "Shidai de jucece, lishi de gongxian," in *Sanxian jianshe jingshen tao fengbei shang ce*, ed. Zhongguo renmin zhengzhi xieshang huiyi Guizhou sheng zhengxie wenshi zi liao weiyuanhui, 1–7. Guiyang: Guizhou sheng zhengxie wenshi zi liao weiyuanhui, 1995.

Chen Zhiqiang and Ming Decai, eds. *Pujiang fengcai*. Beijing: Tuanjie chubanshe, 2016.

Chen Zutao. *Wode qiche shengya*. Beijing: Renmin chubanshe, 2005.

Cheng Zihua. *Cheng Zihua huiyi lu*. Beijing: Jiefangjun chubanshe, 1987.

Dan Lanshan. "Sui Cheng Zihua diaocha da xinan sanxian jianshe." *Taiqian muhou* 6 (2010): 15–21.

Dangdai koushu shi congshu bienweihui, ed. *Dangdai Sichuan yaoshi shilu, Volumes 1–3*. Chengdu: Sichuan renmin chubanshe, 2010.

Dong Ruizhi. *Zongheng chicheng: Da sanxian*. Hong Kong: Zhongguo wenhua chubanshe, 2006.

Dongfeng qiche gongsi li tuixiu renyuan guanli chu. *Jiqi suiyue: Jinian Dongfeng qiche gongsi jianshe 35 zhou nian*. Beijing: Zhongguo shehui chubanshe, 2004.

Duan Haiyan, ed. *Kule nianhua: Tiedaobing nubing fengcailu*. Beijing: Jiefangjun wenyi chubanshe, 2012.

Gao Yangwen. *Fengyu lichen shi ba xujiu (shang, xia)*. Beijing: Yejin gongye chubanshe, 1998.

Gu Mu. *Gu Mu huiyi lu*. Beijing: Zhongyang wenxian chubanshe, 2008.

Gu Xiu. *Licheng huiwang*. Shanghai: Shanghai wenyi chubanshe, 2006.

Guizhou sheng Anshun shi zhengxie xuanjiao wen wei ti weiyuanhui. *Sanxian zai Chunqiu*. Guiyang: Guizhou sheng Anshun shi zhengxie xuanjiao wen wei ti weiyuanhui, 2012.

Han Guobin. *Jiannan de pangang suiye, 1968–1980*. Panzhihua: Panzhihua shiwei danshi yanjiushi bian, 1995.

Hanzhong shi dangan ju. "Xiujian yangan tielu." http://daj.hanzhong.gov.cn/nry.jsp?urltype=news.NewsContentUrl&wbnewsid=10489&wbtreeid=10537. Accessed July 7, 2015.

Huang, Zhengxia. *Jiannan licheng*. Beijing: Xinhua chubanshe, 2007.

Hubei sheng weiyuanhui xuexi wenshi ziliao weiyuanhui. *Hubei sheng wenshi ziliao, Volumes 41–42*. Wuhan: Hubei sheng chubanshe, 1992–1993.

Jia Zhangke. *Ershi si cheng ji: Zhongguo gongren fangcan lu*. Jinan: Shandong huabao chubanshe, 2009.

Jiang Xin, ed. *Qingchun de huimou: Sanxian jianshe zhe de fendou gushi*. Chengdu: Dianzi keji daxue chubanshe, 2012.

Jiangxi "xian sanxian" 9333 chang shilu bian. *Women renmin chang (shang, xia)*. Shanghai: Shanghai renmin chubanshe, 2014.

"Junlu qing" bianji weiyuanhui. *Junhun zao: Jijian gongchengbing meitan budui lao zhanyou shidai fengcai*. Beijing: Junlu qing bianji weiyuanhui, 2006.

Junlu qing: Huiyi zai jijian gongchengbing meitan budui de rizi li. Beijing: Junlu qing bianji weiyuanhui, 2004.

"Leshan Dadu he xiagu tiedaobing bowuguan," Mo Shuyan, www.sohu.com/a/253416199_100223122.

Li Baoliang. *Da sanxian*. Lanzhou: Dunhuang wenyi chubanshe, 2010.

Li Fuchun, "Zai guojia jiwei 1964 nian niandu jihua zuotanhui shang de fayan," August 16, 1964, in *Zhongguo gongchandang yu sanxian*, 61–62.

Lishui shi zhengxie wenshi ziliao weiyuanhui. *Zhenan xiao sanxian jianshe jishi*. Beijing: Zhongguo wenshi chubanshe, 2010.

Liu Fangyin. *Sanxian*. Beijing: Zuojia chubanshe, 2006.

Liu Jianzhang. *Wo de jiushi nian*. Beijing: Zhongguo tiedao chubanshe, 2001.

Liu Qinghua. *Zuihou de guizu*. Beijing: Taihai chubanshe, 2010.

Liu Wanyin. *San xian*. Beijing: Zuojia chubanshe, 2006.

Lu Zhengcao. *Lu Zhengcao huiyilu*. Beijing: Jiefangjun chubanshe, 1988.

Lu Zhonghui, ed. *Minjiang suiyue*. Pengzhhou: Sichuan huabao she youxian gongsi, 2010.

Ma Yunxiang, ed. *Sanxian suiyue*. Chengdu: "Sanxian suiyue" bianwei bianji, 2017.

Nanping shi zhengxie wenshi ziliao weiyuanhui bian. *Nanping wenshi ziliao di wu ji: Nanwang suiyue minbei xiao sanxian jianshe shilu*. Nanping: Nanping shi zhengxie wenshi ziliao weiyuanhui, 1999.

Nie Ronggui. *Chengyu tielu jinxi ji*. Chengdu: Sichuan renmin chubanshe, 1999.

ed. *Sanxian jianshe tao fengbei*. Chengdu: Sichuan renmin chubanshe, 1999.

Nie Rongzhen. *Nie Rongzhen Huiyi lu*. Beijing: Jiefangjun chubanshe, 1986.

Nie Zuoping. "Sanxian rensheng." *Zhongguo guojia dili* 2 (2014). www.dili360.com/cng/article/p5350c3d60bc9c49.htm. Accessed July 7, 2015.

Panzhihua shi zhi bangongshi, ed. *Panzhihua shi zhi, Volumes 1–12*. Panzhihua: Panzhihua shi panzhihua shizhi zazhi shi, 1985–1991.

Panzhihua shi zhengxie wenshi ziliao wenyuanhui. *Panzhihua wenshi ziliao di 7 qi*. Panzhihua: Panzhihua shi danganju, 1992.

Qian Min. "Wo qinshen jingli de xinan sanxian jianshe," in *Xin Zhongguo wangshi: Bulu xiezhen*, ed. Quanguo zhengxie wenshi he kexue weiyuanhui, 32–45. Beijing: Zhongguo wenshi chubanshe, 2011.

Qu Deqian and Zheng Zhubin. *Yidai jiang xing: Kong Qingde*. Beijing: Jiefangjun chubanshe, 2001.

"Sanxian jianshe zai Yichang" bian weihui, ed. *Sanxian jianshe zai Yichang*. Yichang: Yichang zhengxie wenshi ziliao weiyuanhui, 2016.

Shaoyang shi zhengxie wenjiao weiti wenshi xuexi wenyuanhui, ed. *Tiejian fengbei: Shaoyang wenshi teji*. Beijing: Zhongguo wenshi chubanshe, 2007.

Shi Biao, ed. *Zhengcheng: Qianjin zhong de Jiangxi 9304 chang*. Shanghai: Shanghai Daxue chubanshe, 2016.

"Shiyou shiren" Sichuan youqi tian bianweiyui. *Shiyou shiren: Zai Sichuan youqi tian jilu*. Beijing: Shiyou gongye chuban she,1997.

"Shiyou shiren" Changqing youtian bianweiyui. *Shiyou shiren: Zai Changqing youtian jilu*. Beijing: Shiyou gongye chuban she, 1997.

Song Renqiong. *Song Renqiong huiyi lu*. Beijing: Jiefangjun chubanshe, 2007.

Song Shaoming, ed. *Tiedaobing bu liao qing*. Beijing: Jiefangjun chubanshe, 2002.

Tan Chengjian. *Shimian shidai*. Beijing: Xin xing chubanshe, 2012.

Wang Chuncai, ed. *Zhongguo da sanxian baogao wenxue congshu jingxuan, Volumes 1–4*. Chengdu: Sichuan renmin chubanshe, 1997.

Wu Hantao and Li Hebang, eds. *Pujiang wenyun*. Beijing: Tuanjie chubanshe, Beijing, 2016.

Xie Shaopeng. *Xiao sanxian jungong chang de nanwang suiyue*. Jinan: Shandong wenyi chubanshe, 2015.

Xinjiang bingtuan shizhi bianzuan weiyuanhui bongtuan dangwei dangshi yanjiushi. *Xinjiang shengchan jianshe bingtuan shilia xuanji 12*. Ürümqi: Xinjiang renmin chubanshe, 2003.

Xu Chaolin, ed. *Sanxian fengyun: Zhongguo sanxian jianshe wenxuan Guizhou Liupanshui zhuanji*. Beijing: Dangdai zhongguo chubanshe, 2013.

Xu Chi. "Zhou Enlai lingdao women jianshe Panzhihua," *Renmin wang*, March 15, 2018. http://zhouenlai.people.cn/n1/2018/0315/c409117-29869164.html. Accessed October 4, 2018.

Xu Lanru. *Da Sanxian: Bingong daodan*. Changsha: Hunan jiaoyu chubanshe, 2016.

Xu Xiaoling. "Shangou li de guangbo zhan," in *Women renmin chang xia: Jiangxi "xiao sanxian" 9333 chang shilu*, ed. Mao Xiaobing, 725–729. Shanghai: Shanghai renmin chubanshe, 2014.

Xu Youwei, ed. *Kou shu: Xiao sanxian jianshe*. Shanghai: Shanghai jiaoyu chubanshe, 2013.

"Xunfang Jiaozhi tielu (shang): Mimi gongceng yu 'yao zhunbei dazhang'," *Dahe wang*. https://news.dahe.cn/2018/04–10/295006.html. Accessed January 3, 2018.

Yang Chao. *Yang Chao zai Panxi*. Panzhihua: Panzhihua shi danganguan, 2011.

Yan Jianzi, *Zhiliu qingchun zhiliu zhi ge*. Changsha: Hunan renmin chubanshe, 2013.

ed. *Zhiliu suiyue: Zhiliu tiejian Changsha fenzhi zhiqing tuwen ji: 1972–1975, Volumes 1–2*. Changsha: Hunan Renmin chubanshe, 2008.

Yu Qiuli. *Yu Qiuli huiyilu*. Beijing: Jiefangjun chubanshe, 1996.

Zeng Siyu. *Bainian jianzhe*. Dalian: Dalian chubanshe, 2014.

Zhang Chenghan. *Nan zheng bei zhan er shi nian: Exi sanxian jianshe zhengzhan jishi*. Shenyang: Shenyang chubanshe, 2007.

Zhang Hongchun, ed. *Sanxian fengyun Zhongguo sanxian jianshe wenxuan: Zhongguo sanxian jianshe yanjiuhui*. Chengdu: Sichuan renmin chubanshe, 2017.

Zhang Mao. *Raobin zhuanji*. Beijing: Huawen chubanshe, 2003.

Zhang Qing. "Shandong 'xiao sanxian' gongye yicun diaocha baohu yanjiu." PhD diss., Shandong jianzhu daxue, 2013.

Zhang Yujun, ed. *Sanxian jianshe tao fengbei*. Chengdu: Sichuan renmin chubanshe, 1999.

"Zheng Zhen huiyi lu: Zai Gezhouba gongcheng zhihuibu," *China Gezhouba Group Company*, September 6, 2009. www.cggc.ceec.net.cn/art/2015/9/6/art_7369_388024.html. Accessed June 7, 2017.

Zhengxie Guizhou Liupanshui shi weiyuanhui zenshi ziliao weiyuanhui. *Liupanshui wenshi ziliao di liu ji*. Guiyang: Guizhou sheng dikuang ju 113 dizhi dui yinshua chang, 1996.

Zhengxie Zunyi shi huichuan qu weiyuanhui, ed. *Sanxian jianshe zai huichuan: Huichuan qu wenshi ziliao 4*. Chengdu: Zhengxie Zunyi shi huichuan qu weiyuanhui, 2010.

Zhige wang zong bianshe. "Sanxian binggong wei guofang xian zhongshen." *Zhi ge*, July 9, 2010. www.zhige.net/html/2010/0709/13014.html. Acccesed July 22, 2015.

Zhonggong Daqing shiwei dangshi yanjiushi, ed. *Gongye xue daqing xianji lu ji shiliao xuanbian*. Beijing: Zhongyang wenxian chubanshe, 2004.

Zhonggong Liupanshui shiwei danshi yanjiu shi, ed. *Wei wei wu meng shan youyou xiang siqing: Liupanshui shi sanxian jianshe zhe koushu shi*. Beijing: Zhongyang wenxian chubanshe, 2016.

Zhonggong Luzhou shiwei dangshi yanjiushi, ed. *Sanxian jianshe zai Sichuan: Luzhou juan*. Chengdu: Sichuan sanxian jianshe ziliao congshu bianweihui, 2016.

Zhonggong Mianyang shiwei dangshi yanjiushi, ed. *Sanxian jianshe zai Sichuan: Mianyang juan*. Chengdu: Sichuan sanxian jianshe ziliao congshu bianweihui, 2016.

Zhonggong Panzhihua shi dangshi yanjiushi. *Liu zai da liegu de jiyi*. Chengdu: Sichuan cishu chubanshe, 2003.

Panzhihua kaifa jianshe da shiji. Chengdu: Chengdu keji daxue chubanshe, 1994.

Panzhihua kaifa jianshe shi wenxian ziliao xuanbian. Panzhihua: Zhonggong Panzhihhua shiwei dangshi yanjiushi bian, 2000.

Zhonggong Panzhihua shiwei dangshi gongzuo weiyuanhui, ed. *Jianshe Panzhihua de ren*. Chengdu: Chengdu keji daxue chubanshe, 1987–1989.

Zhongguo hangtian bao, ed. *Chong zuo sanxian lu: Wo guo hangtian sanxian jidi jianshe biqin*. Beijing: Zhongguo yuhang chubanshe, 2016.

Zhongguo renmin zhengzhi xieshan huiyi Guizhou sheng zhengxie wenshi zi liao weiyuanhui, ed. *Sanxian jianshe jingshen tao feng bei shang xia ce*. Guiyang: Guizhou sheng zhengxie wenshi ziliao wenyuanhui bian, 1995.

Zhongguo renmin zhengzhi xieshan huiyi Nanchong shi weiyuanhui. *Xiangyu tielu da huizhan: Nanchong minbing shi jishi*. Nanchong: Nanchong jiaoyu xueyuan yinshua chang, 2004.

Zhongguo renmin zhengzhi xieshan huiyi Sichuan sheng Panzhihua shi weiyuanhui. *Panzhihua wenshi ziliao, Volumes 2, 4, 5, 6, 8, 16*. Panzhihua: Zhongguo wenlian chubanshe, 1987, 1989, 1990–1992, 2011.

Zunyi shi defang zhi bianzuan weiyuanhui bangongshi. *Zunyi shi sanxian jianshe zhi*. Beijing: Zhongguo wenshi chubanshe, 2016.

Zunyi shi zhengxie wenshi yu xuexi weiyuanhui. *Zunyi sanxian jianshe qin liji*. Zunyi: Zunyi shi zhengxie wenshi yu xuexi weiyuanhui, 2013.

Factory Gazetteers

523 changzhi bianzuan weiyuanhui. *523 changzhi*. Xi'an: Shaanxi renmin chubanshe, 1996.

5002 changzhi bianji bu. *Chuanbo gongye xitong 5002 changzhi, 1968–1988*. Yunnan: 5002 changzhi bianji bu, 1989.

5113 chang changzhi bianzuan weiyuanhui. *5113 changzhi, 1968–1985*. Lushan: 5113 chang changzhi bianzuan weiyuanhui, 1988.

5123 changzhi bianzuan weiyuanhui. *5123 changzhi di 1 juan (1969–1986)*. "Wu yi er san chang zhi" bian zuan weiyuanhui, 1988.

Changzhi bianshen weiyuanhui. *Changshan redian changzhi, 1969–1985*. Changshan: Changshan redian chang, 1989.

Dongfeng qiche. *Di er qiche zhizao changzhi*. Shiyan: Dongfeng qiche gongsi shizhi bangongshi, 2001.

Donghe yinzhi gongsi 501 changzhi bianji weiyuanhui. *Donghe yin zhi gongsi 501 changzhi*. Beijing: Zhongguo jinrong chubanshe, 1993.

Guangdong sheng Shaoguan gangtie changzhi bianji weiyuanhui. *Shaoguan gangtie changzhi, 1966–1985*. Shaoguan: Guangdong sheng Shaoguan gangtie changzhi bianji weiyuanhui, 1989.

Guizhou xingyi huagong zongchang. *Guizhou xingyi huagong zongchang changzhi (1966–2002)*. Nanning: Guangxi minzu chubanshe, 2003.

Guoying 258 chang changzhi bianzuan weiyuanhui. *Guoying 258 changzhi, 1964–1986*. Beijing: Guoying 258 chang changzhi bianzuan weiyuanhui, 1988.

Guoying Jinshan jixie chang. *Guoying Jinshan jixie chang changzhi (1970–1985)*. Huludao: Guoying Jinshan jixie chang, 1987.

"Hunan sheng Shaodong jiaohua changzhi" bianxie bangongshi. *Hunan sheng Shaodong jiaohua changzhi: 1967–1981*. Shaodong: Hunan sheng Shaodong jiaohua changzhi, 1982.

"Jiangxi chilun xiang zong changzhi" bianzuan bangongshi. *Jiangxi chilun xiang zong chang changzhi, 1969–1990*. Nanchang: "Jiangxi chilun xiang zong changzhi" bianzuan bangongshi, 1992.

Li Genfang and Yunqing Yao, eds. *Zhengzhou lüchuang chang changzhi, 1970–1985*. Zhengzhou: Zhengzhou lüchuang chang, 1986.

Meishan cheliang changzhi bianweihui. *Meishan cheliang changzhi*. Beijing: Zhongguo tiedao chubanshe, 1999.

Panzhihua gangtie jituan gongsi, ed. *Pangang zhi, 1964–1986*. Beijing: Kexue chubanshe, 1994.

Shandong Yimeng yelian chang changzhi bianzuan xiaozu. *Shandong Yimeng yelian changzhi 1966–1985*. Yimeng: Shandong Yimeng yelian chang changzhi bianzuan xiaozu, 1987.

Sichuan jinding jituan emei shuini changzhi bianzhuan weiyuanhui bian. *Emei shuini changzhi, 1965–1994*. Emei: Emeishan yinshua chang, 1999.

Sichuan kongqi yasuo jichang changzhi bianjishi. *Chuan ya changzhi, 1966–1985*. Jianyang: Sichuan kongqi yasuo jichang, 1987.

Tiedao bu Chengdu qiaoliang gongchang changzhi bangongshi. *Tiedao bu Chengdu qiaoliang gongchang zhi: 1966–1992*. Chengdu: Tiedao bu Chengdu qiaoliang gongchang zhi bianzuan lingdao xiaozu, 1995.

Tiedao bu Guiyang cheliang chang. *Gui che changzhi, 1966–1988*. Guiyang: Tiedao bu Guiyang cheliang chang, 1991.

Tiedao bu Tongling jiche changzhi bianzuan weiyuanhui. *Tongling ji che changzhi, 1970–1985*. Tongling xian: Tie dao bu Tongling ji che changzhi bianzuan weiyuanhui, 1989.

"Xiangdong huagong jixie changzhi" bianzuan weiyuanhui. *Xiangdong huagong jixie changzhi, 1971–1990*. Hunan: Xiangdong huagong jixie chang, 1991.

Yejin gongye bu changcheng gang chang si fen chang changzhi bangongshi. *Changcheng gang chang si fen chang changzhi, 1965–1985*. Shanghai: Shanghai shi yinshua chang, 1988.

Yi fangji changzhi, 1966–1986. Yichang: Yichang fangzhi jixie chang, 1988.

Yinhe yibiao changzhi bianzuan xiaozu. *Yinhe yibiao chang zhi (1965–1989)*. Yinchuan: Yinhe yibiao changzhi, 1990.
Yongji dianji changzhi bianzuan weiyuanhui. *Yongji dian ji chang zhi, 1969–1998*. Beijing: Zhongguo tie dao chu ban she, 1999.
Youdian bu Xing'an tongxin shebei chang changzhi bianxiezu. *You dian bu Xing'an tongxin shebei changzhi, 1970–1984*. Xing'an: Youdian bu Xing'an tongxin shebei chang, 1984.
Zengkui Xiao, ed. *Hunan sheng Shaoyang yeya jian chang changzhi, 1966–1990*. Shaoyang: Hunan sheng Shaoyang yeya jian chang, 1992.
Zigong yingzhi hejin chang. *Zigong yingzhi hejin changzhi: 1964–1985*. Zigong: Zigong yingzhi hejin chang, 1986.

Secondary Sources in English

Andreas, Joel. *Rise of the Red Engineers: The Cultural Revolution and the Origins of China's New Class*. Stanford: Stanford University Press, 2009.
Apter, David E. and Tony Saich. *Revolutionary Discourse in Mao's Republic*. Cambridge, MA: Harvard University Press, 1994.
Altehenger, Jennifer. *Legal Lessons: Popularizing Laws in the People's Republic of China, 1949–1989*. Cambridge, MA: Harvard University Asia Center, 2018.
Bachman, David. "Defense Industrialization in Guangdong." *China Quarterly* 166 (2001): 273–304.
Bennett, Gordon. *Yundong: Mass Campaigns in Chinese Communist Leadership*. Berkeley: University of California Press, 1976.
Bernstein, Thomas P. *Up to the Mountains and Down to the Villages : The Transfer of Youth from Urban to Rural China*. New Haven: Yale University Press, 1977.
Bitzinger, Richard A. and J. D. Kenneth Boutin. "China's Defence Industries: Change and Continuity," in *Rising China*, ed. Ron Huisken, 125–143. Sydney: Australian National University Press, 2009.
Bonnin, Michel. *The Lost Generation: The Rustication of China's Educated Youth (1968–1980)*. Hong Kong: The Chinese University Press, 2013.
Bradley, Mark Philip. *Vietnam at War*. Oxford: Oxford University Press, 2009.
Bramall, Chris. *In Praise of Maoist Economic Planning: Living Standards and Economic Development in Sichuan since 1931*. New York: Oxford University Press, 1993.
Brazinsky, Gregg. *Winning the Third World: Sino-American Rivalry during the Cold War*. Chapel Hill: University of North Carolina Press, 2017.
Brown, Jeremy. *City versus Countryside in Maoist China: Negotiating the Divide*. New York: Cambridge University Press, 2012.
"Finding and Using Grassroots Historical Sources from the Mao Era." *Dissertation Reviews*. https://dissertationreviews.wordpress.com/2010/12/15/finding-and-using-grassroots-historical-sources-from-the-mao-era-by-jeremy-brown. Accessed December 3, 2016.
"From Resisting Communists to Resisting America: Civil War and Korean War in Southwest China, 1950–1951," in *Dilemmas of Victory: The Early Years of the People's Republic of China*, eds. Jeremy Brown and Paul G. Pickowicz, 105–129. Cambridge, MA: Harvard University Press, 2007.

Brown, Jeremy and Matthew Johnson, eds. *Maoism at the Grassroots*. Cambridge, MA: Harvard University Press, 2015.

Carter, James M. *Inventing Vietnam: The United States and State Building, 1954–1968*. New York: Cambridge University Press, 2008.

Chamberlin, Paul Thomas. *The Cold War's Killing Fields: Rethinking the Long Peace*. New York: HarperCollins, 2018.

Chan, Anita. *Children of Mao: Personality Development and Political Activism in the Red Guard Generation*. Seattle: University of Washington Press, 1985.

Chan, Anita, Richard Madsen, and Jonathan Unger. *Chen Village: The Recent History of a Peasant Community in Mao's China*. Berkeley: University of California Press, 1992.

Chang, Jung and John Halliday. *Mao: The Unknown Story*. New York: Anchor Books, 2005.

Cheek, Timothy. *The Intellectual in Modern Chinese History*. Cambridge: Cambridge University Press, 2016.

ed. *Mao Zedong and China's Revolutions: A Brief History with Documents*. New York: Palgrave, 2002.

Chen, Chao. *Toleration: Group Governance in a Chinese Third Line Enterprise*. Basingstoke: Palgrave Macmillan, 2018.

Chen, Jian. "China's Changing Policies towards the Third World and the End of the Global Cold War," in *The End of the Cold War: New Perspectives on Regional Conflicts*, eds. Artemy Kalinovsky and Sergey Radchenko, 101–121. London: Routledge, 2011.

"China's Involvement in the Vietnam War, 1964–69." *China Quarterly* 142 (1995): 356–387.

Mao's China and the Cold War. Chapel Hill: University of North Carolina Press, 2001.

Cheng Tiejun and Mark Selden. "The Origins and Social Consequences of China's *Hukou* System." *China Quarterly* 139 (1994): 644–668.

Cheng Yinghong. *Creating the New Man: From Enlightenment Ideals to Socialist Realities*. Honolulu: University of Hawaii Press, 2008.

Ci Jiwei. *Dialectic of the Chinese Revolution: From Utopianism to Hedonism*. Stanford: Stanford University Press, 1994.

Cirincione, Joseph. *Bomb Scare: The History and Future of Nuclear Weapons*. New York: Columbia University Press, 2008.

Clark, Paul. *The Chinese Cultural Revolution: A History*. Cambridge: Cambridge University Press, 2008.

Cliff, Tom. *Oil and Water: Being Han in Xinjiang*. Chicago: The University of Chicago Press, 2016.

"The Post-Mao Reforms in Historical Perspective." *Journal of Asian Studies* 47 (1988): 518–540.

Cohen, Warren I. *America's Response to China: A History of Sino-American Relations*. New York: Columbia University Press, 2010.

Connelly, Matthew. "Taking Off the Cold War Lens: Visions of North–South Conflict during the Algerian War for Independence." *American Historical Review* 105: 3 (June 2000): 739–769.

Cook, Alexander C., ed. *Mao's Little Red Book: A Global History*. Cambridge: Cambridge University Press, 2014.

Crafts, Nicholas and C.K. Harley. "Output Growth and the Industrial Revolution: A Restatement of the Crafts–Harley View." *Economic History Review* 45 (1992): 703–730.

Cumings, Bruce. *Parallax Visions: Making Sense of American–East Asian Relations at the End of the Century*. Durham, NC: Duke University Press, 1999.

David, Kyle. "The Poster Child of the 'Second' Cultural Revolution: Huang Shuai and Shifts in Age Consciousness, 1973–1979." *Modern China* 44:5 (2018): 497–524.

Diamant, Neil J. *Embattled Glory: Veterans, Military Families, and the Politics of Patriotism in China, 1949–2007*. Lanham, MD: Rowman & Littlefield Publishers, 2009.

Revolutionizing the Family: Politics, Love, and Divorce in Urban and Rural China, 1949–1968. Berkeley: University of California Press, 2000.

Dikötter, Frank. *Mao's Great Famine: The History of China's Devastating Catastrophe, 1958–1962*. New York: Walker & Co., 2010.

Dillon, Nara. *Radical Inequalities: China's Revolutionary Welfare State in Comparative Perspective*. Cambridge, MA: Harvard University Press, 2015.

Dittmer, Lowell. *China's Continuous Revolution: The Post-Liberation Epoch, 1949–1981*. Berkeley: University of California Press, 1987.

Economy, Elizabeth C. *By All Means Necessary: How China's Resource Quest Is Changing the World*. Oxford: Oxford University Press, 2014.

Ens-Manning, Kimberley. "The Gendered Politics of Woman-Work: Re-thinking Radicalism in the Great Leap Forward." *Modern China* 32:3 (2006): 349–384.

Ens-Manning, Kimberley and Felix Wemheuer, eds. *Eating Bitterness: New Perspectives on China's Great Leap Forward and Famine*. Vancouver: UBC Press, 2012.

Garver, John. *China's Quest: The History of the Foreign Relations of the People's Republic of China*. Oxford: Oxford University Press, 2016.

Esherick, Joseph. "Ten Theses on the Chinese Revolution." *Modern China* 21 (1995): 45–76.

"Tracking an Iconic Photograph." *PRC History Review* 1:3 (December 2015): 1–5.

Esherick, Joseph, Paul G. Pickowicz, and Andrew G. Walder. *The Chinese Cultural Revolution as History*. Stanford: Stanford University Press, 2006.

Eyferth, Jacob. *Eating Rice from Bamboo Roots: The Social History of a Community of Handicraft Papermakers in Rural Sichuan, 1920–2000*. Cambridge, MA: Harvard University Press, 2009.

"Women's Work and the Politics of Homespun in Socialist China, 1948–1980." *International Review of Social History* 55:4 (December 2012): 1–27.

Fairbank, John K. and Merle Goldman. *China: A New History*. Cambridge, MA: Belknap Press of Harvard University Press, 1998.

Fang Xiaoping. *Barefoot Doctors and Western Medicine in China*. Rochester, NY: University of Rochester Press, 2012.

Farquhar, Judith. *Appetites: Food and Sex in Post-socialist China*. Durham, NC: Duke University Press, 2002.

Feigenbaum, Evan. *China's Techno-warriors: National Security and Strategic Competition from the Nuclear to the Information Age*. Stanford: Stanford University Press, 2003.

Foucault, Michel. *Technologies of the Self: A Seminar with Michel Foucault*, eds. Luther H. Martin, Huck Gutman, and Patrick H. Hutton. Amherst: University of Massachusetts Press, 1988.

Fravel, M. Taylor. "Shifts in Warfare and Party Unity: Explaining China's Changes in Military Strategy." *International Security* 42:3 (Winter 2017–2018): 37–83.

Frazier, Mark W. *The Making of the Chinese Industrial Workplace: State, Revolution, and Labor Management*. Cambridge: Cambridge University Press, 2002.

Friedman, Edward, Paul G. Pickowicz, and Mark Selden. *Chinese Village, Socialist State*. New Haven: Yale University Press, 1991.

Revolution, Resistance, and Reform in Village China. New Haven and London: Yale University Press, 2005.

Friedman, Jeremy. *Shadow Cold War: The Sino-Soviet Competition for the Third World*. Chapel Hill: University of North Carolina Press, 2015.

Gaddis, John Lewis. "The Long Peace: Elements of Stability in the Postwar International System." *International Security* 10 (Spring 1986): 99–142.

Gao Wenqian. *Zhou Enlai: The Last Perfect Revolutionary*. New York: Hachette, 2008.

Gershcenkron, Alexander. *Economic Backwardness in Historical Perspective*. Cambridge, MA: Belknap Press, 1962.

Glosser, Susan L. *Chinese Visions of the Family and State, 1915–1953*. Berkeley: University of California Press, 2003.

Goh, Evelyn. *Constructing the U.S. Rapprochement with China, 1961–1974: From "Red Menace" to "Tacit Ally"*. Cambridge: Cambridge University Press, 2004.

Gompert, David C., Hans Binnendijk, and Bonny Lin. *Blinders, Blunders, and Wars: What America and China Can Learn*. Santa Monica: RAND Corporation, 2014.

Goodman, David S.G., ed. *China's Campaign to "Open Up the West": National, Provincial and Local Perspectives*. Cambridge: Cambridge University Press, 2004.

Gurtov, Mel. "Swords into Market Shares: China's Conversion of Military Industry to Civilian Production." *China Quarterly* 134 (1993): 213–241.

Halsey, Stephen R. *Quest for Power: European Imperialism and the Making of Chinese Statecraft*. Cambridge, MA: Harvard University Press, 2015.

Hellbeck, Jochen. *Revolution on My Mind: Writing a Diary under Stalin*. Cambridge, MA: Harvard University Press, 2009.

Hermes, Walter G. *Truce Tent and Fighting Front*. Washington, DC: Center of Military History, United States Army, 1992.

Hershatter, Gail. *The Gender of Memory: Rural Women and China's Collective Past*. Berkeley: University of California Press, 2013.

Hevia, James L. *English Lessons: The Pedagogy of Imperialism in Nineteenth-Century China*. Durham, NC: Duke University Press, 2003.

Ho, Denise Y. *Curating Revolution: Politics on Display in Mao's China*. Cambridge: Cambridge University Press, 2017.

Honig, Emily. "Socialist Sex: The Cultural Revolution Revisited." *Modern China* 29:2 (2003): 143–175.

Hou Li. *Building for Oil: Daqing and the Formation of the Chinese Socialist State*. Cambridge, MA: Harvard University Press, 2018.

Huang, Jing. *Factionalism in Chinese Communist Politics*. Cambridge: Cambridge University Press, 2000.

Hurst, William. *The Chinese Worker after Socialism*. Cambridge: Cambridge University Press, 2009.

Hung Chang-Tai. *Mao's New World : Political Culture in the Early People's Republic*. Ithaca: Cornell University Press, 2011.

Hunt, Michael H. *The Genesis of Chinese Communist Foreign Policy*. New York: Columbia University Press, 1996.

Hyer, Eric. "China's Arms Merchants: Profits in Command." *China Quarterly* No. 132 (1992): 1101–1118.

Jersild, Austin. *The Sino-Soviet Alliance: An International History*. Chapel Hill: University of North Carolina Press, 2014.

"Joint Statement Following Discussions with Leaders of the People's Republic of China," February 27, 1972. *Foreign Relations of the United States*. Accessed November 10, 2017. https://history.state.gov/historicaldocuments/frus 1969-76v17/d203

Kander, Astrid, Paolo Malanima, and Paul Warde. *Power to the People: Energy in Europe over the Last Five Centuries*. Trenton: Princeton University Press, 2015.

Kaple, Deborah A. *Dream of a Red Factory: The Legacy of High Stalinism in China*. New York: Oxford University Press, 1994.

Karl, Rebecca E. *Mao Zedong and China in the Twentieth-Century World: A Concise History*. Durham, NC: Duke University Press, 2010.

Khan, Sulmaan Wasif. *Muslim, Trader, Nomad, Spy: China's Cold War and the People of the Tibetan Borderlands*. Chapel Hill: University of North Carolina Press, 2006.

Khoo, Nicholas. *Collateral Damage: Sino-Soviet Rivalry and the Termination of the Sino-Vietnamese Alliance*. New York: Columbia University Press, 2011.

Kinzley, Judd. "Crisis and the Development of China's Southwestern Periphery: The Transformation of Panzhihua, 1936–1969." *Modern China* 38 (2012): 559–584.

Kirby, William C. "Engineering China: The Origins of the Chinese Developmental State," in *Becoming Chinese*, edited by Wen-hsin Yeh, 137–160. Berkeley: University of California Press, 2000.

Klinghoffer, Arthur Jay. "Sino-Soviet Relations and the Politics of Oil." *Asian Survey* 16 (1976): 540–552.

Kotkin, Stephen. *Magnetic Mountain: Stalinism as a Civilization*. Berkeley: University of California Press, 1995.

Kueh, Y.Y. *China's New Industrialization Strategy: Was Chairman Mao Really Necessary?* Northhampton: Edward Elgar, 2008.

Kwon, Heonik. *The Other Cold War*. New York: Columbia University Press, 2010.

Lanza, Fabio. *The End of Concern: Maoist China, Activism, and Asian Studies*. Durham: Duke University Press, 2017.

Lardy, Nicholas R. *Economic Growth and Distribution in China*. New York: Cambridge University Press, 1978.

Lawrence, Mark Atwood. *The Vietnam War: A Concise International History*. New York: Oxford University Press, 2008.

Lee, Ching Kwan and Guobin Yang, eds. *Re-Envisioning the Chinese Revolution: The Politics and Poetics of Collective Memories in Reform China*. Stanford: Stanford University Press, 1997.

Leese, Daniel. *Mao Cult: Rhetoric and Ritual in China's Cultural Revolution*. Cambridge: Cambridge University Press, 2011.

Lewis, John W. and Xuetai Li. *China Builds the Bomb*. Stanford: Stanford University Press, 1988.

Liang Qichao. "Renewing the People," in *Sources of Chinese Tradition: From 1600 through the Twentieth Century*, compiled by Wm. Theodore de Bary and Richard Lufrano, 289. New York: Columbia University Press, 2000.

Lei Liu. "'Dog-beating stick': General Zhang Aiping's Contribution to the Modernisation of China's Nuclear Force and Strategy since 1977." *Cold War History* 1 (2018): 485–501.

Li Danhui and Yafeng Xia. *Mao and the Sino-Soviet Split, 1959–1973: A New History*. Lanham: Lexington Books, 2018.

Lieberthal, Kenneth and Michael Oskenberg. *Policy Making in China: Leaders, Structures, and Processes*. Princeton: Princeton University Press, 1988.

Li Huaiyin. *Village China Under Socialism and Reform: A Micro History, 1948–2008*. Palo Alto: Stanford University Press, 2009.

Li Hua-Yu. *Mao and the Economic Stalinization of China, 1948–1953*. Lanham: Rowman and Littlefield, 2006.

Li Xiangqian. "The economic and political impact of the Vietnam War on China in 1964," in *Behind the Bamboo Curtain : China, Vietnam, and the World beyond Asia*, ed. Priscilla Roberts, 173–192. Stanford, Calif.: Stanford University Press, 2006.

Li Xiaobing. *A History of the Modern Chinese Army*. Lexington: University of Kentucky Press, 2007.

Lintner, Bertil. *China's India War: Collision Course on the Roof of the World*. Oxford: Oxford University Press, 2018.

Lu Xiaobo and Elizabeth J. Perry. *Danwei: The Changing Chinese Workplace in Historical and Comparative Perspective*. Armonk: M.E. Sharpe, 1997.

Lüthi, Lorenz. *The Sino-Soviet Split: Cold War in the Communist World*. Princeton: Princeton University Press, 2008.

"The Vietnam War and China's Third-Line Defense Planning before the Cultural Revolution, 1964–1966." *Journal of Cold War Studies* 10 (2008): 26–51.

McEnaney, Laura. "Cold War Mobilization and Domestic Politics: The United States," in *The Cambridge History ofthe Cold War, vol. 1*, eds. Melvyn P. Leffler and Odd Arne Westad, 420–441. Cambridge: Cambridge University Press, 2010.

MacFarquhar, Roderick. *The Origins of the Cultural Revolution, Volume 3, The Coming of the Cataclysm, 1961–1966*. New York: Oxford University Press, 1997.

MacFarquhar, Roderick, Timothy Cheek, and Eugene Wu, eds. *The Secret Speeches of Chairman Mao: From the Hundred Flowers to the Great Leap Forward*. Cambridge, MA: Harvard Contemporary China Series, 1989.

MacFarquhar, Roderick and Michael Schoenhals. *Mao's Last Revolution*. Cambridge, MA: Belknap Press, 2006.

McMahon, Robert J. *The Limits of Empire. The United States and Southeast Asia Since World War II*. New York: Columbia University Press, 1999.

McTurnan, George Kahin. *Intervention: How America Became Involved in Vietnam*. New York: Knopf, 1986.

Maier, Charles S. "The Politics of Productivity: Foundations of American International Economic Policy after World War II." *International Organization* 31 (1977): 607–33.

Mao Tse-tung. *Quotations from Chairman Mao Tse-tung*. New York: Bantam Books, 1967.

Mao Zedong. "Introducing a Co-operative," April 15, 1958. *Marxists Internet Archive*. www.marxists.org/reference/archive/mao/selected-works/volume-8/mswv8_09.htm. Accessed June 25, 2017.

"The Long March," October 1935. *Marxists Internet Archive*. www.marxists.org/reference/archive/mao/selected-works/poems/poems15.htm. Accessed September 5, 2018.

"On Khrushchev's Phony Communism and Its Historical Lessons for the World." *Marxists Internet Archive*, July 14, 1964. www.marxists.org/reference/archive/mao/works/1964/phnycom.htm. Accessed June 2, 2017.

"Serving the People," September 8, 1944. *Marxists Internet Archive*. https://www.marxists.org/reference/archive/mao/selected-works/volume-3/mswv3_19.htm. Accessed August 22, 2018.

"Swimming," 1956. *Marxists Internet Archive*. www.marxists.org/reference/archive/mao/selected-works/poems/poems23.htm. Accessed 27 March 2017.

Masco, Joseph. *The Nuclear Borderlands: The Manhattan Project in Post-Cold War New Mexico*. Princeton: Princeton University Press, 2006.

The Theater of Operations: National Security Affect from the Cold War to the War on Terror. Durham, NC: Duke University Press, 2014.

May, Elaine Taylor. *Homeward Bound: American Families in the Cold War Era*. New York: Basic Books, 1988.

Meisner, Maurice. *Mao's China and After: A History of the People's Republic*. New York: The Free Press, 1999.

Marxism, Maoism, and Utopianism: Eight Essays. Madison: University of Wisconsin Press, 1982.

Meyskens, Covell. "Third Front Railroad and Industrial Modernity in Late Maoist China. "*Twentieth-Century China*, 40: 3 (2015): 238–260.

Miller, Tom. *China's Asian Dream: Empire Building along the New Silk Road*. London: Zed Books, 2017.

Mitter, Rana. "Modernity, Internationalization, and War in the History of Modern China." *The Historical Journal* 48:2 (2005): 523–543.

Mok, Chung-Yuk. "China's motor cities: Industrialization and urban development under state socialism, 1948–90." PhD dissertation, Michigan State University, 1994.

Naughton, Barry. *The Chinese Economy : Transitions and Growth*. Cambridge, MA: MIT Press, 2007.

Nurske, Ragnar. *Problems of Capital Formation in Underdeveloped Countries*. Oxford: Blackwell, 1955.

"Industrial Policy during the Cultural Revolution: Military Preparation, Decentralization, and the Leaps Forward," in *New Perspectives on the Cultural Revolution*, edited by William A. Joseph, Christine P.W. Wong, and David Zweig, 153–182. Cambridge, MA: Harvard University Press, 1991.

"The Third Front: Defense Industrialization in the Chinese Interior." *China Quarterly* 115 (September 1988): 351–386.

O'Donnell, Mary Ann. "Heroes of the Special Zone: Modeling Reform and Its Limits," in *Learning from Shenzhen: China's Post-Mao Experiment from Special Zone to Model City*, eds. Mary O'Donnell, Winnie Wong, and Jonathan Bach, 39–64. Chicago: The University of Chicago Press, 2017.

Pang Laikwan. *The Art of Cloning: Creative Production During China's Cultural Revolution*. London: Verso Books, 2017.

Pantsov, Alexander V. and Steven I. Levine. *Deng Xiaoping: A Revolutionary Life*. Oxford: Oxford University Press, 2015.

Mao: The Real Story. New York: Simon & Schuster, 2013.

Perkins, Dwight H. "Reforming China's Economic System." *Journal of Economic Literature* 26:2 (June 1988): 601–645.

Perry, Elizabeth J. *Patrolling the Revolution: Worker Militias, Citizenship, and the Modern Chinese state*. Lanham: Rowman & Littlefield, 2006.

Perry, Elizabeth J. and Li Xun. *Proletarian Power: Shanghai in the Cultural Revolution*. Boulder: Westview Press, 1997.

Pieper-Mooney, Jadwiga and Fabio Lanza, eds. *De-Centering the Cold War: Global and Local Change*. London: Routledge, 2012.

Pietz, David A. *The Yellow River: The Problem of Water in Modern China*. Cambridge, MA: Harvard University Press, 2015.

Powell, Ralph L. "Great Powers and Atomic Bombs Are 'Paper Tigers'." *China Quarterly* 23 (1965): 55–63.

Priestland, David. "Cold War Mobilisation and Domestic Politics: The Soviet Union," in *The Cambridge History of the Cold War, Volume I: Origins*, eds. Melvyn P. Leffler and Odd Arne Westad, 442–463. (Oxford: Oxford University Press, 2010.

Proquest Historical Newspapers, *The New York Times*, "Cold War."

Radchenko, Sergey. *Two Suns in the Heavens: The Sino-Soviet Struggle for Supremacy*. Stanford: Stanford University Press, 2007.

Riskin, Carl. *China's Political Economy: The Quest for Development since 1949*. New York: Oxford University Press, 1987.

Russo, Alessandro. "The Probable Defeat: Preliminary Notes on the Chinese Cultural Revolution." *positions: asia critique* 6 (1998): 179–202.

Samuelson, Lennart. *Plans for Stalin's War Machine: Tukhachevskii and Military-Economic Planning, 1925–1941*. New York: St. Martin's Press, 2000.

Schivelbusch, Wolfgang. *The Railway Journey: The Industrialization of Time and Space in the 19th Century*. Berkeley: University of California Press, 1986.

Schmalzer, Sigrid. *Red Revolution, Green Revolution: Scientific Farming in Socialist China*. Chicago: University of Chicago Press, 2016.

"Self-Reliant Science: The Impact of the Cold War on Science in Socialist China," in *Science and Technology in the Global Cold War*, eds. Naomi Oreskes and John Krige. Cambridge, MA: MIT Press, 2014.

Schoenhals, Michael. *Doing Things with Words in Chinese Politics: Five Studies*. Berkeley: Institute of East Asian Studies, University of California, Berkeley, 1992.

Schwartz, Benjamin I. "The Reign of Virtue: Some Broad Perspectives on Leader and Party in the Cultural Revolution." *China Quarterly* 35 (1968): 1–17.

Scott, James C. *Seeing like a State: How Certain Schemes to Improve the Human Condition Have Failed*. New Haven: Yale University Press, 1998.

Weapons of the Weak: Everyday Forms of Peasant Resistance. New Haven: Yale University Press, 1985.

Selden, Mark. *The Yenan Way in Revolutionary China*. Cambridge, MA: Harvard University Press, 1971.

Shapiro, Judith. *China's Environmental Challenges*. Cambridge: Polity Press, 2012.

Mao's War against Nature: Politics and the Environment in Revolutionary China. Cambridge and New York: Cambridge University Press, 2001.

Sheng, Michael M. *Battling Western Imperialism: Mao, Stalin, and the United States*. Princeton: Princeton University Press, 1997.

Simon, Denis Fred and Merle Goldman, eds. *Science and Technology in Post-Mao China*. Cambridge, MA: Harvard University Press, 1989.

Smil, Vaclav. *China's Past, China's Future: Energy, Food, Environment*. London: Routledge, 2004.

Solinger, Dorothy J. "China's Floating Population," in *The Paradox of China's Post-Mao Reforms*, eds. Merle Goldman and Roderick MacFarquhar, 220–240. Cambridge, MA: Harvard University Press, 1999.

Spence, Jonathan. *The Search for Modern China*. New York: W.W. Norton, 2012.

Shen Zhihua and Danhui Li. *After Leaning to One Side: China and its Allies in the Cold War*. Stanford: Stanford University Press, 2011.

Sheng Hu. *Imperialism and Chinese Politics*. Peking: Foreign Languages Press, 1955.

Shue, Vivienne. *The Reach of the State: Sketches of the Chinese Body Politic*. Stanford University Press, 1990.

Smith, Aminda. *Thought Reform and China's Dangerous Classes: Reeducation, Resistance, and the People*. Lanham, MD: Rowman & Littlefield, 2013.

Snyder, Jack. *The Ideology of the Offensive: Military Decision Making and the Disasters of 1914*. Ithaca: Cornell University Press, 1984.

Stites, Richard. *Revolutionary Dreams: Utopian Vision and Experimental Life in the Russian Revolution*. Oxford: Oxford University Press, 1988.

Szonyi, Michael. *Cold War Island: Quemoy on the Front Line*. Cambridge: Cambridge University Press, 2008.

Tan Hecheng. *The Killing Wind: A Chinese County's Descent into Madness during the Cultural Revolution*. Oxford: Oxford University Press, 2017.

Tanner, Harold M. *China: A History, Volume 2, From the Great Qing Empire through the People's Republic of China*. New York: Hackett Publishing Company, 2010.

Teiwes, Frederick C. and Warren Sun. *The End of the Maoist Era: Chinese Politics during the Twilight of the Cultural Revolution, 1972–1976*. Armonk: M.E. Sharpe, 2007.

Thaxton, Ralph. *Catastrophe and Contention in Rural China: Mao's Great Leap Famine and the Origins of Righteous Resistance*. New York: Cambridge University Press, 1988.

Thompson, E.P. "Time, Work-Discipline and Industrial Capitalism." *Past & Present* 38 (1967): 56–97.

Thornton, Patricia M. *Disciplining the State: Virtue, Violence, and State-Making in Modern China*. Cambridge, MA: Harvard University Press, 2007.

Tillman, Margaret. *Raising China's Revolutionaries: Modernizing Childhood for Cosmopolitan Nationalists and Liberated Comrades, 1920s–1950s*. New York: Columbia University Press, 2018.

Tilt, Bryan. *Dams and Development in China: The Moral Economy of Water and Power*. New York: Columbia University Press, 2015.

Tsou, Tang. "The Cultural Revolution and the Chinese Political System." *China Quarterly* 38 (1969): 63–78.

U, Eddy. *Disorganizing China: Counter-bureaucracy and the Decline of Socialism*. Stanford: Stanford University Press, 2007.

Vanderbilt, Tom. *Survival City: Adventures among the Ruins of Atomic America*. Chicago: The University of Chicago Press, 2010.

van de Ven, Hans. "The Military in the Republic." *China Quarterly* 150 (July 1997): 352–374.

Vogel, Ezra. *Canton under Communism: Programs and Politics in a Provincial Capital, 1949–1968*. Cambridge, MA: Harvard University Press, 1969.

Deng Xiaoping and the Transformation of China. Cambridge, MA: Harvard University Press, 2013.

Volland, Nicholai. *Socialist Cosmopolitanism: The Chinese Literary Universe, 1945–1965*. New York: Columbia University Press, 2017.

Walder, Andrew. *China under Mao: A Revolution Derailed*. Cambridge, MA: Harvard University Press, 2015.

Communist Neo-traditionalism: Work and Authority in Chinese Industry. 1986: Berkeley: University of California Press.

"Cultural Revolution Radicalism: Variations on a Stalinist Theme," in *New Perspectives on the Cultural Revolution*, eds. William A. Joseph, Christine P.W. Wong, and David Zweig, 41–61. Cambridge, MA: Harvard University Press, 1991.

Fractured Rebellion the Beijing Red Guard Movement. Cambridge, MA: Harvard University Press, 2009.

"Rebellion and Repression in China, 1966–1971." *Social Science History* 38:3–4 (2014): 518–523.

Walder, Andrew G. and Yang Su. "The Cultural Revolution in the Countryside: Scope, Timing and Human Impact." *China Quarterly* 173 (2003): 74–99.

Wang, Ning. *Banished to the Great Northern Wilderness: Political Exile and Re-education in Mao's China*. Ithaca: Cornell University Press, 2017.

Wang, Zheng. *Finding Women in the State: A Socialist Feminist Revolution in the People's Republic of China, 1949–1964*. Berkeley: University of California Press, 2017.

Weart, Spencer R. *The Rise of Nuclear Fear*. Cambridge, MA: Harvard University Press, 2012.

Weeks, Stanley Byron and Charles A. Meconis. *The Armed Forces of the USA in the Asia-Pacific Region*. New York: I.B. Tauris, 2004.

Wei, Nancy and Darryl E. Brock. *Mr. Science and Chairman Mao's Cultural Revolution: Science and Technology in Modern China*. Lanham: Lexington Books, 2012.

Wemheuer, Felix. *Famine Politics in Maoist China and the Soviet Union*. New Haven: Yale University Press, 2014.

Westad, Odd Arne, ed. *Brothers in Arms: The Rise and Fall of the Sino-Soviet Alliance, 1945–1963*. Washington, DC: Woodrow Wilson Center Press, 1998.

The Global Cold War: Third World Interventions and the Making of Our Times. New York: Cambridge University Press, 2005.

White, Lynn T., III. *Policies of Chaos: The Organizational Causes of Violence in China's Cultural Revolution*. Princeton: Princeton University Press, 1989.

Whiting, Allen S. "Sino-Soviet Relations: What Next?" *Annals of the American Academy of Political and Social Science* 476 (1984): 141–155.

Whitson, William W. *The Chinese High Command: A History of Communist Military Politics, 1927–71*. New York: Praeger, 1973.

Wright, Tim. *The Political Economy of the Chinese Coal Industry: Black Gold and Blood-Stained Coal*. London: Routledge, 2012.

Wu Yiching. *The Cultural Revolution at the Margins*. Cambridge, MA: Harvard University Press, 2014.

Xu Guoqi. *Olympic Dreams: China and Sports, 1895–2008*. Cambridge, MA: Harvard University Press, 2008.

Yang, Dali. *Calamity and Reform in China: State, Rural Society, and Institutional Change since the Great Leap Famine*. Stanford: Stanford University Press, 1996.

"Patterns of China's Regional Development Strategy." *China Quarterly* 122 (1990): 230–257.

Yang, Guobin. "Mao Quotations in Factional Battles and Their Afterlives: Episodes from Chongqing," in *Mao's Little Red Book: A Global History*, ed. Alexander C. Cook, 61–75. Cambridge: Cambridge University Press, 2014.

The Red Guard Generation and Political Activism in China. New York: Columbia University Ores, 2016.

Yang, Jisheng. *Tombstone: The Great Chinese Famine, 1958–1962*. London: Allen Lane, 2012.

Yang, Kuisong and Yafeng Xia. "Vacillating between Revolution and Détente: Mao's Changing Psyche and Policy toward the United States, 1969–1976." *Diplomatic History* 34 (2010): 395–423.

Yang, Su. *Collective Killings in Rural China during the Cultural Revolution*. New York: Cambridge University Press, 2011.

Young, Marilyn B. *The Vietnam Wars 1945–1990*. New York: HarperCollins, 1991.

Zeng Yi. *Family Dynamics in China: A Life Table Analysis*. Madison: University of Wisconsin Press, 1991.

Zhai Qing. *China and the Vietnam Wars, 1950–1975*. Chapel Hill: University of North Carolina Press, 2000.

Zhang Shu Guang. "Beijing's Aid to Hanoi and the United States–China Confrontations, 1964–1968," in *Behind the Bamboo Curtain: China, Vietnam, and the World beyond Asia*, ed. Priscilla Roberts, 259–288. Stanford: Stanford University Press, 2006.

"Between 'Paper' and 'Real Tigers': Mao's View of Nuclear Weapons," in *Cold War Statesmen Confront the Bomb*, eds. John Lewis Gaddis, Phillip H. Gordon, Ernest R. May, and Jonathan Rosenberg, 194–215. Oxford: Oxford University Press, 1999.

Economic Cold War: America's Embargo against China and the Sino-Soviet Alliance, 1949–1963. Stanford: Stanford University Press, 2001.

Mao's Military Romanticism: China and the Korean War, 1950–1953. Lawrence: University Press of Kansas, 1995.

Zhang Xiaoming. *Deng Xiaoping's Long War: The Military Conflict between China and Vietnam, 1979–1991*. Chapel Hill: University of North Carolina Press, 2015.

Zhong Xueping and Wang Zheng, eds. *Some of Us: Chinese Women Growing Up in the Mao Era*. New Brunswick: Rutgers University Press, 2001.

Zhou, Xun. *Forgotten Voices of Mao's Great Famine, 1958–1962: An Oral History*. New Haven: Yale University Press, 2013.

Zubok, Vladislav. *A Failed Empire: The Soviet Union in the Cold War from Stalin to Gorbachev*. Chapel Hill: University of North Carolina Press, 2009.

Zubok, Vladislav and Constantine Pleshakov. *Inside the Kremlin's Cold War: From Stalin to Khrushchev*. Cambridge, MA: Harvard University Press, 1996.

Secondary Sources in Chinese

Ai chang ru jia. DVD. Directed by Zhao Ming. Shanghai: Shanghai Film Studio, 1958.

Bo You, Zhu Chaoquan, and Huang Jiandong. "Wang Jie tongzhi 'yi bu pa ku, er bu pa si' de shiji shi zhe yang xuanchuan chuqu de," *Zhongguo gongchandang xinwen wang*. http://dangshi.people.com.cn/GB/144964/145566/8821579.html. Accessed August 19, 2018.

Cao Shuji. "1959–1961 nian Zhongguo de renkou siwang ji qi chengyin." www.yhcw.net/famine/Research/r060628a.html. Accessed June 3, 2016.

Chen Donglin. "San xian jian she shi mo," in *Zhongguo gongchandang yu sanxian jianshe*, ed. Chen Donglin, 3–35. Beijing: Zhonggong dangshi chubanshe, 2015.

Sanxian jianshe: Beizhan shiqi de xibu da kaifa. Beijing: Zhonggong zhongyang dangxiao chubanshe, 2003.

"Zhou Enlai zui jiannan de shike: 1973 'pi Zhou' fengbo kaoshu." *Zhongguo dangdai yanjiusuo*. www.iccs.cn/contents/301/8168_3.html. Accessed July 15, 2016.

Chen Li. "Haoren haoma shang sanxian," *Zhongguo hangtian bao* 8 (2016), 5–6.

Chen Pu. "Sanxian jianhse zhanlue yu xibu mengxiang," in *Sichuan sheng zhonggong dangshi xuehui*, ed. Sanxian jianshe zongheng tan, 2–12. Chengdu: Sichuan renmin chubanshe, 2015.

Chengdu tielu fenju "Xichang tielu fen ju zhi" bianweihui. *Xichang tielu fen ju zhi, 1970–1998*. Chengdu: Chengdu tielu fenju Xichang tielu fenju, 2001.

"Chengkun tielu shang de tie er ju de lieshi linyuan," April 21, 2014, 2018. http://blog.sina.com.cn/s/blog_8812919f0101fry0.html. Accessed September 5.

Cui Yinan and Chen Junfeng. "Sanxian jianshe yu Guangxi chengzhen fazhan yanjiu." *Guangxi shehui kexue*, February 25, 2018.

Dangdai koushu shi congshu bienweihui, ed. *Dangdai Sichuan yaoshi shilu 1*. Chengdu: Sichuan renmin chubanshe, 2010.

Deng Lifeng. "Yuan yue kangmei shulue." *Dangdai zhongyou shi yanjiu* 1:9 (2002): 84–92.

Duan Feng. "Liu Shaoqi 'liang zhong laodong zhidu he liang zhong jiaoyu zhidu' de lilun yu shijian," in *Liu Shaoqi baizhou nian jinian: Quanguo Liu Shaoqi shengping he sixiang yantao hui lunwen ji (xia)*, ed. Zhonggong zhongyang wenxian yanjiu shi guanli bu, 904–915. Beijing: Zhongyang wenxian chubanshe, 1999.

"Duo shuo Pangang yi hao gaolu qi yi chutie, cuo!" *Panzhihua shi danganguan xinxi wang*. www.pzhda.gov.cn/xxgk/daldpzh/620464.shtml. Accessed November 18, 2018.

Feng Hua, "Ni cong liegu zoulai," *Zhongguo shijiu ye jituan youxian gongsi*, June 7, 2016. www.19mcc.com.cn/Sinfo.aspx?t=23&ContentId=3739. Accessed June 13, 2017.

Gansu sanxian jianshe bianjibu. "Guojia jiwei, guojia jianwei guanyu neiqian gongzuo zhong de wenti baogao," in *Gansu sanxian jianshe*, ed. Gansu sanxian jianshe bianjibu, 440–442. Lanzhou: Lanzhou daxue chubanshe, 1993.

Gao Liang. "Guanyu 'xiao sanxian' jianshe de juece." *Dang zhenglun tan (ganbu wenzhai)*, 2010: 44–45.

Ge Weichun and Xu Zhanchu. "Sanxian yanjiu xianzhuang yu Jiangxi xiao sanxian jainshe lishi janjiu. *Yichun xueyuan xuebao*, October 25, 2017.

Guangxi zhuangzu zizhi qu difangzhi bianzuan weiyuanhui. *Guangxi sheng jiaotong zhi*. Nanning: Guangxi renmin chubanshe, 1993.

"Guanyu jiejue sanxian jianku diqu guofang keji gongye liti tuiti renyuan anzhi he zhigong fuqi changqi liangdi fenju wenti de bao gao," in *Sanxian jianshe tiaozheng gaizao youguan zhengce wenjian xuanbian*, ed. Sanxian jianshe tiaozheng gaizao weiyuanhui bian, 13–15. Beijing: Sanxian jianshe tiaozheng gaizao weiyuanhui, 1984.

"Guizhou sheng dianli gongye shi" bian wei hui. *Zhonghua renmin gongheguo dianli gongye shi: Hua zhong juan*. Beijing: Zhongguo dianli chubanshe, 2003.

Guizhou sheng liupanshui difang bianzuan weiyuanhui. *Liupanshui sanxian jianshe zhi*. Beijing: Dangdai zhongguo chubanshe, 2003.

Guojia jiwei sanxianjianshe tiaozheng bangongshi. *Zhongguo da sanxian*. Beijing: Zhongguo huabao chubanshe, 1998.

Guojia tongji ju. *Zhongguo tongji nianjian, 1983*. Beijing: Zhongguo tongji chubanshe, 1983.

Guojia tongji ju guomin jingji zonghe tongji si. *Xin zhongguo 50 nian tongji ziliao huibian*. Beijing: Zhongguo tongji chubanshe, 1999.

Guojia tongjiju shehui tongji gongsi, ed. *Zhongguo laodong gongzi tongji ziliao, 1949–1985*. Beijing: Zhongguo tongji chubanshe, 1987.

Guowuyuan sanxian jianshe tiaozheng gaizao guihua bangong shi sanxian jianshe bianxie zu. *Sanxian jianshe*. Beijing, 1991.

Han Zengtao. "Jiluo U2 feiji de ren: Ji kongjun zhandou yingxiong Yue Zhenhua." *Dangshi bocai* 9 (1996): 30–32.

He Haoju. *Sanxian jianshe yu xibu da kaifa*. Beijing: Dangdai zhongguo yanjiusuo chubanshe, 2003.

Hubei shengzhi gongye zhigao shiyou bianzuan weiyuanhui, ed. *Hubei shengzhi gongye zhigao shiyou*. Jianghan: Hubei renmin chubanshe, 1990.

Jiuquan gangtie gongsi jingli ban gong shi bian. *Jiuquan gangtie gongsi jianshe, fazhan shiliao*. Jiuquan: Jiugang yinshui chang, 1996.

Liang Hua and Liu Jinyi, eds. *Zhongguo shiyou tongshi, 1949–1978*. Beijing: Zhongguo shihua chubanshe, 2003.

Liao Guoliang, Li Shishun, and Xu Yan. *Mao Zedong junshi sixiang fazhan shi*. Beijing: Jiefangjun chubanshe, 1991.

Li Daigeng, ed. *Xin zhongguo dianli gongye fazhan shilue*. Beijing: Qiye guanli chubanshe, 1984.

Li Jinzhu and Chen Yu. *Youpiao yu Zhongguo: Youpiao beihou de gongheguo lishi*. Shanghai: Shanghai kexue jishu wenxian chubanshe, 2011.

Li Ke and Hao Sheng. *Wenhua da geming de renmin jiefangjun*. Beijing: Zhonggong dangshi ziliao chubanshe, 1989.

Li Rui and Wang Chunlei. "Heilongjiang xiao sanxian jianshe diaocha yu pingjia." *Suihua xueyuan xuebao* (2015): 22–24.

Liu Huaqiu. "Deng Xiaoping guoji zhanlüe sixiang lunyao." *Dang de wenxian*, March 2007: 23–31, 46.

Liu Jianmin. "Lun Hebei 'xiao sanxian' jianshe." PhD diss., Hebei shifan daxue, 2004.

Liu Jixian. *Zhongguo jiefangjun jiben jianshe gongchengbing shi*. Beijing: Junshi kexue chubanshe, 2015.

Liu Maocai and Xue Shicheng, eds. *Pangang: Zhongguo gangtie gongye de jiao'ao*. Chongqing: Chongqing chubanshe, 1994.

Liu Zhiqing. "1962 nian de di san cai taihai weiji." *Dangshi bolan* 4 (2004): 9–13.

Ma Quanshan. *Xin zhongguo gongye jingji shi, 1966–1978*. Beijing: Jingji guanli chubanshe, 1998.

Meitan gongye shigaobianyan zu. *Zhongguo meitan gongye: Er shi ba nian shigao, 1949–1976*. Beijing: Meitan gonye shigao bianyanzu, 2001.

Ni Tongzheng, ed. *Sanxian fengyun: Zhongguo sanxianjianshe wenxuan*. Chengdu: Sichuan renmin chubanshe, 2013.

Pang Songzhu, ed. *Mao Zedong shidai de Zhongguo*. Beijing: Zhonggong dangshi chubanshe, 2007.

Panzhihua shi chengxiang jianshe weiyuanhui. *Panzhihua shi chengshi jianshe zhi*. Panzhihua: Panzhihua shi chengxiang jianshe weiyuanhui, 1995.

Panzhihua shi weisheng bianzuan weiyuanhui. *Panzhihua shi weisheng zhi*. Beijing: Minzu chubanshe, 2004.

Shanghai shi difangzhi bangongshi. "Shusong jishu rencai jianshe da xiao sanxian," 2013. www.shtong.gov.cn/node2/node2245/node4471/node56224/node56232/node56234/usero. Accessed March 17, 2013.

Sichuan sheng defang zhi bianzuan weiyuanhui. *Sichuan shengzhi shiyou tianranqi gongye zhi*. Chengdu: Sichuan renmin chubanshe, 1997.

"Sichuan sheng dianli gongye shi" bian wei hui. *Zhonghua renmin gongheguo dianli gongye shi: Hua zhong juan*. Beijing: Zhongguo dianli chubanshe, 2003.

Sichuan sheng Panzhihua shi zhi. *Panzhihua shi zhi*. Chengdu: Chengdu kexue jishu chubanshe, 1994.

Song Yijun and Sun Yanbo. "Liu Shaoqi yu sanxian jianshe de lishi huigu he sikao." *Junshi lishi* 6 (2008): 11–15.

Su Taolin and Zhang Huijian. "20 shji 60 niandai Beijing xian sanxian jianshe." *Dangdai Beijing yanjiu* 1 (2014): 47–49.

Sun Jian. *Zhonghua renmin gongheguo jingji shi: 1949–90 niandai chu*. Beijing: Zhongguo renmin daxue chubanshe, 1992.

Sun Shaoying, ed. *Zhongguo yupiao shi di ba juan*. Beijing: Shangwu yin shu guan, 1999.

Tan Keming. *Shen wadong de jinghou*. Beijing: Zhongyang dangshi chubanshe, 2009.

Tiedaobing shanhou gongzuo lingdao xiaozu. *Zhongguo renmin jiefangjun tiedao bing jianshi*. Beijing: Tiedaobing shanhou gongzuo lingdao xiaozubian, 1986.

Wang Enbao. "Liaoning zai zhiyuan 'sanxian' jianshe zhong de gongxian." *Dangshi Zongheng* 8 (2011): 34–36.

Wang Faxing. "Zhenxing shaoguan huanan zhonggongye jidi de duice yanjiu." *Shaoguan xueyuanbao* 30:1 (2009): 91–95.

Wang Fu. "Jilin 'sanxian' qiye quanbu banqian chushan: Jilin jungong hangye gaige tuokun jishi." *Guofang keji gongye* 3 (2005): 52.

Wang Jiacui. "Guizhou sanxian jianshe yanjiu shulun." *Zunyi shifan xueyuan xuebao* (2014): 21–24.

Wang Tao and Long Fei. "Zhengfu hongguan guihua yu difang chengshihua: Yiwu jihua, sanxian jianshe yu shanxi chengshihua chutan." *Dangdai zhongguo shi yanjiu* 1 (2001): 93–97.

Wang Ziyun. "Shanxi sanxian jianshe de yanjiu." *Shanxi qingnian guanli ganbu xueyuan xuebao*, December 20, 2004.

Wu Li, ed. *Zhonghua renmin gongheguo jingji shi*. Beijing: Zhongguo shidai jingji chubanshe, 2010.

Xie Zhongqing. "1960 niandai Shanghai zhiyuan Jaingxi xiao sanxian jianshe yanjiu." *Jingangshan daxue xuebao* 31:6 (2016): 69–76.

Xu Youwei and Chen Donglin, eds. *Xiao Sanxian jianshe yanjiu luncong, Volumes 1–2*. Shanghai: Shanghai daxue chubanshe, 2015–2016.

Yan Wei. "Hunan sanxian jianshe yanjiu." Master's thesis, Xiangtan daxue, 2007.

Yang Hanqing and Liang Xiangyang. "20 shiji qishi niandai Guangdong de xiao sanxian jianshe." *Hong guangjiao*, July15, 2015.

Yang Xingzheng and Han Qijie, ed. *Yichang: Shuidian zhi du*. Wuhan: Hubei renmin chubanshe, 2005.

Yang Zongmao. *Qingchun jiyi: Yi ge sanxian xuebing de riji*. Beijing: Zhongguo wenlian chubanshe, 2010.

Yejin gongye bu Panzhihua gangtie gongsi. *Pangang shengchan jiansheshi*. Panzhihua: Yejin gongye bu Panzhihua gangtie gongsi, 1983.

Yu Ronggen and Zhang Lanqi, eds. *Dangdai Chongqing jianshi*. Chongqing: Chongqing renmin chubanshe, 2003.

Yuan Yongxin and Zhang Fengying. "Dui 351 ming canjia sanxian jianshe zhe xi fei huanbing qingkuan de diaocha." *Zhiye yu jiankang* 5 (1998): 11–12.

Yue Zhenhua. "Jiluo Mei zhi U-2 feiji zuozhan zhuiji." *Bai nian chao* 6 (2002): 17–22.

Zeng Jie. "'Tielu da huizhan' yu Huaihua chengshi de xingqi (1970–1983)." Master's thesis, Zhongnan daxue, 2012.

Zeng Juan, ed. *Jianshe houfang: Quanguo sanxian jianshe xianqi gaochao*. Changchun: Jilin chuban jituan youxian zeren gongsi, 2010.

Zhang Guobao. "Sulian yuanjian, sanxian jianshe ji daguimo jishujinjin." *Zhongguo jingji zhoubao*, 2014.

Zhang Xueliang, ed. *Fazhan dongle: Xi dian dong song gongcheng jianshe*. Changchun: Jilin chuban jituan youxian zeren gongsi, 2010.

Pieshan zaolu: Xiangqian tielu sheji shigong yu jianshe tongche. Shengyang: Jilin chuban jituan youxianzerengongsi, 2010.

Xi qi dong shu. Changchun: Jilin chuban jituan youxian zeren gongsi, 2010.

Xinan ganxian: Xiangyu tielu sheji shigong yu jianshe tongche. Shenyang: Jilin chuban jituan youxianzerengongsi, 2010.

Xinan tongtu: Chengkuntielu shejishigong yu jianshetongche. Shenyang: Jilin chuban jituan youxianzerengongsi, 2010.

Zhao Dexin, ed. *Zhonghua renmin gongheguo jingji shi 1967–1984*. Zhengzhou: Henan renmin chubanshe, 1991.

Zheng Qian. "Zhonggong jiu da qianhou quanguo de zhanbei gongzuo," in *Zhonggong dangshi ziliao 41*, ed. Zhonggong zhongyang dangshi yanjiushi, 204–233. Beijing: Zhonggong dangshi chubanshe, 1992.

Zheng Sheng. *Zhanlüe tiaozheng: Sanxian jianshe juece yu sheji gongcheng*. Changchun: Jilin chubanshe jituan youxian zeren gongsi, 2010.

Zheng Yougui. *Sanxianjianshe yu xibudakaifa zhong de panzhihua*. Beijing: Dangdai zhongduo chubanshe, 2013.

ed. *Panzhihua kaifa jianshe shi dashiji*. Chengdu: Chengdu keji daxue chubanshe, 1998.

Zhonggong Sichuan shengwei dangshi yanjiu shi, ed. *Zhongguo gongchan dang sichuan lishi dashi ji (1950–1978)*. Chengdu: Sichuan renmin chubanshe, 2000.

Zhonggong zhongyang wenxian yanjiu shi. *Deng Xiaoping nianpu (1949–1976), Volumes 1–2*. Beijing: Zhongyang wenxian chubanshe, 2004.

Liu Shaoqi nianpu, Volumes 1–2. Beijing: Zhongyang wenxian chubanshe, 1996.
Mao Zedong nianpu, Volumes 4–6. Beijing: Zhongyang wenxian chubanshe, 1996.
Zhou Enlai nianpu, Volumes 1–2. Beijing: Zhongyang wenxian chubanshe, 1997.
Zhongguo dianye shizhi bianji weiyuanhui. *Dangdai zhongguo de dianli gongye.* Beijing: Dangdai Zhongguo chubanshe, 1994.
Zhonghua renmin gongheguo dianli gongye shi xibei juan. Beiing: Zhongguo dianli chubanshe, 2001.
Zhongguo qiche gongye shi bianshen weiyuanhui, ed. *Zhongguo qiche gongye shi, 1901–1990.* Beijing: Renmin jiaotong chubanshe, 1996.
"Zhongguo youpiao shi" di ba juan bianweihui. *Zhongguo youpiao shi, di ba juan (1965–1978).* Beijing: Shangwu yin shuguan, 2000.
Zhonghua renmin gongheguo tiedaobu. *Tielu xiujian shiliao, 1949–1962.* Beijing: Zhongguo tiedao chubanshe, 1991.
Tielu xiujian shiliao, 1963–1980. Beijing: Zhongguo tiedao chubanshe, 1991.
Zhonghua renmin gongheguo guojia tongji ju. "1978." www.stats.gov.cn/tjsj/tjgb/ndtjgb/qgndtjgb/200203/t20020331_29991.html. Accessed June 23, 2017.
Zhou Mingzhang. "Dongbei yu zhiyuan sanxian chengshi fazhan." *Kaifang shidai* 2 (2018). www.opentimes.cn/Abstract/9417.html. Accessed July 15, 2018.
"Sanxian jianshe yu Ningxiachengshihua." *Ningxia shehui kexue* (June 2018).
Zhu Cishou. *Zhongguo xiandai gongye shi.* Chongqing: Chongqing chubanshe, 1990.

Sources for Demographic Calculations

Chao Lihua. "'Guofang yixian' de 'sanxian jianshe': Yunnan sanxian jianshe de lishi yanjiu." *Xueshu tanshuo* 4 (2009): 103–108.
"Teshu 'zhanbei jingji': Dui Yunnan sanxian jianshe de lishi renshi." *Chuxiong shifan xueyuan xuebao* 1 (2007): 103–108.
"Yunnan sanxian jianshe tiaozheng gaizao de lishi yanjiu." *Honghe xueyuan xuebao* 4 (2007): 31–34.
Chen Yunsui. "Sichuan sanxian qiye xiagang zhigong qunti zhi teshu xing." *Xinan minzu daxue xuebao* 10 (2007): 197–199.
Dai Anlin. "20 shiji 60–70 niandai hunan 'sanxian' jianshe shuping." *Lunshi bolan (lilun)* (2009): 17–21.
Guangxi sheng difangzhi bianzuan weiyuanhui bangongshi, *Guangxi sheng diqing ku.* http://sd.infobase.gov.cn/ftr/ftr.htm?seachword=%u4E09%u7EBF&K=0&run=11&list=1&page=20. Accessed December 25, 2013.
Guizhou sheng difangzhi bianzuan weiyuanhui bangongshi, *Guizhou sheng difangzhi quanwen shujuku.* http://dfz.gznu.cn/tpi/sysasp/include/index.asp. Accessed January 11, 2013.
Hubei sheng difangzhi bianzuan weiyuanhuibangongshi, *Hubei fangzhi wang.* www.hbdfz.com.cn:8081/was40/dfz/new/search.jsp. Accessed March 22, 2015.
Heilongjiang sheng difangzhi bangongshi, *Heilongjiang shengqing xingxi wang.* http://210.76.63.176. Accessed December 17, 2013.

Liang Yuelan, Chai Yun, and Li Fang, "Shaanxi 'sanxian' jianshe de lishi huigu: Fang Shaanxisheng yuan jinben jianshe weiyuanhui zhuren Ren Jun," *Bai nian chao* (March 2009): 61–65.

Liu Jianmei. "Hebei xao sanxian jianshe de huigu yu pingju." PhD diss., Hebei shifan daxue, 2004.

Liu You'an. "20 shiji qianru ningxia de hanzu yimin." PhD diss., Lanzhou daxue, 2010.

Lu Yun. "Sichuan zhongbu nanbei xian jingji qidai zhongdeng chengshi yu quyu fazhan yanjiu, 1950–2000." Master's thesis, Sichuan daxue, 2003.

Meng Aiqun and Tan Jianjin. "Guangxi sanxian jianshe de gaikuang." *Zhancheng*, February 2008: 14–15, 59.

Shaanxi sheng difangzhi bianzuan weiyuanhui bangongshi, *Shaanxi diqing ku*. http://sd.infobase.gov.cn/ftr/ftr.htm?seachword=%u4E09%u7EBF&K=0&run=11&list=1&page=20. Accessed January 7, 2014.

Shanghai shi difangzhi bangongshi. "Shusong jishu rencai jianshe da xiao sanxian," January 3, 2003. www.shtong.gov.cn/Newsite/node2/node2245/node4471/node56224/node56232/node56234/userobject1ai42781.html. Accessed April 23, 2015.

Shandong sheng difangzhi bangongshi, *Shandong shengqing wang*. http://sd.infobase.gov.cn/ftr/ftr.htm?seachword=%u4E09%u7EBF&K=0&run=11&list=1&page=20. Accessed January 2, 2013.

Shui Junfeng and Fei Jiaxing. "Shilun sanxian jianshe dui leshan diqu jingji shehui fazhan de yingxiang." *Zhonggong leshan shiwei dangxiao xuebao* 4 (2012): 70–73.

Song Renqiong. *Song Renqiong huiyi lu*. Beijing: Jiefangjun chubanshe, 2007, 418–420.

Sun Yanjing and Yue Long. "Lun ershi shiji liu qi shi niandai 'sanxian' jianshe yu Shaanxi gongye." *Xibei daxue xuebao* (April 2003): 36–41.

Tian Mei. "Sanxian jianshe neiqian da yimin." *Hongyan chunqiu* 3 (2006): 25–26.

Wang Enbao. "Liaoning zai zhiyuan 'sanxian' jianshe zhong de gongxian." *Dangshi Zongheng* 8 (2011): 34–36.

Wang Faxing. "Zhenxing shaoguan huanan zhonggongye jidi de duice yanjiu." *Shaoguan xueyuan bao* 1 (2009): 91–95.

Wang Fu. "Jilin 'sanxian' qiye quanbu banqian chushan: Jilin jungong hangye gaige tuokun jishi." *Guofang keji gongye* 3 (2005): 52.

Wang Hongjuan. "Gansu sanxian jianshe." *Hexi xueyuan xuebao* (March 2008): 45–48.

Wang Jingyong. "Guangxi sanxian jianshe guofang gongye yanjiu." Master's thesis, Guangxi shifan daxue, 2007.

Wang Juan. "Qinghai sheng 'sanxian' jianshe shuping." PhD diss., Northwest Normal University, 2013.

Wang Tao and Fei Long, "Zhengfu hongguan guihua yu difang chengshihua." *Dangdai zhongguo shi yanjiu* 1 (2001): 93–97.

"'Xiao sanxian' jianshe." *Fujian dangshi yuekan* 19 (2009): 34.

Xie Zhongqiang. "20 Shiji liu qi shi niandai shanghai shi zhiyuan guofang jianshe shu lue." *Xibei gongye daxue xuebao* 4 (2012): 41–49.

Xu Kaixi, "Hubei Sanxian jianshe de huigu yu qi shi," *Hubei shehui kexue* (October 2013): 23–24.

Yang Linxing. "Yunnan de 'sanxian' jianshe," *Yunnan dang de shenghuo* 1 (2011): 55–56.

Yang Tiancheng. "Liu qi shi niandai sanxian jianshe zhong de gansu jungong." *Fazhan* 11 (2009): 34–36.

Yang Xiaolan. "Huaihua chengshi xingqi yu fazhan yanjiu." Master's thesis, Huanan shifan daxue, 2008.

Zeng Jie. "'Tielu dahuizhan' yu huaihua chengshi de xingqi, 1970–1983." Master's thesis, Zhongnan daxue, 2012.

Zhang De and Zhang Huaiyu. "Dui yunnan sanxian jungong qiye tiaozheng gaizai de yijian." *Jingji wenti tansuo* 12 (1986): 5–7.

Zhang Rui. "Lun Shaanxi 'sanxian jianshe' shiqi de jiantong jianshe." *Xue lilun* (December 2011): 189–190.

Zhao Guoxiang, Zeng Daoming, and Zhang Sanhua. "Sanxian dianzi gongye zai guangyuan," in *Guangyuan shi wenshi ziliao, Volume 6*, 1–16. Guangyuan: Sichuan sheng guangyuan shi weiyuanhui, 1993.

Zhong Jianying. "Liushi niandai fujian de 'xiao sanxian'." *Fujian dangshi yuekan* 5 (1998): 23–25.

Zhou Minzhi. "Hunan sanxian jianshe shimo." *Xiangchao* 7 (2011): 31–34.

Zhu Yanyun. "Lun 20 shiji liu qi shi niandai gansu sanxianjianshe." *Qiqihaier shifan gaodeng zhuanke xuexiao xuebao* (March 2011): 101–102.

Zhu Yanyun. "Lun 'qiwu' qijian gansu sanxian jianshe de tiaozheng gaizao." *Qingnian wenxuejia* 3 (2011): 104–105.

Index

For EU product safety concerns, contact us at Calle de José Abascal, 56–1°, 28003 Madrid, Spain or eugpsr@cambridge.org.

www.ingramcontent.com/pod-product-compliance
Lightning Source LLC
LaVergne TN
LVHW010055220926
848484LV00005BA/1123
9781108489553